Yours Sincerely,
Edwin Forrest

T. B. PETERSON & BROTHERS, PHILADA.

THE LIFE

OF

EDWIN FORREST.

WITH

REMINISCENCES AND PERSONAL RECOLLECTIONS.

BY JAMES REES.
(COLLEY CIBBER.)

WITH PORTRAIT AND AUTOGRAPH.

"HE WAS A MAN, TAKE HIM FOR ALL IN ALL,
I SHALL NOT LOOK UPON HIS LIKE AGAIN."

PHILADELPHIA:
T. B. PETERSON & BROTHERS;
306 CHESTNUT STREET.

TO

THE MEMBERS

OF THE

THEATRICAL PROFESSION

IN

THE UNITED STATES,

THESE

REMINISCENCES

OF

A DISTINGUISHED CO-LABORER

IN THE

CAUSE OF THE DRAMA,

ARE

RESPECTFULLY DEDICATED

BY

THE AUTHOR.

TO THE READER.

SHORTLY after the death of Mr. Edwin Forrest, on account of the intimacy and personal friendship that had existed between us for a period of nearly fifty years, I commenced the publication of a series of articles in the "SUNDAY MERCURY," of Philadelphia, under the head of "Reminiscences" of that distinguished gentleman. The great interest excited by the early numbers, induced me to make some change in my original plan. Since the completion of the series in the "Mercury," I have written several additional chapters, which contain a full history of Mr. Forrest's life, from the time of his birth until his death. I have also made large additions to the articles as originally published in the "Mercury," and they are now submitted to the public, in book form, by one who was endeared to the distinguished actor by the most tender ties of friendship.

On almost every occasion when Mr. Forrest was called upon for a sketch of his early life to accompany some play or book of the drama, he invariably referred such publishers to me, "as being," he said, "more acquainted with his early life, and remembering incidents about him much better than he did himself."

My acquaintance with Mr. Forrest dates from boyhood, and in the latter part of his life, I was his constant companion, and perhaps no one had as many advantages to become acquainted with his professional career, or with the various phases of his character in private life, as myself. These advantages were the result of the confidence Mr. Forrest placed in me. When he was absent from the city, he entrusted his house and its valuable contents to my charge, with money to defray all the current household and any other necessary expenses. I had the sole use of his library during his absence, and the privilege of introducing my friends to view both it and the picture gallery.

It is not egotism which induces me to allude to these facts here, but that my readers may fully understand the personal relationship existing between the subject of this work and its author, and also the motive I had in its composition—A TRIBUTE TO THE MEMORY OF ONE WITH WHOSE NAME A NATION IS SO FAMILIAR.

The portrait of Edwin Forrest, in front of this volume, was engraved expressly for the work, on steel, from the last photograph for which he ever sat. It was taken by the celebrated Philadelphia artist, F. Gutekunst, and Mr. Forrest was so well pleased with it, that he declared he "would never sit for another picture to mortal man." It was alas! too true; for his death followed shortly afterwards.

JAMES REES.

CONTENTS.

CHAPTER IV.

CHAPTER V.

CHAPTER VI.

CHAPTER VII.

CHAPTER VIII.

CHAPTER IX.

CHAPTER X.

CHAPTER XI.

CHAPTER XII.

CHAPTER XIII.

CHAPTER XIV.

CHAPTER XV.

CHAPTER XVI.

CHAPTER XVII.

CHAPTER XVIII.

CHAPTER XIX.

CHAPTER XX.

CHAPTER XXI.

CHAPTER XXII.

CHAPTER XXIII.

CHAPTER XXIV.

CHAPTER XXV.

*

CHAPTER XXVI.

CHAPTER XXVII.

CHAPTER XXVIII.

CHAPTER XXIX.

CHAPTER XXX.

CHAPTER XXXI.

CHAPTER XXXII.

CHAPTER XXXIII.

CHAPTER XXXIV.

CHAPTER XXXV.

CHAPTER XXXVI.

CHAPTER XXXVII.

CHAPTER XXXVIII.

CHAPTER XXXIX.

CHAPTER XL.

CHAPTER XLI.

CHAPTER XLII.

CHAPTER XLIII.

CHAPTER XLIV.

CHAPTER XLV.

CHAPTER XLVI.

CHAPTER XLVII.

CHAPTER XLVIII.

CHAPTER XLIX.

LIFE OF EDWIN FORREST.

CHAPTER I.

INTRODUCTION TO THE WORK.

DR. JOHNSON, speaking of Biographical writing, says:

"No species of writing seems more worthy of cultivation than biography, since none can be more delightful or more useful, none can more certainly enchain the heart by irresistible interest, or more widely diffuse instruction to every diversity of condition." History allows full scope to the writer in the exercise of his pen, if it be impartial, the world will readily acknowledge its truthfulness—if otherwise, it becomes personal, or simply national, and intended to exalt some one, or some nation at the expense of another. History therefore is doubtful, biography truthful. Reminiscences of an individual includes biography and history, and if the author is not swayed by prejudice, the public will find the subject-matter an index to the true character of the person of whom he treats.

One other feature in these reminiscences of Mr. Edwin Forrest, is the lesson they are likely to convey to the young, the aspiring and ambitious. Forrest was the architect of his own fortune, and commanded the Genii of the mind to open to his view the wealth of the intellectual world; into that world, at an early age, he entered, an obscure boy of humble birth, and iron fortune, fighting his way up to an eminence in the profession he had adopted, without those adventitious circumstances which made a Garrick and Kemble great; with Forrest:

> "Ambition was an idol on whose wings,
> Great minds are carried only to extreme
> To be sublimely great, or to be nothing."

The profession of an actor, unfortunately for our stage, is not considered in the same light as are the other learned professions, and yet it requires as much study, application and practice as that of any other coming under the above head. In the question of the character of the stage, and its lawfulness, involves in a great measure that of the actor. If the stage be in itself unlawful, then the actor can lay no claim to the title of a professor—but if it is lawful, both as regards morals, and the requirements of great intellectual power, why is he debarred the admittance into the temple of the universe of letters? The stage has always been considered as a source of moral instruction, as well as of amusement, the profession therefore is not only innocent, but useful and commendable.

A writer has said: "Of the various trades and professions, to which men have recourse, either to gratify their inclinations or to procure a livelihood, there is not one particularly of those called liberal, more laborious, or wasteful of life, than that of an actor, and more especially a tragedian."

To arrive at consummate excellence requires indefatigable study, unwearied practice, and the utmost exertion of the vocal organs; not to mention the violent bodily exercise frequently demanded; and above all, the violent agitation of alternate passions, which though assumed, are often very deeply felt, and which being felt, must naturally impair the vigor of the animal spirits, and "exhaust the lamp of life."

"It does not require the physical or anatomical skill of an M. D.," says the editor of the "Dramatic Mirror," "to understand how intimately the passions and feelings are connected with the bodily frame and affect it; how destructive they often prove to health—how fatal to life itself; and yet, without feeling and passion, what is a player?" A French actor, the Garrick of France, says: "Rules may teach us not to raise the arms above the head; but if passion carries them there, it will be well done." Passion knows more than art. And yet, although we admit this strain upon the mental and physical strength of an actor, still there are but few instances of an actor's career inducing short life. Over exertion, whether on the stage, in the pulpit, or at the bar, has produced fatal results; but this may probably be owing to other causes not apparent to the eye of a casual observer. An eminent French actor, Montfleury, died of his violent exertions in performing Orestes, in the Andromache of Racine. Wm. B. Wood broke a blood vessel while enacting Brutus, and Edwin Forrest was carried out to the green-room on one occasion while playing Lear, in an unconscious state, caused by a rush of blood to the head, and yet, both of these gentlemen lived to a "good old age."

Another remarkable fact in connection with the lives of actors, is that people generally, without thought or reflection say: "Oh! they do not live long; their habits and associations are such as to shorten their lives." This is not so. We admit there are some cases, and fearful ones too, of the death of actors, at an early age, from the causes to which rumor alluded; but they are few, compared to the destruction of human life in other branches of the liberal arts from the same causes. Again, while our alms-houses and prisons are the homes of many who were once the pride and ornaments of society, there is not a single actor, at the present writing, an inmate of either of these institutions. A tree, it is said, is judged by its fruit—that of the stage can therefore be judged by this fact in connection with our criminal records. An idea once advanced that the theatre is an improper source of amusement, becomes in time a serious charge. At different periods of stage history, learned men have advocated the stage as being a "school of virtue"—"a warm incentive to virtue, and a powerful preservative against vice"—"and a perpetual source of the most noble and useful entertainments"—"the mirror of a nation's virtue." By others it has been branded as "the school of impiety"—"the porch of hell"—"the house of the devil"—"the sink of corruption and debauchery." There is one peculiar fact in connection with these antagonistical disputants, and that is, those who defend the drama were the most eminent of the period in which they wrote, viz: "Addison, John Styles, D. D., Wm. Gilpin, author of the Exposition of the New Testament, Rev. I. Plumptree, Dr. Johnson, Richard Cumberland, Dr. Owen,

Milton, Sir Richard Blackmore, and Dr. Watts." As this gentleman's name is so piously identified with our church history, we deem it advisable here to give his opinion of stage performances. In his "Discourse on the Education of Children," he says: "It is granted, that a dramatic representation of the affairs of human life, is by no means sinful in itself; I am inclined to think, that valuable compositions might be made of this kind, such as might entertain a virtuous audience with innocent delight, and even with some good profit. Such have been written in French, and have been acted with applause."—[*Works*, vol. vi. p. 376. *See also Preface to his Horæ Lyricæ.*]

To these we may add the names of the philosopher Plato, Bishop Rundle, Dr. Gregory, and the learned and pious Hugh Blair, D. D. In giving the names of a few of those who advocated the stage—at a time when the stage commanded both notice and respect, it may be well to state that its opponents were quite as numerous, many of whom stood high in the world of letters, but they were more or less influenced by that spirit of fanaticism which no argument, however strong, can ever overcome.

Indiscriminate praise, or indiscriminate censure are alike injurious to any cause, and equally indispose the friends or the enemies of it to an inquiry into its true merits; and when we find such very opposite opinions prevail upon any subject, the *probability* is, that truth lies somewhere between these two extreme points.

Our stage history furnishes numerous instances of this same spirit of opposition, but if we trace it from the year 1752 gradually down to the erection of the old

Chestnut Street Theatre 1793, and follow it step by step to the advent of a class of actors educated in the profession and who had made it a life's study, we have a history of the stage and the drama that finds no parallel in the annals of the world.

Connected with this era in our stage history is the subject of these "Reminiscences," and if we fail to identify him with its legitimate character, it is because a class of actors and sensational dramas have lessened the histrionic art in the estimation of those whose duty it was to maintain, and shield it from these pretenders, to a profession of which they have not the slightest claim. The result has been ruinous to the moral character of our stage, and can only be remedied by a firm determination to discountenance everything that is calculated to lessen its influence as a corrective, as well as a curative of evil.

If the evil attached to a theatre be no part of its inherent quality, but arises merely from the abuse of it, and which is in the power of its frequenters and properly constituted authorities to correct; and if this powerful engine can be further made to promote the cause of virtue, and, with that, indirectly if not directly, the cause of religion, then does it become our duty to separate the evil from the good, and to make it such as all good men and women may frequent. "Next to the church, a theatre should be a place for people to visit, if it is not made unlawful, and contrary to the spirit of our religion. And that visiting acting, or attending it, is inconsistent with the character of a Christian." *John Witherspoon, D. D.*

If the views expressed in these remarks should give offence to those who have control of our theatres, they must attribute them to the desire we have to restore our stage to its former noble and legitimate character; our desire has ever been to see our stage and drama based upon a firm principle, so as to be the arbiters, the guardians, and the guides of the public taste and morals.

CHAPTER II.

EDWIN FORREST'S BIRTH AND PARENTAGE.—HIS ANCESTRY.—EARLY STRUGGLES.—HIS FATHER A RUNNER IN STEPHEN GIRARD'S BANK.—ALEXANDER WILSON, THE ORNITHOLOGIST.—YOUNG FORREST'S TUTOR.—EDWIN A GREAT MIMIC.—HIS EARLY INCLINATION FOR THE STAGE MANIFESTED.—PARENTAL OPPOSITION.—HIS EDUCATION.—A STORE BOY.—PLAY-BOOK AND DAY-BOOK TOO NEAR TO EACH OTHER.—LECTURED BY HIS EMPLOYER.—THE RESULT.

EDWIN FORREST was born in the city of Philadelphia, March 9th, 1806, in what was known as Old Southwark. The small house in which his parents resided was in George Street, and until within a few years could be pointed out as the birth-place of the great tragedian. His father, William Forrest, was a Scotchman, a native of Dumfrieshire, a frontier county of Scotland. In a small village, near Solway Frith, there is a graveyard attached to a small church, upon many a simple slab the stranger will read the name of "Forrest," some of which bear date far back to some distant period. William Forrest came to this country a man grown, and like most of his countrymen was both industrious and saving. It somehow happened that he settled in Trenton, N. J., and there commenced business—failed—and came to Philadelphia.

In 1791, he was engaged at the Dispensary, No. 68 Chestnut Street, old number. In 1794 he again commenced business, and opened a store, No. 26 South Second Street. In 1797, he removed to No. 10 North Front Street. While engaged in mercantile business he was in the habit of going around among merchants and selling goods by sample, in fact, he was what at that time was called a pedler, or, as they termed it in his own country, Scotland, "Commercial Traveller." In the mean time he became acquainted with a Miss Rebecca Lauman, a young lady of German descent, born in this country—the result was she became Mrs. William Forrest. The business in which her husband was engaged did not exactly meet the views of herself and family, for there is an aristocracy even in the middle classes, and the occupation of a pedler of merchandise they considered one step down the social ladder of life. The result was a change of *base*, and we next find him holding a subordinate position in the old United States Bank; place of residence (1802) No. 51 George Street, where he resided up to the year 1810. George Street is to be found on the old city map, as running from No. 24 Gaskell Street to No. 31 German Street. In 1814 the family removed to No. 55 Shippen Street, where they resided until 1818.

At the close of the United States Bank, his friend, Stephen Girard, who had started one of his own, entitled "The Girard Bank," offered him a situation in it, which he retained until the day of his death.

In 1818 the family removed to No. 77 Cedar Street, where shortly afterwards he died. In 1819, we find the name of Mrs. Rebecca Forrest, widow, No. 77 Cedar Street, where she resided up to 1827–8.

The writer of this knew Mrs. Forrest when thus left a widow with six children, as one of the most industrious women of the day. Indeed, industrious she had to be, with a large family, and but little means.

The parents of Edwin Forrest were religious, and regular attendants at church, and he accompanied them frequently. At the early age of seven he displayed wonderful powers of memory, and also those of imitation. It is said that his father first intended him for the Church. He would amuse his parents by reciting from memory, passages of the sermon, and give a tolerable imitation of the minister's voice, manner and style. This happy pulpit aptitude of their son confirmed their pious purpose; but the death of the father put an end at once and forever to his prospects of advancement in any of the liberal professions.

Among the most distinguished men of the day, who discovered the remarkable talents of young Forrest, was Alexander Wilson, the celebrated ornithologist. He selected appropriate passages from authors, and got the "youthful prodigy," as he called him, to recite them. Mr. Wilson was a regular visitor to the family, and would on every occasion listen to the recitations of his pupil, and then reward him by presenting him with the pictures of his great work, entitled "American Ornithology," then passing through the press. Alexander Wilson possessed considerable taste for literature, and published several poems of much beauty. As Forrest was born in 1806, and Wilson died in 1814, the former it will be perceived, at that period was only eight years of age!

Lauman Forrest was the eldest son, he was a morocco dresser, and when we first knew him he was working on Willow Street, above Second. He was the tallest of the family, being over six feet—and to use a familiar expression, was "as straight as an arrow." He used to take Edwin with him to the work shop, where he gave his first recitation *in public*, standing on a marble slab used by the men for dressing leather. His audience were the workmen.

These early dramatic shoots from a fertile brain, tinctured with a Shakesperian hue, soon began to blossom. It may be said that Edwin Forrest was born an actor, for at that early age his readings and recitations were considered as wonderful. Lauman Forrest died in South America; a younger brother died in infancy. William Forrest, the third son, was a printer.

After the death of the father, the three daughters, Henrietta, Caroline and Elenora, opened a millinery store, No. 77 Cedar Street, while their mother added to their scanty means by binding shoes. It was a life-struggle; but they all bore up bravely, and fought the fight that in the end was to be victorious.

Forrest, like most young men of his age and station, received an education such as the limited means of his parents afforded. But what of that, the mind, the incompressible mind, is the tutor of man; it can grasp and bring from unlimited space all the elements which tend to make a genius. It is the mystery, whose power is in itself, to will and control. Mind—

"Makes the body rich;
And as the sun breaks through the darkest clouds,
So honor 'peareth in the meanest habit.
What, is the jay more precious than the lark,
Because his feathers are more beautiful?
Or is the adder better than the eel,
Because his painted skin contents the eye?"

If Forrest's parents had been wealthy, or the school system at that period as it is now, one grand National Seminary, his mind and intellect would have received the impress of the master spirit—education. Still, man is the architect of his own fortunes, and can command, as he advances on to manhood, those agencies which act as tutors to genius.

Forrest was taken from school when he was about ten years of age, a good stout boy for his years. It was necessary for each one to contribute something to the support of the family, and a situation was obtained for him in the store of Mr. Tiers, ship-chandler, on the wharf. His next situation was with Messrs. Baker & Son, importers of German goods. The store was situated on Race Street, below Third, next door to the old tavern of "The King of Prussia." At this time Forrest had a strong inclination to study play-books, and took great delight in hearing talk of theatres and actors. While in the employ of these gentlemen, it so occurred that the writings of one William Shakespeare were not unfrequently found in close proximity with the day-book. Mr. Baker was a very worthy and pious man, and frequently remonstrated with Edwin about his predilection for the stage; and one day remarked, in his own peculiar style and manner of speaking, "Edwin, my boy, this *theoretical infatuation* will be your ruin."

How often are the aged mistaken in giving advice

to the young! for the poor, struggling actor boy, in the year 1829, presented his mother and sisters with a fine house, and gave them a suitable income, from his first earnings as a star; and in that year we find the name of Mrs. Rebecca Forrest in the directory, living at No. 144, old number, North Tenth Street. Father, mother, brother and sisters passed away from earth, and Edwin Forrest, when death laid his cold hand upon him, was the last of his race.

CHAPTER III.

IMITATES THESPIS OF OLD.—FORMS A THESPIAN CLUB. —PLACE OF MEETING.—PLEASING REMINISCENCES. —HE INHALES THE GAS.—DEVELOPS HIS STAGE PROCLIVITIES.—OLD SOUTH STREET THEATRE.—PLAYS A FEMALE PART.—STRANGE DRESS.—SHOWS TEMPER.—PLAYS ANNA IN DOUGLAS.—POOR EDMUND, THE BLIND BOY.—CHARLES S. PORTER AND JAMES H. HACKETT.—AN AMUSING INCIDENT.—SOME ACCOUNT OF THE OLD APOLLO THEATRE.—DROP CURTAIN AND SCENERY.—DESTRUCTION OF THE THEATRE BY FIRE.

THESPIS, a Greek poet, born at Icaria, in Attica, flourished B. C. 576. He is considered as the inventor of tragedy, from his having introduced actors in addition to the chorus. His stage is said to have been a cart; and the faces of the performers were smeared with wine lees, or, according to Suidas, with white lead and vermillion. As regards the latter, the custom as established nearly 2500 years ago is still retained—with the exception of the *white lead,* as the nineteenth century has materially improved the means of beautifying the human face by less injurious cosmetics.

Edwin Forrest, like that great master of art from whose advent we may date tragedy, and equally ambitious to be the founder of a youthful company of comedians, determines to form a Thespian Club.

Various were the modes resorted to, to carry out this object. The first place selected for the purpose was a room in a small house immediately in the rear of Jacob Zelin's tavern, situated on Chestnut Street, below Fifth, north side. In after years this spot was occupied by Parkinson as a confectionery. There were two or three Thespian Societies about this time, and it is a curious fact that it was not until young Forrest took the lead in them that any attention was paid to the properties or costume, nor is there one name among those belonging to either of the others that ever figured on the legitimate stage. Forrest was not more than eleven years of age when, with his little company, he opened in the room mentioned above.

The second attempt was much better, both as regarded his company and locality. The place selected was in the second story of an old house then, and still standing, at the north-west corner of Harmony Court and Hudson's Alley. Here it was that the spirit of Shakespeare animated the soul of the boy that was to assume, in after years, the sole right of being the representative of the ennobling characters of the bard's transcendant creations. There was no boyishness about this Thespian Club—no play-house for children, but for men to see and applaud.

"The Mortonians" was the first association established by amateurs. This company was organized in 1812. The incentive to this was the extraordinary success of Master John Howard Payne, who created a great excitement in this city in the year 1811, and whose genius and talent were not unfrequently compared with those of Cooke, Cooper and Fennell. Payne turned the heads of half the young men of the town. Foremost among those who were eager to become famous was Jackson Gray, his age was about the same as that of Payne. He was a lad in the hardware store of Wayne & Biddle, south-west corner of Market and Front Streets, but subsequently was apprenticed to Jane Aitken, printer. This society soon joined the one established by Edwin Forrest, and the old South Street Theatre became the scene of their youthful efforts to master the art and science of acting. We annex the names of those who were the most active in the cause. Among them will be found several who in after years became popular as actors, while others distinguished themselves in other branches of the liberal arts. Our readers will recognize the names of one or more who rose to eminence as writers, editors, and politicians. Joseph C. Neal, author of "Charcoal Sketches;" M. M. Noah, distinguished both as an editor and dramatic author; Jackson Gray, Anthony Seyfert, Benjamin Mifflin, Washington Dawson, and R. Meers, printers; Harris G. Pearson, Hernizen, Chalkly Baker (this gentleman, better known in after years as a ward politician, kept the old Race Street House, wherein General Andrew Jackson was first spoken of and nominated for the Presidency); Captain Klett, Thomas Reed, Frank Savoy (carpenter); Robert Cooper, J. McKibben, A. Phillips, Charles Webb (subsequently an actor of great merit); Jack Moore (bookbinder, served his time with Robert Desilver); I. C. Higgins (joined Caldwell's company in New Orleans); Fred. Saillac, Robert Laidley (known as an actor of some pretentions to tragedy); Adam Levy (broker); William Carr, Michael Monier, Samuel Ward (subsequently turned his attention to the ministry); West Blair (*rose* to the position of a pilot on board a Mississippi steamer), John Heyl (vocalist). These were all members of the profession; among their friends and youthful companions were Edward King (afterward Judge of the Court), John Swift, Jesse R. Burden, and the writer of these reminiscences. Of the above named, the last two alone are living.

It is melancholy to roll up the curtain of the past, and equally so for memory to people the stage and the auditorium with these, our friends, associates and companions. All gay, happy and full of youthful aspirations for the great future, looking forward, at least some of them, to have their names recorded on the dramatic page, bright stars of the "mimic world." One only of these ever reached any degree of eminence in the profession. And now, he too, is gone, and others gained a name in literature, art and science; others again went down the dark stream of life in sorrow, misery, suicide, ignoble death. Let silence be their epitaph—oblivion their tomb!

"When I remember all
  The friends, so link'd together,
I've seen around me fall,
  Like leaves in wintry weather,

I feel like one
Who treads alone
Some banquet hall deserted,
Whose lights are fled,
Whose garlands dead,
And all but he departed."

One little incident in Edwin Forrest's career we will relate here, as it attracted the attention of Colonel John Swift, and was the cause of that gentleman taking such an interest in his "young *protegé*." We were one evening in the Tivoli Garden, situated on Market Street near Broad, north side, some time in the year 1817, when a professor of chemistry was administering what at that time was called "laughing gas." Some very amusing scenes occurred, arising from its effect on those who inhaled it. At last a fine looking lad, whose age might have been about thirteen years, presented himself to the man of science to be experimented upon. As we have observed, he was a fine looking boy, neck bare, a large shirt collar thrown back over that of a blue roundabout; for boys at that period did not wear men's style of coats. His features were manly, bold, but not forward or impertinent in their varying emotions; he also had a fine head of hair which gathered in clustering curls around his well-formed neck. He was what we should call a model boy. He inhaled the gas; immediately after the bag was removed he started out on the gravel walk, and throwing himself into a position peculiarly dramatic, he recited a portion of Norval's speech and also of Richard III., but ere he got through, the current of his mind changed, and he made a dash at the bystanders, and a race ensued. The effect of the gas passing off, he came to himself, and, looking wildly around upon the laughing crowd, he rushed away and was seen no more in the Garden. That boy was EDWIN FORREST.

OLD SOUTH STREET THEATRE.

The appearance of the old South Street Theatre on the evenings of these Thespian performances was gloomy in the extreme; the stage and the auditorium partly lit up, gave to the wood scenes and old castles a still more sombre hue; added to which two aged musicians, hired for the occasion, gave forth some old Barbara Allen air, which came up from the orchestra like the notes of some ill-fated swan. Then the characters on the stage with long assassin-like cloaks, high brigand hats, with huge feathers, each one grasping awful looking knives, made one's blood chill at the very sight. The audience occasionally indulged in some critical remarks loud enough to be heard by the actors. On one occasion when Forrest was playing the fair Rosolio to Charles S. Porter's Rudolph, a pugnacious boy in the pit made some observations on fair Rosolio's dress. This dress has since been the subject of much comment, and by some denied as being but the creation of our fancy, for we were the first to describe it. The editor of the *Press*, in his obituary notice of Mr. Forrest, mentioned, or rather quoted it from our description given some eighteen years ago, and it may be well to describe it here, as probably many may not have seen the *Press*, or our allusion to it. This play was the Robbers of Calabria. Our account read thus: "Forrest's dress on that occasion was not marked by that artistical taste which has since been such a prominent feature in his impersonation of character. It was one we shall never forget. He wore thick, heavy shoes, coarse woollen stockings, appertaining to a bluish color, a short white dress reaching, with some difficulty, to his knees; on his head he wore a bright scarf, intended to represent a sort of turban fashion of the sixteenth century. Every allusion the lover makes to *her* beauty, and the symmetry of her person, and that matchless excellence which is to be found always in the object of our affections, the audience laughed at most heartily, and well they might, although Forrest and Porter played their respective parts as if no other manifestations than that of delight were given. The pugnacious boy alluded to, however, carried the joke a little too far, for Forrest walked deliberately down to the feeble foot-lights, and, shaking his fist at the pugnacious boy, said in a loud voice, "I'll whip you when the play is over." This silenced the boy, and the play went on.

In after years when speaking of the dress he wore on the occasion, he said: "The dress gave the most trouble, I was under the impression in the morning that I could get one at the theatre. Satisfied of this, I made no attempt to get one, when, to my surprise, I found there was nothing in the theatre wardrobe to suit. Something must be done. I remembered that there was a woman living near the theatre who had a daughter about my size. Away I started, found the woman, and coaxed, begged it of her, and gave her and her daughter a pass to see me in female costume. I carried off the dress in triumph, but, alas! when I put it on, it came, just as you say, to my knees. Judge under what difficulty I played the fair Rosolio."

"Then," he went on, "that rascally boy who annoyed me, and whom I threatened, as you know. Well, after the play was over I looked out for him, and I believe he was looking out for me. It was the hardest fight I ever had, and to this day I cannot tell who conquered. One thing, however, I do remember. We became excellent friends, and he took every opportunity afterward of keeping good order among the boys."

It may be well to state that this "rascally boy" became a wealthy man, and to the day of his death was one of Mr. Forrest's warmest friends.

CHARLES S. PORTER.

One name we purposely omitted on the foregoing list, as it deserves a more special notice—CHARLES S. PORTER. It is a name identified with that of the subject of these reminiscences in the earliest scenes of their amateur performances. Mr. Porter was born in Burlington Co. N. J., July 25th, 1797. His parents removing to the city of Philadelphia, he was placed in the newspaper office of *The Freeman's Journal,* to learn the art of printing. He soon formed the acquaintance of the members of the Amateur Theatrical Clubs, and became one of the stars of the old South Street Theatre. The first time we saw him play, was in the year 1818, on which occasion he played Young Norval, to Forrest's Anna, in the tragedy of Douglas.

It may appear strange to some of our readers in thus speaking of Mr. Forrest's impersonating female characters. It must be observed in this connection that as a boy he was remarkably handsome, and could harmonize his voice so as to imitate most admirably that of a female; then it must be taken into consideration that the audience was composed of the friends of the actors, except on some occasion for a benefit either of a member, or some society.

His second appearance was as Rudolph in The Robbers of Calabria, Forrest playing the part of the beautiful Rosolio. The friendship between these two young men, although Porter was much older, was of the Damon and Pythias order, and continued nearly up to their death. When they were both aged men, a simple circumstance broke the chain of friendship which had linked them together for nearly forty years. We can only say here, without referring to the cause, that Mr. Forrest was to blame.

Mr. Porter was the leading actor at the Old South Street Theatre. On one occasion the play being the Blind Boy, he had occasion to apologize to the audience for the young man who was to have played Edmund, the Blind Boy, and another was called upon *to read the part.* His first appearance is on a bridge, where he is seen, threading his way, with a cane in one hand and the play-book in the other. Whilst his eyes were riveted on the book, his cane was busily engaged in feeling his way. This was too ludicrous, and poor Edmund, the blind boy, had no sympathy from the audience that night. One night we remember reading the following card, printed and stuck against the door of the box office:

> SOUTH STREET THEATRE, 1816.—To-morrow night Chas. S. Porter will enact the Man of Fortitude, being for his benefit. Tickets to be had at the Coffee House, and at Tom Bloxton's. In the evening, at the door of the theatre. Members of Amateur Associations, and his brother typos, please take notice.

Mr. Porter played in all the minor theatres of this city, "Tivoli Garden," "Vauxhall Garden," "Prune Street Theatre," and the "Old Apollo," until his dramatic excellence attracted the attention of William

B. Wood, of the Chestnut Street Theatre, where he became a great favorite with the public. In the year 1826, May 16th, he took a benefit, on which occasion, his friend Edwin Forrest, proffered his services, and played Pierre to Mr. Porter's Jaffier. As he advanced in the profession, he became in time manager, and no man ever enjoyed the confidence of the public as did Mr. Porter when he became the lessee of the Pittsburg and Vicksburg theatres. As manager, actor, gentleman and scholar, Mr. Porter lived and died universally esteemed and regretted. His decease occurred October 5th, 1867.

JAMES H. HACKETT.

The following incident in connection with Charles S. Porter and James H. Hackett, is too good to be lost. Shortly after Mr. Porter left the Old South Street Theatre, he went to New York and offered himself to Messrs. Price and Simpson. He was refused. While in New York he formed the acquaintance of young Hackett, another stage-struck hero, and they concluded to make a theatrical tour on their own "hook," and Newark, N. J., was fixed upon as the most suitable place to make a beginning. The entertainment consisted of readings and recitations. It proved a failure. Hackett had assumed the name of Young, but Porter retained his own. From Newark they proceeded to New Brunswick. Here they were more fortunate. An amusing incident occurred to these aspiring youths while here, which we think worth relating. A military band, composed of young men of the place, had, in the most friendly manner, volunteered to perform for them. A full house was anticipated. From some unforeseen cause they failed to appear. The audience became im patient, to allay which it was necessary that an apology should be made. It is a curious fact in the history of actors that speech-making comprises no part of their study. Hence it is that when it is necessary to address an audience, many of them are worse than the veriest amateur of a Thespian Association. We have known Duff to stammer to such a degree that his remarks were perfectly unintelligible. Even Cooper became nervous, and Jefferson, who was the life and soul of a farce, could not make a speech without exhibiting the utmost confusion. Hackett and Porter were exactly in this position, and were compelled to engage the services of a printer's devil, a real genuine specimen of that mysterious Satanic class, to make the necessary apology. It was to this effect: That in consequence of the non-arrival of the band, Mr. Young would, instead, recite for them young Norval's speech. The "devil," glad of an opportunity to appear on the stage in any character, and paying little or no attention to what had been told him, stepped boldly before the audience. The task, however, he found was not so easy, as the sound of what he had to say, and not the words, were buzzing in his brain. However, he essayed, and thus addressed the audience: "Ladies and gentlemen, the band has not come"—a pause—"the band not being come, Mr. Young will appear as a steed, and give you some novels, and account for himself, being on the 'Camphire Hills.'" This was received with shouts, and when Young appeared, he was hailed with deafening applause. Some looked for the fiery steed, others looked for the novels. Young commenced: "My name is Norval." Some fellow shouted out: "Damn your name"—"on the Grampian Hills, my father, etc." When he came to feeding the flock, another voice yelled out: "Never mind your sheep, give us the novels." The cry became general: "The books! the books!" Young, utterly astonished, rushed off the stage to find Porter and the devil in convulsions of laughter. The band, however, at that moment arrived, and the books were forgotten.

Mr. Hackett was born in the city of New York, March 15th, 1800. He died on Long Island, December 27th, 1871, in the same place where, fifty-five years before, he had formed an Amateur Association, of which he was the leading spirit.

Mr. Forrest's passion for the stage assumed a business character; he intended to follow it as a profession, and for that purpose he devoted all his youthful energies to that end. His was not the mere desire to be considered a Payne or a Betty, he had none of that boyish vanity which would sacrifice art at the shrine of folly. In all that he undertook, and did, he was serious and in earnest. He studied much, and never missed an opportunity of witnessing the advent of some popular star. The stage at that period was, we might say, in its infancy, at least as regarded its national character. An opposition was continually kept up against theatrical amusements, being looked upon as so many branches from the tree of evil, planted as it was said by one William Shakespeare and others, to corrupt the world. Under these circumstances our youthful aspirants for histrionic fame found it an ungracious undertaking. Indeed, to such an extent was this spirit of opposition carried that many of the young men connected with these amateur companies, lost their situations as clerks, and apprentices were actually punished. Jackson Gray, a boy in the store of Wayne & Biddle, hardware merchants; Jack Moore, bookbinder with Robert Desilver, and several others, were compelled to adopt the stage as a profession, in consequence of the prejudice against actors. Men, who in after years fawned upon Mr. Forrest, and flattered him, for they had made the discovery that a profession by which a man became rich, must needs be respectable—had sneered at his youthful efforts when poor.

> "If there is a sin more deeply black than others,
> Distinguish'd from the list of common crimes,
> A legion in itself, and doubly dear
> To the dark prince of hell, it is—HYPOCRISY."

There is not one period of our life to which we refer with more real pleasure than that which was connected with the old theatres. Places of amusement were few; there was but one theatre where the legitimate drama was produced, and that was the Chestnut Street Theatre, better known in after years as "Old Drury."

After the destruction of this time honored Temple, which occurred on Sunday evening, April 2d, 1820, the Walnut Street Theatre then became a prominent place of amusement, under the management of Messrs. Warren & Wood. As the Apollo Theatre was the scene of Mr. Forrest's early dramatic efforts, and up to a certain period in our stage history, was the fashionable resort for the aristocracy of our city, some account of it may not prove uninteresting to our readers.

After the close of the theatre at South and Vernon Streets, in December, 1760, the company of Douglass remained away from the city for more than five years.

The theatre had in the meanwhile fallen into other hands, and Douglass, the manager, therefore took measures to erect a new house, much larger than the first one. It was built at the south-west corner of Cedar, or South Street, and a small street afterwards called Crab Street—at other times Apollo Street and Charles Street — between Fourth and Fifth. This company, which first entitled itself "a company of comedians from London," now assumed the title of "The American Company." Douglass still remained the manager. This continued to be the principal place of amusement up to the erection of the Chestnut Street Theatre (Old Drury) in 1793.

The Apollo was not built entirely of wood, as was supposed; the walls up to the second story were brick; when it was destroyed by fire in 1821, the walls alone remained. When we first visited it, in 1815, it presented more the appearance of a good sized Pennsylvania barn—one large door in the centre, with two small windows on each side of it, were all the architectural features that presented themselves to our view; the whole of the front was painted red. The view from the boxes was intercepted by large pillars, supporting the upper tier and roof. It was lighted by plain oil lamps without globes, a row of which were placed in front of the stage. The scenery was dingy—chamber scenes taken from descriptions of old castles, and altogether the whole presented a dark and sombre appearance. There were two old musicians, to whom we have already alluded, who fiddled away in the orchestra as if life and death depended upon their exertions, and the airs they played sounded as echoes from the tomb. Then the characters on the stage, with costumes combining almost every style of past ages, and with countenances of marked ferocity, making rapid strides, Tarquin-like, toward some innocent victim on whom they were going to inflict some grievous wrong. Much of the scenery was painted by the unfortunate Major Andre, assisted by Captain Delancy, during the time the British had possession of Philadelphia. Mr. Charles Durang, speaking of this old theatre and of the gentlemen we have just named, said:

"They added some very useful and beautiful scenes to the old stock. One scene, from the brush of Andre, deserves record. It was a landscape, presenting a distant champagne country and a winding rivulet extending from the front of the picture to the extreme distance. In the foreground and centre was a gentle cascade, the water exquisitely executed, overshadowed by a group of majestic forest trees. The perspective was excellently preserved; the foliage, verdure, and general coloring, artistically toned and glazed. The subject of this scene and its treatment was eminently indicative of the bland tone of the ill-fated major's mind—ever running in a calm and harmonious mood.

"It was a drop scene, and hung about the middle of the third entrance, as called in stage directions. The name of Andre was inscribed in large black letters on the back of it—thus put, no doubt, by his own hand on its completion, as is sometimes the custom with scenic artists. It was burnt, with the rest of the scenery, at the destruction of the theatre in 1821. It would have been a precious relic at the present day for its very interesting associations.

"Poor Andre little thought, while he was painting

that scene, that in a few short years afterwards it would be used in a national play written on the subject of his capture and death. It was so used in the summer of 1807—on the 4th of July—at the old South Street Theatre, as representing the pass on the banks of the Hudson River where he was taken by the three militiamen. It was the only suitable scene in the house which would answer for the locality without painting one expressly for it. The piece had no merit as a drama, and was only concocted for holiday occasions. It was a sort of hybrid affair—fulsome in dialogue and pantomime, full of Yankee notions and patriotic clap-trap; but incessant laughter and applause of a crowded house, I well remember, rewarded the company's efforts."

The stage-box on the east side, in after years, was fitted up for President Washington whenever he honored the theatre with his presence, at which time The Poor Soldier was played by desire. The drop curtain to which so much interest was attached, was painted by Major Andre. We well remember, when the theatre was destroyed by fire, the extraordinary efforts made by firemen and others to save this curtain from the flames; all attempts however proved unavailing, and that, with many other relics of by-gone days, fell a victim to the all-devouring fiend. After the fire, it was discovered that the walls were not injured, and from its ruins a *distillery* phœnix-like arose. Dunlap, in speaking of the fire, says: "*Once pouring out a mangled stream of good and evil, is now dispensing purely evil.*"

Reminiscences, however, are but retrogressive shadows which cast a gloom over the present, still, as we glance back o'er the past, gleams of sunlight come up to cast a more cheerful ray on the future. Memory leads us—

> "Back
> In mournful mockery o'er the shining track
> Of our young life, and point out every ray
> Of hope, and peace we've lost upon the way."

CHAPTER IV.

HIS FIRST APPEARANCE ON A REGULAR STAGE. — FINDS A FRIEND IN COL. JOHN SWIFT. — THE SPIRIT OF THE BOY FORESHADOWS THE GENIUS OF THE MAN. —YOUNG NORVAL. — THE AMATEUR MERGES INTO THE ACTOR.—PREPARES FOR A WESTERN TOUR.— THE DRAMA IN CINCINNATI. — SOL. SMITH. — THE DRAKE FAMILY. — FORREST'S JOURNEY. — STAGE-COACH ADVENTURE. — MEETS THE HON. SIMON CAMERON. — HIS FIRST APPEARANCE IN CINCINNATI. — THE UPS AND DOWNS OF STAGE LIFE. — THE DREAM OF THE BOY REALIZED IN MANHOOD.

THE same spirit that actuated young Forrest to form amateur companies, extended to others equally enthusiastic and ambitious. Among those who followed the example of this young pioneer were James E. Murdock, Harris G. Pearson, Edmon S. Connor and John R. Scott, these were all Philadelphia *apprentice boys*, and their names are now enrolled among the best of those whose genius and talents gave to our stage "a local habitation and a name."

The limited means of the family debarred him from

taking those lessons in elocution, which are so essential to aid the aspirant for public honors. Nature, however, was an able teacher, and with her assistance he had conquered many difficulties, both in action and speech. Instruction generally is more readily gained through the eye than by means of any other sense; and thus the exhibition of that which is refined and good in our nature has a tendency to lift us above all the mechanical rules of mere art, and creates an enthusiasm and an ambition to appear in real life, like what we have witnessed on the stage. It is action, blended with the emotions, which, by the aid of scenery, may be considered the best teacher for those who are anxious to become actors. Young as Forrest was at that time, he knew there were certain rules to be observed, of which he, as yet, knew but little. He had seen Cooper, whose action arose from the dignity of the character he represented. He saw before him not the mere elocutionist, but the Coriolanus, Damon, and Virginius of history. Everything allied to mere art was no longer stage appendages.

Brilliant talent—great histrionic power—are always to be found with those who studied the art histrionic as a science, and pursued it as one of the learned professions. The light from such stars still linger on the stage to shine like "a good deed in a naughty world." The young actor who selects a great one for his model, should endeavor to imitate his mental as well as his physical qualities. The physical grandeur of the man—his fine perception of the beauties of art—his classical elegance of action and perfect marks of eloquence—present to the student the best models for copy, to form the image he purposes to impersonate. Many young actors imagine themselves perfect, and pay little or no attention to the full latitude of the object they have in view, but form it according to the scanty model of their own capacity. If intellect is not made the medium through which true art is to be carried out on the stage, the aspirant for histrionic fame will never become a master.

Mr. Forrest had Cooper for his classic model, who was the Demosthenes of the drama, and so well did he study in that school that he in time became its Talma. Forrest did not think "himself perfect;" he knew there were certain rules, correct pronunciation, action, elegance and grace to be learned and attained, before he could face an intelligent audience. One year before his first appearance on a regular stage, he placed himself under the tuition of MR. DANIEL MAGINNIS, teacher of elocution, No. 83 Locust Street. *Nature and study did the rest.*

We have said that Colonel John Swift took great interest in young Forrest, and wishing to advance him in the profession he was determined to adopt, waited on William B. Wood, the acting manager of the Walnut Street Theatre, and stated the object of his visit, which was to secure a night for the first appearance of his young *protegé.* The request was promptly refused by Mr. Wood, who remarked: "We have been so unfortunate in the numerous 'first appearances' of late that the young aspirant could hope.for little encouragement of his wishes; the drooping state of the drama furnishes another and stronger reason for our course." The usual arguments were used with some success, for the managers finally consented to give the youthful Roscius one night. Mr. Wood, speaking of Mr.

Forrest, says: "Master Edwin Forrest was sixteen years of age, he was a well-grown young man, with a noble figure, unusually developed for his age, his features powerfully expressive, and of a determination of purpose which discouraged all further objections." As this was the most important event in the life of young Forrest, his first appearance on a regular stage, supported by eminent artists, the cast of the play is equally important in connection with the event. Mr. Wood judged the age of Mr. Forrest from his appearance; at that time he was only *fourteen years of age.*

WALNUT STREET THEATRE.
Monday evening, November 27, 1820.
Will be presented the tragedy (in 5 acts) called
DOUGLAS; OR THE NOBLE SHEPHERD.
Written by Mr. Home.

Young Norval..............By a Young Gentleman of this city.
Lord Randolph..............................Mr. Wheatley.
Glenalvon..................................Mr. W. B. Wood.
Old Norval.................................Mr. Warren.
Norval's Servant...........................Mr. Martin.
First Officer..............................Mr. Scrivener
Second Officer.............................Mr. Carter.
Third Officer..............................Mr. Parker.
Lady Randolph..............................Mrs. Williams.
Anna.......................................Mrs. Jefferson.

Instead of being "one opening night," the success of the "Young Roscius" was so apparent that a repetition of the play was asked for, which soon followed, and with increased approbation. Soon after he added to his reputation by a spirited effort as Frederick, in Lover's Vows, and Octavian, in the Mountaineers. On the occasion of his benefit he recited Goldsmith's celebrated Epilogue in the character of a harlequin, and concluded by turning a somersault through a balloon.

Perhaps a better school, or one more purely legitimate, could not have been selected at the period than this, for the advent of a debutant, nor has there been a company since, which could compete with the old Chestnut Street stock. Forrest enacted Young Norval, with a cast of characters which could not have been equalled in the country then, nor has it been since. Its members were of the old English school, and could trace their tutors from the days of Garrick. The profession with them was an art, and it was looked up to as one of the highest, and respected accordingly. Mr. Wood's Glenalvon we shall never cease to remember, and Warren's Old Norval was one of the gems of the day. Thus, when Forrest stepped on the stage and rehearsed his part, the strict observance of propriety, the marked deference paid to the lady actresses, and all the etiquette of the green-room, laid the foundation of that marked *reverence* for the beauties of the drama, which he has strictly paid at its altar since.

It was in such a school Forrest received his first lesson in the art histrionic. The strict observance of all the rules that compose propriety, the etiquette observed in the green-room, the marked deference paid to the lady actresses—all he said, "made him feel as if he stood in the presence of kings and princes." Such indeed they were as the representatives of those of the "mimic world." Thus, at an age of fourteen, he found himself surrounded with such men as Wood, Warren, Francis, Jefferson, Burke, Darley, Wilson, Green, Wheatley, Hathwell; and ladies, whose names are a part of our stage history, Mesdames Wood, Francis, Williams, Darley, Entwistle, Jefferson, Burke, etc. He went forth from this school with impressions of the most pleasing character—impressions that gave him a high estimate of the drama and a fixed determination to make the stage the stepping-stone to fame. There were times, however, when this resolve wavered, it was when he hesitated between the ring of a circus and the theatre. Saw dust, and the excitement of the equestrian pageantry had their charms; but his good genius came to the rescue and saved him from being the Tatnell* of the first and made him the Garrick of the latter.

After consultation with his friends and the managers, it was resolved that Master Edwin Forrest should abandon the young Roscius plan, and take a wider range through the western country; for that purpose John Swift furnished him with funds, and "he left us," said Mr. Wood, "with favorable auguries for the future."

Cincinnati at that time was the only city where the drama had taken root, from whence a *Forest* was to grow! As this was the second move the young Roscius made on the drama's board, and from which important point in his life we may date his future movements to the highest honor the stage confers on its votaries, some account of the state of the drama in the West at that time may not prove uninteresting.

As early as 1805, some itinerants made their appearance in Cincinnati, and gave readings and recitations, and during several succeeding years, strolling companies, without "name or fame," stopped on their way to the "dark and bloody ground," and gave ex-

* Samuel Tatnell, a celebrated equestrian, who created quite an excitement in Philadelphia, at the Olympic Theatre, in 1822, by his fearless riding. He was the first, we believe, who rode a "fiery steed" without saddle or bridle, in the country, or at least the first of any repute.

4

hibitions, more for the purpose of defraying expenses than anything else. In 1815, a society of young men, amateurs, erected a wooden edifice, for the dramatic muse; no objection seems to have been made against it, by the religious, until a strolling company came, who were permitted to play in it. Then commenced the "tug of war," the "clergy were in arms and eager for the fray," as they always are when the Theatre is the shaft for their venomed darts; it was urged by them that it encouraged a set of wandering vagabonds, and engrossed the time of the people, that it was an idle and demoralizing profession, etc. They were strongly supported by the bigoted—the company vanished, and even the amateurs had to yield to the overwhelming arguments of the clergy, and the temple of the muses, the queen of the arts and sciences, the governess of music, and the concentration of rays from the brightest luminaries in the hemisphere of learning was closed.

Among those who made what is here termed theatrical tours in the far West, was Mr. Wm. Turner. He can claim rank with the earliest pioneers in the drama's cause beyond the Blue Ridge. As early as 1810-11 he performed in various towns of the West, and was a regular visitor at that early period, to many places where the music of the Thespian band had never been heard. In 1815, a Thespian company had a theatre in Cincinnati, from whom Mr. Turner rented it for twelve nights, and performed The Stranger, Othello, School for Scandal, Man and Wife, The Rivals, Richard III., Cure for the Heart Ache, Lover's Vows, Hamlet, Wheel of Fortune, Alexander the Great, Romeo and Juliet, etc. The reader will perceive that the legitimate was decidedly the object of the manager. His company at that period consisted of Mr. Collins, Mr. Caulfield (who died in April, 1815), Morgan, Jefferson, Anderson, Laidly, Bob Laidly, Cargel, Lucas, Turner, Beale, Mrs. Turner, Mrs. Barrett, and Mrs. Milner. This campaign commenced April 3d, 1815.

Mr. Drake and family emigrated to the West in 1815, upon an invitation from Mr. Luke Usher, who had some time previously established theatres in Frankfort and Lexington. The Louisville Theatre, which has since been enlarged to its present size, was built, and in a short time Mr. Drake had the control of all the theatres in Kentucky.

The following persons composed what may properly be termed the Pioneer Company of the West; Messrs. Drake, Blisset, Lewis, Ludlow, S. Drake, Jr., Alexander Drake, Jas. Drake, Mrs. Lewis, Miss Denny, and Miss Julia Drake.

In 1819, a small company under the management of Mr. Blanchard, visited Cincinnati, and performed a few nights in Mr. Dawson's school-room, in Water Street.

The foundation of the Columbia Street Theatre was laid this year, and the company of Messrs. Collins & Jones performed for a short season in the second story of Burrows & Turner's store, corner of Columbia and Walnut Streets. Next year, 1820, the theatre opened with Wives as They Were, with the following persons in the cast. Sir Wm. Dorrillon, Mr. Collins, Bronzely, Mr. Jones, Lord Priorry, Mr. Lucas, Miss Dorrillon, and Mrs. Groshon. Collins was an excellent actor, so was Jones. Mrs. Groshon was deservedly a great favorite; she was an excellent Lady Macbeth. James [illegible]. Scott, since known as "Long Tom Coffin," was a leading member of the company.

A company consisting of Messrs. A. Drake, S. Drake, Jr., Palmer, Fisher, Douglass, Jones, Sol. Smith and Mesdames Morgan, Fisher, and three or four young Fishers', followed. With a company so limited in number, it will be supposed the selection of pieces must have been extremely circumscribed, but this does not appear to have been the case, for we find they performed such pieces as Pizarro, The Poor Gentleman, and other equally full plays. The following was the cast for

PIZARRO.

PIZARRO, ATALIBI,	MR. S. DRAKE.
ROLLA, LAS CASSAS,	MR. FISHER.
ALONZO, OROZIMBO,	MR. A. DRAKE.
HIGH PRIEST	MR. SOL. SMITH !
ALMAGRO	MR. SOL. SMITH ! !
BLIND MAN	MR. SOL. SMITH ! ! !
SENTINEL	MR. SOL. SMITH ! ! ! !
VALVERDE	MR. SOL. SMITH ! ! ! ! !
GUARD	MR. SOL. SMITH ! ! ! ! ! !
THE WHOLE OF THE SPANISH ARMY	MR. SOL. SMITH ! ! ! ! ! ! !

All these seven characters were represented by Mr. Sol. Smith.

We find the name of Sol. Smith among those who formed the company of 1821, acting as prompter. The company consisted of Messrs. Collins, Jones, Cargill, Hays, Henderson, Miss Denny, Mrs. Groshon, Mrs. Jones, Mrs. Hanna, and Miss Seymour, afterwards Mrs. Cargill. Mr. Cooper performed an engagement during the season. On the first night of his engagement, the following whimsical incident occurred. Othello was the play

"The fame of the great tragedian had drawn a crowded audience, composed of every description of persons, and among the rest a country lass of sixteen, whom (not knowing her real name) we will call Peggy. Peggy had never before seen the inside of a playhouse. She entered at the time Othello was making his defence before the duke and senators. The audience were unusually attentive to the play, and Peggy was permitted to walk in the lobby until she arrived at the door of the stage-box, when a gentleman handed her in, without withdrawing his eyes from the celebrated performer, and her beau, a country boy, was obliged to remain in the lobby. Miss Peggy stared about for a moment, as if doubting whether she was in her proper place, till casting her eyes on the stage, she observed several chairs unoccupied. It is probable this circumstance alone would not have induced her to take the *step* she did, but she observed the people on the stage appeared more at their ease than those among whom she was standing, and withal much more sociable, and as fate would have it, just at that moment, Othello, looking nearly towards the place where she was situated, exclaimed:

'Here comes the lady.'

"The senators half rose, in expectation of seeing the 'gentle Desdemona,' when lo! the maiden from the country stepped from the box plump on the stage, and advanced towards the expecting Moor. It is impossible to give any idea of the confusion that followed; the audience clapped and cheered—the duke and senators forgot their dignity—the girl was ready to sink with consternation—even Cooper himself could not help joining in the general mirth. The uproar lasted for several minutes, until the gentleman who had handed her into the box, helped the blushing girl out of her unpleasant situation. It was agreed by all present that a lady never made her debut on any stage with more eclat than Miss Peggy."

Cincinnati at that period was the Athens of the drama beyond the Blue Ridge, but unlike Athens of old, she gave her Thespians something better than a wagon for their exhibition.

The first newspaper printed north of the Ohio River, and the third west of the mountains, was issued at this place, November 9th, 1793, by William Maxwell; its name was the *Sentinel of the Northwestern Territory*, its motto "open to all parties." In 1811 the first public school was erected; and in 1814 we find a seminary was instituted, under the name of the Cincinnati Lancastrian Seminary. In this year the public library, which, for the space of five years, had been struggling with "causes and effects," for an existence, commenced its infantile operations, with eight hundred volumes, the usual number of a private library. To trace the gradual rise of the city, in all the various departments of literature, commerce, etc., would be one of much interest, and productive of much pleasure. In 1831 we find established a wholesome system of education; the Legislature of 1825 having passed a law, laying the foundation of a system of free schools throughout the State; and in addition to which a special act having been passed, making more ample provision in Cincinnati. The city authorities in 1831 commenced operations under this law, and schools have been established in the different districts, sufficient to accommodate all the children of a proper age, and to continue the year round. These schools are free, and open to all classes, without distinction, and are supported by a tax.

In 1815 the population of Cincinnati was about thirty thousand. The increase of this, next to the largest city in the West, will show an account for the extraordinary increase, and the rapid advancement of the arts and sciences through such a vast section of our country, which was a half century ago almost a wilderness. Cincinnati, in 1815, was but a young city, what is she now in 1873? Possessing a population of nearly 220,000!?

Such was the state of the drama in the West, when Edwin Forrest started from Philadelphia, in the year 1822, to join a theatrical company in Cincinnati.

> "When young with sanguine cheer and streamers gay
> We cut our cable—launch into the world,
> And fondly dream each wind and star our friend."

On his way he met with a few obstacles, which his youth naturally incurred, these however he soon overcome. On the route to Pittsburg, at one of the stopping places two gentlemen got on the stage, they were evidently of the better class, in whose conversation Forrest became much interested, and listened with much attention. One of the gentlemen was called by the other, General. After listening some time, chance gave him an opportunity of putting in a word, which he did, and to some purpose, for his two travelling companions became in their turn interested. Boy-like, Forrest told his simple story of how he made his first appearance on the stage, and his ambition to become a great actor. "And so," said the younger of the two, "you are Master Forrest? I am glad to meet you, young sir, as I have heard you surpassed Master Payne in Young Norval. But you have undertaken a great task, and at your age there are so many temptations in your path that it will require the strength of manhood to resist."

"But I will resist, sir, and if I live I will carve for myself a name."

"That you will if you maintain the character you have already, and study with an eye to that object," observed the elder traveller.

Mr. Forrest, in relating this little incident to us, laughed heartily while doing so, "for," says he, "although but sixteen, I really thought myself a second Cooper, and vain enough to think I was capable of holding conversation and maintaining an argument with any one." One of these gentleman—the younger of the two alluded to—was Simon Cameron, and when Mr. Forrest met him in after years, the fulfilment of his ambitious youthful aspirations was the subject of a very pleasing conversation.

In the fall of 1822, Messrs. Collins and Jones opened the Cincinnati Theatre, the company consisting of Messrs. Collins, Jones, Scott, Edwin Forrest, Davis, Eberle, Henderson, Groshon, Mrs. Pelby, Mrs. Riddle, Miss Riddle, Miss Henton, and Miss Eliza Riddle. The opening play was the Soldier's Daughter. Young Malfort by Edwin Forrest.

During the season Mr. Pelby acted as a star, Forrest playing Titus to his Brutus, and Julius to Virginius. It will be perceived that he made a flattering beginning, and everything looked bright before him. With varied success the company played for a short season, and then proceeded to Louisville. Some difficulty arising between the managers and a portion of the company, induced a few of the latter to return to Cincinnati and open the Globe Theatre on Maine street. At this house Forrest played Othello and other characters with much success—"but rather imperfect," says an old friend, "*with scarcely a knowledge of the text.*" The success lie rather in his appearance and voice. Mr. Forrest played Richard III. for his benefit. The same critic said, after seeing his Richard, "that he would in time become a great actor." In conversation with Mr. Forrest, in relation to these early scenes of his life, he said: "The salary I got was so small that I was unable to appear on the street in a decent dress —boots, particularly, gave me the most trouble, for I was compelled to wear my stage boots from the boarding house to the theatre, and from the theatre to the boarding house. On the opposite side of the river there was a large forest, a gloomy place enough, huge oaks, and other tall trees, with a sprinkling of underwood, rendering it a fitting place for me to rehearse my part and try my voice. On a Sunday morning early I would cross the river and seek out the loneliest part of the wood for my purpose. My stage boots—for I had no others—was the only part of my costume that smacked of the shop, my poverty, not my will, rendered this a necessity. Here I would spend the day, reading, spouting and fighting a tree as if it were Richmond and I the Richard.

"I said to Sol. Smith one day that if I ever became a rich man I would purchase that dear old wood—this was said at a time when I really had not a dollar in the world." This wood adjoins the town of Covington, Ky., situated on the Ohio River, opposite Cincinnati, just below the mouth of the Licking River, which separates it from the city of Newport. As Mr. Forrest purchased this woodland in after years, the circumstances which led to his becoming its owner, and which still belongs to his estate, were as follows: When playing a star engagement in Cincinnati years afterwards, Sol. Smith said to him one day, "Forrest, do you remember saying that if ever you became a rich man you would purchase the woods in Covington, where you went in your poverty to avoid society and rehearse your part?"

"Yes, I remember."

"Well, look at that," handing Forrest a bill announcing the sale of valuable property in Covington; the "wood scene" in his youthful memory was particularly described.

"When is the sale to take place?"

"Why to-day; look at the bill."

"Yes, there it is, to begin at ten o'clock precisely; it is now eight. Come, let us be off; it may probably go beyond my figure, however."

The two started, the sale commenced, and it was knocked down to Edwin Forrest, the eminent tragedian.

CHAPTER V.

EARLY STRUGGLES. — TRAGEDY, COMEDY, OR CIRCUS? PLAYS A NEGRO DANDY.—ENGAGES WITH JAMES H. CALDWELL, N. O., FOR THE COMING SEASON.—SUFFERINGS IN THE MEAN TIME.—MAKES A PROVINCIAL TOUR. — ITS RESULTS. — THE RIDDLE FAMILY. — THROWS UP HIS ENGAGEMENT WITH CALDWELL.—JOINS A CIRCUS COMPANY.—SOL. SMITH INDIGNANT. —A PLEASING EPISODE.—GOES TO NEW ORLEANS. —HIS RESOLVE AFTER SEEING CONWAY, THE GREAT TRAGEDIAN.—JANE PLACIDE.—FORREST'S RETURN TO HIS NATIVE CITY.—TRIUMPHANT SUCCESS!

ABOUT this period James H. Caldwell was considered the great Napoleon of the Southern stage. He had erected theatres in the principal cities, more particularly in the South, and New Orleans could boast of having the best temple for the "histrionic muse," as Caldwell called it, and the best company, as he also said, "in the country."

At the suggestion of a friend (Sol. Smith) Mr. Forrest wrote to Caldwell, as also did Smith; the result was that at the commencement of the ensuing season he was regularly enrolled in that gentleman's company at the *enormous salary* of eighteen dollars per week! In the mean time the Cincinnati company struggled on, laboring in its vocation under difficulties. Various attempts were made to keep up with the times, which, at that period, were unusually bad. A new piece written by Mr. Smith was brought out at the Globe, and was quite a success. It was called Modern Fashions. Forrest and Long Tom Coffin Scott (so called in after years) played a pair of dandies. This gave rise to another production, entitled The Tailor in Distress. In this piece Forrest performed the part of a *negro*. Forrest had a decided inclination for comedy; indeed, for a time he actually hesitated between tragedy and comedy, as he did seriously on one occasion between sawdust and the stage. Some of our readers may question this, but as *we know them to be facts*, the record must be received as a truthful version of his early struggles in the mimic world.

As some few months would elapse before he commenced with Caldwell, the company with which he was engaged had to struggle on the best way they could to meet their expenses. This was a hard task, inasmuch as the business in Cincinnati was extremely dull, and little or no encouragement was given to the players. The Globe was therefore given up, and the members of the company scattered in every direction. Forrest and Davis, with the Riddle family, made an excursion into the country and performed at Dayton. They then went to other small towns, and performed with but little success. Indeed, they suffered many privations.

Finding their trip to be one entailing a loss, rather than a profit, they determined to return to Cincinnati. Forrest pawned his stage wardrobe for the purpose of raising money to send the ladies of the company to Newport. The men in the mean time started from Lebanon, on foot, for the same place, a distance of twenty miles. On their way they had to swim a small stream, having no money to pay the ferryman. Too independent to beg, they lived on roasted corn, "as hard," Forrest said, "as Pharaoh's heart." What connection there is between roasted corn and the heart of Pharaoh is a question we very much doubt if Mr. Forrest himself could have answered. This journey, apart from the actual want of food, was a very pleasant one, and Mr. Forrest frequently referred to it as one of the most interesting excursions he ever took!

When they arrived at Newport they played Douglas, and Miss in Her Teens, to a house of seven dollars! They thought it nearly time then to turn their attention to some other business. Some how or other they contrived to get through the summer, and in the fall they joined Collins and Jones, at Lexington, Ky. In the mean time Sol. Smith was getting up a company, and Forrest made application for a situation, but Smith refused, on the ground that Forrest was already under a previous engagement with Caldwell, and he considered the future prospects of his young friend depended much if not altogether upon his adhering to his first contract with the great Southern manager. Forrest, however, insisted upon staying with Sol. Smith, observing: "I would rather remain with you for ten dollars per week than engage with a stranger for eighteen."

Forrest had still another reason for not wishing to fulfil his engagement with Caldwell. There are associations formed in youth which, ere manhood erases them from memory, are stronger than all the arguments of the more advanced or experienced. The Riddle family were talented, and one of them was young and beautiful. There is a certain romance connected with the profession of an actor which throws around him a charm pleasing to the eye of youth and beauty; and thus when as one family they had travelled and suffered together, it did indeed seem hard to separate; and thus it was Forrest determined to break his engagement with Caldwell, and once more appealed to Sol. Smith, but in vain. Provoked at his old friend's opposition, he went immediately to the manager of a circus company, and made an engagement with him as a tumbler and a rider for the term of twelve months. As soon as Smith heard this most extraordinary move on the part of Forrest, he started in pursuit of him, and found him in the ring surrounded by riders, acrobats, vaulters, grooms, and "numerous auxiliaries." Smith had the satisfaction of seeing him throw several flip-flaps, and then running towards the astonished spectator, he shouted out: "What do you think of that, eh?"

Sol. Smith admitted to the writer of this that if he had remained with the circus managers he would have become one of the most daring riders and vaulters that ever appeared in the ring. After much difficulty, in which he was assisted by others, Forrest was induced to give up this engagement and fulfil the one made with Caldwell. This, as the reader will readily perceive, was the most momentous period of the young actor's life. It must also be remembered, as an excuse for his conduct, that he was then only eighteen years of age.

Even after his engagement with Caldwell, this desire for the "ring" did not die out. It still had its attractions, and the youthful athlete often imagined that he was better adapted to the performances of a circus than he was to the more intellectual acquirements of the stage. The moment, however, he gave up the idea of the former, he turned his whole attention to the latter, and the youth who turned flip-flaps in the ring of a circus became in time the finished Shakesperian scholar of the age, and the only man we ever heard read Hamlet up to the standard as prescribed by the author. There may be a difference of opinion in regard to this assertion of ours, but the best critics in this and other countries have invariably viewed the character of Hamlet as one laboring under a mental disease, and as such Shakespeare has drawn him; and if the actor dates the insanity of the prince from his interview with the Ghost, and where he puts "an antic disposition on," he gives but an imperfect impersonation, and makes him "a thing of shreds and patches." We shall allude to this subject hereafter.

We have said that the feats in the ring of a circus in Cincinnati did not put an end to Forrest's desire of becoming a vaulter and a rider. On one occasion, for a wager, however, in another city, he appeared in the ring in a "still vaulting" act, being for the benefit of "Bill Gates," a well-known *attaché* of the circus. Forrest had the privilege in this wager to disguise himself, so as not to be recognized, if possible, by his theatrical friends. His dress consisted of an enormous pair of Turkish trowsers, breast-plate and fly; his feet were adorned with a pair of sheepskin pumps, the kind worn by a numerous train of auxiliaries. But few knew him, however. On another occasion he tendered his services for the benefit of "Charley Young," on which eventful night, the last of his acrobatic feats, he made a flying leap through a barrel of red fire, singeing his hair and eyebrows terribly. To the last moment of Mr. Forrest's life, however, he still exercised with dumb-bells, dead weights, Indian clubs, etc., and other feats of physical exercise, too much, we frequently thought for his advanced years. Others thought so, too, but the spirit of the boy of eighteen only died out with the man of sixty-six.

The South at that period was the El Dorado to actors. Caldwell's reputation as a manager—his high-toned idea of the drama, his desire to give it that attention which would command the respect and admiration of playgoers—was well known. It was under such a manager and in such a theatre Mr. Forrest first began to appreciate the value of true art. Pelby, Conway, Cooper, Booth and others, had shed the light of their genius on the mimic stage, and he determined to catch some of its rays to illuminate his own pathway. With this resolve he entered the Crescent City, and with a like determination he stepped on the stage of the best regulated theatre in the country.

To the credit of Mr. Forrest be it said here, that the first use he made of his earnings was to provide for his mother and sisters. At first his remittances were small. The following incident connected with this noble trait in his character, we introduce here as an episode. Returning to New York, after a successful engagement in the South and West, he met a friend in the lobby of the Bowery Theatre, upon whom he suddenly opened with the following startling declaration, uttered in a triumphal tone: "Thank Heaven, I am not worth a ducat." His friend eagerly inquired the meaning of an assertion so singular and so ambiguous; for he knew Mr. Forrest had netted a large amount of money by his preceding engagements. Said Mr. Forrest: "My mother and sisters were poor, and I have just purchased for them a house in Philadelphia; and all the balance of my funds, I have invested there, for their support. Thank Heaven, I am not worth a ducat." And well might the noble, aspiring, and triumphant adventurer, whose honorable ambition had been always rewarded as it merited,—"thank heaven" that he had already been enabled to obtain the means of benefaction; and that he possessed the exalted magnanimity to apply them in a way so pleasing and grateful to the noblest instincts of humanity. In speaking of this incident he said to us: "After the completion of the purchase, and placing the deed in my mother's hand, *I had actually but one dollar left!*" On that small capital, with a large amount of genius, he started afresh, and once more achieved a fortune and added fresh laurels to his brow.

Forrest made his first appearance in New Orleans on Wednesday evening, February 4th, 1823, as Jaffier, being then only seventeen years of age. On the first of January, 1824, Caldwell opened his new theatre on Camp Street, with Town and Country, Forrest playing Captain Glenroy. During the season Forrest sustained stars, playing Icilius to Mr. Pelby's Brutus. When we take into consideration the fact of his being but a boy, as regards age, this extraordinary precocious talent far surpasses anything of a similar kind on record. If it were not that we have the most positive evidence of his being born on the 9th of March, 1806, we should be induced to rely on William B. Wood's account of his first interview with Master Forrest, and what he said at the time:

"Forrest," says he, "was at this time a well grown young man, with a noble figure, unusually developed for his age, being sixteen, his features powerfully expressive, etc." It does seem reasonable to those who consider that when he enacted Norval at the Walnut Street Theatre, in 1820, he was but fourteen years of age, that Mr. Wood's theory might be sustained of his being sixteen; this would make his age when he joined Caldwell in New Orleans, in 1824, exactly twenty, an age that would in some measure justify a manager in giving him important parts to play. A lad of seventeen enacting Iago to the Othello of a star, and Richmond to his Richard, does indeed seem remarkable, and yet it is so. At the time we knew Mr. Forrest as the *boy* actor, we considered ourselves a *man*—our being Mr. Forrest's senior by four years made the fact very plain to us!

We have something still more remarkable to record in connection with Mr. Forrest's New Orleans engagement, and that is, he enacted King Lear for his benefit, being then in the nineteenth year of his age. Perhaps history does not furnish another instance like it. Lear, a character requiring all the elements that make up the actor, both mentally and physically, is one that few undertake, more particularly as no one had attempted the part since George Frederick Cooke's transcendent genius invested it with so much Shakesperian beauty and power. Forrest's attempt was simply praiseworthy, but from that moment, as he said, "*I determined to make Lear my great character*—that is, if I ever reach a point to command success."

For the first time in his life, Mr. Forrest had here an opportunity of witnessing William A. Conway, whom Caldwell had engaged for a short engagement. This was Mr. Conway's first appearance in New Orleans

His reputation had been the "*evant courier*" to create quite an excitement, and Mr. Caldwell was compelled to sell the tickets at auction to the highest bidder. He opened in Othello on Wednesday, March 2nd, 1825. Mr. Conway's impersonation of the *Moor* astounded the young student; he saw him there on the stage, not as he *had* seen him, not as he imagined him to be from mere reading, but as an untamed animal—grand, majestic, fearful, with Afric's blood flowing in his veins. For the first time Mr. Forrest saw Othello's picture truthfully and fearfully drawn. A character drawn with passions so strong—ill-regulated education, and one whose peculiar notions, mental and physical organization, so learnedly portrayed by the actor, that Forrest gazed in astonishment and felt as if the part of Othello was far beyond his reach. And yet it had been one of his chief studies, but the picture, as drawn by Conway, seemed to him like Martin's great painting (copies of which were then out) of "Satan in Council" —the chief figure towering in fiendish grandeur above all the rest. Shakespeare has drawn a character in the person of Othello that has no parallel in the whole range of the drama. The acting of Conway aroused Forrest from the dreams of the boy to the realities of life—in man. Othello was ever before his eyes in the person of Conway, and he muttered to himself, "*I'll master it yet!*"

Let us introduce an episode here, as it had a bearing on the future prospects of Forrest:

JANE PLACIDE.

This lady was a member of Caldwell's company at that time, and was the innocent cause of a serious quar rel between Forrest and Caldwell; a slight sketch of her life may not be out of place. Forrest, impulsive, brave, and sensitive to an insult of any kind, in the excitement of the moment challenged his manager, who wisely, perhaps, refused it. They then separated; Forrest left for the North, and it is probable this, an unpleasant incident, was a momentous period in his life, as it brought him immediately in connection with the celebrated Edmund Kean, who was playing an engagement in New York about that period.

Jane Placide was born in Charleston, S. C., 1804. She was the daughter of Alexander Placide, well known in the South as a manager. He died in 1812. At an early age she was introduced on the stage as a *danseuse*. She made her first appearance on the stage as an actress, in Norfolk, Va., in 1820, as Violante, in the Honeymoon. Made her first appearance in New Orleans, January 4th, 1823, exactly one month before Mr. Forrest's appearance in that city. When we first saw Miss Placide she was still a member of Mr. Caldwell's company—this was in 1833–34. She was not only a very handsome woman, but one of the most finished actresses in the South. In comedy or tragedy she was alike good, and was the pride of the "mimic world" in that city, as she was acknowledged an *artiste* in the cities of the North. In 1827 she played a star engagement at the Chatham Street Theatre, New York. She soon attained the position she aimed at, and was acknowledged, as we have stated, in the South, as the best native *tragedienne* ever seen there. She died in New Orleans in the height of her popularity, on May 16th, 1835. In the American burying ground, New Orleans, there is a marble slab, on which we read the following:

TO THE MEMORY OF JANE PLACIDE.

"——There's not an hour
Of day, or dreamy night but I am with thee;
There's not a wind but whispers o'er thy name,
And not a flower that sleeps beneath the moon
But in its hues of fragrance tells a tale
Of thee."

EDWIN FORREST'S RESOLVE.

"I'll master it yet," were the words uttered by Forrest as he went over the wonderful points of Shakespeare's great tragedy of Othello; with this resolve and the highest aspirations that ever agitated the mind of youth, he wended his way to Albany, N. Y. He had better inducements to go hither, than those of larger cities could hold out. Charles Gilfert was the manager of the Broadway and Albany theatres, and it was with him Forrest engaged to perform in these cities. Mr. Gilfert, in making his arrangements with Forrest for a limited period, was very careful to have his salary fixed at a low figure—salaries at that period were not quite as high as they are now. By this time Forrest had achieved a certain degree of fame, and when the manager suggested the renewal of his engagement, he said, "I presume the salary will be the same." Forrest looked him full in the face, saying, "My terms sir, are one hundred dollars per week."

The manager laughed—the actor frowned—and yet on the 12th of January, 1827, he received from the manager of the Walnut Street Theatre two hundred dollars per night! A rapid rise in his theatrical career. Before he could command such a price, however, he had to pass through two or three years of much practice and study. Edmund Kean, one of the most extraordinary men of the day, said of Mr. Forrest, "That he was destined to a high station in the theatrical profession." He played Iago to Kean's Othello, and Richmond to his Richard III.

Five years had elapsed since he left the place of his birth—the home of his boyhood—the scene of his early dramatic attempts. He came back full of hope and confidence, and with no intention, as it was near the close of the season, to play. It so happened, however, that Charles S. Porter's benefit was about to take place —that he consented to play for him. The last time these two acted together, it will be recollected, was on the boards of the old South Street Theatre—the one enacted a female part, the other *his* lover. They now appeared on the boards of "Old Drury," two finished actors, in the tragedy of Venice Preserved. Mr. Forrest enacted the part of Jaffier, Mr. Porter, Pierre. This was on the 16th of May, 1826. The result was a decided success. As we observed, it was near the close of the season. Mr. Forrest was announced to play for that night only. So much excitement, however, did this single performance create, that the managers were induced to give him two nights more. Pizarro was selected, and he was announced for Rolla, which character he had to repeat, and with so much surprise to his friends, and the approval of the public, that his engagement might have been still longer extended. It had this effect, for when he did appear subsequently, it was here and elsewhere as the star of the dramatic firmament. Mr. Forrest was announced "from the theatre at Albany." His visit to Philadelphia was during the interval between the closing of the Albany theatre and the opening of the Bowery, with the manager of whom he was engaged.

In the same year Mr. Forrest again returned to New York, and kindly offered his services to an excellent stock actor by the name of Woodhull, to play for his benefit. This was at the Park Theatre, on the 23rd of May, 1826. The play selected was Othello. It was from this hour we may trace the bright career of Mr. Forrest. It is a remarkable circumstance connected with these two benefits, that while it showed the feeling Mr. Forrest entertained for his old friends, though still young in years, it also was the means of bringing himself more considerably before the public of the two largest cities of the country. Several persons claimed the credit of having brought Mr. Forrest out,—among them were Gilfert, Hamblin, Sol. Smith and others. There was no bringing out about it. *Forrest brought himself out.* Neither John Swift or William B. Wood ever made any such claim on the credulity of the public; they gave him a start, and he became the sole architect of his own fortune. He had no patron but his own genius, and well he knew on that he could depend. You cannot darken and degrade genius.

> "———It may rust
> Dimly awhile, but cannot wholly die;
> And when it wakens, it will send its fire
> Intenser forth, and higher."

CHAPTER VI.

GREAT THEATRICAL SEASON, 1825.—KEAN, FORREST, MACREADY, LYDIA KELLY AND THOMAS A. COOPER, THE STARS.—KEAN'S RECEPTION.—FORREST AS DAMON.—HIS ENGAGEMENT AT THE PARK THEATRE, N. Y.—STONE'S TRAGEDY OF METAMORA.—LUCIUS JUNIUS BOOTH.—WILLIAM FORREST.—SKETCH OF HIS LIFE.—AN EPISODE.—JOHN W. FORNEY.—RENEWAL OF EARLY FRIENDSHIP.

THE theatrical season in Philadelphia commenced on the 21st of November, 1825. It was rendered memorable by the second visit of Edmund Kean. Miss Lydia Kelly, Edwin Forrest, William Macready and Thomas A. Cooper were announced as regular stars.

Mr. Kean arrived in New York in 1825, and made his first appearance at the Chestnut Street Theatre on the evening of January 18th, 1826, as Richard III. The writer of this was present, and perhaps, if we except the Anderson riot, a more disgraceful scene never occurred within the walls of a theatre. A bitter feeling was roused against the actor, in consequence of his making some very indiscreet remarks about the "Yankees," during his first visit here, which the people had not forgotten. Rotten eggs, marbles, *buttons*, and other missiles were hurled upon the stage. The appearance of Kean was the signal of assault. The play proceeded in dumb show. It was "Richard" pantomimed!

For awhile the opposition was kept up, until at last he was permitted to address the audience. The play then proceeded, but with occasional hisses. He closed this engagement on the 2nd of February, 1826, having played, without interruption, Richard III., Othello, King Lear, Sir Giles Overreach, Brutus and Hamlet. Our judgment or taste may be at fault when we state that of all the characters in which we saw Mr. Kean, his Sir Giles Overreach is the only one that lives in our remembrance. His Shakesperian characters, although they possessed great merit and power, seemed to us overstrained, in the rendering of which the spirit of the author was lost in the attempt of the actor to produce effects. This was not the case with his Sir Giles Overreach. As a finished portraiture of a grasping villain to obtain money and minister to his ambition, Mr. Kean's copy will ever remain a lasting tribute to his genius and talent.

Mr. Kean's next engagement was on the 12th of June, 1826. Edwin Forrest succeeded him, commencing on the 5th of July with Othello, and although late in the season, drew good houses. This was Forrest's first star engagement. His second engagement was at the Walnut Street Theatre. Previous to which, however, he went to Washington City, where he played Damon for the first time. In a letter to a friend, dated "Washington City, October 14th, 1826," he says; "I play Damon for the first time to-morrow night. * * I shall shortly play with Kean; think of that."

He opened at the Walnut Street Theatre, March 7th, 1827, with Damon. During his engagement he played Othello, Rolla, William Tell, Sir Edward Mortimer, King Lear and Jaffier. On the last night of his engagement, March 24th, 1827, his brother William enacted Pythias to his Damon. We annex the announcement bill:

WALNUT STREET THEATRE.

Positively the last night of
MR. E. FORREST'S ENGAGEMENT.

THIS EVENING, March 24th, 1827,
Will be presented the favorite Tragedy of
DAMON AND PYTHIAS;
OR,
THE TEST OF FRIENDSHIP.

DAMON, a Senator............................MR. E. FORREST.
PYTHIAS, a Soldier, his friend..................MR. W. FORREST.

After which, a comic Farce called
IS HE JEALOUS?
OR,
A PEEP INTO THE BOUDOIR.

The public is respectfully acquainted that Mr. MACREADY will perform for a limited number of nights in this city, previous to his return to Europe, being positively the last engagement he can have the honor of making here.

On Monday, OTHELLO—Othello (for the first and only time here), Mr. Macready.

It will be observed that Mr. Forrest, although but twenty-one years of age, was *sandwiched* between two of the most popular actors of the day—Edmund Kean and William Macready. How did he come forth from this contest? His after history is the answer.

Mr. Forrest's first engagement at the Park Theatre, New York, was on the 17th of October, 1829, when he opened as Damon, and successfully appeared as Ham let, Lear, Iago (to Cooper's Othello), Macbeth, Brutus and Carwin. On the 24th of the same month he began a new engagement as William Tell, and on the 15th of November, 1829, took his benefit, when for the first time on any stage, was represented John A. Stone's tragedy of Metamora; or, The Last of the Wampanoags. It was introduced by a neatly written prologue, the production of Prosper M. Whetmore, spoken by Mr. Barrett, and at its close a sprightly epilogue, written by James Lawson, and recited by Mrs. Hilson.

EDWIN FORREST AND LUCIUS JUNIUS BOOTH.

Perhaps one of the most brilliant engagements of Mr. Forrest in the city of Philadelphia, was the one commencing at the Chestnut Street Theatre, Wednesday, December 8th, 1830. He opened with Damon, Mrs. Sharpe as Calanthe. On Thursday evening, December 9th, Mr. Booth and Mrs. Flynn appeared in the Merchant of Venice. On the 10th, Mr. Forrest produced Metamora—first time at that theatre—with Mrs. Sharpe as Nahmeokee, to a house crowded from pit to dome. Mr. Booth, as Sir Edward Mortimer, on the 11th. On Monday, 13th, Mr. Forrest appeared as William Tell. Our readers will perceive that these two eminent stars appeared on alternate nights. December 14th, Mr. Booth produced David Paul Brown's Sertorius; or, The Roman Patriots. This splendid combination of dramatic talent continued, each in their separate roles, until December 20th, 1830, when the two brilliant stars came together in the great tragedy of Othello. Othello, Edwin Forrest; Iago, Mr. Booth. This was on the occasion of Mr. Forrest's benefit. Perhaps, with the exception of Thomas A. Cooper, with whom Mr. Forrest frequently played, no two more finished artists ever came together than those just named. It was not simply a display of elocutionary powers and the finished touch of true art, but close identification of the actor with the part. If Mr. Forrest's Othello was great, Mr. Booth's Iago was equally so.

At that period Mr. Booth's name was a tower of strength, and his Iago was considered the best on the American Stage, and only equalled by that of William B. Wood, who in this part divided the honor with that excellent tragedian.

MR. WILLIAM FORREST.

This gentleman was born in the city of Philadelphia. His first appearance on the stage was at the Walnut Street Theatre, February 2nd, 1822, as Zaphina, in the play of Mahomet. He was announced as Master William Forrest. He followed his brother to Cincinnati, Ohio, where he was announced as making his first appearance on any stage. He had none of those strong evidences of genius which so distinguished his brother, his voice was a material drawback to stage success. He was an amiable and accomplished gentleman—he was, however, a man of business, and in 1831 we find him one of the firm of Jones, Forrest & Duffy, managers of the Arch Street Theatre, and also of the firm of Duffy & Forrest, Albany, N. Y.

At the close of the Arch Street Theatre season of 1831, the firm was presented by the actors and others, with a silver cup, valued at one hundred dollars, for the honorable manner in which they had discharged all their obligations since they undertook the management of the Arch Street Theatre. The cup was presented by Morton McMichael, Esq., in one of his happiest speeches, and received by Mr. Jones, the senior partner, with a suitable reply, nearly one hundred gentlemen being assembled on the stage, where an elegant collation was prepared, and the song and anecdote enlivened the company, who dispersed about two o'clock, A. M., highly pleased with the events of the evening.

Mr. William Forrest died very suddenly in 1833, universally regretted, his good qualities having endeared him to all with whom he came in contact. It is somewhat singular that the manner of the death of these two brothers should be so similar. Well one moment—the next dead! In the full seeming of good health at night—the next morning lying calm and cold in death! Thus the fate of both. When we saw Edwin Forrest lying on his bed the morning of his death, called thither by the servant in haste, we imagined him in a trance or a stupor. His flesh was warm; no contortion of features, no indication of having suffered pain; so calm in slumber-like, that we immediately commenced bathing his head with cologne water, raising it up, and placing the whole body in a more reclining manner, when of a sudden it flashed upon us—this is death! In less than fifteen minutes we had a doctor at the bedside. All was over. The genial, social gentleman, the great tragedian, had passed away, as had his brother thirty-nine years before. On that calm face the spoiler had forever set his seal of silence.

> "But there beam'd a smile
> So fixed and holy from that marble brow—
> Death gazed and left it there; he dared not steal
> The signet ring of heaven."

At the time of William Forrest's death, his brother was playing an engagement in New Orleans, and the writer of this was also in the Crescent City at the same time. It may probably occur to the reader that our early acquaintance with Mr. Edwin Forrest was still kept up, in another place we have alluded to this; let us introduce here an EPISODE, which will explain in some measure the reason of our not coming together during all the long years intervening between boyhood and manhood.

Our youthful associations were broken off when Mr. Forrest went West in 1822. It was not renewed until John W. Forney, Esq., brought us together some thirty-five years afterward. Mr. Forrest had not the least idea that "Colley Cibber" and his companion in the days of the "Old Apollo," were the same, under that *nom de plume.* Many of our readers are aware that we omitted no opportunity of expressing an opinion of Mr. Forrest's acting; and while giving him all due credit for the opening buds of promise displayed, we never neglected pointing out the thorns which came forth with them. Then he knew us not. As this interview, brought about by Col. Forney, forms a very important epoch in our life, and brought together two persons of entirely different pursuits, we give the circumstances attending it.

Mr. Forrest, looking us full in the face, said: "Not long since, sir, I saw you in New Orleans, sitting with James H. Caldwell, in his private box. Your face then was familiar to me. On another occasion I saw you with Mr. J. Bates, in Cincinnati. I asked him who you were. He replied: 'Oh, a great friend of yours, a Philadelphian.' I also asked Harris G. Pearson the same question, in New Orleans, if he knew you. His reply was: 'Yes, from a boy;' and now, for the first time, I am told by my friend Forney, that James Rees and Colley Cibber are one and the same person." We may as well state here, also, that Col. Forney was equally surprised when he found it necessary to introduce us.

To many it may appear somewhat singular why we did not take an opportunity of making ourselves known to Mr. Forrest during the many years that had intervened. As an actor we admired him, and felt more real pleasure in speaking of him than we imagined we should enjoy in speaking to him. We had heard of his being abrupt and brusque in his manner with strangers, and this would not suit our temperament, so we told him, giving it as our reason for avoiding him. Turning to Col. Forney, he said: "That is honest, and I like it." He caught me by the hand, saying: "Come and see me, for if I am a wild lion abroad, I am at least a tame one at home."

We did call, and often since regretted that such an opinion of Mr. Forrest should have been the means of keeping us so long in ignorance of the many noble and excellent traits in his character. The memory of Mr. Forrest is as dear to us now as was his friendship while living; and the only regret we have is that his epitaph should not have been the public's approbation on his last act instead of its censure. We speak the general sentiment when we say the curtain fell too soon on the last act of the drama of life in which Mr. Forrest played so prominent a part. There should have been an episode, but Heaven decreed it otherwise, and those who should have been remembered in the final close of a great man's life, passed away with the fall of the curtain from all connection, save that of remembrance, with the fortunes or recorded words of friendship of Edwin Forrest. John Swift, Esq., the earliest and staunchest friend he ever had; Col. John W. Forney, who stood by him in the darkest hour of his life—his Pythias and his advocate. Well, the curtain fell, as we have said, too soon. The bell had sounded, the drama was over, and—

"The actor's fame
Knells in the ear of the world."

And the feet of strangers sound unreal in the halls of his splendid mansion, where once was heard those of the friends of his youth and the champions of his fame.

CHAPTER VII.

DRAMATIC AUTHORS.—JOHN AUGUSTUS STONE.—DR. BIRD.—ROBERT T. CONRAD.—JACK CADE.—GLADIATOR.—ORALOOSA.—SUCCESS ATTENDING THEIR PRODUCTION.—SKETCH OF THE LIFE OF THE AUTHOR OF METAMORA.—RICHARD PENN SMITH.—CAIUS MARIUS.

AFTER Mr. Forrest's great success as a youthful star, and having played Othello, so as to divide the honor with Mr. Cooper, he could command, instead of being led, by others. From the year 1830 we date his upward course; from that time forth his ability was universally acknowledged. For several years he was the bright particular star of the "mimic world." Having played all the popular pieces so well known to play-goers, his natural feeling awakened in him a desire to produce something that would bring our own writers before the public. The celebrated Indian play of Metamora brought Mr. Forrest before the public in quite a new character. Our readers are familiar not only with the peculiar characteristics of this play, but also the extraordinary power and aboriginal delineation of Metamora by Edwin Forrest. This drama was indebted for its success almost entirely to the actor, as its literary merits were feeble compared to the productions of a Conrad and a Bird. Mr. Forrest paid the author five hundred dollars for the piece, but subsequently did much more for the unfortunate man who wrote it.

JOHN AUGUSTUS STONE

was born in Concord, N. H., 1801. Made his first appearance on the stage at the Washington Garden Theatre, Boston, as Old Norval in Douglas. In 1821 he married Mrs. Legg. First appeared in New York in 1826, at the Bowery Theatre. Removed to Philadelphia and played at the Prune Street Theatre, also at the Chestnut and Walnut Street Theatres. Mr. Stone produced his tragedy of Fauntleroy in Charleston, S. C. Metamora was first played on the occasion of Mr. Forrest's benefit at the Park Theatre, New York, November 15th, 1829. First produced in this city at the Arch Street Theatre, January 22nd, 1830. Mr. Stone also wrote The Demoniac, Tancred, The Restoration; or, The Diamond Cross, The Ancient Briton, played at the Arch Street Theatre, March 27th, 1833, Golden Fleece, etc. His unhappy death by suicide occurred in this city June 1st, 1834. It was most deliberate, having made two attempts by throwing himself from Spruce Street wharf, Schuylkill;

from the first he was rescued, and led those who saved him to believe it was an accident. A few hours afterward his body was found floating in the dock. Mr. Stone was a man of nervous temperament, and had occasionally displayed symptoms of incipient insanity. Mr. Forrest caused to be erected a neat monument over his grave at Machpelah Cemetery, bearing this inscription:

"In memory of the
Author of 'Metamora,'
By His Friend,
E. FORREST."

What a volume does this simple inscription convey!

As a matter of dramatic history connected with Metamora, we give the cast as originally played in New York.

METAMORA	MR. E. FORREST.
LORD FITZARNOLD	Mr. RICHINGS.
SIR ARTHUR VAUGHN	MR. CHAPMAN.
GUY OF GODALMAN	MR. WOODHULL.
HORATIO	MR. BARRY.
ERRINGTON	MR. LANGTON.
CHURCH	MR. T. PLACIDE.
WOLFE	MR. NIXEM.
TRAMP	MR. POVEY.
HOLYOKE	MR. WHEATLEY.
KAUSHENE	MR. BLAKELEY.
CHILD	MISS PARKER.
OCEANA	MRS. HILSON.
NAHMEOKEE	MRS. SHARPE.

Whatever faults this tragedy may possess as a literary or dramatic production, its real merits keep it living on the stage; and in the character of the hero, no dissenting voice has qualified Mr. Forrest's claim to the highest excellence. It was created for, and entirely fitted all his peculiarities.

The next American author who found a patron in Edwin Forrest was Richard Penn Smith, Esq. On the 12th of January, 1831, he produced Caius, at the

Arch Street Theatre. It was not a success. A writer, speaking of this play, says:—"It was not fairly treated by the actors, and consequently coldly received by the audience." Mr. Forrest paid much better for original plays than the managers, who being able to purchase the best plays of English dramatists for a few shillings, felt little disposition to risk hundreds on native productions. Forrest, however, tried the experiment—risked thousands of dollars and succeeded. In regular succession Mr. Forrest produced several American plays—Dr. Bird's Gladiator, Oraloosa, Broker of Bogota, and Judge Conrad's Jack Cade. The first and the last piece named, probably brought more money into the treasury of a theatre and into that of the actor's, than that of any two other plays in his *repertoire.*

Oraloosa was produced at the Arch Street Theatre October 10th, 1832. It did not produce the effect the Gladiator had—hence its failure. The public had looked for something even better than the hero of the arena, and found an inferior. It lacked plot and incident, the dialogue tame, and, taken altogether, it was a dramatic failure. An incident occurred on its first representation which Mr. Wemyss, in his "Twenty-Six Years of the Life of an Actor," thus relates:—"To me the 10th of October and the tragedy of Oraloosa form no pleasing remembrance—although they can never be forgotten. They have caused me in mimic fight, too real for fancy, the loss of two front teeth, which Edwin Forrest, in the *furore* of acting, displaced from their original stronghold in my mouth by a thrust from his sword at the head of Don Christoval, occasioning some of the wags of the green-room an opportunity of making a bad pun by declaring that

Forrest wished to teach me the proper pronunciation of the name of the play by forcing me to say to him, "*Oh-they-are-loose-sir.*"

As the plays of the Gladiator and Bogota are familiar to our readers, it is not necessary to speak of them here. The latter, however—if we dare express an honest opinion—may be considered in our dramatic volume in the same light that Lear is in that of the English. Superior as the latter is to all others in their country, so is the Broker to all others in our own. The Gladiator, by Dr. Bird, is also familiar to our readers, as is the name of Robert T. Conrad with the play of Jack Cade.

The Gladiator was first produced in Philadelphia at the Arch Street Theatre, on the 24th of October, 1831. Mr. Forrest's Spartacus, from the first night of the Gladiator until the day of his death, was considered the perfection of the art histrionic, and it will long be remembered as one of the gems that shone upon the stage from the brilliant mind of Edwin Forrest. Mr. John R. Scott played Phaisarius, for which he secured a compliment both from Mr. Forrest and the author. There are many passages in the Gladiator of extreme poetic beauty; the language generally is bold and impressive, and at times soars far above the general standard of dramatic literature. The house on the occasion was crowded—in fact, it was a perfect ovation to native talent as displayed by author and actor.

JACK CADE.

Jack Cade, or at least the play by this name, was not originally written for Edwin Forrest. Not long since we had occasion to allude to this play in connection with the author and actor, and as the article forms a link in the chain of our reminiscences—we give it here:

Robert T. Conrad's first production was Conrad of Naples, produced at the Arch Street Theatre, Philadelphia, on the evening of January 17th, 1832, Mr. James E. Murdoch enacting the part of Conrad. Mr. Conrad's crowning effort, however, was Jack Cade, which is now acknowledged as the most successful play ever produced on the American stage. The history of this great American play, and every play has its history, may not prove uninteresting to our readers.

In the year 1835, Robert T. Conrad, Esq., wrote a tragedy for A. A. Addams, at the suggestion of F. C. Weymss, at that time manager of the Walnut Street Theatre. If Mr. Addams approved of the play, he (Mr. Weymss) was to give Mr. Conrad three hundred dollars for the manuscript copy, and a benefit on the third night of its representation. It was called The Noble Yeoman. The title was subsequently altered to Aylmere, and finally to Jack Cade. Addams was delighted with the play, it was accepted, and L. A. Godey and Morton McMichael witnessed the contract between F. C. Weymss and Robert T. Conrad. The document bears date October 2nd, 1835.

On the night of the intended representation, Mr. Addams was seized with a *disease* to which he was subject, and of which he ultimately died. This disease is one of a peculiar character, and is known in the medical world as *mania-à-potu*. In consequence the play was postponed. The part was then given to a young and talented actor by the name of Ingersoll, and against the wishes of Mr. Conrad and the committee.

The piece was first played at the Walnut Street Theatre on the 9th of December, 1835.

Mr. A. A. Addams first enacted the part on the first of February, 1836, and made a failure. The third night the proceeds amounted to only one hundred and eighteen dollars.

In 1839 the first proposition was made to Mr. Edwin Forrest to play the part, providing Judge Conrad would rewrite it. We pass over this portion of the history of Jack Cade as possessing no dramatic interest, until it came into the hands of Mr. Forrest. This gentleman superintended the alterations, adapting certain portions to suit his transcendent powers, and having purchased the sole right and title of the piece from the author, Robert T. Conrad, he prepared himself for its production under the title of Jack Cade.

It was first played at the Park Theatre, New York, on the 24th of May, 1840, under its second title of Aylmere; or, The Kentish Rebellion, but afterwards changed to that of Jack Cade. It was subsequently played at the Arch Street Theatre, Philadelphia, June 16th, 1841, since which time the genius of Mr. Forrest, with his high-wrought dramatic powers, has thrown around the great character of Cade an atmosphere so refined in its elementary principles that no one as yet has been enabled to destroy its influence. The actor and hero of the piece unite and maintain a supremacy over all competitors. Those who have essayed it lacked the fire—the soul, the startling mental and physical powers of this great master of the histrionic art.

In a future chapter we will allude more particularly to these plays and their authors.

CHAPTER VIII.

CONTEMPLATES AN EUROPEAN TOUR. — TAKES LEAVE OF HIS PHILADELPHIA FRIENDS. — HIS SPEECH ON THE OCCASION. — BOWERY THEATRE, N. Y. — THOMAS A. COOPER. — FORREST ENACTS THE PART OF DENTATUS IN THE PLAY OF VIRGINIUS.—BROKER OF BOGOTA. — SKETCH OF THE LIFE OF MR. COOPER. — COMPLIMENTARY DINNER TO MR. FORREST. — TESTIMONIALS.— GOLD MEDAL. — FAREWELL SPEECH. — DEPARTURE TO EUROPE.

MR. FORREST having amassed a fortune, or at least sufficient to justify a cessation from his labors, determined to make the tour of Europe as a private gentleman, and not as a distinguished tragedian. He had read of those lands in which the heroes of the "mimic world" flourished in all their might and glory. He longed to tread the classic ground on which the poets of old immortalized their heroes in inspired verse. To a mind alive to all that appertained to art, the idea of visiting foreign lands is at all times pleasing, but the reality to one of Mr. Forrest's taste and judgment was but the consummation of his boyhood's dream.

On the 2nd of April, 1833, he played his farewell engagement, previous to his departure, at the Arch Street Theatre. The play was King Lear, and it was remarked at the time that his impersonation of the irritable, choleric old king of fourscore and upward, was the most chaste performance that had ever been seen, not even equalled by the elder Kean. After the play Mr. Forrest was unanimously called for; he responded to the call, and thus addressed the audience:

"LADIES AND GENTLEMEN:—I cannot resist the opportunity which now discloses itself, of returning to you my cordial thanks for the very kind manner with which you have been pleased to notice my humble efforts, and for your untired and warm support of my exertions to please you as a tragedian. (Cheers.) But particularly, I feel grateful for the honorable support I have received in my anxious endeavors to give to my country, by fostering the exertions of our literary friends, something like what might be called an American national drama. (Reiterated cheers.) Some time must elapse before we can meet again. I am now going to a foreign land, to study the voluminous book of nature amid the extensive forests, the flowering prairies, and the wild mountain tops; and though I may not be blessed by your smiles in my progress, it shall be my duty to deserve them the more on my return, when next season we shall meet again. Wishing you all, therefore, health and happiness, ladies and gentlemen, with unfeigned gratitude and a lively sense of your favors, I regretfully bid you all adieu!" (Continued cheers.)

On the 27th of November, 1833, Mr. Forrest commenced an engagement at the Bowery Theatre, N. Y., as Damon; followed by Macbeth, Virginius, Rolla, Metamora, Spartacus, Othello, Oraloosa, and Carwin. He was ably supported by Henry Wallack, Mrs. McClure and Mrs. Flynn. This engagement closed on the 23d of December. He commenced a new engagement on the 5th of February, 1834, as Metamora. On the 8th, Mr. Cooper appeared as Pierre, to Forrest's Jaffier and Mrs. McClure's Belvidera. On the 11th, Cooper played Damon, with Forrest as Pythias. On the 12th, Julius Cæsar was played—Cooper as Cassius, Forrest as Marc

Antony. On the 17th, Mr. Cooper took his benefit—playing Virginius—one of his best preserved parts, supported by Hamblin as Icilius! and FORREST as DENTATUS! Miss Priscilla Elizabeth Cooper as Virginia.

Such a combination of dramatic talent is seldom to be found in stage annals; there is also another feature in this connection to which we allude. Mr. Cooper had been Mr. Forrest's idol; he had looked upon him as the great master of the histrionic art, and although not his tutor was the classic model from which he fashioned his own impersonations. At that period Mr. Cooper was only fifty-eight years of age, yet he was far more feeble than others of his own time of life, and it began to show its effect on his acting. Mr. Forrest was at that time in the very prime of life, full of strength, and at the age of twenty-eight a rising star that was to eclipse all other luminaries. Here was the man who in his boyhood looked upon Cooper, the great actor, as some mythical god, to be worshipped, taking an equal part in the great works of the master spirit of the "mimic world," and illustrating by his genius and the powers of art the noblest pictures that were ever drawn by mortal hand. Here was master and pupil contending in the arena for fame—the one having reached its apex, the other striving to gain it. The youthful vine was twining itself around the falling oak, giving it new life—new vigor. Both have now passed away; the laurels that wreathed their brows, and gathered new vigor each succeeding season, still deck their memory; and although ages may pass away, the names of Cooper and Forrest will never be forgotten while the stage and the drama maintain their character and usefulness in the world. On the 15th of July, 1834, Mr. Forrest concluded his last engagement at the Bowery Theatre, previous to his visiting Europe. The play on the occasion was The Broker of Bogota.

As Mr. Cooper's name is identified with our stage history, as well as that of the subject of these Reminiscences, a short sketch of his life may not be out of place.

Thomas Althorpe Cooper was born in London in 1776. At an early age he lost his father, and became the ward of Messrs. Holcroft and Godwin, names well known in British literature and politics, the latter being the celebrated author of "Caleb Williams," "Fleetwood," etc. At the age of nineteen he made his *first* successful appearance on the stage, in London, as Hamlet, under the auspices of his gifted guardians and other gentlemen of learning and influence. Although he had partially failed as Malcolm, in Macbeth, his *first* unsuccessful attempt, he subsequently achieved a triumph in the latter character. Mrs. Merry, after she had retired from the stage, was passing some time in Bath, England, where she received a letter from her husband, telling her that "a most extraordinary lad of nineteen, named Cooper, said to be a ward of Godwin, has created much sensation by his admirable performance of Hamlet, but more of Macbeth."

It was Mrs. Merry who suggested young Cooper to Mr. Wignell, who was in England looking up recruits for the Chestnut Street Theatre. Wignell, at the instance of Mr. and Mrs. Merry, engaged him, offering him a first-class engagement. He made his first appearance in Philadelphia, at the Chestnut Street Theatre, on the 9th of December, 1796, as Macbeth. "At this time," says William B. Wood, "several persons of education condescended to notice the actors and plays. With most of these Fennell and Moreton had won high estimation, and Cooper's *debut* seemed likely to darken the fame of the old favorites."

Cooper made his first appearance in New York Park Theatre, on the 28th of February, 1798, in the part of Hamlet. A writer says, speaking of his *debut:* "With a handsome face and noble person, a fine mellow voice, unusual dignity of manner and grace of action, and in his declamation most forcible and eloquent. As a tragedian he was without a rival." In 1800, Cooper had the honor of acting upon the first theatre ever opened in the City of Washington. The parts in Venice Preserved, on this occasion, were filled thus: Jaffier, Wignell; Pierre, Cooper; Priuli, Warren; Belvidere, Mrs. Merry. In 1802 he entered upon a career of starring, finding it less laborious and far more profitable than the drudgery of a stock actor. He saw Fennell, who was declining in power and estimation, yet receiving in six or eight nights a larger remuneration than he was receiving for three months' regular service.

These two eminent stars came together like two planets, by each other's attraction, and began playing together about the year 1799. Fennell's Othello was his masterpiece, and when Cooper, in the full face of the other's popularity, essayed the part, it was almost a failure, judging by the worst of all rules of criticism —comparison.

Fennell invariably made the Moor *black;* in fact, a decided negro. Cooper tinged his skin to the color of a mulatto; or, more properly speaking, to that of a Moor. Cooper, at first, was very imperfect in the text, as, for instance, when he has to use these words:

"Yet I will not scar that whiter skin than snow, and smooth as monumental alabaster;"

He substituted:

"I will not scar that beauteous form, as white as snow and hard as monumental alabaster."

An actor by the name of Higgins, not to be outdone by Cooper, on one occasion playing the Duke, in Othello, having to say these words:

"Take up this tangled matter at the best," etc.; actually substituted the following:

"Take up the Star Spangled Banner and carry it off to the West."

This is an actual fact. Higgins was a member of the old South Street Theatre Amateur Company. His extraordinary interpretation of the language of Shakespeare was the cause of his leaving the theatre. He went to New Orleans, became a member of Caldwell's company, and when last we saw him in the Crescent City, he was selling lottery tickets and lottery policies, to the demoralization of those who encouraged him.

In 1806 Cooper became manager of the Park Theatre, and afterward associated with Stephen Price, with whom he continued several years, till he resigned management for the more profitable career of starring. His first wife, formerly Mrs. Upton, a daughter of David Johnson, Esq., of N. Y., died in 1808; and by his marriage, in 1812, with the most beautiful and brilliant belle of the city (the Sophy Sparkle of Irving's Salmagundi), Miss Mary Fairlie, daughter of the celebrated wit, Major James Fairlie, and grand-daughter of Gov. Robert Yates. Mr. Cooper became allied to some of the most eminent families in the State, and his society was eagerly courted by all who made pretensions to taste or fashion.

Mr. Cooper visited England in 1803; his reception was cold, for he claimed to be an American actor—a title which at that time, and up to 1845, was far from being a recommendation. In 1828 he again visited England, and was actually hissed and groaned while playing at Drury Lane Theatre. During his first visit to England he played Iago to Cooke's Othello. He subsequently visited Liverpool; he then went to Manchester, and opened with Richard III., Cooke's great part. Upon his appearance, a large audience greeted him with every kind of noise and insult, and shouts for "Cooke! Cooke!" "No Yankee actors!" "Off with him," and other offensive cries. Such was Cooper's reception in England, simply because he was looked upon as a "Yankee."

After his retirement from the stage, the marriage of his amiable and accomplished daughter, Miss Priscilla Elizabeth Cooper, to Robert Tyler, a son of President Tyler, afforded him the advantage of Presidential patronage, and in November, 1841, he was appointed Military Storekeeper to the Arsenal, Frankford, Pa., with the pay and perquisites of a captain of infantry. Subsequently he was appointed to a situation in the New York Custom House, a situation he held until a short time before his death, which took place at Bristol, Pa., April 21st, 1849; aged 73 years.

In the summer of 1834, Mr. Forrest was honored by a public banquet tendered him by his numerous friends in New York, which was attended by some of the most distinguished citizens. Numerous testimonials were shown him by his countrymen as complimentary to his genius and talents. This pleasing event took place on the 25th of July, 1834. Chancellor McCoun presided. On the right of the president was seated the guest in whose honor the feast was provided, and on his left the Hon. Cornelius Lawrence, Mayor of the city. Among the guests were the managers of the several principal theatres. The address of the distinguished president was a brilliant one; he alluded to Mr. Forrest's close identification with what is called the "American Drama." During the short period of eight years, five productions have been written principally through his instrumentality, which else, perhaps would never have found their way into existence. Gentlemen, continued President McCoun:

"I have thus far dwelt on points in the performer's history and character, with which you are all acquainted. There are other topics on which I might touch, did I not fear to invade the heart—not less entitled to your admiration. But there are some feelings, in breasts of honor and delicacy, which, though commendable, cannot brook exposure; as there are plants which flourish in the caves of the ocean, that wither when brought to the light of the day. I shall, therefore, simply say, that in private relations, as in public career, he has *performed well his part*, and made esteem a twin sentiment with admiration in every heart that knows him. I need not tell you, gentlemen, that I speak of Edwin Forrest.

"Mr. Forrest is on the eve of departure for foreign lands. To a man combining so many claims for our regard, it has been thought proper, by his fellow-citizens, to present a farewell token of friendship and respect; a token which may at once serve to keep him mindful that Americans properly appreciate the genius and worth of their own land; and which may testify to foreigners the high place he holds in our esteem.

"Mr. Forrest, I now place this memorial in your hands. —It is one in which many of your countrymen have been emulous to bear a part. It is a proud proof of unusual virtues and talents, and as such may be proudly worn. You will mingle in throngs where jewelled insignia glitter on titled breasts; but yours may justly be the reflection, that few badges of distinction are the reward of qualities so deserving of honor, as those attested by the humbler memorial which now rests upon your bosom."

With these remarks, the President introduced the toast, which was as follows:

"Edwin Forrest: estimable for his virtues—admirable for his talents. Good wishes attend his departure, and warm hearts will greet his return."

The committee appointed to get up the gold medal, presented on the occasion, consisted of: Ogden Hoffman, Fitz-Greene Halleck, Dr. Hosack, Judge Talmadge, William C. Bryant, Washington Irving, William G. Simms, Robert W. Weir, T. H. Perkins, Jr., Philip Hone, and others. The medal was designed by Ingham and engraved by C. C. Durand. It represents Mr. Forrest in profile, surrounded by the words:

"*Histrioni Optimo, Edwino Forrest, Viro-Praestanti;*" and on the reverse, a figure of the Genius of Tragedy, with the following appropriate quotation from the great bard of Avon: "*Great in mouths of wisest censure.*"

The applause which followed the President's speech, and presentation of the medal, fully approved of its sentiments. As soon as it had subsided, Mr. Forrest rose, and though somewhat affected, replied as follows:

"This token of your regard, I need not tell you how dearly I shall prize. I am about to visit foreign lands. In a few months, I shall probably behold the tomb of Garrick—Garrick, the pupil of Johnson, the companion and friend of statesmen and wits—Garrick, who now sleeps surrounded by the relics of the kings and heroes, orators and bards, the magnets of the earth. I shall contemplate the mausoleum which encloses the remains of Talma —Talma, the familiar friend of him, before whom monarchs trembled. I shall tread the classic soil with which is mingled the dust of Roscius—of Roscius, the preceptor of Cicero, whose voice was lifted for him at the forum, and whose tears were shed upon his grave. While I thus behold with deferential awe, the last resting places of those departed monarchs of the drama, how will my bosom kindle with pride at the reflection, that I, so inferior in desert, have yet been honored with a token as proud as ever rewarded their successful efforts. I shall then look upon this memorial; but while my eye is riveted within its 'golden round,' my mind will travel back to this scene and this hour, and my heart will be with you in my native land.

"Mr. President, in conclusion let me express my grateful sense of goodness by proposing, as a sentiment:

"*The Citizens of New York*:—Distinguished not more by intelligence, enterprise and integrity, than by that generous and noble spirit which welcomes the stranger and succors the friendless."

Shortly after this demonstration on the part of his friends, Mr. Forrest might have exclaimed with Hamlet, although with a different result:

Hamlet.—For England?
King.—Ay, Hamlet.
Hamlet.—Come, for England!

CHAPTER IX.

IN EUROPE.—PILGRIM ON THE RHINE.—IN ASIA.—NAPLES.—VENICE.—VERONA.—TOMB OF JULIET.—GLANCE OF TRAVEL.—THE YANKEE IN ST. PETERSBURG.—INTERVIEW WITH GEORGE M. DALLAS.—MOROCCO.—ROME.—THE VATICAN.—VALUE OF A PICTURE.—CASTLE OF ST. ANGELO.—AN INCIDENT.—DELARUE.—A PAGE FROM CLASSIC HISTORY.

IF Mr. Forrest kept a journal of his travels, of which we are not aware, what a theme for one so gifted—a mind richly imbued with classical lore, a soul tuned to poetry, and a lover of all that was beautiful in nature and rich in art, to write and speak about! Suffice for us to say, that he mingled in the festivities of Paris, visited all the places of interest, which the startling events of ages had rendered memorable, and stained its record with blood! How he became a pilgrim of the Danube, wandered over Switzerland, visited the places where the fabulous William Tell was supposed to have held his mythical existence and perform all sorts of mythical deeds. He sailed on the raging Baltic, and travelled on the patriotic ground of Poland. He was seen standing on the lofty parapet of the Kremlin, at Moscow, surveying from its giddy height the sacred city of the mighty Autocrat of all the Russias. He gazed upon the crescent towers of Constantinople, crossed the Euxine, and wandered over portions of Asia

Minor. Then we find him sojourning in Africa, treading upon the soil that gave birth to Othello, whom the great artist painted as one of the most noble and accomplished of the proud children of the Ommades and the Albacides, and who Roderigo profanely called "thick lips," and Iago styled the "Devil." Then at Naples, gazing on the glorious Adriatic, or watching the smoke and fire as they curl and blaze up in terrific grandeur from Vesuvius. For two hundred years this chimney of the earth has thrown out its smoke and flame to admiring millions, and not unfrequently turning that admiration into horror, for death and destruction were around them. Follow him to Venice—there he stands on the Bridge of Sighs, which, like a bracelet, encircles the arm of the bride of the Adriatic. City of Lakes and five hundred bridges, gondoliers and assassins! There, too, he thought of Shylock, as he stood on the Rialto, with its single arch of 187 feet. There, too, was the Doge's palace, and its proud, towering Campanile. Then he gazed on the Corinthian horse, the workmanship of Lysippus, who lived in the time of Alexander the Great, and the winged lion of the Piræus.

Then we see him at Verona, standing beside the sarcophagus of Juliet—the Juliet of Shakespeare's tragedy of Romeo and Juliet. We have simply glanced over places and scenes witnessed by Mr. Forrest in his travels. We will now relate one or two incidents connected with them:

THE YANKEE IN ST. PETERSBURG.

When Mr. Forrest was in St. Petersburg, the Hon. George M. Dallas was the American Minister at the Imperial Court. The great actor and that accomplished statesman met frequently; every attention was paid the former, and facilities afforded him of seeing everything worthy the attention of a traveller. We give the following incident, using our own language, adhering, however, as strictly as memory will permit, to that in which it was related to us by Mr. Forrest.

"I am very much troubled," said Dallas, one day, to Mr. Forrest, "about a countryman of ours."

"Who is he?"

"Well, I really do not know; he seems a sort of Cosmopolite. He says he is from Massachusetts, travelling, as he says, to pick up information."

"Why, how does he trouble you?"

"In this way—he wants me to introduce him to the Emperor."

"And why not?"

"Simply because he is an adventurer, without a single letter of introduction."

"He has his passport?"

"Yes—but his appearance, and my having no knowledge of the man, will not justify such a breach of court etiquette."

Forrest agreed with Mr. Dallas and observed:

"The fellow is probably an impostor."

"No," replied Dallas; "he is a true genuine Yankee—a man of some education—evidently well read, but his dress; he wears large coarse boots over his pantaloons, which, being wide, gives him the appearance of a down-east fisherman. He stands about six feet in height, carries an enormous cane—or rather club—and altogether presents a formidable, if not to the police, a suspicious person. He is, I know, under strict surveillance."

"I should like to see this man."

"So you can, but now comes the most amusing part of my interview with him, when I stated the impracticability of his request, and that I could not take so much liberty with the Emperor, he turned upon his heel saying: 'Well, Squire, I think I shall introduce myself.'"

Some days after this conversation Mr. Forrest called upon Mr. Dallas, and found him somewhat excited.

"I have just returned from the palace, where I had gone on special business, and by appointment. When I was ushered into his majesty's presence, whom do you suppose was with him?"

"Really, I don't know!"

"That Yankee; boots, stick and all."

Forrest laughed outright.

"Yes, there he was, sitting near to the Emperor, and in the most emphatic, as well as familiar manner, was explaining some theory of his, to which the Emperor seemed to listen with much interest. As I approached, the Yankee turned his head, and seeing me, exclaimed:

"'How'd ye do, Squire. You see I am here.'

"To my surprise the Emperor dismissed him with these words:

"'We will talk this matter over again,' and turning to an attendant, said:—'Conduct this gentleman out.' When the visitor had disappeared, the Emperor said:—'A strange man that—a great traveller—a man of wonderful knowledge.'

"I did not contradict him, as I found the fellow had, by some means unknown to me, obtained an interview."

"But how and by what means did he gain admission?"

"In this way, as I subsequently ascertained.

"It seems that he had been all over St. Petersburg, making inquiries relative to the various places of interest, and whenever he could gain admission, apart from places of amusement, he availed himself of the privilege by examining everything thoroughly and telling all he knew about similar establishments in America. What attracted his attention the most were the military schools. Into one of these—the "School of Cadets"—our Yankee found his way. The military schools of Russia receive the special attention of the Emperor. His officers are strict disciplinarians, and study to gain the confidence of their ruler as well as to carry out his plans on all occasions. The commandant of the "School of Cadets" soon discovered that his visitor was no common man; his military knowledge was extensive, and he so won upon the Russian officer that he listened to our Yankee's full description of West Point and other military establishments of the United States with the closest attention. 'You are behind the age, Squire,' says he, 'in many things.' He then went into a full detail of our military system—system of drill, etc. The officer got new ideas from his strange visitor, and remarked: 'I wish the Emperor could have a talk with you, as some of your views would suit him, I feel satisfied.'

"'Just what I want, Squire; our Minister here is a little backward about introducing me, but he is a Philadelphian and don't understand Massachusetts customs. We are a go-ahead people there, and don't stand upon ceremony, Squire.'

"'I think I can manage it; but your costume—'

"'Exactly; our Minister who dresses so fine, and looks as if he had just came out of a bandbox, did look as if I was not the cheese.'

"'Cheese?'

"'Yes, I mean the thing.'

"'I presume it is the fashion of your country?'

"'No, not exactly, only a portion of it, and that portion is called 'Down East.''"

This description of the Yankee's interview was given to Mr. Dallas by the commandant, and as he spoke English fluently, he gave it almost verbatim. It was arranged that at the next visit of the Emperor to the school the Yankee was to be there, and at a given signal was to make his appearance. The interview was effected, and the Emperor became so interested with him that he took him along to the palace.

When Mr. Forrest left St. Petersburg the Yankee was in high favor with the Emperor—indeed, so much that a carriage was allotted him to visit places of interest—he had made a hit at the Court of St. Petersburg. In connection with this incident there is another which occurred while Mr. Dallas was Minister at this place. It is that of a Yankee who had an interview with the Emperor for the purpose of presenting him with an acorn which grew on an oak over the tomb of Washington. Whether this was the same individual or not we are unable to say.

FORREST IN MOROCCO.

Here we find him endeavoring to trace out from its mixed race who were its principal inhabitants; the Berbers, the Amazigs, the Arabs, or the Mahomedans, supposed to be the descendants of those who were driven from Spain in the fifteenth century. Mixed as the inhabitants are, with a large sprinkling of Jews, the dread of Emer-el-Moomeneen, Lord of the true believers, keeps them in fear and awe. This sovereign, or Sultan, possesses absolute power; from him proceed the laws—the lives and properties of his subjects are at his disposal.

Somehow Forrest tamed this mighty monarch—we never learned how. They became friends, and during his sojourn at his court he was treated with marked attention. When he left he was presented with a splendid Arabian stallion. A portrait of this animal, painted by a French artist in Paris, has ever since hung in the art gallery of Mr. Forrest's mansion. Mr. Forrest gave me a very interesting account of how this artist came to paint this portrait for him.

One day just as he came out of his hotel in Paris, a thinly-clad Frenchman addressed him: "Monsieur Forrest, I would speak one word with you. I saw your grand horse in the stable—one fine animal—beautiful. I am a painter of animals—horses particularly. I would like to paint him for you."

Forrest was struck with the appearance of the man, and deeming it an act of charity, he consented, and told the man to bring the picture to him when finished. Those who have seen this *portrait* of the horse pronounce it, as we do, one of the most striking life-like representations of an animal that ever appeared on canvas. The name of this artist was told us, but it now escapes our memory. He subsequently, however, became distinguished in Paris as one of the best animal painters of the day.

FORREST IN ROME.

"This old city," says a writer, "has a never-ending history. One may study the old Roman Republic in its ruins for years; to master the remains of the Roman Empire requires a less time. A long period may be employed in unearthing the vestiges of mediæval and the early Papal Rome, and now in this latter day Rome promises us a new history, perhaps as interesting—perhaps as useful as the one of old." Two thousand years from the dawn of light to our day lie recorded on the stones and the dust of the noble city.

How different is Rome now from what it was when the great actor walked through the halls of the Vatican! The might of Rome then was in the kingly rule of the Pope. All powerful, both temporal as well as spiritual—the one omniscience of Rome as the great Omnipotent is of Heaven and earth; he made his infallibility his sceptre, and his power his diadem. Such was the Pope when Forrest visited Rome. Let us go with him to

THE VATICAN.

The Vatican, the winter residence of the Pope, the largest palace in Europe, attracted much of Mr. Forrest's attention. This splendid palace contains four thousand four hundred and twenty-two halls and galleries, filled with the treasures of ancient and modern art. The library is one of the largest and richest in the world. The picture gallery, containing a collection which, though small in extent—there being not more than fifty—is unsurpassed in real value. This museum, consisting of a series of galleries in which the noblest treasures of art are contained, including, among other rare works, the Laocoon and Apollo Belvidere. Mr. Forrest spent several days here, examining, admiring, wondering, and at last realizing the fact that here, indeed, the gems of true art can be seen. One of the pictures—we think it was "The Transfiguration," by Raphael—in the gallery alluded to, attracted his attention particularly. He asked a priest who had paid him marked attention, and who was also aware of his visitor's profession, which made no difference in his manner, if "there was any price attached to that picture?" The priest looked up in some surprise, saying: "Your State, Pennsylvania, is a rich State—it has inexhaustible coal and iron mines—it has canals, railroads, and large cities—numerous towns and villages, public buildings, colleges, and other institutions of learning—rich in all that industry accumulates and munificence can furnish."

"Well," said Forrest, "Pennsylvania is a rich State, what of that?"

The priest replied, "It does not contain wealth enough to purchase that picture."

"Indeed!" exclaimed the astonished actor; "then my dear sir, if Rome should ever become impoverished we will try to arrange with the State of Pennsylvania for its purchase."

The priest looked up; he saw at once the actor, like himself, was playing a part. Forrest was no great friend to priest-craft, nor had any sympathy with Catholics or their religion.

CASTLE OF ST. ANGELO.

On another occasion, in company with several gentlemen, Forrest visited the castle of "St. Angelo."

Originally it was called the Mausoleum of Hadrian, a rounded pyramid of white marble. For awhile they stood entranced, so much to see—so much to admire and comment upon. All around them were the traces of former greatness. Rome, with its majestic ruins—Rome, in the solemn grandeur of its churches and palaces—Rome, with its endless treasures—Rome, with its church of St. Peter's, built at the expense of the whole Roman world—Rome, the glory of modern architecture—loomed up before them. The Pantheon, the most splendid edifice of ancient Rome—the Vatican, the palace of the Pope—all these were more or less visible to the eye as they stood gazing in wonder and awe.

In one of the pauses of their conversation a voice came up from behind a ruined column, bearing upon its surface the impress of ages, saying, "Mr. Forrest, have you been to see the ruins of the Coliseum?"

Forrest turned around at these words to see from whom they proceeded. There lying at full length on another pillar lay a young man, whom none of the party knew. He went on: "It is a splendid ruin, sir. They say it held one hundred thousand people."

"You know me, it seems?" said Forrest.

"Know you? Why certainly; don't you remember Delarue? I played Richard III. at the Walnut Street Theatre, in imitation of Mr. Booth."

"What! you here? Get up, man, and let me have a good look at you."

Up jumped the eccentric individual, and as he stood before the group, he appeared a *fac-similie* of the great tragedian he could imitate so admirably.

We remember Delarue well. Had his mind been

as well balanced as were his powers of imitation, he would have been an actor of no common order. He was eccentric, and idle. How he ever reached Rome is still a mystery—how he got away, we have every reason to believe, was owing to the group who surrounded him on that occasion.

Delarue made his first appearance on the stage at the Chestnut Street Theatre in 1827, as Sylvester Daggerwood, in which he gave imitations of the leading actors of the day with great fidelity. What became of him we know not. The last we heard of him was in 1852; he was then living in New York.

Mr. Forrest's European tour will probably be found among his papers, written by himself. We know he had made notes of his travels, but, as he stated to us, they were simply memorandums. We have alluded, *en passant*, to many places he visited. His visit to the tomb of Shakespeare forms an important place in his notes, and connects him with the bard as one of his most ardent admirers and the representative of the immortal heroes of the tragic muse! Mr. Forrest met with some of the most gifted gentlemen of Europe, with whom he conversed and became their honored guest. He came home imbued with the spirit of poetry, romance and history. The drama appeared to him as the great link connecting the past with the present, in which the actor became the medium of conveying to the latter the likeness of the great men who flourished, died, and would have been forgotten, had it not been for the actor. His mind was enriched by foreign study and observation, and to the last hour of his life he had numerous anecdotes to relate and pleasing instances to record.

If you spoke to him of Greece and Rome, their ancient history, and ruined grandeur, he would describe to you the temple of Theseus, and the glorious Parthenon, perched aloft on the rocky Acropolis. He would carry you away with him over the bridge beyond Cephisus, and down the high road into the shady walks of the grove of Academus, where Plato, the pupil of Socrates, introduced his disciples, maintaining the immortality of the soul. He would tell you of the altar of the Muses, whose votaries may in some degree be said to hallow literature with a divine sanction. Yonder to the east, near the Marathon road, he would point out to you on the map, the Cynosarges, or school of the cynic philosophers; near the gate of the Piræus is the Museum, a building dedicated to the liberal arts, and to the Goddess whose name it bears. The superb structure to the left is the Odeum, beyond it is the Lyceum where Aristotle instructed his disciples. The building on the left of the Odeum is the Great Theatre, to which the Athenians flocked to weep at the tragedies of Æschylus, Sophocles and Euripides, to be convulsed with laughter at the farcical satires of Aristophanes, or to be delighted with the polished wit of the chaste and elegant Meander.

To such a mind as that of Mr. Forrest's, were not these scenes now but the *débris* of former grandeur, sufficient to interest and impress upon it the glorious age wherever the classic Muses revelled as it were, in the Elysium of fabled gods?

CHAPTER X.

FORREST'S RETURN FROM HIS EUROPEAN TOUR.—HIS RECEPTION.—APPEARS AT THE CHESTNUT STREET THEATRE.—SPEECH.—PARK THEATRE, N. Y.—FAREWELL ENGAGEMENT.—IMMENSE SUCCESS.—ADDRESSES THE AUDIENCE.—HIS DEPARTURE.—APPEARANCE ON THE ENGLISH STAGE.—KINDLY RECEIVED.—PUBLIC DINNERS TENDERED HIM BY THE GARRICK CLUB!—PRESENTS, ETC.—HIS MARRIAGE.

MR. FORREST, as our readers are aware, did not appear upon the stage during his European pleasure tour, as it was distinctly understood before he left the country that it was not his intention to do so. But he made arrangements to play there in October of the year of his return home.

CHESTNUT STREET THEATRE.

Mr. Forrest's first appearance in Philadelphia, after his return from his delightful journey, was on Monday, September 5th, 1836. He opened at the Chestnut Street Theatre, with Damon, and probably since the days of Cooke a greater rush has not been known at our theatres. During his engagement the orchestra was thrown open and additional space given to the pit. As early as five o'clock in the afternoon, the streets in the vicinity of the theatre began to exhibit the gathering of the populace, and long before the hour of opening—half-past six o'clock—the whole of Chestnut Street opposite to Old Drury was nearly a solid mass of human beings. The doors were opened with great caution, and much care was taken that no rush should be made; but so anxious were the people without to gain admission into the theatre, that hundreds became wedged together so immovably that they were obliged to stand and swelter with the patience of martyrs. Finally, they were admitted, only to make room for fresh crowds. Long before Damon appeared in character, the house was filled to overflowing, not a niche nor corner being vacant from pit to gallery. When Damon did appear, the pit and boxes rose as one man, and a roar of welcome, hoarse, loud and long, echoed through the theatre. Ladies waved their handkerchiefs, gentlemen their hats; indeed, to such an extent was this carried, that the Roman signification of ovation could not apply to the reception Mr. Forrest met on this occasion. The actor bowed and bowed, until the act became a spectacle of dumb iteration. At last order was restored; the play went on, and never did Forrest perform with more credit to the author of the play and himself. When the curtain fell, the calls for Forrest were loud and deafening; he appeared and bowed again, until the pit and boxes, which were alive with waving handkerchiefs, were stilled into a temporary calm. He said:

"Ladies and gentlemen, for this warm peal of hearts and hands I have only strength to say, in my present exhausted state, *I thank you.* It has served to convince me of the grateful truth that neither time nor distance has been able to alienate from me your kind regards. I am unable to speak what I wish; but I can sincerely declare that you make me *proud* this evening. And the remembrance of this cordial greeting, after no common absence—given to me here, in this city of my birth and my affections—shall go down with me, to my latest hour. as one of the happiest scenes of my professional life."

On Tuesday, he played Othello, and Spartacus on Wednesday, which character he repeated on Thursday. On Friday evening he took his farewell benefit, playing Spartacus. The house was literally crammed; indeed, there was no diminution of numbers during his whole engagement. A considerable trade was carried on in tickets outside of the theatre, which had been obtained at the risk of broken limbs.

He immediately repaired to New York, to finish an engagement there, and played every night up to the 15th of September, to overwhelming houses. He received $500 per night—notwithstanding which the manager must have cleared $1000 each night. The New York *Spirit of the Times* said: "A raft of tickets were bought by a speculator for the few last performances and sold at auction at fifty per cent. profit. Mr. Forrest has appeared as Damon, Othello, Spartacus, and Lear, and never to such manifest advantage. We have no doubt of his triumphant success in London as the first tragedian of the age."

Mr. Forrest bade farewell to his countrymen at the Park Theatre, in Othello. The house was crowded to the ceiling, and would have been uncomfortably crammed with hundreds more, had not many been, fortunately for those who were present, deterred from coming by the advanced prices at which numbers of tickets were purchased on speculation, which led to the belief that there would be no room. Some of the box tickets were sold at auction, and brought the enormous price of twenty-five dollars each. Mr. Forrest's acting was powerful and finished. At the close he was called out, and addressed the audience in his usual felicitous manner—spoke of his being content to repose on the good opinion of his countrymen, but that the solicitations to appear at Covent Garden were too flattering not to comply with them, and which he wished more particularly, to accept, to show that he believed that an English audience will receive with a cordial welcome an American actor. "They will," cried an honest John Bull. "I'm sure they will," replied Mr. Forrest, very happily. Thunders of applause followed. He alluded to the kind reception he had met with in his *debut*, when a youth, before a New York audience, in the part he had just performed; spoke of the effect that this had had on his ambition, and that their approbation had stamped him as an actor. He bade an affectionate farewell, and the audience, amidst the waving of handkerchiefs from the ladies, gave six heartfelt cheers in return.

Mr. Forrest, in the speech, alluded to his appearing at Covent Garden. The following, from a London paper, explains the change made in this arrangement:

MR. FORREST IN ENGLAND.

"We were as convinced as of our political existence, that Mr. Willis Jones would have nothing whatever to do with Covent Garden Theatre. We stated this in the most positive manner on Sunday last, and we are now enabled to confirm it. At the same time, when we published this prediction, or rather assertion, we had no idea that Mr. Jones was intent upon having an interest in one or the other of the two large theatres, and certainly not that there was any likelihood of his vesting such interest in Drury Lane. The simple fact turns out that Bunn has completely jockeyed Osbaldiston, and has secured to himself one of the greatest cards that has lately been played in London. Mr. Willis Jones, having some time since entered into a compact with the celebrated American tragedian, Mr. Forrest, to produce him on one of the principal London theatres, together with the original plays in which he has made so great a hit in transatlantic lands, has entered into an arrangement with Bunn for the use of Drury Lane Theatre for such purposes; and in the event of Mr. Forrest making the hit in London which is so fully anticipated, Mr. Jones is empowered to have a given number of nights throughout the season for the purpose of exhibiting Mr. Forrest in the range of his principal characters. We do not know, and have no desire to inquire into the pecuniary arrangements between Bunn and Willis Jones; but we hear they are extremely liberal on both sides, and will no doubt end in ample remuneration to all parties concerned.

"From every report we have heard, Mr. Forrest is a young man of most extraordinary abilities, and by the exercise of them has already amassed a large fortune in his native country. He is stated to possess a noble figure, and considered one of the finest men that has ever appeared on the stage, being gifted with a powerful mind and every possible requisite for his profession. The 'hiatus histrionicus,' left by the death of Kean and the retirement of Young, is therefore at length likely to be filled up, and the play-goer no longer be subjected to the tricky attempts or drowsy fulminations of the brace of bravoes who have lately been sickening him on the boards of Covent Garden."

The following account of Mr. Forrest's appearance on the English stage, is from the London *Chronicle* of the 17th of October, 1836.

"Mr. Edwin Forrest, the eminent American tragedian, whose first appearance, last evening, on the British stage (before one of the most crowded audiences ever assembled in any theatre), elicited those enthusiastic testimonials of success which have stamped him one of the greatest actors that ever graced the English theatre, will, in consequence of the unbounded applause with which he was received in the new tragedy of the Gladiator, have the honor of repeating the character of Spartacus, three times every week until further notice.

"When Mr. Forrest opened in England, at the Theatre Royal, Drury Lane, on the evening of October 17th, 1836, as an American actor in an American play, it was under circumstances particularly favorable. We had been puffing third, fourth and fifth rate actors here, and sending them back loaded with gold; and it would have certainly been very strange if they, in return, prejudice aside, could not receive one favorably from this country. Indeed, his triumph was great; and, as a matter of history, we furnish a few items attending his advent upon the British stage. The writer, after giving an account of the opening, etc., says:

"'On his *entree*, the whole house rose and gave him *three times three.* The applause lasted three or four minutes, and what, with hands and hearts, the waving of kerchiefs by the ladies and gentlemen in all the private boxes and the dress circles, and the spontaneous burst of enthusiasm, his reception was more flattering than his most sanguine friends could have anticipated. On being called for at the close of the play, the applause was truly deafening. He repeats the character three times a week, until further notice. Victory sits perched upon his beaver, and he must and will support her without losing a single feather.'"

The play was Dr. Bird's Gladiator, which was not received, however, with the same warmth by the audience as was the actor. Another paper, speaking of the *debut*, says:

"His reception was enthusiastic, and had he failed, he could not have attributed the misfortune to coldness of reception. He was greeted from all parts of a very full house. He did not fail. He was eminently successful, and the impression produced by him in Spartacus, was such that we doubt whether the same character could be safely ventured upon by any other man now upon the stage, at least in presence of the audience which witnessed the performance that night."

Another says:

"Mr. Forrest's reception on his arrival was the most flattering. He has been sought after by men whose kindly attention cannot be otherwise than gratifying to his pride, and the numerous acts of courtesy and hospitality bestowed upon him, were calculated speedily to remove the impression from his mind that he was a stranger in a strange land."

We shall have occasion to speak more particularly of Mr. Forrest's reception in London, when we come to his third visit, and his second engagement. He startled the "John Bulls" by his masterly delineations of Othello and Lear, and his Gladiator opened to their view in the drama's perspective another phase in classic literature. Charles Kean, that miserable specimen of English mendacity, jealous of Forrest's triumphs, had attempted to lessen his fame by retailing his petty spite to the "penny-a-liners" of the London press. A correspondent of the New York *Evening Star*, writing home, said:

"Forrest's success has been unprecedented. When I last wrote he had only appeared as Spartacus, and I doubted, to confess the truth, whether he had *mind* enough to play more intellectual characters. Charles Kean led me into the mistake, by speaking of Mr. Forrest as a 'giant—one who could throw a man across the stage'—and I was led to think that he had more muscle than genius. But his Othello is considered the finest thing that was ever witnessed on the British stage. The *Athenæum* (no mean authority,) places it far above Kean's, (I mean *the* Kean, not the boy imitator,) and the *Atlas*, fastidious to a fault in dramatics and letters, says 'If we observe that, since the days of Kean, we have had no actor capable of approaching his excellence, and that in many parts Mr. Forrest was equal, and in some few superior to that great tragedian, we shall have discharged all that we desire to say on that point.' "

One of their own critics said, in speaking of his Othello:

"The first scene between Othello and Iago was played by Mr. Forrest in a subdued tone, to which our actors have not accustomed us. Slow to suspect, Othello hovers over the abyss before he takes the fatal plunge. Mr. Forrest embodied this view of the opening of the temptation with great skill. Through the terrible scenes that follow he rose to a height of grandeur which places him at the head of living actors in England. In one particular passage he drew down an expression of admiration, such as we have seldom before witnessed in a London theatre. The passage to which we allude is that beginning or rather ending with

"'I had rather be a toad,
And live upon the vapors of a dungeon,' etc.

"The look of ghastly horror with which the utterance of this passage was accompanied electrified the audience, who rising in all parts of the house, continued for several minutes to greet the performer with most enthusiastic applause."

His King Lear was considered the best witnessed since the great Garrick and Cooke had made it their speciality.

These criticisms gave offence to the once prejudiced Englishmen, and laid the foundation for a determined opposition to everything that was calculated to pale the lustre of their own stars. Lesser ones had leave to shine—greater ones must be put out.

During this visit Mr. Forrest was not only highly honored, but for awhile became quite a lion in London.

The Garrick club gave him a dinner, at which Sergeant Talfourd, the author of Ion, presided. From Charles Kemble and Stephen Price he received three swords, once severally the property of John Kemble, Kean, and Talma. An original portrait in oil, of Garrick, was presented to him, and his own, in the character of Macbeth in the dagger scene, was exhibited at the Somerset House.

During this visit (1837) he married Miss Catharine Sinclair, daughter of John Sinclair, the well known vocalist. Had the tragedian foreseen the cloud that was to darken his latter days beyond the fair vision that stood blushing beside him at the altar, he would have hesitated even there. But all was sunshine then, and the future to him was a sealed book. Better, far better would it have been had he won the Swiss maiden who crossed his path on one of the mountain slopes of that fair land, instead of the beautiful and accomplished daughter of England! But—

> "There's a divinity that shapes our ends,
> Rough hew them how we will."

CHAPTER XI.

OTHELLO.—ITS ORIGINAL PLOT.—NOTED ACTORS IN THE PART.—FIRST OTHELLO IN THIS COUNTRY.—MR. FORREST'S CONCEPTION OF THE CHARACTER.—SIGNOR SALVINI COMPARED WITH FORREST.—AN ITALIAN VERSION.

IN the last chapter we left Mr. Forrest enjoying all the honors heaped upon him by a people's unbiassed opinion of his histrionic abilities, and having also taken a part in a comedy entitled The Honeymoon, to conclude with the play of The Stranger, in which the lady was accused of playing Mrs. Haller in private life. Leaving Mr. Forrest for a while in his domestic difficulties, acting a part so entirely out of his line, we will speak further of him in tragedy—the tragedy of the "mimic stage" of life, in which his noble nature in the character of the Moor found the counterpart of Consuelo in the character of Iago.

OTHELLO.

Giovanni Giralda Cynthio's Hecatommithi contains the original story of this tragedy, but no English version of the work of the time of Shakespeare has yet been discovered, though an imperfect French translation, by Gabriel Chappuys, was published at Paris in 1584. Malone originally assigned 1611, Chalmus, 1614, and Dr. Drake, 1612, as the date of the composition of this tragedy. Malone subsequently altered his time to 1604, affirming that the play was acted that year.

Vertue's MSS. shows, however, that it was performed at court before James I., 1613, but it is supposed that Shakespeare derived Othello's simile of the never-ebbing current of the Pontick Sea, Act III., Scene 3, from Dr. Philomon Holland's translation of Pliny's Natural History, London, 1601, folio book II., Chapter 97.

Othello was entered at Stationers' Hall, October 16th, 1621, and appeared in quarto in the year following, but there are many minute differences between this edition and the folio of 1623.

For the first act of this play the scene lies in Venice, but during the remainder at a seaport in the Isle of Cyprus, and a few days appeared to include all the action.

For the historical period, Solyman II. formed his design against Cyprus in 1569, and captured it in 1571, which being the only attempt that the Turks ever made upon the Island after it came into the Venetian powers in 1473, the circumstances must be placed in some part of the interval.

The play relates—Act I., Scene 3—that there was a junction of the Turkish fleet at Rhodes, for the invasion of Cyprus, to which it was first sailing; then it returned to Rhodes; and then, meeting another squadron, resumed its way to Cyprus. The real date, therefore, is May 1570, when Mustapha, the general of Solyman, attacked the Island.

This tragedy was originally performed at the Globe and Black-Friars' Theatres, Othello and Iago being played by Burbage and Taylor. Spranger Barry is said to have made the finest Moor on the stage; and he was also admirably supported by his wife, formerly Mrs. Dancer, whom he taught to perform Desdemona. The other most eminent actors in the principal parts have been Betterton, Booth, Garrick, Henderson, Cooke, Young and Kean; and Mr. C. Kemble as Cassio. The modern alteration of Othello was produced by J. P. Kemble, at Covent Garden in 1804, for which house Mr. J. R. Planché published a series of accurate historical costumes in 1825.

The first performances of Othello in this country was at the "Theatre" in Nassau street, New York, December 23rd, 1751; Othello, Mr. Upton. This man was an Englishman, and the treacherous agent of Hallam, who had sent him over from London in advance, to make arrangements for the company. He cheated his employers, and endeavored to palm himself off as an actor, but failed most signally. Its second representation was on the 11th of April, 1767, at the John Street Theatre, New York. Othello, Mr. Douglass; Desdemona, Miss Cheer.

Othello, like Lear, seems to have been studiously avoided by the pioneers of the drama in this country. Mr. John Henry was the first great representative in the part, although not the first who essayed it. Dunlap says: "Mr. Henry was full six feet in height, and had been uncommonly handsome. He played Othello better, we believe, than any man had done before him in America." It is also recorded of him that he wore the uniform of a British officer, his face black and hair woolly. This must not appear strange, however improper, for Dunlap says: "When the writer saw John Kemble, in 1786, play the Moor, he wore a suit of modern military of scarlet and gold lace—coat, waistcoat and breeches. He wore white silk stockings, his face was black, and his hair long and black, cued in the military fashion of the day."

Heretofore it has been an invariable custom to dress him as an Ottomite. The custom of Venice should be preserved in all its details. Painters, designers and actors have differed from one another very widely in relation to the costume of Othello. There can be but one opinion upon this point, for Vicillo, a contemporary of Shakespeare, describes the dress of the Venetian General, as follows: "Gown of crimson velvet, with loose sleeves, over which was a mantle cloth of gold, buttoned over the shoulder, with massive gold buttons. His cap was of crimson velvet, and he bore a silver baton, like those which are still the official designations of the field marshals of Europe."

Othello, according to Venetian laws, predicated on motives of policy, could not hold this office unless he was a Christian by profession; he must have assumed the appropriate costume as much as if he had been a Frenchman, a German or a Neapolitan. Would the Catholic Church, at that period paramount in all things, have permitted a turbaned Turk, an Ottomite, to lead their armies? Would Christian knights and gentlemen, jealous of their honor and religion, have served under a Mahommedan? Othello himself says:

"Are we turned Turks, and to ourselves do that
Which Heaven hath forbid the Ottomites?
For Christian shame!"

——"In Aleppo once
Where a malignant and turban'd Turk
Beat a Venetian,
I took by the throat," etc.

James Fennell, when he came to this country in 1793, brought with him the reputation of being the best Othello on the English stage. Cooper, Conway, and in fact the most eminent tragedians of the day, made it one of their studies. As regards the dressing of the part, and the color of Othello's skin, there cannot be a question of doubt if the author is strictly adhered to. Othello was unquestionably one of the most noble and accomplished of the negro race. Such Shakespeare makes him; and all the saponaceous compounds that ever emanated from a "critic's brain" cannot wash that color out. If the Moor had been one of the proud race of the Ommacides, and the Abbasides, as is contended, it would not have affected his social position or debarred him from being received on a social footing with the proudest of the Venetian republic. But such was not the case, as the very language and words of

Shakespeare prove. Messrs. Fennell, Henry, Cooper, Conway, and others of lesser note, up to a certain period, painted him *black*. Subsequently, more from local causes than a critical analysis of the character, the color of Othello's skin was changed to that of the Mulatto, or rather the Quadroon. Mr. Forrest conformed to the "custom of the country," and made him one of the mixed breed. Mr. Forrest's Othello was, however, a living portraiture of the noble Moor's mind, power and intellect; it was grand in conception and powerful in rendition. Gradually from the excess of his love—gradually to the first instillation of Iago's poison into his brain—does Othello rise up grandly before us. From the moment, a flash, as if it were from hell, darts across his mind, revealing as he imagines the guilt of Desdemona, he becomes the incarnation of that

——" Green-eyed monster
Which doth make the meat it feeds on."

He towers in crime, he grasps the reins of passion and drives on furiously to his own destruction!

Othello is a character that chiefly depends upon the actor to invest it with a living truth, for it "lays siege" to the bosom, while Richard and Macbeth, to the head. The first agitates, softens and subdues the heart; the others elevate and astonish the imagination. Thomas A. Cooper and Edwin Forrest were the only two actors whose impersonations of these three characters struck us as being truthful to nature and art.

Mr. Forrest's great *forte* in tragedy was his forcible delineation of the deep and terrible passions of the soul, and perhaps of this, Othello affords the most striking illustration. His exhibition of what was majestic and beautiful in sentiment, when connected with the powerful influences exercised by feeling, were always considered by critics as being impossible for any one to equal. He stood alone the "noblest Roman of them all."

In his Othello we recognized the great master of the histrionic art. No man—not even the great Kean himself, or the cold, mechanical Macready—ever uttered these words as Mr. Forrest did, conveying in the fullest manner to the audience the great mental strife going on within. His form drooping, limbs powerless, reason palsied, he seemed as if life itself was going out with each word:

——"O! now, forever,
Farewell the tranquil mind! farewell content!
Farewell the plumed troop, and the big wars
That make ambition virtue! O! farewell!
Farewell the neighing steed, and the shrill trump,
The spirit-stirring drum, the ear-piercing fife,

* * * * * * *

Pride, pomp, and circumstances of glorious war!

* * * * * * *

Othello's occupation's gone."

Our readers will remember how Mr. Forrest rendered that terrible passage:

——"I had rather be a toad,
And live upon the vapor of a dungeon," etc.

Forrest, in delineating the various passions which agitate and excite the jealous Moor, has had no equal; indeed, few actors possess the physical and mental powers so happily blended, as did this great artist, so as to enable them to give full force to language requiring the highest order of genius and talent, as well as the masterly touches of true genius combined—the only two qualities calculated to make a great actor. All others have failed. During Mr. Forrest's first visit to England, professionally, his Othello was the subject of much comment. The John Bulls' could not bring themselves to believe that an American actor could achieve a triumph over a Kean and a Macready. Jealousy came very near depriving Mr. Forrest of an opportunity of achieving this triumph. The critic of the London *Morning Herald*, in October, 1836, speaking of Mr. Forrest's Othello, says :—"From this moment the actor was determined not to lose hold of the minds of the audience, and duly kept his hold. When a conviction of the guilt of Desdemona first came full upon him, and he exclaims, 'I had rather be a toad!' his emotion and gesticulation were absolutely terrific, though neither coarse nor overacted. Here (and we are aware of the hazardous assertion) Mr. Forrest really appeared to leave behind him the best Othello of them all. Three distinct rounds of applause rewarded his successful exertion."

In the address to the Senate, Mr. Forrest gave two new readings, which have been adopted as the standard, being in conformity to the true meaning of the author. We do not give them as of sufficient importance to elicit criticism, but simply to show the care and attention he bestowed on the text of his favorite author. For example:

——"Rude am I in my speech,
And little bless'd with the set phrase of peace;
For since these arms of mine had seven years' pith,
Till now, some nine moons wasted, they have us'd
Their dearest action in the tented field;
And little of this great world can I speak
More than pertains to feats of broil and battle;
And, therefore, little shall I grace my cause
In *speaking* for myself."

We do not recollect an instance in which this was not read:

"In speaking for *myself*."

The other reading was of still greater importance. It is in the passage where he describes the anxiety with which Desdemona used to listen to his recitals:

"She'd come again, and with a greedy ear
Devour up my discourse, which I observing,
Took once a pliant hour, and found *good* means
To draw from her a prayer of earnest heart," etc.

In connection with the tragedy of Othello, there is an interpolation of six lines in the speech of Othello before the Senate, which have perplexed the critics and actors considerably. They take the place of those extravagant lines, commencing with

"And portance in my travel's history,
Wherein of antres vast, and deserts idle,
Rough quarries, rocks, and hills whose heads touch heaven,"

and

"The Anthropophagi, and men whose heads
Do grow beneath their shoulders," etc.

Such sights as described by Othello fully sustain Iago's remark that Othello won his bride by telling fantastical lines. All these are omitted, and the following most happily substituted:

"Of battles bravely, hardly fought; of victories
For which the conqueror mourned,
So many fell. Sometimes I told
The story of a siege in which I had to combat
Plague and famine; soldiers unpaid,
Fearful to fight, but bold in dangerous mutiny."

In a prompt-book of Covent Garden, not printed in the text, but interwritten upon a blank leaf, these lines, it is said, were first discovered. We have a copy of Othello, wherein they are to be found as given above. The play has the following title:

OTHELLO,
A Tragedy, by Shakespeare,
As performed at the
THEATRE ROYAL, DRURY LANE,
Regulated from the Prompt-Book,
WITH PERMISSION OF THE MANAGERS,
By Mr. Hopkins, *Prompter*.
An INTRODUCTION and NOTES,
Critical and Illustrative,
Are added by the
AUTHORS OF THE DRAMATIC CENSOR,
London.
Printed for John Bell, near Exeter Exchange,
In the Strand,
MDCCLXXVII.

SALVINI.

An Italian artist, by the name of Salvini, with an Italian company, recently arrived in this country, and his Othello has been said by critics to be superior to that of Mr. Forrest's. We admit the talents of this Italian, and that of his company, but cannot endorse him as being the Othello of the world! Our opinion of him we give here in connection with the great tragedy:

The Italian stage and actors are but little known to us, although the history of their drama dates back to a very early period. After the extinction of the Latin Theatres, the Italian drama degenerated into vulgarity and its profession strolled from town to town. It languished thus, until the twelfth century, when it gradually recovered its vigor and admitted the embellishment of dialogue. Then came a lapse of years, during which the Italian stage, and the drama, were lost sight of by the people.

The Academy of Sienna was the first body of persons who set the example of composing and representing correct comedies. In the seventeenth century the hired actors, who until that period had acted extempore, were known as *improvisatori*, now performed any piece which had not been previously printed. This was the commencement of the legitimate drama in Italy, which was subsequently enhanced by the translation of the Plays of Shakespeare. These gave a somewhat different tone and character to their tragedies.

Salvini is a specimen of the Italian and Shakespeare schools combined. His conception of the character is in the main correct, but in carrying it out he overacts, or rather, we should say, gives it an Italian coloring. In the First Act, where Othello shows the most love, he was not quite up to the standard of an impassioned lover. He did not show that warmth of love for Desdemona which so distinguished Mr. Forrest in the part, but in the bursts of passion his every outbreak reminded us of that gentleman. Exaggeration in the impassioned scenes of the drama is not at all times considered a fault, as for instance in King Lear, Virginius, Damon, and Othello, the actor is justified in stretching the power of declamation to its climax.

The Third Act, which has always been considered the test of an actor's ability, was one grand display of the histrionic art, and never surpassed, within our recollection, but by one man, and that one, the great Othello of the American stage:

EDWIN FORREST.

In this act, and in fact throughout the Fourth and Fifth, he bore such a striking likeness to this gentleman, both in voice and in action, that it seemed as if the spirit of the great actor, now in Heaven, was present on this occasion. The genius of Shakespeare dwells with but few actors, and when it does fire the soul, it makes such actors as Cooke, Cooper, Kean, Conway, the elder Booth, Edwin Forrest and SALVINI.

We have spoken of the actor generally, there are however one or two points in his acting which marred the harmony as a perfect whole. The first is the savage treatment he inflicts upon Iago. Jealousy, we admit, is a strong passion, but it seldom shows itself on the advise of another's dishonor. Forrest's manner was not of the tiger kind, Salvini's is, for he not only dashes Iago to the ground, but it seemed to us that he *kicked him when down.*

In the last interview with Desdemona he seemed like a tiger weaving across his cage, he ranges to and fro along the furthest limits of the stage, now stealing away from her with long strides and avoiding her approaches, and now turning fiercely round upon her and rolling his black eyes, by turns agitated by irresolution, touched by tenderness, or goading himself into rage, until, at last, like a storm, he seizes her and bears her away to her death. After the deed has been accomplished, what can exceed the horror of his ghastly face, as he looks out between the curtains, which he gathers about him when he hears Emilia's knock—or the anguish and remorse of that wild, terrible cry, as he leans over her dead body after he knows her innocence, or the savage rage of that sudden scream with which he leaps upon Iago.

To this we may add, as not being Shakesperian nor soldier like, the cutting his throat with a sort of butcher's knife. It is not a refined method of dying, nor is it consistent with the noble bearing of Othello, who exclaimed even in the moment of wild excitement: "Behold! I have a weapon," and then when he says, in a more subdued, yet equally determined manner, bent on the act of suicide, "I took by the throat the circumcised dog, and smote him thus—"

In the original copy of Othello, following the words "smote him thus," we find this in brackets [*stabs himself*]. Salvini adopts the butcher's mode, and not that of the more refined method of making his quietus.

Again, as Othello has to speak after the deed, we question if he would be enabled to do so with a "slit wizzen." The words he has to say are these:

> "I kiss'd thee, ere I kill'd thee: no way but this,
> Killing myself to die upon a kiss.—"

CHAPTER XII.

FORREST RETURNS HOME WITH HIS BRIDE.—HIS RECEPTION.—GRAND DINNER.—HIS OLD FRIENDS AROUND HIM.—JOHN SWIFT, MORTON McMICHAEL, LOUIS A. GODEY, ETC.

MR. FORREST, accompanied by his wife, arrived home in 1837. Perhaps no married couple ever approached our shores upon whose countenances there glowed the light of love more bright, and upon the brow of one a more brilliant wreath of fame never entwined its laurelled leaves. Little did he think then, with his smiling bride beside him, that in time a dark cloud was to darken their future happiness. Little did he dream that years of misery were to follow this marriage, and that his fame and fortune were to be imperilled by it. But the die was cast, confidence destroyed, and man and wife parted forever!

Immediately on his return, he began an engagement at the Park Theatre, New York, where he achieved a triumph unequalled in stage history. The receipts for the first night exceeded four thousand dollars!

OLD DRURY, CHESTNUT STREET.

This theatre opened for the fall season on the 18th of August, 1837, with "Every One has His Fault." The stars announced, were Edwin Forrest, the elder Vandenhoff, Hackett, Jim Crow Rice, Ellen Tree, Charles Horn, Bedouin Arabs, Miss Horton, Mr. Brough, and Mr. and Mrs. Wood, vocalists.

On the 15th of November, 1837, Mr. Forrest appeared as Othello, Mr. E. S. Connor playing Iago; on the 27th, Broker of Bogota; and for one month continued to fill the theatre, closing a very brilliant engagement, the first and only one of the kind at the Chestnut Street Theatre; over the head of all the brilliant stars named above, Forrest, and Forrest only, was the card. Miss Turpin and Miss Clifton closed the year 1837.

The friends of Mr. Forrest, who felt as if his triumph in England was a compliment to our country, and a homage the British nation paid to American talent, tendered him a public dinner. On the 15th of December, 1837, this event took place at the Merchant's Hotel, North Fourth street, above Market. On that day about two hundred gentlemen, including many of the most eminent of our fellow-citizens, and a number of distinguished strangers, sat down to a sumptuous dinner, prepared by Mr. Sanderson. The following named gentlemen had been previously appointed officers, viz:—

President.—NICHOLAS BIDDLE.

Vice-Presidents.

HON. JOS. R. INGERSOLL,	HON. JOHN SWIFT,
DR. SAMUEL JACKSON,	COL. JAMES PAGE,
COL. JOHN P. WETHERILL,	WM. D. LEWIS, ESQ.

Stewards.

MORTON McMICHAEL,	WM. H. HART,
R. T. CONRAD,	F. A. HUBER,
C. INGERSOLL,	N. C. FOSTER,
R. PENN SMITH,	JAMES GOODMAN,
THOS. HART,	ADAM WOELPPER,

ROBERT MORRIS.

Among the invited guests were several members of the press, and of the dramatic profession—William B. Wood, R. C. Maywood, E. S. Connor, F. C. Wemyss, Charles Porter, and others.

In consequence of severe indisposition, Mr. Biddle was unable to attend, and he addressed the following note to one of the committee of arrangements.

"PHILADELPHIA, Dec. 15th, 1837.

"HON. ROBERT T. CONRAD.

"MY DEAR SIR:—I regret much that indisposition will prevent me from joining your festival to-day. Feeling, as I do, an intense nationality, which makes the fame of every citizen the common property of the country, I rejoice at all the developments of intellectual power among our countrymen in every walk of life, and I am always anxious to do honor to high faculties combined with personal worth. Such a union the common voice ascribes to Mr. Forrest, and I would have gladly added my own applause to the general homage. But this is impracticable now, and I can therefore only convey through you a sentiment which, if it wants the vigorous expression of health, has at least a sick man's sincerity. It is:

"The genius of our country, whenever and wherever displayed—honor to its triumphs in every field of fame.

"With great regard, yours,

"NICHOLAS BIDDLE."

At five o'clock the company sat down to the table, which occupied the whole of the spacious dining hall, the HON. JOSEPH R. INGERSOLL being in the chair. Mr. Forrest, the guest of the day, was placed at his right; and on his left were Chief-Justice Gibson, Judge Rogers of the Supreme Court, Recorder Robert T. Conrad, and other judicial officers. Many gentlemen of high literary distinction were present. Messrs. Dunlop, Banks, Bell, Doran, and other members of the Convention, then sitting in the city, to revise the Constitution of the State, were at the table; among the professional persons who joined in the festivity, we particularly noticed Dr. Jackson, of the University of Pennsylvania, Professor Mitchell, and Dr. Colhoun, the Dean of Jefferson College. Mr. Leggett, of New York, the early friend of Mr. Forrest, was present by invitation.

After the cloth was removed, many speeches were made, and among those who spoke at length, were Col. John Swift, James Page, and Joseph R. Chandler. The latter, in the course of his remarks, made allusion to Jack Cade and Caius Marius, and concluded by offering the health of the Recorder of the city, Robert T. Conrad, to which that gentleman replied as follows—

"To those who are acquainted with the gentleman who has just taken his seat, no act of generosity or kindness coming from him can be wholly unexpected. I will not, therefore, plead, in extenuation of my inability to return a suitable acknowledgment, the surprise which his flattering reference to me, and the still more flattering manner in which that reference was received, have excited. I may, however, regret that the excess of his kindness deprives me of the power of speaking the gratitude which it inspires —a gratitude which is only rendered more profound by a reference to our home literature. The press has domesticated it in the poor man's cottage, and made it with all its holy and humanizing influences, universal as the rains of spring, or the sun of summer. To be, or to have been, connected with an agent so mighty and beneficent, is no slight honor. The first minds of the age have been associated with the press. Several of the choicest spirits around this board have labored in that field; and, if I do not err, the gentleman who is prevented by illness from presiding here to-day, "our absent Banquo" —the accomplished Biddle, was, at one time, connected with the periodical press. Of the profession, as now constituted in this country, I do not hesitate to affirm, that it comprises an almost unrivalled amount of genius and public spirit—thousands of gifted men, whose minds flow through society, like rills through the meadow—

———"'That, with a livelier green,
Betrays the secret of their silent course.'

"The gentleman who called me up is, himself, an instance of the truth of this remark—one who would adorn and illustrate any walk of public life, however arduous or however elevated. In our own city, the corps is composed of men who would do honor to any community—men as enlightened and liberal, as high-minded and warm-hearted as any in the land. Their craft has been considered, by some, an ungentle one, and many have regarded editors as a species of intellectual gladiators, who cut and hack each other 'for the diversion of Romans:' but in this city, at least, such is not the fact; for, while they have won the confidence and applause of the public, they have done what is more difficult and more honorable—they have maintained feelings of almost fraternal kindness for each other. It is to be wished that such were the spirit of the press everywhere. The priests who minister in the great temple of knowledge are, or ought to be, always and everywhere, brothers.

"I would be proud to bear this testimony in favor of the press at any time; but I do it the more eagerly on the present occasion, as I see at this board a valued and estimable member of the press, from whom I venture to hope for a response. His station would do honor to any man—the man would reflect honor on any station. No one has done more to cultivate the elevated, refined, or friendly spirit that characterizes the Philadelphia press—no one has directed the energies of that press to the accomplishment of milder or nobler purposes. In such hands the giant power of the press will always be safe—its influences beneficent—its triumphs stainless—*victoria sine glade.* I have only to add the hope that he may long continue to grace the councils of the city and the State, and, for many and many a year to come, give us each day the daily bread of the mind. I tender as a sentiment,

"'RICHARD PENN SMITH, whose early connection with the public press of our city was the precursor of its present success—whose accomplishment as a scholar, whose talents as a writer, are made more attractive by his attachment as a friend, his feelings as a man, and his courtesy as a gentleman.'"

In reply, Mr. Smith arose and said:

"MR. PRESIDENT:—I find myself in the position of the needy knife grinder—'Story! God bless you! I have none to tell, sir.' You, sir, are an experienced member of the Philadelphia bar, and consequently cannot imagine *how hard* it is to make a speech after the pointed and eloquent addresses that have just been made; but, sir, you have also been a member of Congress, and can fully understand *how hard* it is to listen to a succession of speeches without relief or interruption. The repetition of the words *how hard* reminds me of a benevolent being who visited the principal penitentiaries of Europe for the purpose of alleviating the condition of their distressed inmates. I at present feel myself in the position of a prisoner, and the most feasible escape that occurs is to call upon my friend, the benevolent Howard, to relieve me from my difficulties and cheer me with a song."

The President called upon Brough and Howard for a duett, which was given.

After the song, Mr. Smith responded to the compliment contained in Mr. Chandler's address, and said, that he must confess himself a genuine Yankee in his literary pursuits, for he had commenced business in various branches, but had been constant to none. As a newspaper editor, he had his day—a stormy one, without a ray of sunshine. As a novelist, his productions were *Forsaken*, and somewhat *Deformed;* but the organ of philoprogenitiveness was so strongly developed, that they were never *Disowned.* Mr. Smith here paid a just tribute to the talents of Irving, Cooper, Kennedy, Sedgwick, and other distinguished novelists of the day. He touched upon his career as a dramatist, and begged permission to speak in kindly terms of his productions, as the Roman adage fully applied to them —*de mortuis nil nisi bonum.* He referred with pleasure to his intercourse with Mr. Forrest, for whom he wrote his tragedy entitled Caius Marius, but regretted that even the transcendant talents of his friend could not save his hero from perishing among the ruins of Carthage.

Mr. Smith, in speaking of the American drama, said, that on such an occasion, it would be unpardonable to overlook one who stood foremost in the ranks of our dramatic writers. A gentleman who had distinguished himself by his various talents as an artist and an author; and whose dramatic works would ultimately secure him an enviable fame. He regretted that age, and the inclement season, prevented his participation in the festivities of the occasion. He referred to William Dunlap, of New York. Mr. Smith read the following letter:

"NEW YORK, December 11th, 1837.

"GENTLEMEN:—I received on the evening of the 9th instant, your polite letter, doing me the honor of requesting my presence at a public dinner to be given to Edwin Forrest on the 15th instant. Nothing but the progress of winter, which I see around me, and feel within, could prevent my testifying in person how highly I appreciate the invitation of the committee and the gentleman to whom the public mark of esteem is to be given. Permit me to offer a toast:

"'The American Actor, who both in public and private life upholds the honor of his country: Edwin Forrest.'

"WILLIAM DUNLAP."

Mr. President, said Mr. Smith, I will offer you a toast which I have no doubt will be cordially responded to.

"WILLIAM DUNLAP. The Nestor of the American Drama. May he live to see the edifice become what his foundation promised."

Now commenced the crowning scene of the evening. Chief-Justice Gibson rose in his place, and said:

"The friends of the drama are desirous of paying a merited tribute of respect and esteem to one of the most distinguished and successful of its sons. Well approved usage, upon occasions not dissimilar, has pointed to this our cheerful greeting as a fitting method for carrying their desires into effect. It combines the compliment of public and unequivocal demonstration with the kindness and cordiality of social intercourse. It serves to express at once opinions the result of deliberate judgment, and sentiments warm and faithful from the heart.

"To our guest we owe much for having devoted to the profession which he has selected an uncommon energy of character and peculiar personal aptitudes. They are both adapted to the happiest illustrations of an art, which in the absence of either would want a finished representative; but by a rare combination of faculties in him, he is enabled effectually 'to hold the mirror up to Nature.' It is an art, in the rational pleasures and substantial advantages derived from which, all are free to participate, and a large proportion of the educated and liberal minded avail themselves of the privilege—an art which for thousands of years has been practised with success, admired and esteemed; and the men who have adorned it by their talents have received the well-earned plaudits of their age, and the honors of a cherished name.

"To our guest we owe especial thanks that he has been a prompt, uniform and liberal patron of his art. Dramatic genius and merit have never appealed to him for aid in vain. He has devoted the best directed generosity, and some of his most brilliant professional efforts, to their cause.

"To our guest we owe unmeasured thanks that he has done much by his personal exertion, study and example, to identify our stage with the classic drama, and that he has made the more than modern Æschylus, the myriad-minded Shakespeare, ours.

"We owe him thanks, as members of a well-regulated community, that by the course and current of his domestic life, the reproaches that are sometimes cast upon his profession have been signally disarmed. And in this moment of joyous festivity, we feel that we owe him unnumbered thanks, that he has offered us an opportunity to express for him an unfeigned and cordial regard. These sentiments are embraced in a brief but comprehensive toast, which I will ask leave to offer, 'The stage (and then turning to Mr. Forrest) and its Master.'"

A peal of three-times-three followed the speech and sentiment, after which Mr. Forrest, rising, with great power and effect, returned his thanks in an able and appropriate address, which was made with good discretion. His delivery was natural, forcible and unaffected; and in many passages, all who heard him were moved to tears. At the allusion to his earliest and best friend, Col. John Swift, the Mayor of the city, the whole company rose, and, by a common impulse, gave six good cheers. Mr. Forrest said:—

"Mr. President and Gentlemen:—I feel too deeply the honor this day rendered me, to be able to express myself in terms of adequate meaning. There are times when the tongue is at best a poor interpreter of the heart. The strongest emotions do not always clothe themselves in the strongest language. The words which rise to my lips seem too cold and vapid to denote truly the sentiments which prompt them; they lack that terseness and energy which the occasion deserves.

"The actor usually comes before the public in a 'fiction, in a dream of passion,' and his aim is to suit his utterance and the '*havior* of the visage' to the unreal situation. But the resources of my art do not avail me here. This is no pageant of the stage, to be forgotten with the hour, nor this an audience drawn to view its mimic scenes. I stand amidst a numerous throng of the chiefest denizens of my native city, convened to do me honor; and this costly banquet they present to me, a magnificent token of their regard. I feel, indeed, that I am no actor here. My bosom throbs with undissembled agitation, and in the grateful tumult of my thoughts I cannot 'beget a temperance to give smoothness' to my acknowledgments for so proud a tribute. In the simplest form of speech, then, let me assure you, from my inmost heart I thank you.

"I have but recently returned from England, after performing many nights on those boards where the master-spirits of the stage achieved their noblest triumphs. You have heard from other sources with what kindness I was received, and with what bounteous applause my efforts were rewarded. Throughout my sojourn abroad, I experienced only the most candid and liberal treatment from the public, and the most elegant and cordial hospitality in private. But I rejoice that the time has come round which brings me again to the point from which I started, which places me among those friends whose partial kindness discovered the first unfoldings of my mind, and watched it with assiduous care through all the stages of its subsequent development. The applause of foreign audiences was soothing to my pride, but that which I received at home had aroused a deeper sentiment. The people of England bestowed their approbation on the results of long practice and severe study, but my countrymen gave me theirs in generous anticipation of those results; *they* looked with indulgence on the completed statue; *you* marked with interest, from day to day, the progress of the work, till the rough block, by gradual change, assumed the present form. Let me hope that it may yet be sculptured to great symmetry and smoothness, and better deserve your lavish regard. The sounds and sights which greet me here are linked with thrilling associations. Among the voices which welcome me to-night, I distinguish some which were raised in kind approval of my earliest efforts. Among the faces which surround this board I trace lineaments deeply stamped on my memory in that expression of benevolent encouragement with which they regarded my juvenile attempts and cheered me onward in the outset of my career. I look on your features, sir (said Mr. Forrest, addressing himself to the Mayor of the city, John Swift, who occupied a seat by his right), and my mind glides over a long interval of time, to a scene I can never forget. Four lustres are now nearly completed since the event occurred to which I allude.

"A crowd was gathered, one evening, in the Tivoli Garden to behold the curious varieties of delirium men exhibited on inhaling nitrous oxide. Several years had then elapsed since the great chemist of England had made known the singular properties of exhilarating gas; and strange antics performed under its influence by distinguished philosophers, poets and statesmen of Europe, were then on record. It was yet, however, a novelty with us, and the public experiments drew throngs to witness them. Among those to whom the intoxicating agent was administered on the occasion referred to, there chanced to be a little unfriended boy who, in the instant ecstasy which the subtle fluid inspired, threw himself into a tragic attitude, and commenced declaiming a passage from one of Shakespeare's plays: 'What ho!' he cried, 'young Richmond, ho! 'tis Richard calls. I hate thee, Harry, for thy blood of Lancaster!' But the effect of the ærial draught was brief as it was sudden and irresistible. The boy, awaking as from a dream, was surprised to find himself the centre of attraction, '*the observed of all observers.*' Abashed at his novel and awkward position, he shrunk timidly from the glances of the spectators, and would have stolen in haste away; but a stranger stepped from the crowd, and taking him kindly by the hand, pronounced words which thrilled through him with a spell-like influence. 'This lad,' said he, 'has the germ of tragic greatness in him. The exhilarating gas has given him no new power; it has only revealed one which lay dormant in him before. It needs only to be cherished and cultivated to bring goodly fruit.'

"Gentlemen, the present chief magistrate of our city was that benevolent stranger, and your guest to-night was that unfriended boy. If the prophecy has been in any degree fulfilled—if since that time I have attained some eminence in my profession, let my full heart acknowledge that the inspiriting prediction, followed as it was with repeated acts of delicate and considerate kindness, exercised the happiest influence on the result. It was a word in season. It was a kindly greeting calculated to arouse all the energies of my nature and direct them to a particular aim. Prophecy oftentimes shapes the event which it seems to foretell. One shout of friendly confidence at the beginning of a race may nerve the runner with strength to win the goal. Happy he, who, on accomplishing his round, is received with generous welcome by the same friends that cheered him at the start. Among such friends I stand. You listened with inspiring praise and augury to the immature efforts of the boy, and you now honor with this proud token of your approbation the achievements of the man. You nurtured me in the bud and early blossom of my life, and 'labored to make me full of growing;' if you have succeeded, the harvest is your own."

Mayor Swift had made an allusion to an incident in Forrest's early history—that of inhaling laughing gas at the Tivoli Garden, on Market Street. This caused a roar of laughter, in which no one joined more heartily than the tragedian himself. (See Chapter III.)

Some remarks were made at that time by the press as regards the exclusive character of this dinner. It was said that a dinner to an actor was the reward of literary services rendered to his country, and that invitations should have been given to the members of the profession, who for years assisted the great actor to sustain the dramatic, as well as the literary character of the American stage. There were many actors living at the time, whose names should have been included among those of the press, the politicians, lawyers and doctors. William B. Wood, Maywood, Wemyss, E. S. Connor, Charles S. Porter, and Howard, the vocalist, were the only members of the profession present. As a compliment to Mr. Forrest, this dinner was a flattering mark of the estimation in which his talent was held in his native city. Some fifteen years ago, in giving an account of this dinner, in connection with a short sketch of Mr. Forrest's life, we said:

"Time and space would fail us to accord even a brief notice to the various addresses on this festive event. His Honor the Mayor, as the tide of reminiscences swept past, gave vent to the obvious expressions flowing from the fountain of feeling—the heart. He did honor to the involuntary bursts of applause by gently wiping his well-deluged eyes—a weakness, if ye please so to call it, that seemed contagious. The noble Chief-Justice Gibson relaxed from legal dignity and reserve, and amused the company from his well-stored anecdotal repository, with plain-spoken and racy facts. Joseph R. Chandler, Col. James Page, Richard Penn Smith, Morton McMichael, Dr. Jackson, and others, kept the tables joyous with piquant jest, repartee, and sprightly anecdote; and, as one of the editors of our press said, 'our brother of the *United States Gazette* was full of point and pith, teeming with peculiar aptitude of allusion, from gay to grave.' The songs and duets, by Messrs. Russell, Brough, Howard, and our old amateur friend H. E. Levenstein, were excellent, and as tastefully swallowed as the sparkling champagne, some of the bottles of which were with a very felicitous conceit marked the 'Forrest Brand,' while the name of the chief guest was woven in wreaths which encircled the sugared pyramids of confection, and was also embossed in white sugared letters, in the cakes and pastry of the dessert."

Letters were received from Washington Irving

and other distinguished literary gentlemen, complimentary to the guest, apologetic of non-attendance.

William B. Wood, in his "Personal Recollections of the Stage," sums up this pleasing event in Mr. Forrest's life in *five lines*:—"*During this season the citizens of Philadelphia honored their distinguished townsman, Edwin Forrest, with a splendid dinner, under circumstances which must have proved highly gratifying to him.*"

CHAPTER XIII.

KING LEAR.—ORIGIN OF THE PLOT.—CHRONICLE HISTORY OF KING LEAR.—SHAKESPEARE'S LEAR.—BETTERTON.—BURBAGE.—BARTON BOOTH.—KEMBLE'S ADAPTATION.—WILLIAM DUNLAP'S OPINION OF FORREST'S LEAR.—MR. FORREST'S CONCEPTION OF THE CHARACTER.—EXTRAORDINARY TALENT DISPLAYED IN ITS RENDITION.—CRITICAL NOTICES BY THE AUTHOR.—THRILLING INCIDENT DURING MR. FORREST'S PERFORMANCE OF LEAR.—FIRST PERFORMANCE OF KING LEAR IN AMERICA.—THE CAST.

MR. FORREST'S career was now one of a succession of triumphs. We shall have very little to say about his engagements North or South, nor of any other until his departure to fulfil another engagement in Europe. Our readers will perceive that in our desultory style we have not strictly adhered to the biographical order of composition, but used the more general term—Reminiscences. Our object is to place

Mr. Forrest before the American people in two distinct characters, the one private, the other dramatic.

Perhaps no man belonging to the profession rendered these two characters more distinct than did Mr. Forrest. Garrick, Kemble, Cooke, Kean, Booth and Fennell, acted all the time, and were alike distinguished for their actions off the stage, which were as much in character as were those on the stage.

To prove this, it would be necessary for us to give a sketch of the life of these gentlemen, which is quite out of the question in connection with these reminiscences. Many of our readers, however, can bear witness to the truth of these remarks, as relates to two or three of those named. Nor is it necessary to add, there are many now living to whom they will apply with equal force.

It is said of one of those named above:

> "Hide the goblet from his lip,
> He must glut in his thoughts while his brethren sip;
> Should his proboscis once in its hollow be tombed
> All its liquor would hiss, and its sides be consum'd."

Not alone to this prominent actor will these lines apply. Although we do not allude to them here as forming a stage trait of character, yet the indulgence of the "wine cup," not unfrequently was the means of destroying both the private and dramatic character of many a member of the profession.

While Mr. Forrest was winning laurels elsewhere, let us leave him for the present, and say something of his

KING LEAR.

> *Lear*—"You must bear with me!
> Pray now, forget and forgive; I am old and foolish."
> *Act IV.; Scene* 7.

This great tragedy—the most finished, bold, and next to Hamlet in its intellectual and philosophical characteristics—was written when the author was in the very prime of life and the full vigor and maturity of his genius. It is deeply stamped with all the most marked peculiarities of the style and cast of thought predominant in all his later works.

THE OLD PLAY OF KING LEAR.

The old "Chronicle" History of King Leir, as it is called on the title-page, was entered at Stationers' Hall in 1564; the author's name is unknown. It was played by Henslowe's company, on the 6th of April, 1593. Shakespeare's King Lear, could not have been composed until after 1603, because it contains several singular names of spirits, taken from Samuel Hansnet's Declaration of "Popish Imposters," then first published. Malone confidently thought that the substitution of "Britishman" for "Englishman" in Edgar's repetition of the old verse, act iii., scene 4, proved the piece to have been written *after* James I. had been proclaimed the first sovereign of Great Britain, October 1st, 1604. He therefore referred the play to 1605, and Dr. Drake to 1604.

As this entry is somewhat curious, we annex it:—

"26 *November*, 1607.—*Na. Butler and Jo. Busby. Entred for their copie under t' hande of Sur Geo. Bucke, Kt. and the wardens a booke called Mr. Willm. Shakespeare, his historye of King Lear, as yt was played before the King's Majestie at Whitehall, upon St. Stephen's night, at Christmas last, by his Majestie's servants playing usually at the Globe on the Bank side.*"

There is no doubt but the two plays owe their origin to a literal translation of King Lear of the Britons, and his Three Daughters, from a portion of the Welsh history by Tysilio, who wrote in the sixth century; the MSS. of which are now in the Bodleian library. The legend was frequently quoted by Geoffery of Monmouth, and then translated in Holinshead's Chronicles, whence Shakespeare certainly derived it.

In the old Welsh legend, it reads that Lear had no sons, but three daughters, whose names were Gonilla, Ragun and Cordilla, whom he loved most tenderly, but especially his youngest daughter Cordilla. When he became old he thought of dividing the Isle of Britain, as a portion for his daughters. But to make a trial of their affection and duty to him, and to know who deserved the best part of the kingdom, he asked each of them who loved him most. Gonilla, the eldest, made answer, "that she loved him more than her own soul." The father replied — "Since you regard my old age before your own soul, my dearest daughter, I will repay your affection, and you shall be married to the man you desire, and the third part of my kingdom shall be your portion." The question was proposed to Ragun, the second daughter, who replied, "that she could not express her tender affection for her dear father, but she loved him above all creatures;" the father answered, "that he loved her as much, and would bestow the same upon her as his eldest daughter, Gonilla." Cordilla, perceiving how they betrayed her credulous father with flattery, thought of making a suitable reply to his question; when being asked she said:—"My dear father, although there are some who profess to love you beyond bounds, yet I love you, my dear father, as much as it is the duty of a daughter to love her father, neither more or less, and take this as my answer—how much you have, so much is your value, and so I love you."

The choleric king takes offence at this and to use a familiar phrase, "cut her off with a shilling." In the old play the words are thus given. Gonilla says:—

"As much as child e'er loved, or father found;
A love that makes breath poor, and speech unable;
Beyond all manner of so much I love you."

Ragun, equally affectionate, says:—

"I am made of that same metal as my sister,
And prize me at her worth. In my true heart;
I find she names my very deed of love;
Only she comes too short, that I profess
Myself an enemy to all other joys,
Which the most precious square of sense possesses,
And find I am alone felicitate
In your highness' love."

Cordilla's response is beautifully expressive:—

"I love your majesty—
According to my bond; nor more, nor less."

It is not our purpose to point out passages which have a seeming resemblance, seeming indeed they are, for Shakespeare's play founded upon these mere sketches, is a triumph so immense, that all minor productions are but the A, B, C to the dramatic art, at whose head he alone will ever stand.

In the old play, Lear has a friend called Percillus, who never excites our interest as does that of Kent in the later and greater play by the immortal bard, Shakespeare.

The characters of both performances are nearly the same; but while in the old play, they are comparatively only instruments of utterance, Shakespeare breathes a spirit of life into his historical personages, and they live again in his lines. Shakespeare may be criticised for a century, but after all we shall only arrive at this point—that we admire him above all others, because he is, more than all others, the poet of actual existence.

SHAKESPEARE'S LEAR.

The story of Lear was originally related by Geoffrey of Monmouth, and thence translated in "Holinshead's Chronicles," whence Shakespeare certainly derived it; though he seems to have been more indebted to an anonymous play, entered at Stationers' Hall, May 14th, 1594. Several passages in Shakespeare's Lear, lead to the conclusion that he read John Higgins' poem of "Queen Cordela," in part i. of the "Mirror for Magistrates," 1587, and also the episode of "Gloucester and Sons," as well as the "Narrative of the Blind King of Paphlagonia," in "Sir Philip Sidney's Arcadia." Shakespeare composed Lear in 1603. There can be no doubt of this, from the fact that he uses the names of certain spirits taken from Samuel Hansnet's "Declaration of Popish Imposters," then just published. There are many curious facts connected with Lear. The story of Lear bears date eight hundred years before Christ. He was the eldest son of Bladud, and is said to have governed "his country for sixty years."

In 1681, Nahum Tate's edition of this tragedy appeared at the Duke's Theatre, in which the fool was omitted. Coleman's version, in 1763, was a failure.

The full title of Shakespeare's play was, "History of the Life and Death of King Lear and his Three Daughters, with the Unfortunate Life of Edgar, Sonne and Heire of the Earl of Gloucester, and his Sullen and Assumed Humour of Tom of Bedlam. As it was plaid before the King's Majesty at Whitehall uppon St. Stephen's night, in Christmas hollidaies. By his Majesty's Servants, playing usually at the Globe on the Bank Side. 4to. 1608."

Tate and Coleman's we have alluded to. The great play, however, upon this subject, prior to the time Shakespeare's was written, is the one dated 1594, and entitled "The True Chronicle History in King Leir and His Three Daughters, Gonerill, Regan, and Cordella. As it hath been divers and sundry times lately acted. 4to. 1605." Shakespeare's Lear, differs materially from this version.

There is no doubt but Shakespeare borrowed the *idea* of the curse from the Œdipus, of Sophocles, although it had not then been translated. Shakespeare must have read it in the original, if he read it at all. The similarity, however, is not so striking as to accuse him of plagiarism, nor so startling as to lessen his claim to originality. We annex a portion from Œdipus:

> "Get thee hence, thou hast no father here
> Detested wretch—thou vilest of the vile—
> And take these curses with thee on thy head,
> Which I call down; by arms thy native land
> Never may'st thou recover, nor again
> Visit the vales of Argos: may'st thou die
> Slain by a brother's hand, and may thy hand
> Slay him by whom thou art to exile driv'n.
> These curses I call on thee, and invoke
> The parent gloom of Erebus abhorr'd,
> To give thee in his dark tartarian realms
> A mansion."

The curse of Œdipus is prophetic of the fate of his sons. To give the terrible one of Lear otherwise than as a curse would destroy all its terrible meaning and mar its power. Lear himself says: "*'Tis the untented woundings of a father's curse.*"

From tradition we learn that Betterton and Barton Booth rendered the curse more as a prayer than as a terrible imprecation. Indeed, there are those who consider it in that light still. Those who so construe it are not Shakesperian scholars, or versed in the holiness of prayer. Garrick gave it after the traditionary manner of Burbage, with fierce and rapid vehemence. Kemble, however, uttered it as a curse, made up of unmixed wrath.

Mr. Forrest's name is identified with the character of Lear, as were those of Burbage, Betterton, Barton Booth, Garrick and Kemble. Barton Booth first appeared on the stage in 1701. He was celebrated in Shakespeare's Othello and Hamlet's Ghost, these being his master-pieces. He was likewise the original Cato. It is a curious fact connected with all the great English actors, that their Lear, if we except, perhaps, Garrick, never created so much excitement in the dramatic world as has that of Mr. Forrest's. Betterton and Booth were considered great in the part, nor was it until 1742 that their reputation grew dim beneath the blaze of genius Garrick threw around it. John. P. Kemble, in 1801, produced his own adaptation of the tragedy at Drury Lane, and at Covent Garden, in 1808.

Mr. Edwin Forrest *re*-created Lear, as Richelieu did France, infusing into it new life, new power, and carrying out to the very *letter* the *spirit* of the author.

One great feature in Mr. Forrest's impersonation

was his identification with the peculiar characteristics of the part. Lear is not governed by one passion alone; there is a blending of rage, grief and indignation and what may be termed a tumultuous combination of them altogether. The words and the actions (as far as the author conveys them) of Lear are written out, and described for an old man of four-score years, and added to the extraordinary incidents of the tragedy, render it one of the most difficult to portray.

> "*Pray do not mock me.*
> *I am a very foolish, fond old man,*
> *Four-score and upward, and to deal plainly,*
> *I fear I am not in my perfect mind.*"
> *Act IV.; Scene* 7.

When Forrest enacted King Lear in New York, in 1827-'8, William Dunlap, "the father," so-called, "of the American stage," speaking of this performance at the time, said:

> "That young man is not merely superior to other representatives of Lear of the present day, but in portraying the passions, sufferings and insanity of the generous, hasty, heart-broken old monarch, with a degree of energy, pathos and fidelity, he even surpasses the wonderful efforts of George Frederick Cooke."

Leigh Hunt subsequently endorsed Dunlap's opinion, by saying some years afterwards, that he considered his King Lear as the best impersonation of the character that has ever been given on the English stage within his recollection.

There was one feature in Mr. Forrest's Lear, and that is, he was the only actor who ever attempted the herculean task of carrying out the physical infirmity, as well as the irritability of Lear, and keeping up the nervous tremor and the varying passions, acting upon old age from the first to last, so as not to mar the harmony existing in the terrible whirlwind by which they are agitated. The great beauty of Mr. Forrest's Lear was what we might term "artistic harmony." Cooke's Lear, never could stand the test of criticism. He destroyed all harmony of words and action by a sort of rugged rumbling, and what musicians call *staccato*. Forrest's, on the contrary, was harmonic, and given in *legato*—denoting smoothness. Some critics have accused Mr. Forrest of rant, and too much display of violence and uncontrolled passion. Lear is all passion. "Come not between the dragon and his wrath," is in itself a text for the actor. If this is a fault, it is Shakespeare, and not the actor, who is to blame. In Lear, as in Hamlet, the author's object was to represent the beginning and course of insanity. Old age struggling with wrong and insult is one of the startling features of this great tragedy.

Lear, in the early scenes, bears but the scars of mind upon his brow—the thought of years—not their decrepitude. His course had been one of might and power, and he determines to maintain them. The scene with Kent, in Act I., shows this, as also his fearful curse on Goneril. Here we have the monarch a dragon in his wrath; but when the startling facts break upon him that his children are turned traitors to his will, reason receives an additional blow, and the old king totters to his ruin. Mr. Forrest never for a single moment lost sight of the physical and mental condition of Lear; hence he gave the insane portions so true to nature that they appalled the audience, and we behold him—though crowned with a wreath of straw—"every inch a king."

Mr. Forrest had studied the theory of insanity with a student's care—a knowledge of which is so essential to a proper delineation of several of the characters in the plays of Shakespeare. It was this knowledge that made his Hamlet the Hamlet of Shakespeare, and gave to that of Macbeth, its psychological cast, and illustrates the true theory of apparitions—*the mind's disease.* "Is this a dagger which I see before me?" is one of the visions the condition of the mind conjures up. It was this knowledge that gave Mr. Forrest an advantage over others far less studious. He made the study of insanity a specialty, visited insane asylums and other places both here and in Europe, and with artistic exactness, carried out in his renditions all those mental peculiarities and eccentricities that critics recognize as truthful, and not as the mere ebullitions of a disposition and temper naturally fiery and irritable. Our readers—many of them, at least—will remember the terrible scene in Lear, where he appears fantastically dressed, and exclaims:—"No! they cannot touch me, for I am the king himself!"

The pauses in Mr. Forrest's readings have been quoted as faults. Pauses are not unfrequently the lights and shades of sentences that give effect to impersonations; Shakespeare himself says:

> "Give me leave to read philosophy,
> And while I pause serve in your harmony."

In Lear, we see the ebb and flow of feeling, its pauses and feverish starts, its impatience of opposition, and its accumulating force. The passion of Lear is like the tempest—it has its pauses and its outbreaks. "Blow winds and crack your cheeks! rage! blow!" etc., is one of the loftiest examples of apostrophe that is to be found in the English language. Then comes the pause in the tempest. "My wits began to fail." It is here the power of Mr. Forrest shone forth in fearful grandeur—it is here by action he conveyed to the audience the foreshadowing of Lear's madness. The twitching of the fingers—the motion of the body—the pressing together of the hands—in fact, every peculiar trait denoting insanity—told that the mind of Lear was gone. This scene kept the house spell-bound; the silence throughout was painful.

> "Come on, boy! how dost my boy? Art cold?
> I am cold myself."

These words were uttered in tones that no other actor we ever heard was capable of giving. A writer once said that the Lear of Shakespeare cannot be acted. It is true that the greatness of Lear is beyond the reach of common minds; it is full of intellect, madness, passion and insanity, dramatically worked up. To give these it required a Garrick, a Cooke and a Kean in England, but it remained for our own country to give us a Lear that eclipsed them all. Forrest's Lear lives with the fame of Shakespeare.

We give a few extracts from articles written by us at various times during Mr. Forrest's performance of Lear. They were written long before our personal relations with the great actor commenced. Nothing that we ever wrote since spoke more favorably of him than what we said then. *He was at all times a great actor.*

[FIRST EXTRACT.]

"The great beauty of Mr. Forrest's Lear is what we might term 'artistic harmony.' Cooke's Lear never could stand the test of criticism. He destroyed all harmony of words and action by a sort of rugged rumbling, and what musicians call *staccato*, resembling more a watchman's rattle than anything else in nature. And yet Cooke was great in one or two things; one was where he says: '*No, Regan, thou shalt never have my curse*,' and the other where he exclaims:—'*Who put my man i' the stocks?*' In the loftier passages of Lear he was not great. The character of Lear has been drawn by Shakespeare, bold, warm-hearted and direct; if for a moment he smothers his rage, he never conceals it; his passion, when most repressed, is a subterraneous wind that is heard with a deep sound as it rushes along; when that passion is released, it is indeed, a 'tempest,' and as you may say a 'whirlwind.' And yet there is music in it—wild and fearful music. Such is Lear—such Mr. Forrest's conception, such his rendition. Our readers will understand that we have never praised nor spoken in commendatory terms of Mr. Forrest, unless he came up to our notion of how and in what manner a part should be played. We have tradition for our comparisons, and a proper appreciation of true art to distinguish between the two extremes—good and bad. Nor do we rely upon our own judgment altogether, critically speaking, but the effect good acting has upon us physically as well as mentally. Impressions from the seal of genius, like those on the device of a picture, live on with us through life. The artist may devise a new one, but the first still remains. *Mr. Forrest's Lear was great.* This opinion the public 'has sealed with *its* seal.'

"Mr. Forrest's mad scene surpassed all his former efforts. From his first entrance into the forest until the last, it was one continued chain of wild grandeur. The audience listened entranced—pent up feeling, feelings of sorrow, sympathy with his grief, seemed ready to give vent in tears; and had it continued, we feel satisfied that a sense of overpowering nature would have outspoken—grief would have had vent."

[SECOND EXTRACT.]

"Mr. Forrest's King Lear has never been equalled. We have seen all the great actors in the part since 1815, and never in a single instance, found one that could grasp, with a master's hand, all those terrible elements of passion with which it abounds, as he does. Lear, in every age since its introduction on the stage, has been considered one of the most difficult characters of Shakespeare. Chilled from age, choleric, peevish and overbearing, with sufficient cause to make him so, the actor who attempts its delineation must be quick of conception, skilful and ready to depict these several characteristics.

"Some critics have endeavored to parallel the terrific curse of Lear, with that of Œdipus upon his sons in the 'Œdipus Coloneus' of Sophocles, but there is no comparison. The one is prophetic of the fate of his offspring, the other appeals to universal feeling, working on the ungrateful child, as he imagines, pangs similar to those which she inflicts.

"Readers of the Bible have no difficulty in tracing to its hallowed pages many of the beautiful as well as the terrible passages which abound in the plays of Shakespeare. Job furnishes several, and the CIXth Psalm may be quoted as furnishing materials for the curse of Lear."

[THIRD EXTRACT.]

"Taken in all, it was a grand performance. The man who can play Lear as it deserves to be played, must not only possess high genius, fine taste and uncommon physical energy, but he must have passed into the shadows of age, and endured sharp trial and bitter sorrow. Mr. Forrest has all these requisites, and they blend together in an impressive picture whose sombre yet powerful colors are stamped upon the soul of him who looks thereon. The tremendous grief of the crownless king, his awful wrath, his madness, his tears, his death—all these are drawn with a wonderful vividness and reality, which go straight to the heart. We remember nothing more touching on the stage than the struggles of the poor old man when he feels reason tottering upon her throne, and then yielding to the irresistible pressure of a mighty woe, sinks into the semi-oblivion of a harmless lunacy. And in the climax of the closing scene, where he bends over the corpse of his daughter, looks into her still eyes, presses her pulseless heart, watches for the dumb lips to open once more, and then whispers, in broken, tremulous voice: '*Cordelia! Cordelia! stay a little!*' what an infinite depth of pathos is there in it all! It is the sublimity of sorrow, the acme of an anguish whose appropriate consummation is death."

[FOURTH EXTRACT.]

"Mr. Forrest's King Lear is one of his best parts, and he stands alone the Lear of his time. From the moment he appears on the stage until the final close of this great tragedy, he never loses sight of the true character of Lear. His bursts of passion are beyond the power of pen to describe; they are the outbreaks of an abused man driven to desperation by the cruel treatment of his daughters. Mr. Forrest's delineation of the choleric king is so extremely natural, that his individuality is lost in the masterly portraiture he presents us with. Perhaps there is not in the whole range of dramatic writing anything to equal the terrific curse in Act I. There is no attempt to make the mere dramatic art subservient to the actor's purpose solely, but it is to give us Lear and Shakespeare, and not Lear and the actor. Mr. Forrest's great starting-point in Lear, is where he utters the curse on Goneril, Act I. Let any one not a theatre-goer, read this awful malediction, and then imagine what an effect it would have on an audience when given by Mr. Forrest. It is sublime even in the terror it creates. Mr. Forrest's utterance of this passage is, perhaps, the most startling and thrilling that was ever heard upon the stage; there is no dramatic preparation for its coming, no foreshadowing it by any inaction previous; it comes upon us a part and portion of the great play in all its terrific grandeur. Age in anger, age in arms to crush base ingratitude, age in passion, yet governed by reason, throws itself on its knees and exclaims in awful wrath—'Hear, nature, hear. Dear Goddess, hear!' then he invokes the curse, during which the house was hushed into silence, the audience seemed to feel the oppression, for the very air was stilled; and a sense of some powerful influence pervading, held the breath as it were in abeyance. As he progressed in its utterance, he arose in grandeur, awful in his terrible sublimity; and when he reached its climax, and exclaimed, 'Away! away!' the audience awoke as from a fearful spell, and sound again broke upon the awful stillness which its delivery caused.

"In the third act, where his mind totters between reason and madness, he held the audience spell-bound by the magic of his art. His defiance of the elements was grand and magnificent; it was Ajax-like, gigantic, awful, fearful in its sublimity.

"Throughout the part, Mr. Forrest never for a moment missed the 'cue' of age. He looked a king, 'aye, every inch a king,' even in his moods of grief. We do not speak of Mr. Forrest's Lear as a production of to-day, nor do we say that he plays it better now than he did years ago. Then, as now, he was the finished artist, and those who speak of faults to be corrected under their instruction, have other motives, which sway their opinions, than those which constitute the basis of that peculiar art called criticism. The man, not the artist, is the target of their venomed shaft."

We might follow Mr. Forrest through each and every scene of this great play, and point out passages which struck us as being of great force and power; but to speak of his Lear in detached parts, is not our purpose, as it would seem to question its general and harmonic whole, not only as a great piece of dramatic art, but conveying to us, by the power of genius, the original by a seeming optical illusion. Where everything was so grand, so imposing and so natural, it would be a very difficult matter for the most astute critic to distinguish one single brighter gem than those from the brilliant cluster he presents to us. In connection with Mr. Forrest's Lear, we annex the following incident, which occurred in New Orleans some thirty years ago, on the occasion of his playing King Lear in that city. During the utterance of the curse we heard a strange sound proceeding from a gentleman sitting beside us—a sound so strange and unnatural, which induced us to turn suddenly round. The fearful words of the curse were ringing in our ears as uttered by the only living actor capable of giving it with that fierceness and rapid vehemence so essential to render it effective. That it was so in this instance there was no mistake. To our horror, we found the eyes of the gentleman fixed, his mouth open, and a death-like paleness overspreading his face. His hands were clenched together, and it was evident that all voluntary motion was suspended. Instinctively we caught him by the shoulders, and with a sudden jerk, caused a reaction of the blood. He gave a gasp, and uttered a deep, heavy sigh. As he gazed around, it was like one awaking from a troubled sleep. The awful curse, so fearfully uttered, was still ringing in his ears. It had taken away the man's breath, and my shaking him caused him to recover. "One moment more, sir," he said, "and I should have been a dead man." Looking towards the stage, he continued: "Is he gone?" Being answered that the *terrible old man* was not there, he, like Richard, "was himself again."

King Lear was first played in this country, January 14th, 1754, and as a matter of dramatic history, we give a copy of the original cast:

KING LEAR	MR. MALONE.
KENT	MR. HALLAM.
GLOSTER	MR. BELL.
EDGAR	MR. SINGLETON.
EDMUND	MR. CLARKSON.
CORNWALL	MR. MILLER.
ALBANY	MR. ADCOCK.
BURGUNDY	MR. HULETT.
USHER	MR. RIGBY.
ATTENDANTS	MASTERS HALLAM.
CORDELIA	MRS. HALLAM.
REGAN	MRS. ADCOCK.
GONERIL	MISS BECCELEY.
FANTHER	MRS. RIGBY.

CHAPTER XIV.

MR. FORREST A STUDENT.—MEN WITH WHOM HE ASSOCIATED.—DAMON, HIS GREAT TRIUMPH IN THE PART.—VIRGINIUS.—ENGLISH CRITICISM.—CORIOLANUS.—RICHELIEU.

MR. FORREST'S position before the American people, in the years 1828, '30, '31, was one that, while it astonished the English clique, delighted his friends, and it required all his energy and genius to maintain it. The school in which he was educated, the associations he had formed in his western tour, and his limited time for study, were considered as so many drawbacks to his future success. How he studied, when and where, and acquired, as it were, the mastery over the elements of the dramatic art, are questions that the midnight lamp, which saw him hovering over old tomes, old plays, and the annotations from gifted minds, alone can answer. Forrest did not, at one period of his career, like the elder Booth, A. A. Addams, and others, associate with the lowest of the profession, or the "oyster critics" of the press. He formed the acquaintance of such men as George P. Morris, M. M. Noah, William C. Bryant, William Leggett, James Dunlap, Joseph R. Ingersoll, Jesse R. Burden, Morton McMichael, Chief-Justice Gibson, Judge Rogers, Col. John Swift, Dr. Samuel Jackson, Louis A. Godey, John W. Forney, Henry Clay, George M. Dallas, Daniel

Webster, and his idol of Democracy, and of a *Man*—General Andrew Jackson. We do not give these names as myths in his catalogue of associates, advisers, and friends; but names of men who took a pride in the rising genius of the American stage.

Forrest spent many a pleasant hour with Old Hickory, at the Hermitage, and held converse with the most talented men of the country. These were men, gentlemen, who had no other object in view, when they took young Forrest by the hand, than to advance him in the profession he had adopted. They could well say with Hamlet:

> "Nay, do not think I flatter;
> For what advancement may I hope from thee,
> That no revenue hast, but thy good spirits,
> To feed and clothe thee? Why should the poor be flatter'd?"

They did not "crook the pregnant hinges of the knee where thrift may follow fawning," but made his pathway to fame and fortune pleasant by proper encouragement and advice. These he did not disregard; hence success.

From the time he achieved a triumph in the character of Damon, over the impression Cooper had made upon the public, he bounded upward, coming forth from obscurity as it were, Pallas-like, fully panoplied to battle in the "Mimic World," and he was carried along the stream of time by the mere efforts of his genius, guided by a strong will, until he reached the topmost round of the dramatic ladder, upon whose pinnacle was the word—"EXCELSIOR!"

We have alluded to Forrest's Damon, in connection with which let us speak of his Brutus. Mr. Forrest was no imitator—his style was entirely original. His declamatory powers were of a most startling character, and his frenzied passion, as evidenced in Brutus, were truly appalling. An unanimous cry of "bravo!" not unfrequently burst from the audience, elicited by the beauty, force, and power of the delivery of thrilling passages. We well remember his Brutus (John Howard Payne's Brutus), the Brutus of his prime, as it was for all time. We well remember the deep and smothered rage of the rising storm as it gathered force to hurl destruction on the tyrants of Rome; before us stands the stern avenger of his country's wrongs; we hear the deep tones of his rich and mellow voice, in that great struggle between a father's love and love of country.

> "Nature must have way;
> I will perform all that a Roman should;
> I cannot feel less than a father ought."

These lines were delivered with so much feeling that tears were freely shed by the spell-bound audience. Brutus was Forrest's great and first effort in Roman characters; but, to make his footing sure, Damon had to be essayed. Cooper's Damon had stood the test of all the critics of the day. His figure, his face, his voice breathing forth the high-toned grandeur of human greatness, blended with harmony, all combined to make his impersonations of the Roman characters master pictures of the art. He might have been surpassed by Kean as Lear, Othello, and Richard III.; but as Damon, Coriolanus, and Virginius, he had then no equal in the world! Kean was eminently successful as Richard and Othello; but when he would rival Cooper in the proud unbending characters of the Roman school —those godlike spirits who rose out of the desolation of war—who brooded over the ruins of their country's greatness, or triumphed over the vestiges of their own blighted fortunes—whose mighty souls bore up amidst the ruins and sorrows of a nation, and finally gave freedom to the people, and prosperity to the land—it was here, and only here, Kean and his imitators failed, and Cooper stood alone, the noblest Roman of them all. Such was the reputation of Cooper, when Edwin Forrest, the youthful athlete of the dramatic ring, stepped forth to compete with him in Roman characters. We shall never forget his first essay as Damon, when as an acknowledged star, he appeared before the largest audience ever assembled within the walls of a theatre. From that night he was the acknowledged Damon of the American stage.

We remember as if it were but yesterday, instead of almost a half century, the effect produced in what is called "the Lucullus scene." It is where he calls for his horse; the slave hesitates. Damon repeats his request, yet Lucullus stirs not; and when his master sternly commands him to obedience, the trembling slave tells what he had done:—

> *Luc.* "When I beheld the means of saving you,
> I could not hold my hand—my heart was in it;
> And in my heart, the hope of giving life
> And liberty to Damon; and—
> *Damon.* Go on,
> I am listening to thee.
> *Luc.* And in the hope to save you,
> I slew your steed.
> *Damon.* Almighty gods!"

As he uttered the expression, "Almighty gods!" he stood the picture of mute despair. Lucullus gazes upon the terrible look and convulsive movements of his master in silent horror. Directly the delirious fury of Damon is turned upon his slave; for a moment his eyes, like those of a tiger ready to spring upon his prey, are fixed on the trembling victim ; in the next he seizes him by the throat. The slave struggles, but in vain. The hands of his master are upon him ; his screams avail not. The desperate Damon drags him towards a yawning precipice ; his eyes flash maniac fires—his features convulsed—the slave struggling, but in vain, to escape the dreadful doom before him. During the scene the audience were held spell-bound ; nor was it until the master and slave disappeared, that the pent-up feelings gave way and the intensity caused by the scene found vent in a suppressed sigh of relief. The next grand scene in this play, so full of "natural glory," is where Damon reaches the scaffold in time to save Pythias from the death his friendship for his friend was about to bring upon him. They meet ; they embrace ; the voice of Dionysius is heard calling "Damon!" who, when he hears it, rushes towards the scaffold and ascends it. Drawing his figure proudly up he gazes for a moment upon the spectators with unflinching eyes : then turning toward the place whence the voice came, exclaims :

"Damon is here—look at me.
I am standing on my throne—as proud a one
As yon illumined mountain, when the sun
Makes his last stand. Let him look on me too;
He never did behold a spectacle
More full of natural glory.
All Syracuse starts up upon her hills,
And lifts her hundred thousands hands. (*Shouts heard.*)
She shouts! Hark, how she shouts. Oh, Dionysius,
When wert thou in thy life hailed with a peal
Of hearts and hands like that? Shout again—
Again—until the mountains echo back your clamor,
And the great sea joins in that mighty voice.
Tell me, slaves, where is your tyrant?
Why stands he hence aloof—where is your master—
What is become of Dionysius?
I would behold and laugh at him."

As the recollection of Mr. Forrest's Damon is so fresh in the memory of our readers, and who can bear witness to its greatness, it is unnecessary for us to say more.

VIRGINIUS.

In no other character, if we except Coriolanus, has the actor's figure and general bearing been shown to such advantage as it is in Virginius. The massive, yet compact form—the bold, free drawing of the frame (to speak in a painter's phrase)—the surprising strength and the ponderous grace which Mr. Forrest displayed in this character, presented to the audience the most perfect picture of a Roman hero that was ever displayed on the stage. During Mr. Forrest's last engagement in Philadelphia (1871), we wrote a notice of his Virginius, from which we make the following extract:

"In the earlier scenes where domestic ease and parental affection blend with the martial roughness of the warrior, Mr. Forrest pleased us much. The picture scene was full of familiar touches, and truth of feeling. In the passage, too, where Virginius prepares for the dreadful rescue of his daughter's honor, the calm, natural tone of voice gave a terrible significance to the brief arrangements for the deed. When he sent Icilius to join his friends, for instance, Mr. Forrest delivered the command in that tone of calm urgency which people assume under an impending calamity; giving to monstrous events an air of danger blended with the certainty of averting them. When Virginius says to his daughter, '*I hope you never play the truant!*' it was with the fond raillery of an affectionate parent. Conscious of the truth of his child, he asks the question, knowing the reply she would make. Mr. Forrest, during this passage, was beyond description; it was a gem: '*You are so happy when I am kind to you! Am I not always kind? I never spoke an angry word to you in all my life, Virginia,*' etc. And '*whose face is this you have given to Achilles?*' was asked not angrily, or as a demand, but in the manner of curious inquiry. We remember Mr. Hamblin in this scene, making the inquiry in a tone of anger, startling Virginia by his harshness. Mr. Forrest was very fine in the scene where he gives Virginia in marriage to Icilius. Also grand in the one wherein Lucius informs him he is summoned to Rome to answer to the charge of Caius Claudius. '*Did he not strike him dead?*' came from the lips of Mr. Forrest as man never uttered them. Not Cooper, the Virginius of his day, equalled Mr. Forrest in this, the most exciting scene in the play. The scene in the forum awed the house into silence, and when the eyes of Virginius rested on the knife as it laid on the shambles, the pent-up feelings of the audience gave vent by a sigh of relief, for they saw, what Virginius did, the means, and the only means, of saving the honor of his child."

An English critic, speaking of Mr. Forrest's Virginius, at Drury Lane, said:

"In the passage, too, where Virginius prepares for the dreadful rescue of his daughter's honor, the calm natural tone of voice gave terrible significance to the brief arrangements of the deed. * * Sheridan Knowles, the author, played Dentatus. Mr. Matthews is a respectable and useful actor; but he looks so very *un*-Roman in Appius Claudius, and is so deficient in animal spirits and lusty imperiousness, that the groundwork of the story lost in probability what it gained in odiousness by the tame and premeditated viciousness of the Decemvir. Such a man as Mr. Matthews's Appius was not the one to carry his schemes of luxurious outrage by public force, and in the face of danger—more especially when opposed to such a presence as that of Mr. Forrest in Virginius."

CORIOLANUS.

The materials of this great drama were derived chiefly from the memoirs of Coriolanus, contained in the "lives of the noble Grecians and Romans," compared together by that grave, learned philosopher and historiographer, Plutarch of Chœronea, translated by Thomas North, Esq., 1579, and this one great hero was selected from the others by Shakespeare for *immortality*. The character is one that few actors attempt—indeed, there are but few capable of rendering it in a manner calculated to impress it with the Roman attributes of the hero. Mr. Cooper and Mr. Forrest are the only two who made the character a stage illusion by a truthful picture of this superb production of the great master of arts—Shakespeare.

In 1864, during Mr. Forrest's engagement at the "Academy of Music," in Philadelphia, we wrote an extended notice of his Coriolanus, from which we make the following extracts:

"Monday evening, November 21st, 1864, will long be remembered in dramatic annals. It will form an era in the drama, and add another page to its history.

"The Academy of Music was literally crammed on this occasion, to witness Mr. Edwin Forrest reappear, after many years, in his great character of Coriolanus. It was placed upon the stage in a manner and style of excellence never surpassed. The stage throughout the action of the piece gave us a view of Rome in her grandeur, and the artistes in the play peopled it with the characters and personages of the day; the present was forgotten—the imagination swayed by the illusion of the whole scene, and the action of the play, carried us back to Rome, and the territories of the Volscians and the Antiales.

"Coriolanus, is not a familiar stage piece. Not because it is deficient in any of those dramatic elements which constitute a perfect whole, but from the fact that few artistes are enabled to grasp them, and bring their conflicting physical and mental qualities together. Coriolanus is one vast store-house of phrases, from the political, common-place language of the rabble to the high-toned argumentative reasoning of the hero, wherein, as Hazlitt says, 'The language of poetry naturally falls in with language of power.'

"Mr. Forrest's early impersonation of this character, that is, years ago, when youth excused exaggeration, was simply a creature of his elocutionary teaching. It had the peculiarities of a school that has done more to spoil actors than ever was accomplished by injudicious criticism. And this is saying a great deal. But as he threw off the trappings of art, which encased genius, and erased the water colors of her pictures, his own creation placed Coriolanus before us on this occasion a most finished and brilliant picture. It is one to grace the walls of the Academy among the proudest productions of the age—a fadeless gem of true art.

"The Roman manliness of his face and figure, the haughty dignity of his carriage, and the fire of his eye, united to the *abandon* with which he entered the arena to contend against *remembered stars*, conspired, on this occasion, to render his Coriolanus one of the most finished, striking and classical performances that was ever exhibited on the American stage. Sublime in giving utterance to its language, noble in the expression of its sentiments—fiery, nay, even furious, yet dignified—he threw around it a grandeur, pen is inadequate to describe. Throughout he was great—uniformly so—there was no husbanding his powers for the mere purpose of making a point, no subdued emotion for the display of unnatural bursts of passion, no tameness on the one hand, no unnecessary rant on the other.

"Mr. Forrest stands alone in this character; look back over the 'mimic world,' and whose name nears itself to his in the past? Not Vandenhoff's, who was considered the model of the classic school of acting, and the representative of the heroes of its poets. We witnessed this gentleman's impersonation of the character in the year 1838. Lacking all those physical qualities so essential to the great character—qualities that invest the artist with power to look and act the part, he failed to render it either striking or interesting; in fact, it created neither wonder nor surprise. It was a reading of Shakespeare—words without looks, words without action; a Coriolanus without a body or a soul—a painted figure only. Forrest's Coriolanus is now a living picture. Vandenhoff's hangs beside it a painted one of—'still life.'"

Of Mr. Forrest's Richelieu it is scarcely necessary for us to say much. It is familiar to all, and all acknowledge its superiority over that of all others. Vandenhoff failed in it; Macready rendered it ridiculous; Booth the younger, Connor—in fact all who essayed the part—most signally failed in making it other than a galvanic attempt to resuscitate a dead body. Now that the actor master of the art has gone, who will rule the stage and sustain its classic character? Not Edwin Booth; he has not the physical or mental capacity. Who can now take the lead in the rank of actors? who assume the sceptre? who wear the crown? There is one man, and the only man who, if he knew his own worth as we know and appreciate it, whose name should now become the synonom of Edwin Forrest, and that man is E. L. Davenport, the best living actor on the stage. Let us return to "Richelieu."

As we have said, it is not necessary to call attention to those beauties with which this play is studded, and which Mr. Forrest displayed with so much power, skill and judgment. His rendition of the wily Cardinal will ever be remembered as one of his greatest stage productions. Who can ever forget the great scene where Baradas, insisting on Julia's obedience to the king's command to return to the palace, exclaims:

"Ay, is it so?
Then wakes the power, which in the age of iron,
Burst forth to curb the great, and raise the low.
Mark, where she stands, around her form I draw
The awful circle of our solemn church!
Set but a foot within that holy ground,
And on thy head—yea, though it wore a crown—
I launch the curse of Rome!
Baradas. I dare not brave you!
I do but speak the orders of my king.
The church, your rank, power, very word, my lord,

Suffice you for resistance:—blame yourself,
If it should cost you power!
Richelieu. That's *my* stake! Ah!
Dark gamester! *what is thine!* Look to it well—
Lose not a trick. By this same hour to-morrow
Thou shalt have France, or I thy head!"

His startling energy of this passage our readers will well remember, and the applause which invariably followed. Again, when overhearing Baradas sneeringly whisper:

"His mind
And life are breaking fast,"

he cries aloud, while his aged frame trembles with excess of rage:

"Irreverent ribald!
If so, beware the falling ruins! Hark!
I tell thee, scorner of these whitening hairs,
When this snow melteth there shall come a flood!
Avaunt! my name is Richelieu—I defy thee!
Walk blindfold on; behind thee stalks the headsman,
Ha! ha!—how pale he is! Heaven save my country!"

We need not speak of the *denouement* of this play, as the masterly performance of Mr. Forrest invested the whole with an interest no other actor ever gave it. Richelieu died out with this great actor.

The remark was made, when Macready and others performed Richelieu, that the play was not an acting one, and gave as an excuse for their failure that it was better adapted to the closet than the stage. It was not until Mr. Forrest enacted the part, and by his powerful genius transferred to the stage the life-like visions the gifted author had set in letters of gold, that these wonderful critics discovered the difference between true art and false conception. Forrest took the play from their hands, and showed to the world the power of dramatic art, how it could conjure up the mighty dead, and bid the long-laid spirits stalk—show the "swelling triumph and the curtained crime"—made "slumbering kings his mighty voice obey," and Richelieu's greatness subdue a king and foil his foes.

CHAPTER XV.

HAMLET.—ORIGIN OF THE TRAGEDY.—THE ORIGINAL HAMLET.—ACTORS GREAT IN THE PART.—CRITICISM ON KEMBLE.—WILLIAM B. WOOD.—MR. FORREST'S HAMLET.—HAMLET'S INSANITY.—WILLIAM A. CONWAY.

THIS great tragedy has long been a fruitful subject for critics, and some of our best writers have exercised their talents and displayed much erudition in their endeavors to prove Shakespeare was all wrong in his *conception of* the character of Hamlet.

ORIGIN OF THE TRAGEDY.

A drama of the same name and subject as the present, is supposed to have been exhibited before the year 1589; and Malone imagined that Shakespeare only altered it, using likewise the black-letter "Historie of Hamblett." The story itself was originally derived from the "Historiæ Danicæ" of Saxo Grammaticus; translated by Belleforest in his Novels, and rendered into English in the above narrative.

Dr. Percy's copy of Speght's edition of Chaucer, once belonged to Gabriel Harvey, who had written his name at both the commencement and conclusion, with the date of 1598, and several notes between; one of which was "The younger sort take much delight in Shakespeare's Venus and Adonis, but his Lucrece, and his Tragedy of Hamlet, Prince of Denmarke, have it in them to please the wiser sort." The original composition of Hamlet is therefore placed in 1597, with revisions and additions to 1600. The earliest entry of it at Stationers' Hall, is July 26th, 1602, and a copy of the play in its imperfect state, dated 1603, and supposed to have been printed from a spurious original, was first discovered in the beginning of 1825. Another edition appeared in 1604, "newly imprinted and enlarged, to almost as much again as it was;" the variations in which are both numerous and striking.

In 1771, Garrick produced this tragedy at Drury Lane, all the parts being sacrificed to that of Hamlet; but after his death the original was restored, and the modern adaptation is that by John P. Kemble, brought out at Drury Lane, in 1800, and at Covent Garden, in 1804. The scene of Hamlet is at the Castle and Court of Elsinoir, and the action apparently occupies some months. The story is entirely fabulous, and is placed by Saxo at an impossible period of antiquity; but perhaps it may be safely referred to the end of the tenth, or the beginning of the eleventh century, during the invasions of England by the Danes; to which period Mr. Planché has adapted the series of historical costumes prepared for it, for Covent Garden, in 1825.

The original Hamlet was Richard Burbage. Joseph Taylor, instructed by Shakespeare to play Hamlet, and from the remembrance of his performance Sir William Duvencent is said to have instructed Betterton. Following these, who were celebrated in the part, are the names of Barton Booth, (this gentleman was celebrated as Othello, and Hamlet, and the original Cato,) David Garrick, John P. Kemble, Young, G. F. Cooke, Edmund Kean, William Macready, Thomas A. Cooper, Lucius Junius Booth, William A. Conway, EDWIN FORREST, James E. Murdock, E. L. Davenport and Edwin Booth. Although we have given the names of those who were distinguished in the part, still several of them were open to severe and just criticism. A misconception of the character has invariably lessened the claims of an actor to be considered the Hamlet of Shakespeare's creation.

The idea of Hamlet being a genuine madman, seldom enters the mind of an actor, in consequence of which they labor under a perplexity to impersonate or illustrate the character satisfactorily to the audience. Whether the great Kemble took this view of the mental condition of Hamlet or not, can only be judged by the criticism written at the time. William B. Wood, who witnessed his representation of it in London, only speaks of the effect the Ghost scene had upon him, and when we questioned him more closely upon that gentleman's manners and style, he said: "His interview with the Ghost made me shudder; his look of horror, as he gazed upon the shadowy form before him, communicated itself to the house, for that gaze invested the spirit with all the attributes of the grave."

Mr. Wood's admiration of Kemble did not extend beyond the interview with the Ghost. We remember distinctly, when we asked why he never essayed the part, he said: "By G—d, sir, there is no man now living who can play it."

Another critic, not quite so enthusiastic as Mr. Wood, speaking of Kemble's Hamlet, said:

"Again, before the performance of the play, where his assumed character is to be of more service to him, he meets Ophelia, and, wishing probably to deepen the impression of his madness on the minds of the Court, he speaks incoherently, indeed, but sometimes in a strain of melancholy truth and sound advice to this 'fair lady.' During all these scenes we think Hamlet is 'more in sorrow than in anger,' whereas Mr. Kemble makes him bang a door on one side, half burst a lock on the other, insult Ophelia by a most *exalted* tone of voice, and, indeed, 'out-herod Herod.'

"Mr. Elliston emphasized the word *my*. The writer on Kemble says the emphasis should be placed on '*sins*,' although he admits the possibility of '*my*' being correct.

"Mr. Kemble reads this line, 'Great pith and moment,' 'Great *pitch* and moment.' The writer goes on to say that Mr. Kemble 'wanted to conciliate the galleries;' but as he gives no reason why, we presume he *pitched* into new reading."

Hallam, who was the first to play Hamlet in the Colonies, although young at the time (1761), had witnessed Garrick's inimitable acting in this part, and the remembrance of which added materially to the cause of his success.

Cooper subsequently became the Hamlet of the American stage. Fennell had also achieved success in the part. Conway subsequently made or rather created a great sensation in the character of Hamlet, from the fact of giving it a shadow of himself, whose melancholy tone of mind subsequently resulted in his death. Of Mr. Edwin Forrest's Hamlet, it is said by the ablest critics, *that he was the best reader of the part of any who ever attempted it in this country*.

Forrest had Cooper for his classic model, who was the Demosthenes of the drama, and so well did he study in that school, that he, in time, became its Talma.

Kean was its Raphael in producing picturesque

grandeur, and its Garrick in impassioned eloquence. Mr. Forrest, young as he was then, with these eminent actors before him, the idols of the people, saw at a glance that the great secret of their success was their mental quality; it was the mind that gave vigor, grace and beauty to their limbs, fire to their eyes and classic beauty to their impersonations. Mere physique was nothing to be compared to intellect.

He did not, as many of our young actors do, study the mere personal peculiarities of their model, and also certain intonations and *nasal* imperfections of the voice, leaving the mental quality entirely out of the question; he studied the latter, and after mastering all its difficulties, he soon made the mere mechanical yield to the master spirit—*mind.*

His "bold brow" bore the scars of mental labor, the thoughts of years, "not their decrepitude," while that of others bore the scars of mental failure, leaving the physique a barren waste. Study makes the body rich, its want

> "The leafless desert of the mind,
> The waste of feelings unemployed."

Many actors of the modern school are idealists; that is, they are unable to draw the line of distinction between a bodiless substance, and objects which are the immediate emanations of the mind. These are called ideas which give form and figure to shapeless matter.

Mr. Forrest's conception and rendition of Hamlet were those of a close student and a finished artist. It was a triumphant refutation of the sneers of those who called him a mere physical actor. There is a certain class of idealists to whom matter is a great bugbear. They measure a man's mental calibre by his weight in the scales. In the eyes of these critics, the very qualities which commend an artist to the many, are so many blemishes.

Mr. Forrest's delineation of character was not given hastily or carelessly; there was a startling finish in all he undertook, which left a favorable impression ever afterward. His dying scenes were death's protraitures. There is nothing more difficult in the whole range of dramatic art than are its death scenes. Mr. Forrest invested them with a solemn reality; they were sublime (if we may use the word) pictures, which made the sense of death more in apprehension than the supposed horror attending it.

In the art gallery of the stage there are many striking pictures. There we see Mr. Forrest as Othello. There we see him as Damon, in all his Roman grandeur, Damon in his agony, Damon in his triumph. There we see him as Virginius, Coriolanus, Macbeth, King Lear, Richelieu, Jack Cade, The Gladiator, Metamora, etc. These glorious pictures are now the proudest in the histrionic gallery, and will never grow dim while the image of him who gave them life lives in our memory.

The first time we witnessed Mr. Forrest's Hamlet, was at the old Chestnut Street Theatre, in 1827. He was then but twenty-one years of age! What could be expected of one so young? And yet it was a beautiful but not a philosophical Hamlet. He had studied it carefully from an acting copy, and took the accepted notion of Hamlet's assuming a madness, instead of making that assumption a phase in his actual insanity. Hamlet, after the interview with his father's spirit, has announced his probable intent to "bear himself strange and odd, and put an antic disposition on." This is very well; but how is it that in the opening soliloquy he meditates suicide, having no other cause than the marriage of his mother with his uncle. To one so young, surrounded with everything to please his taste as well as his ambition, is this marriage a sufficient cause for suicide, or even its contemplation? Dark thoughts of self-destruction enters his mind, and he exclaims:

> "O that this too, too solid flesh would melt,
> Thaw, and resolve itself into a dew.
> Or that the Everlasting had not fixed
> His canon 'gainst self-slaughter."

Thus it will be seen that the mind of Hamlet was diseased, and a deep-settled melancholy had taken full possession of his mind. We have said this much here, because in all our subsequent articles on this great play, we invariably had occasion to trace the failure of actors in this part, to their mixing the real insanity of Hamlet with his simulating it in after scenes, which is in fact but another shade of the mad fiend's "wing flapping o'er his head." Space will not permit us to enter more fully into the metaphysical, or, as Shakespeare rendered it, *super-naturalia*, character of Hamlet, but we will give the Prince's own words. After a long spell of insanity he comes to his senses, and says, when he takes the hand of Laertes, previous to the trial of skill with foils:

> *Hamlet.* "Give me your pardon, sir; I've done you wrong;
> But pardon it, as you are a gentleman.
> This presence knows, and you must needs have heard,
> How I am punish'd with a sore distraction.
> What I have done
> That might your nature, honor, and exception,
> Roughly awake, *I here proclaim was madness.*
> Was't Hamlet wrong'd Laertes? Never, Hamlet.
> If Hamlet from himself be ta'en away,
> And when he's not himself does wrong Laertes,

> Then Hamlet does it not. Hamlet denies it.
> Who does it then? His madness. If't be so,
> Hamlet is of the faction that is wrong'd;
> His madness is poor Hamlet's enemy.
> Sir, in this audience
> Let my disclaiming from a purposed evil
> Free me so far in your most generous thoughts,
> That I have shot mine arrow o'er the house
> And hurt my brother."

This we think unquestionable authority, and to the psychologist has left nothing to be desired, having, as we think, established Hamlet's real madness.

It was not until many years afterward, that Mr. Forrest's Hamlet soared above all the other Hamlets' of the day, for his illustration of the character from a mad-point of view, rendered it not only perfectly plain, but satisfactory to the audience.

We spoke of Mr. Forrest's Hamlet in 1827, somewhat freely, and alluded to several passages as being given, not only too rapidly, but with an imperfect knowledge of the author's meaning.

To one of these we will allude here, as it is connected with a very pleasing incident which occurred in his library a short time before his death. One of the passages we criticised at that time (1827) was the manner he rendered this passage:

> "I'll call thee Hamlet!
> King! Father! Royal Dane!—Oh, answer me!"

He gave it thus:

> "I'll call thee Hamlet!
> King! Father! Royal Dane, O answer me!"

Hamlet knows not by what gracious or acceptable title to salute the spectre; it comes in such a questionable shape, that he addresses it by the several appellative terms which distinguished his father while living. "Royal Dane" is used precisely in the same sense as are those of the others; indeed, it is a vocative climax. Being so, it should read as we have given it above. Several errors of a youthful construction on the text of Shakespeare marked Mr. Forrest's first attempt of Hamlet, all of which, with one exception, he long since corrected, and that one he maintained to the last.

We have in one or more instances alluded to Mr. William A. Conway, in connection with Hamlet. We will speak of him here. In the year 1823, this gentleman made his first appearance in America. He was the first actor we ever witnessed in the character of Hamlet *who made us feel uncomfortable;* for it seemed then, to our youthful imagination, as if he himself had the cue for passion that Hamlet had. We do not say it was a great performance, but it had that about it which impressed the audience with the painful idea that the actor, as well as the hero of the play, was *mad!* Subsequent events in the life of this gentleman, resulting in a melancholy death, fully sustained this impression. Mr. Conway was of the Fennell school; his person tall and commanding, and he possessed the rare merit of being a most elegant scholar and reader. The celebrated speech commencing with, "To be or not to be," etc., as given by him, seemed as if he intended to make his quietus then and there. During its delivery the audience seemed lost in wonder, not so much from the beautiful reading, but from a painful feeling he created that he was fearfully in earnest. This was the impression it made upon us—it was a thrilling delineation of a phase of insanity under which the actor himself was laboring. Mr. Conway's temperament, added to a morbid state of mind, rendered him fully capable of grasping the peculiar elements of which the character of Hamlet is composed; for those who assume sorrow, or affect grief, in general overact the part, because their natures do not assimilate with that of the character. We would not have our Hamlet's mad, but we would have them so to represent the part as to make that appear natural, which in less skilful hands, would seem quite the reverse. Tacitus uses this phrase when speaking of this class: "*Nulli jactantius moerent, quam qui maxime lactantur.*"

The Hamlet of Mr. Conway was marked by a striking identification with the mental peculiarities as drawn by Shakespeare, investing it with all the attributes that make up the real and imaginary wrongs under which Hamlet is supposed to labor. The whole of the interview with his mother was given in a most impassioned manner; it was stern, decided, positive, but neither in the delivery of the words nor in his actions did he forget that she was his mother· and when he gave these lines, it was with a deep sense of a wrong inflicted upon him by her conduct, and he the only living person to show up that wrong, and check her further progress in crime:

> "Good-night; but go not to my uncle's bed;
> Assume a virtue, if you have it not.
> Once more good-night!
> And when you are desirous to be blessed,
> I'll a blessing beg of you."

We well remember with what enthusiasm this whole scene was received. If we are more favorably disposed towards the memory of Mr. Conway in this great character, it is because we have seen no one up to this period, who could *melancholize* the part to the extent he did.

CHAPTER XVI.

LATE AT REHEARSAL.—RICHELIEU IN A PASSION.—AN AMUSING INCIDENT.—THE EXCITED CRITIC.—KING LEAR'S WIG.—ALMOST A DUEL.—ANDREW JACKSON ALLEN.—A SATISFACTORY EXCUSE.—FORREST MEETS HIS MATCH.—ROMAN CITIZENS.—POWERFUL ACTING.

DURING the years intervening between Mr. Forrest's first and second professional visit to England, he pursued with an artist's assiduity the duties of his dramatic career. It was a triumphant one; he was everywhere greeted with applause, and the press, with but few exceptions, spoke highly of his performances. Before we follow him to England, we propose to relate a few anecdotes and incidents connected with the theatre during his starring engagements.

An old writer has said, "If you have anything worth communicating in return, I hope you will not refuse the trouble of giving me the intelligence; not only as we are all of us rationally fond, you know, of news, but because interesting anecdotes afford examples which may be of use in respect to our own conduct."

LATE AT REHEARSAL.

Many acts of kindness, blended with the Divine attribute, charity, are daily performed by men of wealth, of which the world is not advised. In almost every case of this kind which came under our knowledge, in connection with Mr. Forrest, it was the desire of that gentleman that publicity should not be given. We shall have occasion hereafter to speak of his charities; in the mean time we give "Late at Rehearsal."

On one occasion Mr. Forrest was fulfilling an engagement in New York; the morning rehearsal of an important play was delayed some time by the non-arrival of one of the company. The part he had in the piece was a minor one, but very important to the actor, particularly in the first act. Mr. Forrest became impatient; he walked up and down the stage in no very mild humor—the manager and the company very uneasy. At last the truant came—a quiet, gentlemanly man, heretofore remarkable for close attention to business and rehearsals. Mr. Forrest, much excited, addressed him:—"Sir, you have kept these ladies and gentlemen waiting a full half hour. You cannot be ignorant, sir, of the importance of a rehearsal in which every member of the company take part." At that moment the actor raised his eyes and met those of Mr. Forrest—they were watery—grief was visible in every varying expression of his face. Forrest stopped—he could not add another word. The actor spoke:—"Mr. Forrest, I ask your pardon. I—I could not come sooner;" here tears came into his eyes. "I have met with a serious loss. My son—my only son—died last night. I—I hurried here as soon as I could, and—"

"Say no more," was the actor's reply. He knew the man to be poor, with a family; he also knew him to be correct in his habits. His anger was gone.

"Step aside, sir; I wish to speak to you," was the great actor's answer to the sad cause of the man's absence. "You have no business here; go home immediately; we will endeavor to get on without you, and take this from one who sympathizes in your grief." So saying, he slipped a fifty dollar note into his hand. Then turning suddenly round, exclaimed in a loud voice:—"Let us go on with the rehearsal."

RICHELIEU IN A PASSION.

Forrest was once playing an engagement at Pittsburg. Already dressed for the character of Richelieu, he was in the act of going on the stage in the first scene, when he discovered that the sleeve of the dress he wore was either too short or drawn up; he called to his dresser, and told him to pull the sleeve down, so as the lace frill would show. The man commenced pulling the robe instead of the under-sleeve, when Forrest, in a loud voice, exclaimed:—"Hell and fury! what are you about? The under-sleeve, d——n you." Being near the first entrance, he was heard in front, and a round of applause followed—the audience imagining it part of the play. "What are they applauding?" exclaimed Forrest. The prompter promptly replied:—"Your first speech, sir, off the stage."

AN AMUSING INCIDENT.

The following pleasing dramatic incident has been given in connection with more "Rolla's" than one. It actually occurred, however—no matter who the "Rolla" was on the occasion.

"Some years ago, when the play of Rolla was very *popular*, the manager found it very difficult to procure a child to play a part in that piece, which the reader well remembers is essential to its interest and final *tableau.* Having on one occasion procured a smart, intelligent child, by sundry presents and kind promises, it was inducted in its new vocation, and during rehearsal, promised fair to make a decided hit at night. Among the presents was a pair of red shoes, of which the little thing was extremely proud. At night everything went on well. In the first act the child is placed on the stage by its mother, who rushes out when she hears her husband's (Alonzo's) voice; two soldiers then enter and carry the child off to Pizarro's camp. Some delay having occurred, these two soldiers did not come in time, and the child looking round and wondering what it was all about, proudly walked down to the footlights, then putting out her feet, exclaimed:—'Look at my pretty red shoes.' The audience looked and shouted. The child, somewhat alarmed at this note of admiration, started and ran back just in time to be carried off by the two tardy soldiers. The applause continued for some time. That child made a hit."

THE EXCITED CRITIC.

On one occasion, while playing Virginius in a Western city, he noticed a man in the pit who seemed to enter into the spirit of the play by his never taking his eyes off the actor, watching his every motion with an earnestness that made Virginius feel uncomfortable. In the fifth act, when Virginius kills Virginia in the market-house, the house was perfectly spell-bound. The man in the pit manifested considerable emotion; he would start up and clutch his hands, thus attracting the attention of those around him.

At last, when Virginius returns to his home, mind distraught, and calls for his daughter, "Virginia, Virginia," in a broken voice, the man in the pit started up in actual fury, and shouted out:—"You killed her in the market house, you d——d villain!"

This was too much for the house. One loud shout

testified its appreciation of the critic's judgment, as well as his manner of expressing it. Forrest left.

The following incident connected with Mr. Forrest's Lear, is thus related by T. H. Morrell, Esq., New York, November 20th, 1872:

"About eighteen years ago, Mr. Forrest was playing an engagement at the old Broadway Theatre, near Anthony Street, their duration generally extending from fifty to seventy-five consecutive nights, and at that time considered a feat unparalleled in the annals of the stage. One night, while performing the role of King Lear, with Barry, Conway, Davidge, Whiting, Madame Ponisi, Mrs. Abbott and other well known favorites in the cast, in the last scene of the second act, when depicting the frenzy of the noble old monarch, whose brain was overwrought with passion, and maddened by the injuries of his unnatural daughters, Goneril and Regan, in the excitement of the moment Mr. Forrest tore the wig of whitened hair from his head and hurled it some twenty feet towards the footlights. The effect was a striking one, and the wig thus removed revealed to the audience a head of glossy raven locks, forming a strange contrast to the hoary beard still appended, and fastened by a white cord to the actor's chin. The situation was one that on an ordinary occasion would have caused embarrassment both to actor and spectator, but not so there. Among that vast audience not a single titter could be heard, and scarce a smile was discernible. Enchained, enraptured by the mighty master's art,

'A man of kingly stature and of kingly voice,'

delineating to the perfect life a mightier master's genius, two thousand silent listeners still gazed with eyes bedimmed upon the mimic scene before them. Nor did the pause or actor hesitate. Still did that voice, superbly grand, so rich in infinite pathos and of beauty—the most remarkable for compass, melody and power of any on the stage—speak forth in anguish and in sorrow, that fierce denunciation of the outraged king and father. Nearly two decades have passed away since that memorable engagement, and the 'old Broadway' is among 'the scenes that were,' as are also two other 'temples of the drama,' in which the veteran so often delighted the thousands who thronged to witness those characters in which he alone was capable of presenting the finest examples of feeling, dramatic passion and artistic beauty."

ALMOST A DUEL.

Playing Claude Melnotte out West, he found, as usual, much difficulty with actors at rehearsal. A young man who played an important part, disputed his business with the great actor with much spirit, saying: "I have as much right to my opinion, or the part I have to play, as you have, sir."

"Indeed," exclaimed Forrest, "and who are you, sir?"

"A gentleman."

"Indeed, I am glad to hear it."

"Probably," replied the young man, "for it is seldom you associate with them."

This was too much for Forrest; he burst out in great fury, and in no measured terms expressed his opinion of *the gentleman.*

The young man made no other reply than quietly remarking: "Ladies are present, and I never use improper language or bluster before them." Bowing, he left the stage.

After the rehearsal was over, and Forrest started to the hotel where he was stopping, the first person he met was the actor in question.

"A word with you, Mr. Forrest."

"I have no time, sir."

"Then take time; for what I have to say to you requires both time and attention. You insulted me, sir—insulted me in the presence of ladies, and I here demand an apology."

"Apology?"

"Yes, sir; for insulting me. I never submit to an insult, and you have to apologize or fight me. You may say I am but an actor—so are you—and being an actor, I claim also that of the character of a gentleman."

"Well, sir, suppose I refuse?"

"Then I insult you here in the open street—man to man. Sir, I am your equal in strength and science."

Forrest looked in astonishment upon the young man, who stood so boldly up before him; he admired his spirit and gentlemanly manner; he found he had to deal with a man, and his better nature acknowledged it.

"Well, sir, I will accept your challenge. It is my misfortune to meet so many of the profession, ignorant of their duties, in my travels, that the violence of my temper not unfrequently gets the better of my judgment."

"This, Mr. Forrest, is almost an apology."

"No, it is not—not sufficient—bring with you to my hotel as many of those whom you may wish to consult, before we meet in deadly strife, and who were present on the occasion. You shall have satisfaction, and ample; it shall never be said that I wronged a man unjustly."

It is unnecessary to say that the whole matter was amicably arranged, and that Mr. Forrest made a foe a friend. It was after this scene Mr. Forrest relaxed most wonderfully from his old violence of temper and manner. Forrest was an excellent story-teller, and liked nothing better than to tell the following anecdote in the green-room, if he found all the ladies of the company assembled. In his hotel, in St. Louis, there was a colored barber who always shaved Mr. Forrest, and was an intense admirer of the great tragedian. While performing his functions one morning, the following conversation ensued:

"We's going to play Othello, to-night, Massa Forrest."

"We? Who do you mean?"

"Me, sar, an' de oder colored gemmen. I wish you'd come and see us, sar."

"Well, perhaps I would if I had time. Where do you play?"

"Down in the servants' hall, sar. We'se got a good company."

"Oh! indeed. Good company, eh? Are your actresses good?"

"Well, Massa Forrest, dat's just whar de trouble is. We ain't got no actresses."

"No actresses!"

"Well, sar, we can't get no colored ladies to play on top of de stage."

"Why not?"

"Well, sar, dey won't do it; they tinks it so degrading, sar."

Mr. Forrest always told this with immense point, and thoroughly enjoyed the indignation with which the actresses invariably received it.

THE GERMAN DESDEMONA.

On one occasion Forrest was playing an engagement out West. The company was limited in numbers, and the leading actress was of German extraction and had not as yet mastered the English language; nor had she the least idea of the characters, particularly those of Shakespeare, in which she appeared. On the occasion of his playing Othello, this lady of course, took that of Desdemona. Forrest's description of this performance, as frequently told when he was "in the vein," was rich beyond expression, exaggerated to a certain extent; yet he said the main features were strictly true. In the scene where she is sent for to corroborate Othello's story of his love and whole course of wooing, when her father says:

> "Come hither, gentle mistress.
> Do you perceive in all this noble company
> Where you most owe obedience?"

She answered him thus:

> "My noble fader, I do see here many peoples,
> You are my fader; I owe you much duty,
> Mine life, and education, and all dese things.
> But dare is mine husband, dat black man;
> I likes him de most, I prefers him to you all the
> time. Ha—ha."

So saying, she made a rush at the Moor and nearly upset him; she clung to him, uttering ha—ha. The audience was delighted, for the actress was a great favorite.

As Forrest intended to play Macbeth, he was very much worried about his Lady Macbeth; there was no one to play it but this lady. He waited upon her to talk the matter over; he asked her if she had ever played Lady Macbeth.

"Eh, who is de lady, eh? I never knew her—never played her."

"Did you never hear of the great play of Macbeth, by William Shakespeare?"

"Eh, me do know him; but I will soon learn de part; fetch it to me, I learn it."

"My dear madame, if you have never played the

part, nor heard of the play, it would take months to do so—it is no common character."

"Eh, common? me no play common characters."

"You misunderstand me; this is a great character —one that requires months and years of study. We will change the play to something else."

"No! me play Macbeth; I learn her in three days, eh?"

Forrest would not risk it, to the lady's great surprise, saying, "Me learn her in three days, eh?"

TEACHING A PROMPTER A LESSON.

On one occasion, while acting Claude Melnotte at the old National Theatre, Philadelphia (where the Continental Hotel now stands), and while that establishment was under the management of Wemyss & Oxley, he exposed the prompter, Mr. Collingbourne, in a most emphatic manner. It is perhaps necessary to apprise the reader that all letters which are read upon the stage during a performance are previously written by the prompter. By some mistake, on this occasion, the "written letter" which Beauseant sends to Melnotte in the first act got mislaid, and the servant in the piece brought on to Mr. Forrest a blank document. The tragedian opened it as usual, and instead of finding the words, "Young man, I know thy secret, etc., etc.," he found a spotless piece of foolscap. Forrest rushed up the stage furiously, and hurling the dumb missive at the servant's head, exclaimed, "Bring me a written letter!" There was considerable of a "stage wait" before the proper letter could be found, and the audience was greatly amazed and annoyed at the sudden interruption of the scene and the actor's anger.

Poor Collingbourne afterwards confessed that he was "frightened out of his wits."

ANDREW JACKSON ALLEN.

This individual, better know as "Dummy Allen," travelled with Mr. Forrest on his professional tour as his "costumer." He was born in New York, December, 1776. In 1787, he appeared as a child in the John Street Theatre, New York, from which circumstance he boasted being the paternal parent of the Histrionic tribe. He was attached to various theatres in New York in subordinate situations. He was connected with the National Theatre in 1838, and in 1852, he took a benefit at the Lyceum, Broadway. Allen was very deaf, and consequently very annoying to those with whom he played, who not unfrequently took an unkind revenge on his misfortune, by misleading him with an inaudible movement of the lips during the performance, to which he thought he must reply, his speeches being often quite *mal-apropos.* On one occasion, when an actor's lips seemed to move beyond the cue by which he was to reply, he exclaimed aloud: "What is all this? Are you going to do all the talking? Stop, or I'll go off the stage." The audience roared with laughter.

Allen possessed a patent for the manufacture of gold and silver leather, much used upon stage costume. He died in New York, October, 30th, 1853.

The name of Andrew Jackson Allen, with the exception of his paternal appellation, was entirely gratuitous. He was a great admirer of the general. During Mr. Forrest's professional visit to Europe, Allen accom panied him as his costumer. On one occasion a dinner was given by some of the minor actors of the theatre, to which Allen was invited. In reply to a toast complimentary to America, Allen rose and made some remarks, in the course of which he spoke of "the Boy" as the greatest actor of the age. "Where," he shouted, "is there another to equal him? Where," he exclaimed in high tragic notes, "will you find him?" An excited individual, carried away by the eloquence of the speaker, shouted out: "Hear! hear!" It is customary in England, when anything good or startling is said by the speaker, for the audience to cry, "Hear! hear!"

Allen, taking the words literally, shouted in return: "Where? Show me the man!"

"Hear! hear!" was heard from several voices.

"Where?" roared Allen; "where is he. Show me the man; bring him up."

"Hear! hear!"

"Where?"

"Hear! hear!" resounded through the room.

As soon as they discovered that Allen misunderstood them, they kept up the excitement until Allen, becoming enraged at not seeing the equal to Forrest, rushed from the room, exclaiming: "I should like to see the man that can beat the "Boy."

On another occasion, at some festival given to Mr. Forrest, Allen was present, and becoming very loquacious, the great tragedian said to him: "Come, come, Allen, you had better go home and attend to your *silver leather*" (a theatrical decoration upon which Mr. Allen prided himself as the inventor). At this remark, it is said the Great American Costumer, as he styled himself, rose up indignant, and banging his hat upon his head, stammered out—"B-B what ud your Bacbeth or Richard be bidout by silber leather." An impediment in Allen's speech, and his indignant manner, created an uproarious scene.

A SATISFACTORY EXCUSE.

Mr. Forrest was once playing in Richmond, Va., when one of the minor actors annoyed him terribly by persisting in reading his few lines in Richelieu incorrectly. Forrest showed him several times how to do it, but to no purpose, and then commenced abusing him. "Look here, Mr. Forrest," finally said the poor fellow, in sheer despair, "if I could read it in that way I wouldn't be getting six dollars a week here." Forrest said only: "You are right; I ought not to expect much for that sum," and left him alone, but on the conclusion of the engagement sent him a check for forty dollars, with a recommendation to act up to the worth of that.

MR. FORREST MEETS HIS MATCH.

To use a slang word, he was extremely apt to "bully" all in the theatre, from the manager down. But he once met his match. It was when he was playing at the old Broadway Theatre, near Pearl Street. His pieces were followed by an exhibition of lions by their tamer, a certain Herr Driesbach. Forrest was one day saying that he had never been afraid in all his life—could not imagine the emotion. Driesbach made no remark at the time, but in the evening, when the curtain had fallen, invited Forrest home with him. Forrest assented, and the two, entering a house, walked a long distance, through many devious passages, all dark, until finally Driesbach, opening a door, said:

"This way, Mr. Forrest." Forrest entered, and immediately heard the door slammed and locked behind him. He had not time to express any surprise at this, for at the same moment he felt something soft rubbing against his leg, and, putting out his hand, touched what felt like a cat's back. A rasping growl saluted the motion, and he saw two fiery, glaring eyeballs looking up at him. "Are you afraid, Mr. Forrest?" asked Driesbach, invisible in the darkness. "Not a bit." Driesbach said something; the growl deepened and became hoarser, the back began to arch and the eyes to shine more fiercely. Forrest held out for two or three minutes; but the symptoms became so terrifying that he owned up in so many words that he was afraid. "Now let me out, you infernal scoundrel," he said to the lion-tamer; "and I'll break every bone in your body." He was imprudent there, for Driesbach kept him, not daring to move a finger, with the lion rubbing against his leg all the time, until Forrest promised not only immunity, but a champagne supper into the bargain.

ROMAN CITIZENS.

Nearly every actor who has ever played with Mr. Forrest, has his own little anecdote to tell of Forrest's grim humor or scathing sarcasm, but such anecdotes mainly depend for appreciation upon an imitation of the tragedian's voice and manner. That Mr. Forrest had abundant humor of its kind no one can doubt. A remark of his made in Baltimore, a few years ago, has become famous as a stage tradition. Mr. Forrest's legs were a theme of great admiration to the world at large, and of no little pride to himself. The play was Vir-

13

ginius, and Mr. Forrest, in the costume of the Roman General, was standing at the wings in his usual firm attitude, and with his usual scornful smile gazing at the actors and supernumeraries standing on the stage. The lower limbs of the actors for the most part being plentifully padded, presented a respectable appearance, but the poor supers, being, as is usually the case in American theatres, mere overgrown boys, and having no pads, their limbs were ridiculous, and the fleshings with which they were covered being a world too wide for their shrunk shanks, their appearance roused the ire of Mr. Forrest. Mr. Ford, the manager, passing at the time, Forrest called his attention to the supers, and said: "Mr. Ford, for heaven's sake what are those?" "Those," said the manager, "are Roman citizens, Mr. Forrest." "Roman citizens! Ye Gods! Did Romans have legs like those?"

The air of utter disgust attending the words was indescribable, and Forrest stalked on the stage as if he could devour the Roman citizens, legs and all.

POWERFUL ACTING.

The last almanac issued by the English theatrical paper known as the *Era*, gave some amusing but apocryphal anecdotes of "powerful" American acting. On one occasion, Mr. Edwin Forrest, then a young man, gave a tremendous display of really powerful acting. He was supposed to represent a Roman warrior, and to be attacked by six minions of a detested tyrant. At the rehearsals, Mr. Forrest found a great deal of fault with the supers who condescended to play the minions. They were too tame. They didn't lay hold of him. They wouldn't go in as if it were a real fight. Mr.

Forrest stormed and threatened; the supers sulked and consulted. At length the captain of the supers inquired in his local slang, "Yer wan this to be a bully fight, eh?" "I do," replied Mr. Forrest. "All right," rejoined the captain; and then the rehearsal quietly proceeded. In the evening the little theatre was crowded, and Mr. Forrest was enthusiastically received. When the fighting scene occurred, the great tragedian took the centre of the stage, and the six minions entered rapidly and deployed in skirmishing order. At the cue "Seize him!" one minion assumed a pugilistic attitude, and struck a blow straight from the shoulder upon the prominent nose of the Roman hero, another raised him about six inches from the stage by a well-directed kick, and the others made ready to rush in for a decisive tussle. For a moment Mr. Forrest stood astounded, his broad chest heaving with rage, his great eyes flashing fire, his sturdy legs planted like columns upon the stage. Then came the few minutes of powerful acting, at the end of which one super was seen sticking head foremost in the bass drum in the orchestra, four were having their wounds dressed in the green-room, and one finding himself in the flies, rushed out upon the roof of the theatre, and shouted "Fire!" at the top of his voice; while Mr. Forrest, called before the curtain, bowed his thanks pantingly to the applauding audience, who looked upon the whole affair as part of the piece, and "had never seen Forrest act so splendidly."

CHAPTER XVII.

MR. FORREST'S MEDICAL KNOWLEDGE.—FORREST AND SHAKESPEARE.—THE TURKISH BATH.—SHORT LETTER.—INCIDENT IN AN INSANE ASYLUM.—HEREDITARY GOUT.—QUACK MEDICINE.

WE are not about to speak of Mr. Forrest's medical knowledge as being derived from a University education and a regular course of study; there was no diploma given, nor fees paid to professors. A knowledge—superficial, it is true—may be attained of various diseases without devoting years to study. In the first place, he studied the various phases of insanity, visited asylums both in this country and in Europe, held frequent conversations with the celebrated Dr. Rush, and more recently with Dr. Gross, one of our most eminent physicians. He studied with an eye to render his knowledge available to his profession. It was this knowledge that made his King Lear, Hamlet, and Virginius so great. The study of medicine is not, we think, a proper expression, at least in its application to Mr. Forrest—we should say the study of man—and it was here he laid the foundation for his knowledge of the former by close study of the latter. Again, he had studied the anatomy of the human frame; he could talk well upon the subject; he had all the physiological and technical terms at his tongue's end, and could hold "learned discourse" with men of science upon the subject.

Mr. Forrest believed firmly in the power of electricity in curing many diseases, both by the battery, and by manipulation. He possessed great power himself, by bringing his influence to act upon a body weaker than his own. The writer of this found almost immediate relief from a severe nervous headache under the manipulating power exercised upon him by Mr. Forrest.

Mr. Forrest studied the insane characters of Shakespeare from that great author's instructive physiological knowledge, as well as he did from those whom he visited in the asylums. What numerous texts did he find in Shakespeare to study! In Macbeth, he found the cue to that monarch's acts; in Lear, almost every phase of insanity, induced by old age, wrong and passion. In Hamlet, the monomania leading him to meditate suicide—in fact, Shakespeare studied from this point—furnishes the actor with all the traits essential to the proper rendition of the character. A writer, speaking upon this subject, says:—"Upon no subjects, perhaps, has this extraordinary man (speaking of Shakespeare) been more curiously manifested than those of physiology and psychology. In fact, we believe a very complete physiological and psychological system could be educed from the writings of Shakepeare—a system in complete accordance, in almost every essential particular with that which we now possess, as the result of the scientific research and experience of the last two centuries."

Our readers will observe, at least that portion who have carefully studied Shakespeare, a striking similarity between that great author and the subject of these reminiscences. The latter, like the former, was a poor boy—the one held horses at the theatre entrance, the other formed amateur companies, and became an actor, as did the holder of horses; the one became a great author, the other a great actor; the one wrote plays, and the other acted them.

Although it did not require so many years of study, to make Forrest a great actor, as it did Shakespeare to become the master spirit of English literature, still it took both time and application to learn something of other professions to be as perfect in, as that of his own.

Shakespeare, who never studied medicine as a science, displays in his writings considerable knowledge of diseases to which the human system is subject. Dryden says: "In him we find all arts and sciences, all moral and natural philosophy, without knowing that he ever studied them."

Shakespeare, as the young actor-poet, became the companion of gentlemen—the teacher of a court, the delight of his sovereign, and the "darling of the nation."

Forrest, at an early age became the companion of gentlemen, and at the age of fourteen, under their auspices, became the Roscius of the American stage.

Shakespeare, it is said, was a butcher's boy—a wool dealer and a glover's boy. Forrest was a ship-chandler's boy, and a shop boy in a German notion house.

Shakespeare was born in a pleasant English home, of good Protestant parents; he went to the village school and learned grammar.

Forrest was born in a pleasant home, of good Protestant parents; he went to school and learned to read and write.

Shakespeare's heart was warmed by "sitting at goodmen's feasts."

Forrest's heart was warmed by sitting at a good mother's simple fare.

What was said of Shakespeare can be said of Forrest: "No matter what his struggles may have been while yet a young man, if he go through with honor and health untouched, his early trials would but add to the enjoyment of life in after years. But if in setting out he chanced to be a little wild, he would all the more likely be made acquainted with a great variety of strange people, and get a near view of their characters and habits."

Our readers must understand that Mr. Forrest's knowledge of medicine, and the interest he took in the sufferings of others, was entirely of a philanthropic character. He had but one complaint, that of gout, and to the cure of which he devoted both time and money.

Mr. Forrest placed great virtue in the Turkish bath, and had one made in his own house, to which he resorted, we often thought, too frequently for his health. In a letter he wrote to us on one occasion, wherein alluding to a portion of the one we had sent him, he says; "I am sorry to hear that you still suffer from headache. Why cannot you be persuaded to try the efficacy of the Turkish bath, which equalizes the circulations of the body and purifies the blood more effectually than any medicine can do? Try it first at a temperature of 140°," etc., etc.

I did not try it, and still live!

He read almost every book that came out on the subject of medicine, cures, etc. He had read numerous essays on gout and rheumatism. But neither the essays nor the doctors could drive the former from his system. He did not, however, generally lend himself to quacks, but on one occasion he did; the result of this man's nostrum came near killing him. The shortest letter which Mr. Forrest probably ever wrote, was to request the writer to procure a certain book on medicine for him, the merits and character of which we had been discussing. Here it is:

"MONDAY NIGHT.

"MY DEAR MR. REES:—Please get me the book.

"Yours, "EDWIN FORREST."

We have said that Mr. Forrest, in studying Lear, visited insane asylums, and the "Old Man's Home," for the purpose of catching the peculiar traits of the "mind's disease," as well as the walk and actions of the aged. How admirably he carried out these sad phases of humanity on the stage we all know.

Mere imitation, however, does not constitute originality in art; in the language of criticism, it is called invention. Had Mr. Forrest merely imitated others, he never could have established a style of acting peculiarly his own. For instance, had he followed others in their rendition of Lear, we should have had a mere copy instead of a great original. He went beyond Cooper's and Kean's views of the choleric King—even back to those of a Shakespeare. To produce a great picture, he first studied the character, and then sought a model among the old men of our city. One he selected—a poor, aged, tottering creature—fourscore and upwards, and whose peculiar walk and action he watched with an artist's eagerness. In the language of Dryden he said: "I have followed him everywhere,

I know not with what success, but I am sure with diligence enough; my images are, many of them, copied from him, and the rest are imitations of him."—[*Dryden; Letter I.—Sir R. Howard.*

On one occasion, speaking of his visit to hospitals and insane asylums, he related a thrilling incident which occurred during his visit to one of these institutions in Paris.

Among the insane was a man whose whole appearance and manners were those of a sane person. During the conversation with the keeper, he noticed the eyes of this man intensely fixed upon him. A pause occurring in their discussion upon some point, the keeper turned his head for a moment; in the next, Mr. Forrest found himself seized with maniac fury by the man with staring eyes, and thrown completely over his head; it was the work of an instant; he had scarcely time—stunned as he was—to defend himself from the infuriate man, nor was it until two or three attendants arrived, that he could be secured.

Mr. Forrest was well versed in homœopathic cures, and could tell you what medicine was necessary to be taken for almost any disease. He was not, however, a convert to the system, although he occasionally took these sugared doses. Living as Mr. Forrest did, alone, the many dark hours of his dreary life no doubt had an effect upon his spirits. He did not court society; hence the few who visited him were the old friends of his early days. To talk over past scenes, recall the reminiscences of youth, fight over again the mimic battles of the stage—these visits seemed to give him new life; his full, sonorous voice sounded through his library like the notes of some Cathedral organ—

there was music in it. The writer of this had frequent opportunities of noticing the rise and progress of his thermometer of health, and although it slightly varied, there were times when the indications would have puzzled the most scientific.

One day, when he seemed unusually depressed, we asked him, very cautiously, however, if he did not, at times, suffer from a fullness of the head, as it had frequently struck us that there were apparent symptoms of a determination of blood to that region. "Oh, no!" he said, "from here up," pointing to the seat of the gout, "I am all right; were it not for this hereditary curse, I would be as well as ever."

"Hereditary?" I exclaimed.

"Yes; but not from my parents. But from my grandfather, it came down to the third generation; hence the phrase, the sins—you know the rest."

Although we did not express it, the thought struck us that the victim in the third generation was the most likely to transmit it to his posterity.

Our reason for asking the above question was that we had observed, more particularly a short time before his death, certain symptoms which we thought tended to apoplexy; such as the stoppage of the flux and reflux of his spirits, as if the usual voluntary motion of the nerves was unnatural. At times his face would be flushed, at others pale and cadaverous. Again, he was all life and animation; and at no time did he appear in better health than he did a few days before his death. And yet that insidious foe to man, apoplexy, in an instant did its fearful work.

Mr. Forrest had collected a number of cures for various diseases; and whenever he heard of a case for which he had an authenticated remedy, he either recommended it, or sent it to those afflicted.

We think Mr. Forrest's attention was drawn to the study of medicine in consequence of his meeting so many passages in Shakespeare alluding to the science. In conversation with him upon the subject, we felt assured that part of his study of medicine was based more upon curiosity than a desire to master its mysteries. We allude here to medicine generally; for he studied the phases of insanity for a far different purpose. Like many amateurs, more particularly those of the middle ages, the study of chemistry, and pharmacy, excited his curiosity; and those who were familiar with his dressing-room found a perfect laboratory; and had he lived in the age of Alchemy and Astrology, he would have been taken for an investigator of the visible phenomena of matter. And yet he could not tell you why and wherefore this vast collection of bottles was made, for what purpose, what object, beyond the remark — "Merely for experiments!" These he never tried upon himself internally, we know; externally, some of them were used; but with little or no effect for what they were intended, viz.: cure of the gout.

We have shown a striking similarity between the youth of Shakespeare and of Forrest; in age, this similarity still existed; and perhaps in no one more striking illustration, than that we have given in that of the study of medicine. He would frequently quote passages having some allusion to his own ailment; as, for instance, when groaning under a severe attack of gout, he would exclaim: "I am like the owner of a foul disease. To keep it from divulging let it feed, even on the pith of life."

Any one conversant with Shakespeare knew full well that he never omitted an opportunity of exhibiting his knowledge of other professions beside that of his own—not egotistically given, but to carry out the peculiar characteristics of the personages of his dramas. With Mr. Forrest this peculiarity was equally discernible; but, like Shakespeare, never displayed but in connection with the philosophy of his art. *Forrest had less vanity than any other actor that ever trod the stage.*

It may be said of Mr. Forrest as it was said of Shakespeare; "Let us, therefore, intelligently admire Shakespeare's varied knowledge of the common affairs of life, by considering his vast capacity in connection with the fact that this knowledge of his, at which we are so much astonished, is of that kind and degree that comes from observation, and not by special study or daily practice."

Health and disease are questions of such importance, that it would be strange indeed if their phenomena had found no place in Shakespeare's writings. Equally strange would it have been if Mr. Forrest, who suffered so much from an hereditary disease, had not bestowed some attention to the nature of the disorder by which he was afflicted.

In striving to gain relief from recipes he came across, or in consequence of becoming interested in other diseases, apart from that of his own, he left behind him some very valuable recipes, among which is an invaluable one for the cure of "St. Vitus's dance"—(*Chorea.*)

CHAPTER XVIII.

ENGLISH PREJUDICE AGAINST AMERICAN AUTHORS AND ACTORS.—ORIGIN OF THEIR DRAMA, NOT AS LEGITIMATE AS OUR OWN.—SOME ACCOUNT OF BOOTH'S RECEPTION IN LONDON.—FORREST'S SECOND PROFESSIONAL VISIT.—ITS RESULT.

IT is said that "genius knows no country," yet it has been shown that prejudice gives it a *locale* when prejudice sways the judgment. England has always claimed the honor of giving birth to whatever genius and talent America imagined was indigenous to its soil. It is our purpose to speak more particularly of the stage and drama in this connection. It is true, their literary treasures have been accumulating from Alfred, Bede and Chaucer, through a succession of centuries, swelling up the vast catalogue of science with the most enlightened and intellectual names that have gilded the firmament of letters in any age or hemisphere. *Ours* can scarcely be estimated more than seventy years, and yet the origin of the English drama, springing as it did from the corruptions of the Catholic Church, with its Miracle plays, followed by the "Mysteries and Moralities," was by no means creditable either to the morals or the literature of the age, while that of ours can boast of a more classical origin, and the character of our earliest productions of a far more legitimate character.

In England, the first spectacle of a dramatic nature was the Miracle play of St. Catharine, mentioned by Matthew Paris as having been written by Geoffrey, a Norman, afterwards Abbott of St. Albans, and performed at Dunstaple Abbey, in the year 1110.

The ancient religious dramas were distinguished by the names of Mysteries, precursors of the regular drama, which consisted of a dramatic representation of religious subjects, from the New or Old Testament, apocryphal stories, or lives of the saints, which were of the nature of tragedy, representing the acts of martyrdom of a saint of the Church. Some of these pieces consisted of a single subject only, as "The Conversion of St. Paul," "The Casting out of the evil Spirits from Mary Magdalene," etc.

The devil was frequently one of the persons of these mysteries. He was constantly attended by the vice, or clown, whose chief business was to play to his Satanic Majesty, tricks, and strike him with his wooden dagger till he roared, which always elicited bursts of laughter. Adam and Eve were represented in a state of actual nudity, and so late as James I., a pastoral was played before the queen and her women, in which some of the characters were almost naked. Such is the origin of England's early stage history!

The first play written in this country was by Benjamin Coleman, in 1690, entitled Gustavus Vasa, and performed by the students of Harvard College. The first piece performed was Shakespeare's Richard III., by a regular company of comedians, New York, Monday, 5th of May, 1750; Richard III., by Thomas Kean.

Such being the origin of our drama, there was no necessity of making holy matters subjects for amusement. It was probably well for us that the Church of America had more respect for the Bible than those who made religion a *farce* and the saints its *characters.*

A drama like ours, having no monks nor priests to control it, would naturally produce good actors. So it did, and how a few of them were treated in England from sheer prejudice and a determination to encourage nothing but of indigenous growth, we purpose to show. To such an extent was this national feeling carried, that actors of English birth, whose reputations were made in this country, and were considered as American actors, by education, actually found no favor among their own countrymen. Among these was

JUNIUS BRUTUS BOOTH.

He was born at St. Pancras, near London, 1796; made his first appearance on the American stage, as a star, at Petersburg, Virginia, in 1821. It was probably more Booth's fault, rather than English prejudice, that rendered him unpopular in London. He strongly contested the palm with Kean of being the better Richard; but a striking similarity, or rather as the critics call it, imitation of that great actor, materially lessened his claims. He however, found in this country more just and liberal criticism, and to the last divided honors with the best actors of both hemispheres. We pass over others who were coldly received in England and come to Edwin Forrest's second professional tour to that country. As the name of Charles William Macready will be closely connected with the events arising out of this visit, it is necessary to say something of that gentleman here.

Mr. Macready was born March 3rd, 1793, in London.

In September, 1826, he came to this country with the reputation of being the best actor on the English stage. He opened at the Park Theatre, New York, October 2nd, as Virginius. The receipts of the house were $1680. On January 10th, 1827, he appeared in Philadelphia, at the Chestnut Street Theatre, as Macbeth; returned to England in 1827. In 1843 he re-visited America, acting in all the principal cities in the United States. It was during this visit that the merits of the actor were freely discussed, and his cold, stately, mechanical style, compared with the gushing genius of a Kean, Booth and Forrest, found but few advocates; these were chiefly Englishmen, who were in some manner connected with the press. The New York *Herald* had critics, as well as prejudiced writers, who endeavored by every means to extol Mr. Macready at the expense of Mr. Forrest. In New Orleans, a certain Henry Percy Leonard, an Englishman, commenced a series of articles against Mr. Forrest, while at the same time he applauded Macready. The writer of these articles was in that city at the time, and not having the same opinion of the actor, nor a very high estimate of the moral and social character of "Percy" himself, he exposed the man and his motives. During Mr. Macready's engagement in Philadelphia it is well known how we defended Mr. Forrest against those who were the advocates of the English actor: the result of our labors was the removal of our name from the free list, by Mr. E. A. Marshall, the manager, influenced by Charles William Macready.

Thus was the attempt made to muzzle the press, and silence, if possible, independent criticism; and to this bold movement on the part of Mr. Macready, was he indebted for a more correct estimate of his dramatic ability than that fulsome flattery had given him. It also tended to place Mr. Forrest's claim much higher, and lessened those of the great mechanical actor.

Mr. Marshall subsequently apologized to us for acting as he did in erasing our name from the list—*it was because Macready desired it:* observing, "my poverty and not my will yielded to the great man's demand." Macready returned to England, disappointed, soured, and revengeful. In Forrest he found his superior, who came out of this *test* the conqueror, and the acknowledged master of the American stage.

Shortly after Mr. Macready's departure, Mr. Forrest made his arrangements to fulfil his engagement in London. Unconscious of the storm that awaited him—unprepared for the malice of the disappointed—he arrived in England, and made his appearance at the Princess' Theatre, February 17th, 1845. As we have said, he was totally unprepared for the reception he met with. The London press had not attacked him in advance—he knew nothing of a premeditated design to drive him from the stage; the curtain rose; the actor appeared; he was greeted with hisses and groans from a large portion of the audience. It was evident that a combination was formed against him; not alone because he was a superior actor, but because he was an American. The insult was, in an eminent degree, national. The fame of a great actor is the property of his country; and when we, in good faith, entrusted that property to England, it should have been respected, not abused. Never yet did the American people refuse to render justice to English actors; even those of mediocre ability were kindly received, many of whom have made our country their home, and become naturalized citizens.

That Macready was instrumental in getting up this opposition, none dare deny; the proofs are beyond a question of doubt. His friend, John Forster, editor of the *Examiner*, was busily engaged in writing against Edwin Forrest during his engagement in 1845. As an evidence of his mendacity, we give the following from the *Examiner* of the 22nd of February, 1845:—

"Our old acquaintance, Mr. Forrest, the American tragedian, has played Othello at the Princess' Theatre during the past week, and it would seem from the account (we did not see the tragedy), with entire abatement of that 'sound and fury,' which distinguished his performance nine years ago. 'Nor should you do it too terribly,' says that excellent dramatic critic, Peter Quince, 'for you would fright the Duchess and the ladies.' According to the *Times*, the too terrible has subsided into the too tame. But we must venture to think the change a clear improvement, and great gain to the audience."

Who but Mr. Forster, the creature at that time, of Mr. Macready, could display such venom and vulgarity? Contrast the following notice of Forrest's Lear, written by Douglas Jerrold, London, March 9th, 1845, with the low, vulgar article from the *Examiner*.

EDWIN FORREST, AS KING LEAR.

"A more truthful, feeling and artistical display of genuine acting, we never witnessed. From the first scene to the last, he was the Lear of our immortal bard. Not a line, look or gesture told of Mr. Forrest, but Lear was Lear from the first scene to the last. We never saw madness so perfectly portrayed. It is true to nature—painfully so; and to the utter absence of mannerism, affectation, noisy declamation, and striving for effect, may, nay must, be attributed the histrionic triumph achieved by Mr. Forrest in this difficult part. By his display of Thursday evening, Mr. Forrest has stamped himself a man of genius. We candidly confess we did not think it was in him, and we were much electrified, as was every one in the house. The whole audience, in fact, were taken by surprise; and the unanimous cheering at the conclusion of each act, must have convinced Mr. Forrest how much his performance was appreciated. He must have been gratified, for the expressions of delight which greeted him were as heartfelt as they were merited. The imprecation at the conclusion of the first act, was most impressively and admirably delivered, and drew down thunders of applause from one and all. We never heard this awful curse so powerfully uttered. It was dreadful from its intenseness and reality. Had we space we could point out numberless excellencies in Mr. Forrest's performance. A more talented exhibition we never wish to see; it is impossible to imagine anything more intellectual. The care and study bestowed upon this part must have been great, and the actor has identified himself most completely with it. It is refreshing, now-a-days, to see one of Shakespeare's plays so brought before us, and we feel exceedingly obliged to Mr. Forrest for having reminded us of the palmy days of Kemble and Kean; and when we add that his Lear is equal in every respect to that of the two mighty tragedians whose names are hallowed by the admirers of genius, we think we can scarcely bestow higher praise."

CHAPTER XIX.

MR. FORREST.—RECEPTION IN ENGLAND.—COMBINATION.—INTRIGUE.—MACREADY'S COMPLICITY WITH FORSTER.—FORREST AND MACREADY MEET IN PARIS AND AT EDINBURG.—PAS DE MOUCHOIR, DISTASTEFUL. TO FORREST.—BULWER AND HIS PLAYS.—CORRESPONDENCE BETWEEN AUTHOR AND ACTOR.—THE PRESS TAKES PART.—JOHN FORSTER OF THE EXAMINER.

MR. MACREADY had previously been in this country, and played engagements in every city, and made a fortune. He was extolled by a portion of the press, and leniently treated by those who did not consider him a great actor. But instead of returning this kindness, he acted openly towards Mr. Forrest as his determined foe. In Paris, Mr. Macready and Mr. Forrest met. The latter was anxious to appear on the French boards, but Mr. Macready threw obstacles in the way, and this was the first time that the two parties were enemies. Mr. Mitchell, the enterprising lessee of the St. James Theatre, in London, took an English company of actors to the French capital, with Mr. Macready at the head of the list. Macready was to be the hero—the great attraction of Paris. He failed, however, to draw money to the treasury, and Mr. Mitchell lost a large sum by the speculation. Mr.

Forrest had letters of introduction to Mr. Mitchell from his friends in London; but Macready was jealous, lest Forrest should prove the greater star, and he cautioned Mitchell not to allow Forrest to appear. The result was that Mr. Mitchell refused to see Mr. Forrest.

The parties returned to London. The hypocrisy of Macready is apparent in his note of invitation to Mr. Forrest to dine with him. The latter, knowing the intrigue that had been carried on in Paris between Macready and Mitchell, declined the invitation, as every high-minded man should. This refusal induced the friends of Macready to get up a story to the effect that *Forrest was offended because he was not invited!* Is it likely that Forrest could take offence at such a trifle, when, at the same time, he was invited to dine with many of the leading nobility of England, but especially of Scotland, where he passed several months as their guest? It will be seen that in every movement of Mr. Macready, jealousy of the great American actor was the prominent cause.

> "Of all the passions, Jealousy
> Exacts the hardest services, and pays
> The bitterest wages. Its service is—
> To watch an enemy's success; its wages—
> To be sure of it."

The next mean act towards the American actor, brought through the influence of Macready, was when Mr. Forrest appeared at the Princess' Theatre, in London. Macready had been endeavoring for a long time to effect an engagement with some London manager, but was unsuccessful. The success of Forrest stung him, and he resolved to "put him down." It was said at the time that he or his friends actually hired men to visit the theatre and hiss Forrest off the stage, and he was consequently received with a shower of hisses before he was heard! This mean conduct was followed up by the press, by which Mr. Forrest was most outrageously assailed, and not him alone, but his country, which was proud to own him as one of her sons.

Having the evidence of the origin of these assaults, is it to be wondered at that Mr. Forrest felt indignant against a man whom his countrymen had honored and treated with courtesy? [The evidence of Mr. Macready's complicity with John Forster and others, to hiss Mr. Forrest will be given when we come to the Astor Place Opera House riot.]

We now come to the first outbreak of Mr. Forrest, and it is one we regretted at the time and to which we objected. Forrest and Macready met in Edinburg. Macready was playing Hamlet at the Theatre Royal. Forrest was present. During the beginning of the piece, Mr. Forrest applauded several times, and, as we are informed by an eye-witness, he started the applause when some brilliant effect had been given to a passage, so that the whole house followed. But now comes Forrest's great error, which Mr. Macready never forgave —the error of hissing that gentleman for introducing the *pas de mouchoir* at the close of the play scene, and performing sundry other similar antics. This act of Mr. Forrest drew the attention of the Dublin audience to this scene, when Mr. Macready repeated the play a few nights subsequently. The editor of the Edinburg *Weekly Chronicle*, March 14th, 1846, says: "On Monday he personated Hamlet, when he again introduced the *pas de mouchoir*. A few injudicious admirers attempted to applaud the harlequinade, which elicited hisses from so many of the audience that we fear our contemporary, the *Scotsman*, will be unable to enjoy the satisfaction of individually stigmatizing the offenders." Mr. Forrest should have remembered that Hamlet, being mad, was just as likely to dance a horn-pipe as anything else. This was not original with Mr. Macready, as we saw it done on the boards of old Drury (Chestnut Street Theatre) long before Mr. Macready's name or fame had reached this country.

Out of this incident Macready contrived to create a great deal of sympathy for himself. He was at the time part proprietor of the London *Examiner*. Forster, who did all things to please Macready, gave a false coloring to the whole affair, denouncing Forrest in the *Examiner* and other papers.

Had Mr. Macready received Mr. Forrest in London as one gentleman and actor should have received another, and extended to him that courtesy Mr. Forrest had shown him here, how much rancor, ill feeling, and even *bloodshed* might have been avoided. But ingratitude not unfrequently finds its reward, but alas! too late at times to remedy the evil it produces in society. The innocent often suffer for the guilty acts of others.

"Not faster yonder rowers' might
Fling from their oars the spray;
Not faster yonder rippling bright
That tracks the shallop's course in light,
Melts in the lake away,
Than men from memory erase
The benefits of former days."

But Mr. Macready's persecution did not stop here. Forrest desired to appear in London in Bulwer's plays of Lady of Lyons, and Richelieu. To obtain this he had to apply to the author. He reasoned upon this principle, that if the Garrick Club deemed him worthy of the compliment of a dinner in 1836, and Macready and Kemble honored the festival with their presence, he might ask with a good grace the privilege of playing the production of one of their honored members. The following correspondence will enable the reader to answer the question, why Mr. Bulwer refused to allow Mr. Forrest to appear in plays in which Mr. Macready had acquired a high reputation:

"26 REGENT STREET, LONDON.

"SIR:—Being desirous of producing at the Princess' Theatre the plays of Richelieu and the Lady of Lyons, I take the liberty of addressing you to know if you have any objection to them being represented there, and what would be the author's nightly fee.

"I have the honor to be, yours, with the highest respect, "EDWIN FORREST.

"To SIR E. L. BULWER, Bart."

"MARCH 4th, 1845.

"SIR:—I regret that, having invariably declined to allow the representation of my plays, nightly, at any metropolitan theatre, I cannot comply with your request. I could not allow Richelieu and the Lady of Lyons to be performed for a less period than ten nights each, *upon a payment beforehand of fifty guineas for the two*, and supposing that the twenty performances were included within five weeks—at which time the right of performance (supposing that accident prevented the completing the twenty representations) would cease—and return entirely at my disposal.

"I am, sir, your obedient servant,

"E. L. BULWER.

"E. FORREST, Esq."

Mr. Bulwer did not even condescend to reply to Mr. Forrest's note until nearly ten days had expired. The reader will perceive from this correspondence that Mr. Bulwer knew it would be impossible for Mr. Forrest to comply with his conditions. What influence was brought to bear upon the author during these ten days?

It was ascertained that Macready and Bulwer had been much together, and that the former had prevailed on the latter not to allow Forrest the use of his compositions. [The correspondence between Mr. Forrest and Mr. Macready upon this subject will be given in their proper place, as it was not published until 1848–9.]

Shortly after Mr. Forrest's death, an article appeared in the New York *Clipper*, headed "Edwin Forrest in London. Personal Reminiscences of him. By Le Voila." The article contains very little of interest beyond table gossip, having more of romance about it than reality. One passage, however, we give here, as it contains an allusion to the subject upon which we are engaged in this number:

"The visit made to London in 1845 exerted a wonderful influence upon the subsequent career of Mr. Forrest—an influence much more enduring and profound than his most intimate friends in this country could truly imagine. In the spring of 1846 the writer passed some weeks in a pleasure-visit to the British metropolis, and, while in company with Mr. Charles H. Peabody, the originator of the once famous *Knickerbocker Magazine*, and of the very popular *Parlor Journal*, I renewed an acquaintance with Mr. Forrest which, in America, had been almost formal. At that moment our tragedian was engaged in a controversy, through the colums of the *Times*, with Mr. Macready, and although his communications were suffered courteously, to appear in that daily, the general tone and temper of the press were decidedly hostile to him as an actor. It is due to Mr. Forrest to say that he had never decried the artistic ability of his presumptive rival, who, however, belonged to that traditional school of imitators of the Kemble family, so popular in London, and comparatively unknown to us, preferring, as we did, that style of acting proceeding from Garrick, through John Frederick Cooke, Edmund Kean, and the elder Booth. Neither did Forrest hiss Macready for his performance of Hamlet, but merely gave expression to his displeasure at his rendition of an isolated point in the tragedy. In the scene wherein the prince invites the court to the play, Mr. Macready preceded the royal cortege, waving a pocket-handkerchief, while executing a sort of waltz around the stage. This decidedly ludicrous exhibition of madness in philosophic gentlemen of mature years, which Mr. Forrest humorously designated as a *pas de mouchoir*, undoubtedly excited his imagination, and he, unguardedly, gave vent to his disapprobation in a half-stifled hiss. Probably it would have been wiser in the American to have allowed the free-born Britain to have capered in perfect silence, for the over zealous friends of Macready misconstrued both the intent and the extent of his indiscretion, and a howl went forth throughout the length and breadth of the land that 'Forrest had had the presumption to hiss Macready.'

"Our tragedian had been well received by crowded audiences at the Princess', but having been criticised, as he considered, unjustly, and by parties in the interest of Macready—notably Mr. Forster, of the *Examiner*—he had resolved neither to renew the engagement or to accept any others made before his unpleasantness with the English actor occurred. He was, when the writer met him, merely stopping in London with his wife, on a visit to her family, preparatory to a tour on the European continent. I had recently made a prolonged visit to Wales, and on my way towards London had indulged in a sort of pilgrimage on the footsteps of Owen Glendower, visiting many of the localities mentioned in Shakespeare's Henry IV. A description of these places interested Mr. Forrest deeply, as I found him to be well versed in the earlier dramatic literature, and most anxious to obtain all manner of books relating to the Elizabethan stage. After this casual meeting, Mr. Forrest exhibited towards me the greatest friendship, as the companionship of a brother American, with ample leisure on his hands, was an agreeable break in the monotony of a residence amid a community for which he entertained little respect, and which he was commencing almost to hate."

The attacks made upon Mr. Forrest by the English press were followed up here, in which the New York

Herald took the lead. The following article first appeared in this country in the *Herald*, while Mr. Forrest was playing in Liverpool, after a stormy engagement in London. It may be well to state, however, that he triumphed even there over his enemies, received high testimonials from the gentlemen of the press and the literary talent of the metropolis. We give the article as it appeared in the New York *Herald* and republished in *Scott's Weekly Paper*, of Philadelphia, with editorial remarks. The writer of this was interested in *Scott's Weekly Paper*, and used its columns in defending Mr. Forrest from his enemies:

MR. FORREST IN EUROPE.—ATTACKS OF THE ENGLISH PRESS. —A CORRUPTING INFLUENCE.—PALTRY COMPARISONS.

"'The Liverpool *Mercury* states that Mr. Edwin Forrest has taken his departure suddenly in the good ship Rochester. Mr. Forrest was advertised to take his farewell benefit at Liverpool, but did not do so. It is certain that he felt much disappointed at his reception on this, his last visit; but in reality he has no one but himself to blame. He engaged at a theatre not fitted for the representation —he played parts in which the public had seen him in other and better pieces—parts too in which that public had awarded the palm of superiority to Macready and Charles Kean. The only novelty he attempted was *Metamora*, and no talent could uphold such a drama as that. Had Mr. Forrest offered anything at once new and endurable, the public would not have deserted him. Many characters were suggested for him—Zanga, Bajazet, Octavian, Gambia, amid the rest—but he stuck to Macbeth, Lear, and one or two other parts, in which it was evident the public mind had been made up not to acknowledge him. The general opinion appeared to be, that on his physical abilities (not on his mental ones) he must rely. John Bull was prepared to receive him with open arms as a melodrama actor, not as a tragedian. We are informed that he will make a tour of the States, and then quit the stage forever. He is the first American actor, and his absence will create a void not speedily to be filled up.'

"The above article first appeared in this country in the New York *Herald*, and has since travelled the rounds of the American press, without note or comment. Our object in copying it, is to express astonishment at some of the assertions therein, and to say that it is with no little degree of surprise that we have noticed articles of a similar tenor copied into our papers, as if every word they contained were solemn truths.

"It was undoubtedly copied into our papers like that of many others, and taken as all such criticisms are, with a certain degree of allowance, nor were the comments of the press unfavorable to the American tragedian. It was well known here that a determined opposition was made against Mr. Forrest, and we were prepared for it.

"The Liverpool *Mercury* says Mr. Forrest appeared in parts 'in which that public had awarded the palm of superiority to Macready and Charles Kean.' Good gracious, Max—Will some one take this man away. This Liverpool *Mercury* man, we mean. Macready and Charles Kean! Really, if anything had been wanting to *prove* the pre-paid, well bought English press, we have it here. Charles Kean awarded the palm of superiority over Edwin Forrest! It is too ludicrous, yet it is but a repetition of the vile slang that has been hurled at Mr. Forrest since his appearance at the Princess', in London, some eighteen months ago.

"And what was the cause of all that violent opposition?

"Mr. Macready had been in this country, and although our toadying press bespattered him, and his acting, with fulsome praise, his trip was a failure—a lamentable failure—not from opposition by any one press in the country, but from the lack of merit. The automaton style of Mr. Macready pleased not; the genius—the fire—the originality—the pathos—the natural development of the passions—the soul-stirring, invigorating style of Forrest—*the* Kean style—was wanting, and mechanism was not relished—Mr. Macready's mannerism failed, while Mr. Forrest's genius triumphed.

"Mr. Forrest visited Europe.

"It is well known that he had scarcely made his appearance ere disapprobation was manifested—and we have Mr. N. P. Willis for authority, and he in this has not been denied or doubted—by persons who acknowledge that it was from no ill-will to Mr. Forrest, but *they were paid to hiss him.* Who paid them?

"The press was violent in its opposition. Why?

"Mr. Forrest refused to *buy* their praise, and stood, as he had done for twenty-five years previously, upon his individual *merit as an actor.* With the people he was successful; and the great force of his acting, and the rapturous applause that attended it, in King Lear, *compelled* the London press—the *Times* among them—to acknowledge they had never seen it equalled! And yet it is gravely stated in the above, that the 'palm of superiority had been awarded to Macready and Charles Kean in that very character.

"Talent is confined to no clime—it knows no locality, and the people of this country have been prolific in their homage to merit *from abroad*—seldom bestowing much upon that of home origin. Hence, the abuse of 'the first American actor' by the British press. We have not the courage to sustain talent of our own while we lavish adulations upon doubtful merit of other climes.

"'The characters of Zanga, Bajazet, Octavian, Gambia, etc., had been suggested *for* him,' says the Liverpool *Mercury*, 'but he would stick to Macbeth, Lear and one or two other parts.' Suggested for him, indeed. Probably, the *Mercury* man was grieved that Mr. Forrest stuck to those characters—particularly if he is so friendly to the other gentlemen—for *Mr. Forrest is the only living representative of the two characters named, with others of the Shakesperian caste.* This is placed beyond all doubt by the honest dramatic critics of all countries."

Many have confounded John Forster, of the *Examiner*, with John Foster, the celebrated Essayist and eloquent Baptist clergyman. He was a man of the purest heart, and of the most exalted intellect. He cultivated letters, for that enlarged the sphere of his usefulness, and taught him (to use his own words) "to live along the progression of sublime attainment."

John Forster, whom Mr. Macready "has the honor to call friend," was cast in a different mould.

CHAPTER XX.

FORREST HISSES MACREADY.—THE RIGHT OF DOING SO QUESTIONED.—COMBINATIONS IMPROPER.—ARE ACTORS COMPETENT CRITICS?—HAMLET'S INSANE ACTIONS.—FORREST VS. SNOBBISM IN GOTHAM.—THE RIGHTS OF HISSING AT THEATRES CONSIDERED.

IN the last chapter we spoke of Mr. Forrest's hissing Macready on the 2nd of March, 1846, while that gentleman was playing Hamlet at the Theatre Royal, Edinburg—whether from personal considerations or upon critical grounds, are questions a difference of opinion has never yet reconciled. At the time this incident occurred, we wrote the following article, which is the only one to which we believe Mr. Forrest ever made an exception; but that mattered little to us. We wrote as we thought then, and see no reason now to suppress the article in connection with these "Reminiscences." The following is an extract from the article:

"As we purpose to allude to some of the facts in relation to what are termed 'the Macready Riots,' as a preliminary to which we shall briefly state that on Forrest's visit to England in 1845, a regular organized band of ruffians were hired by some person or persons to hiss him off, while at the same time the press, under, it is said, the conduct of a few popular actors, made a decided attack upon him, in which criticism, courtesy and all the rights of hospitality were most outrageously abused. *An editor of one of these presses was a personal friend of Mr. Macready, of which he boasted in this country.*

* * * * * * *

"Mr. Forrest hissed Mr. Macready for introducing a fancy dance in 'Hamlet'—we should have hissed him for attempting to muzzle the press, but, as we are opposed to that system of criticism, we adopted the more legitimate mode—the *pen.*

"We now come to that portion of Mr. Forrest's life which we are reluctantly compelled to censure—and that is, the hissing of Mr. Macready at the time and place mentioned. The play was 'Hamlet.' Whatever cause, beyond the real one given, Mr. Forrest imagined or conceived he had, to insult a brother actor thus publicly, it displayed a passionate temper and that lack of courtesy due to those who are endeavoring to amuse and instruct their fellow-men. In the first place, an actor has no right to hiss; his position before the public is as its servant. As well might a member of Congress hiss a brother member because he does not pronounce a word right, or agree with the critic in opinions under discussion. Nor has any one individual a right to hiss an actor; if there be anything he does not like, he can retire; is the house to be disturbed because one man is not pleased? are five hundred persons to be debarred the pleasure they derive, because one is dissatisfied? No! nor is there anything to justify hissing, but palpable neglect, indecency and vulgarity; and even then, one man has no right to disturb five hundred, whose views and ideas of what constitutes morality, differ from his. When Mr. Forrest hissed Mr. Macready, he was, it is true, an auditor, and a brother actor. Mr. Macready's notion of Hamlet differed from Mr. Forrest's, and he hissed. What would Mr. Forrest have thought of Mr. Booth, if that gentleman hissed his Richard III.?

* * * * * * *

"Combinations have been formed by a few individuals to hiss an actor off the stage for personal reasons, and in almost every instance they have succeeded, simply because the audience did not exercise its right to put them out. Every star has some peculiar business on the stage, or new reading, at least, differing from others. Mr. Forrest has many, and what would he think of those who, to use his own words, 'have the right' to hiss, compel and force an actor to act, do, perform and read in accordance with their dictation? No! it is all wrong; the pen is the only weapon to be used in criticism; nor should the theatre become the arena for the display and exercise of that most delicate art.

"Dr. Johnson, in paper No. 25 of 'The Idler,' speaking upon this subject, uses the following strong and forcible language:—'I have always considered those combinations which are formed in the play-house, as acts of fraud or cruelty. He that applauds him who does not deserve praise, is endeavoring to deceive the public. He that hisses in malice or in sport is an oppressor and a robber.'

"Mr. Forrest, in his published letter defending his right to hiss, falls into several errors, which we most sincerely regret. In the first place, he says: 'Mr. Macready thought fit to introduce a fancy dance into his performance of Hamlet.' In the second place, he contends that 'a man can manifest his pleasure or displeasure after the recognized mode.' Thirdly, an actor, in his capacity as a spectator, has a right to hiss, because, 'from the nature of his studies, he is much more competent to judge of a theatrical performance than any *soi-disant* critic, who has never himself been an actor!'

"Having already shown the fallacy of such reasons, we now ask, what is the recognized mode alluded to? Who are to constitute themselves critics under the new system? No one individual, we contend, has the right to disturb the house; it must be two-thirds or none. The minority cannot put down the majority. Hence there are no recognized modes but those of the *pen* and the *press*. For one man to hiss an actor is a direct insult, not only to him but to the audience.

"The next point is, are actors, from the nature of their studies, competent to be critics? We contend they are not. They are actors, and invariably have notions peculiarly their own; and from the very 'nature of their studies,' are incapable of judging or correcting the errors of their brother artists. It is true, an actor will criticise; but are his criticisms just? Are not actors, like poets, hemmed in by an atmosphere of their own—each thinking that he excels, and forming ideas and opinions directly opposite to those of the author himself, as is frequently the case? The critic's art is above that of the actor. The one identifies himself with the image prepared for him, and he presents himself before us, for our approval or censure. The question is, whether the actor or the audience should be the judge. If the actor, then the critic's art ceases at once. When a writer in London criticised Kemble's dress in Othello, that actor admitted its truth, and gave as a reason, that if he were to dress the character as the authority called for, it would be too weighty for him; and hence the error even to this day. Who was right here—the actor or the critic? This critic did not correct Kemble while on the stage; on the contrary, he adopted the only legitimate mode, and that was, and is, the pen. Shakespeare, an actor and author, never presumed to criticise. He created subjects for the critic's pen. 'Addison wrote and Addison criticised,' is a well-known phrase. So did Dr. Johnson. But neither of these great men were actors. In fact, to the credit of the stage be it said, no one has ever presumed to set himself up as a censor over his brother actors.

"We seldom hear one actor speak well of another; the same with authors and painters. They are all superlative in their own estimation, and yet we are told, 'from the nature of their studies, they are the best critics.' The fact is, an actor may deem himself honored when the critic notices him. Criticism was, in the golden days of the drama, considered the highest order of writing; and when Addison wrote and Johnson criticised, the actor would have cut a bad figure in entering the list against such odds. Criticism and the rules which govern it are, we contend, incompatible with the actor's position as well as his studies.

"'True criticism,' says Blair, 'is the application of taste and good sense to the several fine arts. The object which it proposes is, to distinguish what is beautiful and what is faulty in every performance; from particular instances to ascend in general principles; and so to form rules or conclusions concerning the several kinds of beauty in works of genius. Criticism is, therefore, above all the arts.'"

We think an actor is excusable in introducing by action any ridiculous folly in the scene of what Forrest called a fancy dance. Hamlet being mad, the audience, when the fit is on him, is prepared for almost any sort of outbreak. Our readers, however, must not take our view of this particular phase in Hamlet's insanity from the acting copy. The following, from the folio of 1623, will show Hamlet's mental condition in a very different light from the text of the modern acting copy:

> *King.*—" Give me some light. Away!
> *All.*—Lights—lights—lights!
> [*Exeunt all but Hamlet and Horatio.*]
> *Ham.*—Why let the stricken deer go weep,
> The hart ungalled play;
> For some must watch, while some must sleep;
> Thus runs the world away.
> Would not this, sir, and a forest of feathers (if the rest of my fortunes turn Turk with me), with two provincial roses on my razed shoes, get me a fellowship in a cry of players, sir?
> *Hor.*—Half a share.
> *Ham.*—A whole one, I,
> For thou dost know, O Damon, dear!
> This realm dismantled was
> Of Jove himself; and now reigns here
> A very—very—paiock!"

The word peacock was introduced by Pope; nor are we enabled to discover by the oldest authorities why in the old quartos, as well as in the folio of 1623, it is written paiocke, and in one of the quartos paioc, which the folio of 1632 changes to pajock. If Shakespeare intended to apply the word to Hamlet, or to the King of Denmark, as being a very—very "peacock," it is equally difficult to determine; but there it is, and we take it as an evidence of Hamlet's insanity. Shakespeare may have borrowed the idea from Pliny, who in speaking of this "proud and conceited fowl," says:

"The peacock farre surpasseth all the rest of this kind, as well as for beautie, as also for wit and understanding that he hath; but principally for the pride and glorie that hee taketh in himselfe. For perceiving at any time that he is praised, and well liked, he spreadeth his tail around, shewing and setting out his colors to the most, which shine againe like precious stones."

Hamlet in this scene acts in such a manner as to induce him to ask Horatio if he would not make a good actor, to which his friend readily assents; hence the words, "forest of feathers," etc. Horatio, to humor Hamlet in his "peacock" conceit, as he struts about the stage, uttering unmeaning words, says: "You would be entitled to half a share," which was the pay of a second-rate actor. Hamlet claims a higher rank, and exclaims: "A whole one."

In connection with these disjointed words, a fancy dance we do not think would be out of place. At least we do not consider it sufficient cause for public censure, coming as it did in a *hiss*. The action might elicit criticism, which even then would be simply a difence of opinion.

On one occasion when Mr. Macready enacted Hamlet here, he assumed in this scene the manners of a silly youth, tossed his head right and left, and skipped back and forth across the stage five or six times.

Actors, in Shakespeare's time, had no salaries as now. The receipts were divided into shares, of which the proprietors of the theatres, or "house-keepers," as they were called, had some; and each actor had one or more shares, or parts of a share, according to his rank or interest. In 1608, the Blackfriars Theatre was held by eleven members of the company, on twenty shares, of which Shakespeare owned four, while some others had but a half share each.

It was certainly a great oversight in Shakespeare to introduce, in the tragedy of Hamlet, incidents and illusions occurring some four hundred years after the supposed transactions upon which the play was founded. The history of Hamlet, or Hamleth, is found in the Danish historian, Saxo-Gramaticus, who died about 1204. The works of this historian are in Latin, and in Shakespeare's time had not been translated into any modern language. Shakespeare, therefore, must have read the original. That Shakespeare adopted the same period of action as related by Saxo-Gramaticus, there can be no doubt; hence the passages alluded to as occurring in the seventeenth century, can only be set down as anachronisms, or merely thrown in as local hits, at actors and others of the period. Hamlet's advice to the players may be also quoted: "To split the ears of the groundlings," etc., could not apply to the stage in Denmark in the twelfth or thirteenth centuries.

THE RIGHT OF HISSING AT THEATRES.

The right of individuals to hiss in public places, seems to be but imperfectly understood. It has long since been decided, both here and in Europe, that a man has the right to hiss, and denounce publicly anything that is offensive to morals and the expression of sentiments tolerating murder, arson, and treason. As regards the right of hissing in a theatre, the very character of such exhibitions requires some potent power to keep both manager and actor within the bounds of decency.

Lord Mansfield, in the case of Mr. Macklin, stated that a British audience had a right to express their applause or disapprobation of plays and actors in the usual manner; but if it could be proved that any person or persons went night after night to the theatre for the purpose of preventing an actor exercising his profession, or to injure the manager or proprietors, such person or persons would not only be subject to an action at law, but might be indicted for the offence. Indeed, we can go back to the year 1629, when a company of French players, chiefly females, who had been expelled from their own country for indecent exhibitions, appeared at Blackfriars, London; they were hissed, hooted, and pippin-pelted from the stage. If we had been as moral in the year 1819, when the French ballet company appeared here and shocked modesty with their short skirts and low-neck dresses, our stage would have been far more respectable than it ever has been since.

In Prynni's Histriomastix, 1634, is inserted a marginal note in these words: "Some Frenchwomen, or monsters rather, in Michaelmas term, 1629, attempted to act a French play at the Blackfriars play-house, an impudent, shameful, unwomanish, graceless, if not more than wantonish, attempt." Another account says: "Furthermore you should know that last daye, certaine vagrant French players, who had beene expelled from their owne countrey, and those women did attempt thereby, giving just offence to all virtuous and well-disposed persons in this town, to act a certain lascivious and unchaste comedye in the French tongue, at the Blackfrairs. Glad I am to saye they were hissed, hooted, and pippin-pelted from the stage, etc."

In the old English theatres, as well as in those of our own, the audience expressed its disapprobation or approbation in much the same manner as they do now, by clapping of hands, exclamations, hisses, groans, and by various imitations, such as that of cats, dogs, cocks, etc. Marston, in the introduction to his "What You

Like," 1607, says: "Monsieur Snuff,* Monsieur Mew, and Cavaliere Blirt, are three of the most to be-feared auditors;" and farther on he asks if the poet's resolve shall be "struck through with the blirt of a goose breath?" So that the technical phrase of "treating an actor with goose" was understood at a very early period of our stage history. Indeed, the audience in the year 1654 had the complete control of the theatres. Edmund Gayton, in his "Festivous Notes on Don Quixote," says: "I have known upon one of these festivals, but especially at Shrovetide, when the players have been appointed, notwithstanding their bills to the contrary, to act what the major part of the company had a mind to; sometimes 'Tamerlane,' sometimes 'Jugurth,' sometimes the 'Jew of Malta,' and sometimes parts of all these; and at last, none of the three taking, they were forced to undress and put off their tragic habits, and conclude the day with the 'Merry Milkmaids.'"

A very commendable instance of the audience censuring improprieties of an author, and the author acquiescing and altering them, is to be seen in a note to the prologue to "Sir John Cockle at Court," by Dodsley. In the prologue are these two lines:

"Small faults we hope with candor you'll excuse,
Nor harshly treat a self-convicted muse."

These two lines were added after the first night's per-

* The use of tobacco and snuff was oftentimes very offensive to the actor, the consumption of which on the stage is mentioned by innumerable authorities; but it should seem from a line in the epigams of Sir John Davies and Christopher Madon, printed 1598, that at that period it was a service of some danger, and generally objected;

"He dares to take tobacco on the stage."

In 1638, women smoked tobacco in the theatre as well as men.

formance, and the author thanked "the town" for so judiciously correcting the abuses. Collier, p. 271, says: "The duties incumbent upon the frequenters of theatres are, undoubtedly, great, since they are, in part, the patrons and support of the theatre, and are in a great measure those who give the law to its professors, by the applause and censure and attendance which they give to particular exhibitions and performers. If the amusement be vicious, the company are all accessory to the mischief of the place; for, were there no audience, we should have no action."

An audience constitutes itself the judge in deciding upon the question of the right to "hiss in a theatre," from the fact that we have no censorship over plays, or laws prohibiting indecent exhibitions, or if we have they are not enforced. An actor who comes on the stage in a state of intoxication insults the audience; the manager in permitting it, alike insults it. There is but one way to resent this insult, and that is to hiss him off the stage. Or, if an actor so far forgets himself as to use vulgar or indecent language, he subjects himself to this mode of expressing the disapprobation of the persons present. Again, if a manager should engage a police officer to remove the individual who so expresses his objections to indecency, he sustains the actor in his vulgarity, or the drunkard in his beastiality.

CHAPTER XXI.

RICHARD III.—COLLEY CIBBER'S VERSION.—FIRST RICHARD IN AMERICA. —ACTORS CELEBRATED IN THE PART.—FORREST'S RICHARD, NOT SHAKESPEARE'S.—HE ADHERES TO HISTORY.—QUESTION OF DRESS.

IN our last chapter we left Mr. Forrest in England. As we shall not bring him on the stage again until the year 1849, we will fill up the interval with personal and dramatic matters which we think will be equally interesting to our readers. In this part we will speak of

MR. FORREST'S RICHARD III.,

which met with but little favor from the press. Some account of this great and popular tragedy in connection with Mr. Forrest's rendition of the character, may not be considered out of place in these Reminiscences.

In the commencement of this drama, which, in the original title, is stated to be "The Life and Death of Richard III.," the historical action is somewhat confused, since it opens with George, Duke of Clarence, being committed to the tower, in the beginning of 1478; whilst the second scene brings in the funeral of Henry VI., who is commonly reported to have been murdered, May 23rd, 1471. It closes with the death of Richard, in the battle of Bosworth Field, August 22nd, 1485; and thus it may be said to comprise the space of fourteen years. The scene is laid in London and various parts of England.

There seems to have been several dramas and other pieces written upon this point of history before Shakespeare produced his tragedy, but he does not appear to have used any of them. Mr. Boswell supposed, however, that an "Interlude of Richard III., with the death of Edward IV., the smothering of the two princes, the end of Shore's wife, and the contention of the Houses of Lancaster and York," published in 1594, had so great a resemblance to this play, that the author must have seen it before he composed his own. It is, notwithstanding, one of the worst of the ancient Interludes, and has but few traces of likeness.

Richard III. was probably written in 1593 or 1594; it appears entered at Stationers' Hall, October 20th, 1597. In 1700, Colley Cibber's alteration of this tragedy was produced at Drury Lane, from which the licenser obliterated the whole of the first act, observing that the distresses and murder of Henry VI. would too much remind weak persons of James II., then in exile at St. Germains. It was thus performed for several years, and was always very popular and successful, which Stevens attributes partly to Cibber's revision. The modern adaptation of Richard was made by John P. Kemble from both Shakespeare and Cibber, and was published by him as acted at Covent Garden in 1810. This version is remarkably feeble; and when Garrick produced Colley Cibber's version at Goodman's Fields, his utterance of the line—"Off with his head; so much for Buckingham," drew down thunders of applause, and these words first set the seal on Garrick's popularity, and of course sustained Cibber's version. The introduction of cannon and fire-arms startled old stagers, and unwise critics shouted out "anachronism!" Not so. The battle of Bosworth Field was fought on the 22nd of August, 1485. Great guns were invented in 1330: used by the Moors at the siege of Algeciras, in Spain, in 1344; used at the battle of Cressy, in 1346, when Edward had four pieces of cannon, which gained him the battle. They were used at the siege of Calais, in 1347; in Denmark, 1354; at sea, by Venice against Genoa, 1377. First used in England, at the siege of Berwick, 1405; first used in Spain, 1406.

Colley Cibber's version has been criticised and condemned ever since its introduction on the stage. It was considered by Shakesperian scholars as a desecration, and yet it has maintained a place upon the stage ever since. Shakespeare's Richard, as written, would not be acknowledged now by play-goers. Garrick, Mossop, Kemble, Cooke, Cooper, Kean, and Forrest have played Garrick's version, and this fact gives its authority. A writer says: "Great as these names are, that of Shakespeare is surely well worth a myriad of them." And yet, with all these criticisms and reflections on the Richard of Cibber, actors all agree that if he had only added to the original the two lines which at all times elicit applause, he would have merited a higher compliment than he has for a general revision of it. The lines are these:

"Off with his head; so much for Buckingham;"

and

"Richard is himself again."

That our readers may appreciate Cibber's alterations and additions, we add the following:

"The aspiring youth that fired the Ephesian dome,
Outlives in fame the pious fool that raised it."
ACT III. SCENE 1.

"——Hark, from the tents,
The armorers accomplishing the knights,
With clink of hammers closing rivets up,
Give dreadful note of preparation.

"I've lately had two spiders
Crawling upon my startled hopes—
Now, tho' thy friendly hand has brushed 'em from me,
Yet still they crawl offensive to my eyes;
I would have some kind friend to tread upon 'em."
ACT IV. SCENE 3.*

THOMAS KEAN—THE FIRST RICHARD III. IN AMERICA.

This gentleman was a man of talent. Little, however, is known of his history. He arrived in Philadelphia from the West Indies, in 1747–8, and played with the "American Amateur Company" in 1748–9, in a temporary building in what was known as "Little Dock Street." In connection with a Mr. Murray, he made arrangements to open a theatre in New York. There was no theatre at that time in that city. Their arrival was thus announced in the "Gazette" of February, 20th, 1749:

"Last week arrived here a company of comedians from Philadelphia, who, we hear, have taken a convenient room for their purpose in one of the buildings lately belonging to the Hon. Rip Van Dam, deceased, in Nassau Street, where they intend to perform as long as the season lasts, provided they meet with suitable encouragement."

The announcement of the managers was as follows:

* William Hazlett, however, seems to have had a very different opinion of Colley Cibber's version, for, speaking of it, he says: "The manner in which Shakespeare's plays have been generally altered, or rather mangled by modern mechanists, is a disgrace to the English stage. The patchwork 'Richard III.' which is acted under the sanction of his name, and which was manufactured by Cibber, is a striking example of this remark."

By his Excellency's permission, at the theatre, in Nassau Street.
On MONDAY, the 5th day of March (1750),
will be presented the Historical Play of
KING RICHARD III.,
wrote originally by Shakespeare, and altered by Colley Cibber, Esq.
Pit, 5 shillings. Gallery, 3 shillings.

This was the first representation of Richard III. on record in the Colonies. Thomas Kean was the Richard. As this was the first acknowledged theatrical company in the country, we give the names of its members as far as they could be found in the play-bills of the day: Kean, Tremaine, Murray, Woodham, Iago, Scott, Leigh, Smith, Moore, Marks, Master Murray, Miss Osborne, Miss Nancy George, Mrs. Taylor, Mrs. Osborne, Mrs. Leigh, and Mrs. Davis.

The most celebrated Richard's in this country since Hallam's advent, were Cooper, Booth, Fennell, Cooke, Kean and Edwin Forrest. All these great actors, except Mr. Forrest, adhered to traditionary authority for portraying the character; the latter gave us a version of his own. He represented the crook-backed tyrant somewhat different from the general idea we have of his personal appearance, but he gave us Richard as he contended was the proper view of the character, as towering and lofty, equally impetuous and commanding; haughty, violent and subtle; bold and treacherous; confident in his strength as well as in his cunning; raised by high birth and higher by his genius and his crimes; a royal usurper, a princely hypocrite—a tyrant and a murderer of the house of Plantagenet. Is an actor not justified in fashioning his appearance to suit the character? Although deformed, would not this restless and sanguinary Richard, conscious of his strength of will—his power of intellect—his daring courage—his elevated station—lessen that deformity by the same arts he uses to disguise his murderous purposes? Mr. Forrest's Richard was a great conception, and powerful in delineation; he seemed the first tempter approaching his prey, clothed with all the attributes of the basilisk to charm and allure. Shakespeare has been accused of exaggerating the personal appearance of Richard, as well as that of his character. It will be observed, however, that the only one who descants upon his personal defects is Richard himself; hence the actor may infer that he distorts his person by viewing it through a mental glass, thus magnifying each and every defect.

Richard III. and the Duke of Buckingham were both remarkable for their love of finery. This love of dress on the part of Richard did not develop itself until the effect of his extraordinary scene with Lady Anne became apparent; it was then he exclaimed:

"My dukedom to a beggarly denier,
I do *mistake* my person all this while;
Upon my life, *she finds*, although I cannot,
Myself to be a marvellous proper man;
I'll be at charges for a looking-glass,
And entertain a score or two of tailors,
To study fashion to adorn my body;
Since I am crept in favor with myself,
I will maintain it with some little cost," etc.

Why may we not infer that when Richard speaks of himself as being deformed and unfinished, and that the dogs barked at him as he passed along the streets, he it is, and not Shakespeare, who magnifies his deformities? He mentally conjures up these defects, and contrasting his person with those who compose his brother's court, falls into a state of inquietude, and rails at nature for sending him into—"this breathing world scarce half made up." Such, it is true, Shakespeare fashions his mind, and puts words into his mouth equally express-ive; but does not the interview with Lady Anne change this "fashion" of his mind and induce him to engage a score or two of tailors to "study fashions to adorn" his body?

Mr. Forrest took this view of Richard, and conveyed the idea of his deformity more by words than the presentation of an actual picture. If the other characters in the tragedy looked upon Richard as one at whom the very dogs barked, or that Shakespeare intended him to represent, stronger allusions would have been made to his personal appearance throughout the play. [*See Sir Thomas Moore's* "Relation of Richard," *and also* "Fuller's Church History."]

Mr. Forrest's portrait of Richard was taken from a copy of the original, as lithographed for the fifth volume of the "Parton Letters"—this being historical, and taken in connection with the flattering description of the old Countess of Desmond, who had danced with him when he was Duke of Gloster, and is stated to have declared that he was the handsomest man in the room except his brother, King Edward VI.

We called Mr. Forrest's attention to the portrait of Richard, as drawn by Shakespeare, and it was from this he should fashion his person; indeed, the very language required it. "Your Richard," we observed, "will never be popular if you insist upon representing him in the light the Countess of Desmond places him."

"But her description, and that of Sir Thomas Moore, are historical."

"True; but it is not Shakespeare. Kean made him a 'painted devil.' The usurper considered his deformity as a neglect of nature, and supposes himself justified in taking revenge on the human society from which he is excluded by his 'mis-shapen trunk.' The difference between Kean and yourself is, that while he makes him

> "'Deformed, unfinished, sent before my time
> Into this breathing world, scarce half made up,
> And that so lamely and unfashionable,
> That dogs bark at me as I halt by them,'

you make up a very proper man."

"True; yet, if tradition had not thrown around the character these objectionable features, would not my version be more acceptable to the audience?"

"No, for tradition has given to the stage a Richard; you must trace it back to Shakespeare, even to the first representative under the eye of the immortal author himself. You cannot depart from this. Had Kean, Booth, and Cooper changed this traditionary picture, we question if Richard III. would be as popular as it is now. It is the character that renders it great; take that away, and what is left?"

"This, I admit, is a strong argument, but still I cannot so distort Richard."

"Then, let me advise you to present him in the two pictures, one historical, the other Shakespeare."

"How so?"

"You make him history from the first to the last. Why not make him Shakespeare up to the wooing of Lady Anne? He is here in all his deformity, for she says:

> "'Blush, blush, thou lump of foul deformity.'

These words will not apply to your Richard, but to that of Shakespeare's. Still, the lady listens to his vows, and is won by a tongue that can wheedle the devil."

"Well, what then?"

"Why, after this, follow history. Carry out the words of Richard; change your dress, and appear 'a very proper man, as fashioned by a score of tailors.'"

Forrest laughed outright, and admitted the philosophy, if he did not the correctness of our criticism.

Apart from Mr. Forrest's conception of the character of Richard, it was a masterly performance, and if he could have impressed his audience with the same idea he had of it, we should have had an American actor to claim the honor of being the best that ever trod the stage. As it is, the Richard of Kean, and of Booth, overshadows that of Edwin Forrest's.

CHAPTER XXII.

MACBETH.—NEW READINGS.—CRITICISMS. — DIVERSITY OF OPINION ABOUT CERTAIN PASSAGES.—ENGLISH NOTICE OF FORREST'S MACBETH.—FORREST ELATED. —WRITES AN INJUDICIOUS LETTER HOME. — YOUTH AN EXCUSE.

PROPRIETY of fiction, solemnity, grandeur, and variety of action, are the chief features of this sublime tragedy, which has been pronounced in the Theatre, "the highest of all dramatic enjoyments." As it formed an important feature in Mr. Forrest's *repertorie* of plays, and, indeed, in that of all other great actors, a few historic facts connected with it may not be out of place in these Reminiscences.

MACBETH.

The progress of the action of this play is fearfully rapid, and seems to include but a few days; though its precise historical duration cannot be ascertained. Boethus and Buchanan state that Duncan was murdered by his cousin-german, Macbeth, about A. D. 1040 or 1045; and that the latter was slain by Macbeth in A. D. 1057 or 1061.

The original narrative of these events is contained in the Scotorium Historiæ, of Hector Boethus; whence it was translated into Scotch by John Bellenden, and afterwards into English by Raphael Hollinshed, from whose chronicle Shakespeare closely copied. Malone placed the composition of the drama in 1606; and it has been regarded as the medium of dexterous and graceful flattery to James I., who was the issue of Banquo, and first united the three kingdoms of Britain; at the same time that the play adopted his well known notions on the subject of Demonology. Shakespeare derived much of his incantations from a manuscript tragic comedy, without date, by Thomas Middleton, called The Witch. We give the following extracts from The Witch; and it will appear very evident that Shakespeare had read the piece, and made considerable use of it.

Hecate.—(*Ascending with the spirit.*)
"Now I go, now I fly,
Malkin my sweet spirit and I.
Oh! what a dainty pleasure 'tis
To ride in the air,
Where the moon shines fair," etc.

* * * *

A charm song—(The witches going about the cauldron.)

"Black spirits and white, red spirits and gray:
Mingle, mingle, mingle; you that mingle may."

* * * * *

1st Witch.—"Here's the blood of a bat;
Hecate.—Put in that; oh! put in that.
2d Witch.—Here's a libbard's bane;
Hecate.—Put in again.
1st Witch.—The juice of toad; the oil of adder;
2d Witch.—Those will make the yonker madder," etc.

In 1674, William Davenant altered the tragedy of Macbeth, introduced songs and the celebrated music of Matthew Locke. It was brought out in great splendor at the Duke's, Dorset Garden.

The modern revival was produced at Drury Lane in 1789, by John P. Kemble, and published in 1803, as performed at Covent Garden. The part of Macbeth was one of this great actor's most admirable efforts, as it had also been of Garrick's. Mrs. Siddons played the character of Lady Macbeth on the 2nd of February, 1785; previous to which Mrs. Pritchard was considered by far the most perfect Lady Macbeth of the age.

Macbeth was first performed in this country by Hallam's company, March 3rd, 1768; Macbeth, Mr. Hallam, Lady Macbeth, Mrs. Douglass.

Mr. Thomas A. Cooper, George Frederick Cooke, Edmund Kean, Lucius Junius Booth and E. L. Davenport, have distinguished themselves in the character of Macbeth. But public opinion, both in Europe and America has, we believe, decided that Mr. Edwin Forrest's Macbeth is on the stage record given as only equalled by that of Garrick's. Mr. Macready's style of acting, although termed classical, was too cold and mechanical for the American people, and his delineations, or rather portraitures of the heroes of Shakespeare's plays, were deficient in the skill and management of the *chiaro-scuro*. His pictures generally were ungraceful—not from any deficiency on his part—but a habit he had of attudinizing on mechanical rather than natural principles.

Cooper, Fennel, and Edwin Forrest, relied more for effect on their assuming the character than in the endeavor to fashion the character to suit themselves. Thus, in their impersonations of Roman characters, they stood before us the panoplied spirits of the mighty dead.

> "Name to me yon Archen chief for bulk
> Conspicuous and for port. Taller indeed
> I may perceive than he, but with these eyes
> *Saw never yet such dignity and grace.*"

Macbeth is one of the noblest creations of Shakespeare, and yet it was not one of Mr. Forrest's parts. It was at our suggestion he played it on one or more occasions, giving a reason for leaving it out of his *role* that he could not find a Lady Macbeth to aid him in rendering it in an effective manner. "You may remember," said he, one day, "an article you wrote on the character of Macbeth, wherein you suggested a new business. I called the attention of Miss Wemyss (Mrs. Duffield) to the point, and stated that I endeavored on several occasions to have the passage given as you suggested." We annex the following extract from the article to which Mr. Forrest referred:

"The character of Lady Macbeth has been the theme of many able criticisms. Mrs. Siddons has clearly analyzed it, and Mrs. Jamieson in her characteristics of Shakespeare's female characters, most learnedly discusses the various questions relative to the sinfulness and crimes of this vile specimen of the most vicious of her sex. Lady Macbeth is not merely a fiend—one whose soul has lost its divine attribute, and whose purposes are murderous and bloody—but she is a woman of powerful intellect, and hence the influence she exercises over her husband. A writer speaking of her says: 'She overpowers Macbeth's mind and beats down his doubts and fears—not by superior talent, but by violence of will, by intensity of purpose. She does not even hear the whispers of conscience. They are drowned in the whirlwind of her own thoughts. She has intellectually the terrible beauty of the Medusa of classic art.'

"Holinshead, speaking of Lady Macbeth, describes her 'As burning with unquenchable desire to be a Queen.'

"Schlegel, the accomplished German lecturer on the plays of Shakespeare, says: 'The wife of Macbeth conjured him not to let the opportunity slip of murdering the King. She urges him on with fiery eloquence, which has all the sophisms at command that serve to throw a false grandeur over crime.

* * * * * * * *

"Macbeth following immediately the receipt of the letter he had written to his wife announcing his arrival, is received by her with these words:

> "'Great Glamis! worthy Cawdor!
> Greater than both by the all hail hereafter.'

"To which Macbeth answers:

> "'My dearest love, Duncan comes here to-night.'

"How does Lady Macbeth receive this intelligence from her lord? In the same tone, but with a decided marked emphasis, with the eyes fixed on those of her husband, as if to read his inmost soul, she exclaims:

> "'And when goes hence?'

"Macbeth sees not the deep hellish glance—feels not the presence of a demon—'top full of direst cruelty'—the dream of murder, the vision raised by the Weird Sisters—all have passed from his mind, and he naturally replies, 'to-morrow.' At that moment he meets the eye of his wife—like an electric shock, the infernal spark acts upon his already overcharged brain—he starts, gazes as if upon the fabled basilisk, and mutters in fear and dread, as if in presence of a supernatural being,

"'As he purposes.'

"Here it is they fully understand each other; thoughts and feelings are read and exchanged—he looks through the windows of her mind into her very soul, and the dim chambers of his brain, the charnel house of bad thoughts are lit up with hellish fires; he gazes upon his evil genius —she speaks:

"'O, never
Shall sun that morrow see!'

"The author here, who never loses sight of nature and truth, fully explains why Lady Macbeth gives her free thoughts speech—

"'Your face, my Thane, is a book, where men
May read strange matters. To beguile the time,
Look like the time—bear welcome in your eye,
Your hand, your tongue; look like the innocent flower,
But be a serpent under it. He that is coming
Must be provided for—and you shall put
This night's great business into my despatch,' etc.

"Lady Macbeth here takes the business at once in hand, for why? because his nature

"'Is too full of the milk of human kindness,
To catch the nearest way.'"

Mr. Forrest's Macbeth was a most finished performance—it was grand in conception, and Shakesperian throughout. It is true, much of the real action of the play falls upon the actress, and the audience in many scenes entirely loses sight of Macbeth, in the interest they take in the bloody queen. The moment an actor finds the leading actress of a company to be considered a great Lady Macbeth, that moment he leaves Macbeth out from his *role*. We do not say Mr. Forrest displayed any such selfishness; on the contrary, he gave as a reason that generally the Lady

Macbeth's were very inferior. He, however, spoke highly of Mrs. J. W. Wallack and Mrs. Duffield in connection with the character.

Mr. Forrest's Macbeth was also a great part before he left for England; and although his conception of the character did not assimilate with our own, yet it made, as it did everywhere, a most powerful impression. We annex another extract from a London paper:

"Mr. Forrest's Macbeth was a masterly portraiture of the irresolute, ambitious and guilty Thane; too elaborate, perhaps, and overworked for some who take the simplicity of nature for their standard of excellence; yet distinguished by those exquisite touches which mediocrity can never reach, and which it is the province of genius only to impart. In many instances, Mr. Forrest differed from the accustomed reading with judicious effect, in others he was not so happy. The delivery of his share of the dialogue in a whisper, after the murder was committed, produced a marked effect upon the auditory, and was a bold and original thought, and skilfully carried into execution."

Mr. Forrest threw around his impersonation of this character, an air of wild, startling romance, which we consider as perfectly just, for the whole play of Macbeth, with its witches, its ghosts, and its music, is a melo-dramatic play, and as such was rendered by Mr. Forrest.

It may be noticed that Mr. Forrest, like Macready, did not, in the commencement of a play, draw largely upon his powers, great as they were. In Othello, Damon and Virginius, it was his habit to commence with a low voice and with a minimum of action. He allowed the passion of the piece to lead him on, circumstance by circumstance, until he reached, what, like Milton, he might call

"The height of his great argument."

If, in Lear there is a more immediate development of power, it is because Shakespeare's creation rendered it necessary in that case. In the character of Macbeth, we have an especial example of the actor's keeping himself up for the greater scenes; every moment in the play adds to the causes of his excitement, and draws out the passion in greater dignity and grandeur. When Macbeth first meets the witches the thought of evil has not crossed his mind—ambition has not entered it—and crime has been undreamed of. But their prophecies startle him—and while his mind is thus in the commencement of its feverish anticipations, there comes the fulfilment of one prophecy, for Rosse hails him Thane of Cawdor—an accession of dignity which the weird sisters had just forwarned him of. Then commences the swell of ambition, and step by step it is consummated; as the river, small at its source, is swelling to a mighty flood, by the accession of auxiliary streams, until it reach the mighty ocean.

We have always objected to Mr. Forrest's reading this passage thus:

> "If it were done, when 'tis done, then 'twere well
> It were done quickly, if the assassination
> Could trammel up the consequence, and catch,
> With his surcease success."

The old reading merely implies that if the deed is to be committed, the sooner the better. Mr. Forrest brought out a new and fuller meaning; that the deed (as elevating him to empire) would be well if it were done; and that if the murder could ensure success to his aims, it should be quickly done. The doubt is, not so much whether Duncan should be removed, as whether his removal would effect Macbeth's purpose of usurpation, Duncan's son being yet alive.

In our humble opinion the passage should be read thus:

> "If it were done, when 't is done, then 't were well
> It were done quickly. If the assassination
> Could trammel up the consequence, and catch,
> With his surcease, success; that but *this blow*
> Might be the be-all and the end-all *here*,
> BUT *here* upon this bank and shoal of time—
> We'd *jump the life* TO COME."

The meaning in other phrase is this. 'T were well it were done quickly, if, when 't is done, it were *done*, or at an end. If the assassination at the same moment that it ends Duncan's life, would ensure success—if the crown could be enjoyed, Macbeth would stand the chance of what might happen in the future state.

As this oft-mooted question possesses some degree of interest, from the fact that Mr. Forrest invariably read it as quoted above, it may be well to state here that he had high authority for its use. Writers, at least, dramatic ones, agree that there is what may be called "embarrassment in the language." Yet will it be found admirably suited to the character of Macbeth. Still ambiguity is not exactly a fault of Shakespeare.

> "It were done quickly (on the instant); if the assassination
> Could trammel up the consequence," etc.

sounds well; but does it not sound equally so to read it thus:

> ——"if the assassination
> Could trammel up the consequence, and catch
> With his surcease success; that but this blow," etc.

The dispute is simply on the application of terms. Macbeth begins the soliloquy in a measured tone: "If it were done"—*i. e.*, if the act of the murder were performed, even when Duncan was asleep, and was the final issue of the business—

> ——"then 't were well
> It were done quickly."

He then commenced, taking a new view of the matter:

> ——"If the assassination
> Could trammel up the consequence,"

—which implies merely the attainment of the object he aimed at, and which was conveyed in these words:

> ——"and catch
> With his surcease success"——

The question would here suggest itself, if there should not be a full period at the word "success," and the commencement of the next passage be looked upon as a new idea which strikes Macbeth at the moment, as thus:

> ——"that but this blow
> Might be the be-all, and the end-all here;"

and that he would run no risk as to futurity? Worldly ambition is the first cause of this strange soliloquy, and fear of what comes after death the second. He grows still more nervous the further he argues the matter, and finally concludes to

> ——"proceed no further in this business."

Dr. Jonson proposed an emendation of "its surcease," instead of "his." Seymour, in his notes on Shakespeare, says:—"'His' would wipe out a capital beauty in this speech. Macbeth enters, ruminating upon an action he is about to commit, and now for the first time discloses it; imperfectly, however, by the use of 'his,' instead of the substantive to which in his mind it has reference; and of 'surcease' instead of a word of more open meaning.

There are many passages in the play of Macbeth which have afforded food for criticism, time out or mind, not one of them deserving the time and attention devoted to them. Shakespeare has given us a standard, and as these very passages are given in the folio of 1623 properly, and it is to be presumed correctly punctuated, we see no good reason why they should be changed to suit different notions. To some of these we will allude. Mr. Forrest was a stickler to the text of Shakespeare, but he not unfrequently, unintentionally, we know, deviated somewhat from the original. We called his attention to his reading of the following passage, as a direct deviation from the text. Macbeth, addressing the ghost, says:

"Hence! horrible! shadow!
Unreal! mockery! hence!"

Contrast this with the text, and the general manner of reading it:

"Hence horrible shadow!
Unreal mockery, hence!"

[Old edition.]

Mr. Cooper was at one period severely criticised for reading that well-known passage—"If trembling, I inhibit thee," thus: using *inhabit* instead of *inhibit*. The fact is, this is the original, and is to be found in old English folios. Pope changed it to *inhibit*, as was said, through his ignorance of old English literature. The true and literal meaning of the word is to be found in the following reading:

"If trembling I do *house* me then, protest me
The baby of a girl."

Macbeth wishes the Ghost distinctly to know that he will not seek a habitation, or stay at home, on the occasion of his challenge. Inhibit is a substitute word, and does not carry out the idea of the poet.

Pope did not show his ignorance of "old English literature," inasmuch as the definition given by good authorities to the true meaning and application of the words are nearly the same: "Inhabit"—to have, to hold, or keep himself, to dwell, to reside, to remain or abide. "Inhibit"—to hold, to restrain, to withhold, to prevent, to forbid. In an old edition of Macbeth the passage is given thus:

"Be alive againe
And dare me to the desert with thy sword
If trembling, I inhabit (inhibit) then protest mee
The baby of a girle."

There is another passage which a diversity of opinion has made popular, and is one which we think the actor is justified in reading either way. Mr. Forrest read it thus:

"Hang out our banners on the outward walls,
The cry is still they come."

Others again, read it thus:

"Hang out our banners. On the outward walls
The cry is, still 'they come.'"

It frequently struck us that the latter was the most correct: as banners on the outward walls of the old castles would not have been in accordance with Scottish customs; the banner was generally placed in the centre, or keep. Even in times of peace, this banner was often raised; but in time of war it was the signal of defiance. This being the case, and the "outward walls" lined with armed men, it may be read with equal dramatic effect, thus:

> "Hang out our banners:—
> On the outer wall the cry is still they come."

As those on the outward walls had much better opportunity of seeing the approach of the enemy than those inside, it is natural to suppose the cry would come from them.

With all our admiration of Mr. Forrest, his genius, judgment, and general character, we cannot pass over one period in his dramatic career without comment. He too readily fell a victim to the flattery of the English press, whose criticisms he extolled at the expense of our own. Not that alone, but he cast a reflection on the literary taste and character of the community at large. We contend, and with reason too, that there is as much theatrical talent in this country as there is in England, and that our critics are far more independent than those of that country. The history of the English drama furnishes us many instances of the mendacity of the press; and when it openly advocates the claims of *prostitutes* and *noble seducers*, it is not to be wondered at that the pure character of our drama and press becomes infected, when writers and actors from abroad come among us and exercise their influence here over both the press and the stage.

Having already spoken of the press, and its favorable notice during Mr. Forrest's first visit to Europe, we now introduce Mr. Forrest's letter. That he wrote it under the pleasing emotions created by his success, we do not question; and the remembrance of certain critiques published in this country, written by foreigners, were no doubt rankling in his breast. Every allowance must be made; but if the tenor of the letter be true, we can only regret the absence of a standard of criticism amongst us, and thank the American tragedian for enlightening us on the subject. We give the letter entire, that we may not be accused of publishing a garbled statement of it. We have italicized the passages alluded to:

"——My success in England has been very great. While the people evinced no great admiration of the Gladiator, they came in crowds to witness my personation of Othello, Lear and Macbeth. I commenced my engagement on the 17th of October, 1837, at Old Drury, and terminated it on the 19th of December, having acted in all thirty-two nights, and represented those three characters of Shakespeare twenty-four out of the thirty-two, namely, Othello nine times, Macbeth seven, and King Lear eight—this last having been repeated oftener by me than by any other actor on the London boards, in the same space of time, except Kean alone. This approbation of my Shakespeare parts gives me peculiar pleasure, as it refutes the opinions very confidently expressed by a certain *clique* at home, that I would fail in those characters before a London audience.

"But it is not only from my reception within the walls of the theatre that I have reason to be pleased with my English friends. I have received many grateful kindnesses in their hospitable homes, and in their intellectual circles have drank both instruction and delight. I suppose you saw in the newspapers that a dinner was given to me by the Garrick Club. Sergeant Talfourd presided, and made a very happy and complimentary speech, to which I replied. Charles Kemble and Mr. Macready were there. The latter gentleman has behaved in the handsomest manner to me. Before I arrived in England he had spoken of me in the most flattering terms, and on my arrival he embraced the earliest opportunity to call upon me, since which time he has extended to me many delicate courtesies and attentions, all showing the native kindness of his heart, and great refinement and good breeding. The dinner at the Garrick was attended by many of the most distinguished men.

"I feel under great obligations to Mr. Stephen Price, who has shown me not only the hospitalities which he knows so well how to perform, but many other attentions which have been of great service to me, and which, from his long experience in theatrical matters, he was more competent to render than any other person. He has done me the honor to present me with a copy of Shakespeare, and a Richard's sword, which were the property of Kean. Would that he could bestow upon me his *mantle* instead of his weapon! Mr. Charles Kemble, too, has tendered me, in the kindest manner, two swords, one of which belonged to his truly eminent brother, and the other to the great Talma, the theatrical idol of the *grand nation*.

"The London press, as you probably have noticed, have been divided concerning my professional merits; though as a good republican I ought to be satisfied, seeing I had an overwhelming majority on my side. There is a degree of dignity and critical precision and force in their articles generally (I speak of those against as well as for me, and others, also, of which my acting was not the subject), *that place them far above the newspaper criticisms of stage performances which we meet with in our country. Their comments always show one thing—that they have read and appreciated the writing of their chief dramatists; while with us there are many who would hardly know, were it not for the actors, that Shakespeare had ever existed. The audiences, too, have a quick and keen perception of the beauties of the drama. They seem, from the timeliness and proportion of their applause, to possess a previous knowledge of the text. They applaud warmly, but seasonably. They do not interrupt a passion, and oblige the actor to sustain it beyond the propriety of nature; but if he delineates it forcibly and truly, they reward him in the intervals of the dialogue.* Variations from the accustomed modes, though not in any palpable new readings, which, for the most part are bad readings, for there is generally but one mode positively correct, and that has not been left for us to discover; but slight changes in emphasis, tone, or action, delicate shadings and pencilings, are observed with singular and most gratifying quickness. *You find that your study of Shakespeare has not been thrown away; that your attempt to grasp the character in its 'gross and scope,' as well as in its detail, so as not merely to know how to speak what is written, but to preserve its truth and keeping in a new succession of incidents, could it be exposed to them—you find that this is seen and appreciated by the audience; and the evidence that they see and feel, is given with an emphasis and heartiness that make the theatre shake.*"

The only cause Mr. Forrest had to question the Shakesperian knowledge of his countrymen, was a few isolated criticisms upon his acting, which we can prove in every instance emanated from foreign pens.

CHAPTER XXIII.

HOME.—LETTERS TO THE AUTHOR.—FORREST THINKS OF HOME.—POSTAL MATTERS.—QUACK MEDICINE.—DEATH IN THE POT.—GLAD TO HEAR OF FORNEY'S RESIGNATION.—A LEAKY HOUSE.—BAD ACTORS.—CRITICISM.—JOSEPH McARDLE.

WE have numerous letters from Mr. Forrest. The selection here made is to show the character of the man as drawn from an epistolary point of view. In fact, a man's letters are the index to his mind. They show a love of home, of friends, and those who make up his household. They show that, although absent, the heart is still linked to home.

We often thought how appropriate the following lines of Goldsmith were to Mr. Forrest; for, although he had not those tender ties to bind him to home—ties of wife and children—still he had all the feeling which links man to his homestead. It will be seen from a few extracts we have made from his letters, that although there was no one to welcome him—no kindred, no one to hurry through the long corridors of his splendid mansion, and clasp him with fond arms—no one to cry out, "Papa's come!"—yet the home had a charm, its only charm—his library; this he called "the soul of his household." To him it was. We give the lines which we deemed so applicable to Mr. Forrest:

HOME.

"In all my wand'rings round this world of care
In all my grief—and God has given my share—
I still had hopes, my latest hours to crown,
Amid these humble bowers to lay me down;
To husband out life's taper at the close,
And keep the flame from wasting my repose;
I still had hopes, for pride attends me still,
Amidst the swains to show my book-learned skill,
Around my fire an evening group to draw,
And tell of all I felt and all I saw;
And as a hare, whom hounds and horns pursue,
Pants to the place from whence at first he flew,
I still had hopes, my long vexations past,
Here to return, *and die at home at last.*"

LETTERS.

"You have frequently promised me to make a collection of my letters (if in truth there be any which deserves a preference), and give them to the public. I have selected them accordingly."

During Mr. Forrest's absence from the city we had charge of his house, as stated in a former part of these reminiscences. A large willow tree stood immediately in the rear of his library, whose branches overshadowed the whole portion of his back building, keeping the sunlight (in which he so often basked) from penetrating into the room. We had this tree cut down, and in a letter describing the appearance of the library, the effect of the light upon each object within its range, and the cheerfulness prevailing in the absence of the dark shade from the tree, we received a letter from him, from which we make the following extract:

"CINCINNATI, OHIO, November 1st, 1871.

"JAMES REES, ESQ.:—*Dear Friend:*— * * * How much I wish I could have stood with you in the library on Sunday, amid the pleasant memories of that 'Soul of the Household.' Your vivid description of the scene made me sigh for home again. With many thanks, my dear friend, for kind and thoughtful offices in my behalf,

"I am yours truly,

"EDWIN FORREST.

"P. S.—Mr. McArdle's regards to you, and thanks you for kind remembrances of him."

"KANSAS CITY (Mo.), December 27th, 1871.

"DEAR FRIEND REES:—I received your letter without date, but postmarked the 13th inst., at Nashville (Tenn.), the other day, together with the letters you did me the favor to forward from my house. * * * I am glad to hear that everything is right about the homestead, and that the garden is improved by sunlight cheerfulness, since the shade trees were removed. I long to see it under the influence of bright skies again. I wrote and sent you a long letter from Galveston, Texas, which, as you have not acknowledged, I suppose has been purloined with other letters containing money which I sent to others. I will never again trust money in a post office letter."

The attention of the postal department about this time was called to the sad state of the post office in Texas, and to the loss of letters between certain points in that State and Northern cities. Several special agents were detailed to examine into the matter. The following gentlemen were selected from the department for that purpose: Major E. R. Petherbridge, Col. E. K. Shannetts, and Col. John Peddrick. The account given to the department being a "state affair," we can only allude to it here. Suffice however to say there have been fewer complaints made since. This is in part owing to the "Money Order System," which should be as universal as it is safe.

Mr. Forrest goes on to say in this letter:

"I herewith send you some newspaper notices, and would call your attention to the long article on Lear, from the New Orleans *Republican*, which is evidently written with unusual power, struggling through former prejudices. It is, however, well worth reading.

* * * * * *

"I had an awful attack of the gout while in Galveston, brought on by taking a medicine for the cure of that disease. The doctor told me it would reproduce all the excessive paroxysms of the gout, which I must bear, and so finally cure it. But my professional duties prevented me from going through the 'grinding mill,' until such time as I shall have leisure to endure and win. I have the utmost confidence in the curative qualities of the medicine, which is as pleasant to imbibe as a mint julep in 'fly time.' Only think of that; a physic which is at once delicious and curative. I will give it a fair trial next summer, if I live, etc.

"EDWIN FORREST."

All that we have to say here is, that the medicine, so delightful to the sense of taste, came very near sending the victim of its trials to an untimely grave. We do not think we ever saw a man nearer death's door than was Mr. Forrest after he had taken four bottles of this most vile nostrum. We use the word vile in its application to the nature, not the taste of the medicine. We suggested to Mr. Forrest, after he recovered from the attack, to put this label on the few remaining bottles left:

"There is death in the pot."—2 Kings, iv: 40.

We had enclosed to Mr. Forrest, during his engagement at Pittsburg, an article written by some *astute critic* of this city, on Mr. E. L. Davenport's Hamlet, wherein it was said that that gentleman read a line thus:

"Nymph, in thy *horizons*
Be all my sins remember'd."

Now, Mr. Davenport said nothing of the sort, but the sapient critic's ear depended more upon that organ than he did upon common sense and critical acumen. Even, however, if Mr. Davenport had used the word "horizons," instead of "orisons," he had authority for it, although the *critic* knew it not. Extract from Mr. Forrest's letter:

"ST. CHARLES HOTEL,
"PITTSBURG, January 28th, 1872.

"JAMES REES, ESQ:—*Dear Friend:*—I duly received your favor of 24th instant. Send you herein two checks; one of them for $128.50, due G. B. Moore, and the other, Frank W. Taylor, for $21.50, per bills rendered. Mr. Rubert's bill you will please pay when due from funds already in your hands, and also Mr. Ralston's account, as per your statement, $23.91.

"Mr. E. L. Davenport has authority for his saying in Hamlet "horizon," for it is given so in the 3d, 4th and 5th quartos, as well as in the 1st. The H is a cockney superfluity, etc."

"PITTSBURG, Pa., February 22nd, 1872.

"A friend of mine, Mr. James P. Barr, editor and proprietor of the *Daily Post*, in this city, will call to see the pictures, library, etc., in my house, corner of Broad and Master streets. I am sure you will find much pleasure in extending to him any affable courtesies, for 'he is a good one, and his worthiness doth challenge much respect.' I am glad to hear everything is right at the house, and that the trees and bushes in the garden have been pruned and trimmed under your careful instructions. Those apple trees required a good deal of pruning. I look forward with great pleasure to the opening of spring, when I shall be at home once more to enjoy in peace its calm and pleasant comforts after the turmoil and excitement consequent upon the discharge of my professional labors and the weariness of continued travel. * * * *

"I was glad to hear friend Forney has resigned his office of Collector of the Port of Philadelphia, and hereafter if he makes any change in the future, let it be for the highest post of honor—the Senate of the United States.

"You did just what was right in having the roofs repaired and painted when they so much needed it, and without consulting me, for such delay might have proved very injurious to the property. I am glad you acted so promptly and efficiently, and the bills for the work are not too high. [The reason we acted so promptly was, that during a very heavy rain the water came through the ceiling of the picture-gallery, and one or two rooms in the attic were inundated.] * * * * * *

"As the girls, Lizzie and Kate, must need money, pay the former $42, and the latter $35, and oblige

"Yours truly, "EDWIN FORREST."

"PITTSBURG, PA., January 22nd, 1872.

"DEAR FRIEND REES:—Your letter of the 19th inst. is just received, which I should have got yesterday but that I arrived here after the post-office had closed. Your letter of the 10th inst. I duly received at St. Louis. Many thanks for your kind and friendly attentions to my affairs during my absence. Make yourself at home in my library, for I often picture you 'in my mind's eye' seated near the Dramatic collection, and poring over the works of your favorite authors. Have you published your article entitled 'Shakespeare and Bacon?' * * * I wish you could have seen some of the plays as we acted them at St. Louis. Oh! such a wretched company—worse than I ever met with—all wretchedly bad; but one woman reached the depths of d——n. She got *through* Desdemona, knowing only about fifteen lines of the Shakespérian text, all the rest being improvised and attempted to be uttered with the sweet German accent, mingled with Cuban *patois* and negro French! The representative of fair Desdemona was, as I learned, a native Cuban, and afterwards educated at Munich. It was the —— thing I ever saw, and yet some of the St. Louis papers actually commended her performance.

"Yours, truly, "EDWIN FORREST."

We had called Mr. Forrest's attention to a passage in Othello, as rendered in the acting copy, to read: "Thou hadst better have been born a dog, Iago," etc., instead of as printed in the folio of 1623, thus:

> "Thou hadst been better have been born a dog,
> Than answer my wak'd wrath."

This omission of the word "Iago," and transposition of the words "been" and "better," seems to have been changed long subsequent to the early quarto and folio editions of Shakespeare's plays. Mr. Forrest's reply to us was to this effect:

> "PHILADELPHIA, November 19th, 1869.
>
> "MY DEAR MR. REES:—The line in the first four folios reads: 'Thou hadst been better have been born a dog,' which is evidently a blunder of the type-setter. Shakespeare never involved a sentence in that way. Garrick, Kemble, Cooke and Kean spoke the line as I do, thus: 'Thou hadst better have been born a dog, Iago;' which is both the measure and rhythm, etc.
>
> "EDWIN FORREST."

Subsequently, we told Mr. Forrest that it was scarcely possible the "type-setter" would take the liberty of changing a whole sentence, and substituting a word to make the measure and the rhythm more perfect, at least in his estimation; a liberty that type-setters have no right to take with the author's copy.

We are under the impression that this change in the original text was made about the year 1750. In Cumberland's edition of the "British Theatre," London, 1829, there is an allusion made to this passage, but as we have no copy of the work, we cannot quote the passage here. We have a prompter's copy of Othello, as performed at Drury Lane Theatre, published with notes in the year 1777, with the modern interpretation of the passage.

"PHILADELPHIA, November 29th, 1869.

"JAMES REES, ESQ.—*Dear Sir*:—I have just received your note of this day. I thank you for correcting my mistake about Othello. I erroneously supposed it had not been printed until its appearance in the folio of 1623. I was wrong; I had confounded it with Macbeth. Othello, in quarto form, was printed by N. O. for Thomas Wathlery, in 1622; and another edition, *without date*, after that; and another still, printed by A. M., for Richard Hawkins, in 1630. I have no copy of the quarto of 1622.

"EDWIN FORREST."

The first published edition of Othello was in a quarto pamphlet (1622), the original of which has now become one of the scarcest of books, for which rich bibliomaniacs have paid fabulous prices.

Whenever Mr. Forrest heard of any one of his friends being sick, he inquired very particularly about the nature of the disease. In 1868, the writer of this had a very severe attack of *erysipelas*. It affected the head and eyes particularly, and for awhile kept us from the office. Mr. Forrest had been looking over medical books, and having obtained a knowledge of this terrible complaint, he found, as he thought, a radical cure, and sent us immediately the following note:

"PHILADELPHIA, November 14th, 1868.

"JAMES REES, ESQ.—*My Dear Sir*:—I should like to have a friendly chat with you to-morrow, say about twelve o'clock, if you can make it convenient to call at my house. Among other things, I should like to discuss the best means of cure for the *erysipelas*. Yours truly,

"EDWIN FORREST."

The recipe given us, and which we used, has been mislaid, the loss of which we most sincerely regret.

JOSEPH McARDLE, ESQ.

The name of this gentleman is mentioned in one of the letters given before. Our readers are no doubt aware that he was Mr. Forrest's business agent, in whose hands the tragedian placed the whole management of his dramatic engagements, arranging terms, etc., thus giving him full control over all financial matters connected with his performances. A more energetic, faithful and reliable man does not exist than Mr. Joseph McArdle. An intimate acquaintance of Mr. Forrest's for upwards of thirty years, fifteen of which he had been his faithful steward, he enjoyed not only the confidence of his employer, but was his companion and friend. To the writer of this Mr. Forrest often expressed the high esteem he had of Mr. McArdle: who, he said, was "*reliable, trustworthy, and studied my interests more than his own. As a business man he has no equal. I do not know what I should do without him.*" Such was Mr. Forrest's opinion of Mr. Joseph McArdle.

The executors of the estate of the deceased will no doubt retain this gentleman as one of the active agents of the "Edwin Forrest Home," which was the intention of the testator, as the writer of this can fully testify.

"Man proposes, but God disposes."

CHAPTER XXIV.

MR. FORREST'S RELIGION.—LOVER OF NATURE.—LETTER TO A FRIEND.—"MY MOTHER."—WAS SHAKESPEARE A ROMAN CATHOLIC?—MUSIC IN CATHEDRALS.—KING JOHN.—SHAKESPEARE AND THE BIBLE.

"Nature is the glass reflecting God,
As by the sea reflected is the sun,
Too glorious to be gazed on in his sphere."

AS regards Mr. Forrest's religious belief, we do not think there is a man living enabled to connect it with any of the prominent denominations of the day. His was a belief founded upon the principles which governed humanity, and considered as a direct law emanating from Deity. "Deity," he observed, "must be just, otherwise man could not have the reverence for his laws which is so essential to a proper appreciation of his Divine character." He respected the church and her members, but never expressed an opinion in favor of any particular one. Forrest admired everything that was beautiful in nature and art. He would talk to you of flowers—give their botanical names; and also those of various plants. When riding out with him through the romantic grounds of the Park, every object of a natural character attracted his attention. Nature to him in these rides was the medium through which he raised his eyes to Deity; and he would quote some favorite author in praise of her wondrous charms, and then refer to others speaking of Him, their creator. His remarks and observations, as we rode along the banks of the Wissahickon, evidenced a mind imbued with the true spirit of religion; the religion of the soul—not of the church. It was during these rambles over hills and valleys, along streams and through woods —we learned more of Mr. Forrest and his belief— more of his inner life—than we did in the many years of his active dramatic career. We knew him then in the "Mimic World"—we know him now in the great. In the first, he was the creature of art; in the second, he was the student of nature.

It was, at one time, stated that Mr. Forrest had been converted; rumor gave it out that he was studying for the ministry. He wrote a letter to a friend, from which we make an extract:—

"But in answer to your questions, my good friend, for I know you are animated only by a sincere regard for my spiritual as well as for my temporal welfare, I am happy to assure you that the painful attack of inflammatory rheumatism, with which for the last three months I have combatted, is now quite overcome, and I think I may safely say that, with the return of more genial weather, I shall be restored once more to a sound and pristine health.

"Then, for the state of my mind; I do not know the time since, when a boy, I blew sportive bladders in the beamy sun, that it ever was so tranquil and serene as in the present hour. Having profited by the leisure given me by my lengthened illness seriously to review the past and carefully consider the future, both for time and for eternity, I have, with a chastened spirit, beheld with many regrets that there was much in the past that might have been improved—more, perhaps, in the acts of omission than in acts of commission; for I feel sustained that my whole conduct has been actuated solely by an honest desire to adhere strictly to the rule of right; that the past has been characterized as I trust the future will be—to love my friends; to hate my enemies—for I cannot be a hypocrite—and to live in accordance with the Divine precept: 'As ye would that men should do to you, do ye also to them likewise.'

"And now for that 'higher welfare' of which you speak. I can only say that, believing as I sincerely do, in the justice, the mercy, the wisdom, and the love of Him who knoweth the secrets of our hearts, I hope I may with

> "'An unfaltering trust approach my grave
> Like one who wraps the drapery of his couch
> About him, and lies down to pleasant dreams.'"

In speaking one day of the many temptations to which youth was subject, and of those whose connections with the stage had brought them to an untimely grave, we asked—"How is it that you have escaped all these dangerous quicksands? Few men have had such temptations held out to them as you have; few men of your age and impulsive nature have resisted them."

"True," he said, "I have had temptations, nor have I resisted them on the instant; the moment, however, when on the eve of becoming the inebriate or the gambler, and disgracing my profession, the words of my mother came up, angel-like, and checked me in my career. I may have faults; I have elicited censure from the world; but I flattered myself that the correction of youthful errors, and strict attention to my duties as an actor, have, in a measure, redeemed these faults. To the early lessons taught by my mother, and those of the good old pastor of St. Paul's Church, am I indebted for all the good that is in me. I do not say that they have made me what the world calls a religious man, but they taught me to appreciate all that is good and noble in man; and to love and admire all that is bright and beautiful in the world, with due reverence to Him who created it." The words, "To my Mother!" as spoken by Mr. Forrest, sounded as the heart's epitaph

TO HER MEMORY.

Mr. Forrest at one time conceived the notion that Shakespeare was a Roman Catholic; there is nothing in the writings of this great man to justify that idea. Nearly all the passages in the works of Shakespeare—of a religious or doctrinal character—have at different times been brought before the reader. The object was to disabuse the mind of Catholics, that Shakespeare did not belong to their order. In 1843, nearly all the passages in the several plays of the bard, of this character, were published by Sir Frederick B. Watson, K. C. H., in a very elegant volume, printed for the benefit of the members of the two principal theatres of London. We called Mr. Forrest's attention to this little book, as also to other passages, not included in this work, wherein Shakespeare denounces the Church of Rome in the most unmeasured terms. It may be said that these denunciations are those of the personages of the plays, and not the sentiments of the author. True, in some cases, we admit this is the case, for Lord Byron was denounced an infidel for the words he puts into the mouth of *Lucifer* in his great poem of "Cain." But no true Catholic would put words into the mouth of the historical or fictitious character of his dramas denouncing the church of which he was a member, particularly that of the Church of Rome—sacred from the corner-stone to the big toe of the Pope.

Shakespeare was no Catholic—neither was Mr. Forrest. Mr. Forrest always spoke in the highest terms of the music of our churches—more particularly that of the Catholic. "The latter reminds me," said he, "of a passage in an old rare book; the original is not in my library, but it is quoted in a work on the stage. I will read it to you." Taking it from the shelf, he said:— "The author, it seems, was speaking of the origin of the 'Ode and Chorus' in honor of the heathen gods, and connecting them with the psalms of David and the song of Moses, on the deliverance of the Israelites from their Egyptian oppressors, and goes on to say:—'The music of the Temple was unquestionably beyond all conception — magnificent and grand. Many of the psalms are little dramas, and were sung as dialogue; a part by the priests, and answers to their parts were finely interwoven, when at other times all Israel joined in chorus. Psalm ii.: ch. xxxv., and many others, are fine specimens of this sort of poetry. The style of their music was probably much more solemn and simple than ours, and the instruments whereby it was conducted, powerful in a high degree. Perhaps nothing so nearly represented the joys of Heaven above, like the singing of the psalms of David in the temples of old.'

"Only imagine," says he, "all Israel joining in chorus. I think," he continued, "the Catholics are the only denomination at the present who take this view of music in their churches, and that is one reason while in Europe I visited them on every occasion my time and business permitted."

Mr. Forrest, while in Paris, went in company with the Rev. E. L. Magoon, of Philadelphia, to hear a celebrated Catholic priest, whose reputation as an orator was national and historical. The music of the choir, he said, surpassed anything he ever heard. If we mistake not, the Royal family were present. The priest, he said, fully sustained his reputation as an orator—fully carried out the ancient idea that oratory was a fundamental principle—and frequently inculcated that the orator ought to be an accomplished scholar, and conversant in every part of learning.

The passages to which we called Mr. Forrest's attention in defence of our argument, that Shakespeare was no Catholic, we annex. Shakespeare was baptized in the ordinary way; the old broken font in which the poet was christened, still exists; it is, however, but a fragment, the upper portion only remaining. It is now in possession of the family of Mr. Heritage, a builder at Stratford. It was here Shakespeare was christened, at an established place of worship in the parish. He was educated and brought up in the Protestant faith, by good Protestant parents, in which faith he lived and died. He was certainly not a Catholic when he wrote "King John," first printed in 1596. This passage alone in sufficient to show the absurdity of his being other than a true Protestant:

King John—Act III. Scene 1.
K. Philip.—" Here comes the holy legate of Rome.

[Enter *Pandulph.*]
Pandulph.—Hail, you anointed deputies of heaven.
To thee, King John, my holy errand is.
I, Pandulph, of fair Milan, Cardinal,
And from Pope Innocent, the legate here,
Do in his name religiously demand,
Why thou against the church, our holy mother,
So wilfully dost spurn; and, force perforce
Keep Stephen Langton, chosen Archbishop
Of Canterbury, from that Holy See? * * *
King John.—What earthly name to interrogatories
Can task the free breath of a sacred King?
Thou canst not, Cardinal, devise a name
So slight, unworthy and ridiculous,
To charge me to an answer, as the Pope.

Tell him this tale; and from the mouth of England,
Add thus much more,—that no Italian priest
Shall tithe or toll in our dominions.

* * * * * * *

So tell the Pope; all reverence set apart
To him, and his usurp'd authority.
K. Philip.—Brother of England, you blaspheme in this.
K. John.—Though you, and all the kings of Christendom,
Are led so grossly by this meddling priest,
Dreading the curse that money may buy out,
And by the merit of vile gold, dross, dust,
Purchase corrupted pardon of a man,
Who, in that sale, sells pardon from himself;
Though you, and all the rest, so grossly led,
This juggling witchcraft with revenue cherish;
Yet I, alone, do me oppose
Against the Pope, and count his friends my foes.
Pandulph.—Then by the lawful power that I have,
Thou shalt stand cursed and excommunicate."

In the first part of King Henry VI. our readers will find the following (Act I., Scene 3)—a scene between Winchester and Gloster:

Win.—"How now, ambitious Humphrey! What means this?
Glos.—Piel'd priest, dost thou command me to be shut out? *
Win.—I do, thou most usurping proditer,
And not protector, of the king and realm.
Glos.—Stand back, thou manifest conspirator;
Thou that contriv'dst to murder our dear lord;
Thou that giv'st whores indulgence to sin. †
I'll canvas thee in thy broad cardinal's hat,
If thou proceed in this thy insolence.
Win.—Nay, stand thou back; I will not budge a foot.
This be Damascus; be thou cursed Cain, ‡
To slay thy brother Abel, if thou wilt.
Glos.—I will not stay thee, but I'll drive thee back.
Thy scarlet robes, as a child's bearing cloth,
I'll use to carry thee out of this place.

* "Piel'd priest." Piel'd is what is now usually spelt peel'd, and in the folio of 1623 the orthgraphy is *pield.* It occurs in the same sense in Measure for Measure. The allusion is to the shaven crown of the Bishop of Winchester.

† The public stews in Southwalk were under the jurisdiction of the Bishop of Winchester. In the office book of the court all fees were entered that were paid by the keepers of these brothels—the church reaping the advantages of these pests to society.

‡ "This be Damascus, be thou cursed Cain," etc. In "The Travels of Sir John Mandeville," we find this passage :—"And in that place, where Damascus was founded, Kayn sloughe Abel his brother."

Win.—Do what thou dar'st. I'll beard thee to thy face,
Glos.—What! Am I dar'd and bearded to my face?
Draw, men, for all this privileged place;
Blue coats to tawny coats.* Priest, beware your beard,
[Gloster and his men attack the bishop.]
I mean to tug it, and cuff you soundly.
Under my feet I stamp thy cardinal's hat,
In spite of pope or dignities of church;
Here by the cheeks I drag thee up and down.
Win.—Gloster, thou'lt answer this before the pope.
Glos.—Winchester goose! † I cry—a rope! a rope!
Now bear them hence; why do you let them stay?
Thee I'll chase hence, thou wolf in sheep's array.
Out, tawny coats! out, scarlet hypocrite." ‡

When these passages were brought before Mr. Forrest, and which he made copies himself from the folio of 1623, he gave one of his peculiar smiles, and said, "Shakespeare was a great man, sir."

Shakespeare's familiarity with the Bible we consider one of the most striking proofs of his religious tendencies. This knowledge far surpasses that of his legal and medical acquirements, and ranks second only to that of his literary attainments. The Bible and Shakespeare are synonymed. In fact we may sum up his wonderful power and genius in the one line of Dr. Johnson, who in praise of Shakespeare says:

"That he exhausted worlds, and then imagined new."

* Tawny coats were worn by the attendants of the Bishop. Stow, in a passage quoted by Stevens, speaks on one occasion of the Bishop of London, who was "attended on by a goodly company of gentlemen in tawny coats." Gloster's men wore blue coats.

† "Winchester goose." That the reader may better understand the terrible words of Gloster addressed to the Bishop and the insult aimed at his church, the word goose was a particular stage of the disease contracted in the stews. Hence Gloster bestows the epithet on the bishop in derision and scorn, referring to his licentious life so strongly painted in Act III., Scene 1, of this most extraordinary play.

‡ We have no doubt but Shakespeare introduced these terrible passages against the Church of Rome to please Queen Elizabeth, she having been trained up in a hatred of Popery.

CHAPTER XXV.

MR. FORREST'S CHARITY.—HOW HE DISPENSED IT.—THE ACTOR'S WIDOW.—THE DUTIFUL SON.—PLEASING INCIDENT.—LIBERAL TO HIS PARTY.—FORREST AND THE POOR.—AN UNJUST DEMAND UPON HIS PURSE.

FROM the time Mr. Forrest achieved his great triumph over the prejudice which gave to other countries all the honor and profits derived from stage talent and dramatic literature, he, like some fabled god, bounded over the mimic world and became its ruler.

Fortune flowed in upon him in golden streams, and in time he became a millionaire. Many persons have an idea that Mr. Forrest worshipped the "almighty dollar." Not so. He was liberal, and nothing offended him more than to have his private charities the subject of comment. The writer of this had many opportunities of witnessing the exercise of this great virtue in Mr. Forrest. The word charity in modern acceptation implies the giving of alms to the poor. The New Testament, however, does not give it that signification altogether. Clarke, in his Commentaries, says: "It appears that the word charity, in the New Testament, does not signify (as we use it) only alms to the poor, but that universal love and good will towards all men, which includes both it and all other virtues; the constant practice of which universal charity is indeed worshipping God in spirit and in truth." [This comment is upon I. Corinthians; Chap. xiii.; v. 2.]

In Mr. Forrest's case, no thought of his charities being a coverlid for a man's sins, or a mere shadow of religion, ever crossed his mind. With him to assist a fellow-creature was a duty, and in almost every case the act of giving was on the instant a case of distress was brought before him. Not long since the editor of a paper in this city said, among other things, speaking of Mr. Forrest, that he "has never been noted for any particular action in favor of the unfortunate members of the profession." This is untrue. Mr. Forrest has given in public and private charity upwards of forty thousand dollars! It would be useless for us to reason with those who doubt this; for, unless we placed before them the figures, they would not be convinced. It is not for us to open Mr. Forrest's private memorandum book and produce the proof, as there are many living whose names are on the list who were the recipients of his bounty. Mr. Forrest's charity was like that of Esreff's, in the following beautiful tradition:

"Zaccher and Esreff begged Morah, their tutor, to permit them to visit the curiosities of Aleppo. He gave them a few aspers to expend as they thought proper; and on their return, he inquired how they had bestowed the money. 'I,' said Zaccher, 'bought some of the finest dates Syria ever produced: the taste was exquisite.' 'And I,' said Esreff, 'met a poor woman, with an infant at her breast; her cries pierced me; I gave her my aspers, and grieved that I had not more.' 'The dates,' said Morah to Zaccher, 'are gone; but Esreff's charity will be a lasting blessing, and contribute to his happiness, not only in this life, but in that to come.'"

We could write a small volume upon the subject of Mr. Forrest's charities—speak of incidents, scenes of distress, cases of gratitude and ingratitude arising from them. Some of these are of such a nature as to render them apochryphal in the estimation of those who knew but little of Mr. Forrest's inner-life. Few would believe that he took his cloak from his back, and wrapped it around a half-frozen, wretched man, and had him taken care of. Such, however, was the fact. As we have said, our purpose is not to parade instances of this kind before our readers. They have nothing to do with the subject of these Reminiscences, of whose stage-life and public career it is alone our purpose to speak. Still we deem it necessary to allude to his charities, as his reticence and that of the recipients of his bounty have given rise to reports of his lack of this virtue and love of money; both are false and unjust to his memory.

One or two instances, however, will show the manner of Mr. Forrest's dispensing charity. Every winter —more particularly what is called a hard one—orders were left at the grocers from whom Mr. Forrest purchased his supplies, to refuse no poor person wanting credit, and the bills were to be sent to him for settlement. It was left with the grocer to discriminate who were to be the recipients of his bounty. This plan was suggested by Miss Elenora, sister of Mr. Forrest, and during the latter part of her life she superintended the carrying out of this praiseworthy system. This estimable lady, the last of her kindred, died June 3rd, 1871. In a notice of her death, which we wrote at the time, and published in *The Press*, we made an allusion to this fact, in the following language:

"Kind, gentle, with a hand open to charity, she did not remain at home awaiting the call of the destitute and suffering; but when the storms and the tempests of winter came, and the poor were suffering, bearing their poverty and wretchedness in silence, it was her hand that came forth unsolicited to aid them."

An interesting incident occurred, to which the attention of Mr. Forrest was called by a letter written by a member of a well-known firm in this city, at the request of the widow of an old actor, who, with two children, was in actual want. The object of the writer was to dispose of a picture she had, suitable, as she thought, to the taste of the tragedian. To this letter, bearing the address of the gentleman who wrote it, there came no reply, nor did he hear anything more of the subject until several weeks had passed, when he ascertained that the widow and her children had been taken from their wretched home and placed in more comfortable lodgings. The gentleman who superintended her removal, purchased additional furniture, and gladdened the widow's heart, was an agent of Edwin Forrest. The picture still hangs in the neat little parlor of its owner.

We could furnish other instances equally interesting, and as characteristic of the man, but space will not permit. A short time before his death, he showed us a letter he had received from a young man, to this effect: In looking over the papers of his father, who died on his way to New Orleans, the young man (his son) found a memorandum stating: "Due Edwin Forrest, Two Hundred Dollars (money borrowed)." The letter requested Mr. Forrest to inform him if such was the case. In reply he said it was, and that he held a due bill for that amount. The letter shown us was to say that if the due bill was forwarded to Mr. Forrest's agent, or friend, it would be paid.

Mr. Forrest's answer, which he read us, was noble, generous and kind—saying: "Not a cent will I receive from you to pay a debt of your father's—and my friend. The due bill I hold was pressed upon me by your father. I knew the man—knew his worth, and had he lived it would have been paid. I will take nothing from his children; the due bill, which I had long since forgotten, is 'cancelled.'" This letter was sent—the son's reply was equally noble, stating, that they were enabled to pay it, that the family were not straitened in circumstances, and that, for his father's memory, he hoped Mr. Forrest would not refuse the amount sent by the same mail in a draft.

The gentleman alluded to here, whose name if given, would be recognized as holding a high position in our stage history, was a Philadelphian by birth, and an old, valued and much regretted friend of him who lives to record these facts.

Col. John W. Forney, in his admirable book, entitled "Anecdotes of Public Men," speaking of Mr. Forrest, says:

> "He gave liberally to the Union cause without being a Republican. Though he did not unite with us when we sung 'John Brown,' none could have been more graceful and ready in contributing to the general pleasure."

In a future part of these "Reminiscences" we will give the balance of the article from Col. Forney's book which the reader will find in that work, on page 77.

The fact is, Mr. Forrest, unlike other wealthy men, performed acts of benevolence when and where they were beneficial, and not for newspaper notoriety. His *true* friends knew his good qualities—the public generally knew him only as an ACTOR.

Mr. Forrest, at one time, was highly censured for refusing to act for the benefit of the poor in his native city, during a winter of unusual severity. The committee appointed for the purpose of carrying out this laudable object was composed of some of the wealthiest men in the city, who considered they had a right to dispose of his services as they thought proper, and actually wanted him to give his night's service and its result for the poor. These very (rich) men would contribute the price of a ticket, and asked of Mr. Forrest five hundred dollars. As a matter of course, he refused his professional services. This was considered in the light of a crime—an actor dared to fly in the face of a committee who had the generosity to buy a ticket valued at one dollar and fifty cents—all for the poor. The press took up the matter, and was shocked at Mr. Forrest's want of liberality in refusing to give five hundred dollars, when these men—many of them far wealthier than the actor—were giving their mite in the shape of the price of a ticket. It was monstrous—an outrage—and not to be endured! Mr. Forrest made this proposition to the committee, that if the gentlemen who were so clamorous on the subject of his refusal, were to show him the list and the amount attached to their respective names, he would double the highest sum mentioned—if five hundred, he would give a thousand! This they declined, and we believe it has never been known how much was subscribed, nor the amount paid over to the poor of the city. Mr. Forrest did not forget the poor during that hard and severe winter.

CHAPTER XXVI.

CORIOLANUS.—ITS ORIGIN.—THE ACTOR.—MR. FORREST'S IMPERSONATION OF THE CHARACTER.—THE MARBLE STATUE.—MR. THOMAS BALL, THE SCULPTOR.—SPLENDID SPECIMEN OF ART.—A PERSPECTIVE GLANCE OF THE ACTOR'S HOME.

IN Chapter XIV. of these Reminiscences we alluded to the play of Coriolanus in connection with Mr. Forrest. As that gentleman's impersonation of the character furnished the subject for a celebrated sculptor to produce a marble portrait statue of the eminent tragedian as Caius Marcius Coriolanus, we devote another portion of these Reminiscences to the Play, the Actor and the Sculptor.

This fine production of art will be a prominent feature in the "Forrest Home."

THE PLAY.

As we said before, this inimitable drama was derived chiefly from the memoirs of Coriolanus contained in the "Lives of the noble Grecians and Romanes compared together, by that grave learned Philosopher and Historiographer, Plutarch of Cheronea;" translated by Thomas North, Esq., Comptroller of the Household to Queen Elizabeth. London, 1579.

The scene is laid in Rome, and partly in the territories of the Volscians and Antiates, and the action commences with the secession to the Mons Sacer in the year of Rome, 262, and ends with the death of Coriolanus, Y. R. 266.

There is no entry of this play earlier than that of the folio of 1623; but from a slight resemblance between the language of the fable told by Meneius in the first scene, and that of the same apologue in Camden's Remains, published in 1605. Malone supposes the passage to have been imitated from that volume. From the history above mentioned Shakespeare has taken many of the speeches, and such alterations were made as were necessary to form them into blank verse. He assigns the production, however, to 1609 or 1610, partly because most of the other plays of Shakespeare have been reasonably referred to other years, and therefore the present might be most naturally ascribed to a time when he had not ceased to write, and was probably otherwise unemployed, and partly from Volumnia mentioning the mulberry the while, species of which were brought into England in great quantities.

A tragedy of the same name and subject as the present, by James Thompson, was produced at Covent Garden in 1748, for the benefit of the author's family, by the zeal of Sir George Lyttleton; which raised a considerable sum, though it added nothing to the poet's fame. In 1755, Thomas Sheridan brought out Coriolanus; or, the Roman Matron, at the same theatre, composed from both Shakespeare and Thompson, which had some success, being assisted by a splendid ovation. The best revisal, however, was that also taken from both authors by John P. Kemble, produced originally at Drury Lane, in February, 1789, and sometimes ascribed to Wrighten, the prompter. It was again brought out by the same excellent performer, with some additions from Thompson, at Covent Garden, November 3rd, 1806, in which his Coriolanus and the Volumnia of Mrs. Siddons, formed the proudest display of even their magnificent histrionic powers. It was in the part of the Roman General that Mr. Kemble took leave of the stage, at the above theatre, on Monday, June 23rd, 1817.

THE ACTOR.

The only American actor who had distinguished himself in Coriolanus was Mr. Edwin Forrest. His splendid figure, his surprising strength and yet ponderous grace, if we may be allowed the expression, of his fine frame, make a perfect picture of the Roman warrior. "He is," says a London critic, "more like the creation of Polidora de Carravaggio's triumphant victors than the sculptured Apollo of the Academy." Added to which, he possessed the fire of genius, which alone gives life and animation to the picture.

Mr. Forrest, both by education and national proclivities, was peculiarly adapted to this character. The argument of the play is decidedly opposed to the aristocracy, although the characters speak for and against it. Liberty and slavery—the privilege of the few and the claims of the many—are alike ably as well as politically handled. Mr. Forrest's sarcastic mode of speaking, when these subjects are introduced, was one of his striking features. Coriolanus, however, is not a republican; he rates the people as if he were a god to punish, and not a man of their infirmity.

In 1864, we wrote the following article, being one of several we had written upon his Coriolanus, and the last:—"It seems to us that this version of Coriolanus is of a more modern date than any one adapted to the stage that we have witnessed. Whose version is it? The commendations which from time to time have been given to three great actors—Kemble, Cooke and Conway—speak of a play intact with the fame of Shakespeare. There is not only a heavy discount in this piece of language, but a very large percentage taken from its original dramatic construction.

"We have always opposed this pruning system, as having a tendency to lessen the stage attractions of any piece, though it be even one of Shakespeare's. It is true, Coriolanus stands out in bold relief—the prominent figure in the picture. Yet, the shades of light, so essential to give it effect, are so scattered that the harmony of the whole is materially marred. There is no blending of character to bring out the real beauties of the picture.

"We have spoken of Mr. Forrest's Coriolanus as being great. It is so, whatever difference of opinion may exist upon the subject. Our praises of Mr. Forrest are the expression of an opinion formed years ago, and are strengthened by his progressive improvements in the art. They have no other standard. We speak of an artist without regard to name or country, friend or enemy. In the gigantic school of art, among the clustered gems that grace the walls of the Academy, we criticise the *work*—not the *man*.

"Coriolanus is a peculiar character. He is the creature of a mother's pride, and what he does 'is to please her, and to be partly proud.' But he is not partly proud; he was 'thoroughly and extremely proud, even to the altitude of his virtue.' He is at times the slave of passion, then of subdued emotion; at others, furious, mad, or blinded, if you please; but in all and through all the method is principled. All these conflicting elements were handled by Mr. Forrest, as Franklin handled and subdued the lightning, bringing it submissive to his will. Again, the pride of Coriolanus is that of a noble; it is tinctured with the prejudices of his education, and assumes at times more the shape of insult to those around him than a distant reserve to preserve his dignity. Coriolanus has lain, as it were, for many years—silent, cold, classic, it has slept in its lettered tomb, or, like an encrusted diamond, in its gemmed mine. Mr. Forrest has raised it from its coffined home, and while gazing upon its motionless form, as it lays in its motionless classic beauty before him, he studied its history, scientifically anatomized it, and, as he read the burning pages describing the man of *his* time, he breathed upon it the genius of the actor, and gave life to its poetic creation. It came forth the Coriolanus of Shakespeare, full of life and action.

"It was the diamond of the *mind*, fashioned into beauty by the artiste. We have spoken of Mr. Forrest's Coriolanus as a masterly whole—it would be lost labor to particularize its parts. Its colossal grandeur cannot be improved by additions, nor its beauty lessened by the shafts of envious criticism.

"Mr. Forrest's Coriolanus was a most masterly performance; the Roman manliness of his face and figure, the haughty dignity of his carriage, and the fire of his eye, conspired to render his impersonation of the character one of the most striking performances that was ever exhibited upon the stage.

"The mode in which Mr. Forrest pronounced the word Coriolanus has from his authority become generally prevalent. Mr. Forrest could at all times be taken as the standard of correct pronunciation, either of names or words. He threw the accent on the second syllable of this derivative word Coriolanus, because the accent rests upon the second syllable in the primitive word, *Corioli.* As uttered by some actors, slurring the first syllable, it is drawled out *Cow-ri-o-lanus,* but should be pronounced short and quick as accented above.

"It is a question, however, if by throwing the accent on the second syllable it would not tend to lengthen the word, as far as sound goes; for the breath in the pronunciation of any long word cannot be conveniently suspended till the last syllable, which is long in this instance, as the other is short. Hamblin, we think it was, who, like Kemble, was troubled with asthma, invariably adopted this course for breath-sake. And pronounced it thus—Corio-*lanus.* We leave it to the more learned to decide the question."

THE STATUE.

THOMAS BALL'S MARBLE PORTRAIT STATUE OF EDWIN FORREST AS CAIUS MARCIUS CORIOLANUS.—This work, the result of personal friendship, owes its existence to the persistent efforts of a few of Mr. Forrest's intimate friends, who, so long ago as the year 1862, applied unsuccessfully to Mr. Forrest for his permission and the sittings necessary for its execution.

In January, 1863, Mr. Forrest having consented to give to Mr. Thomas Ball the desired facilities, the model was made in Philadelphia, and in 1865 Mr. Ball went to Italy to complete the statue in marble. The following extract is from a letter written at Florence after the completion of the large model:

"While Ball has succeeded in giving a most striking personal likeness of the great actor, he has imparted to the statue the inspiration of the Roman Consul. There is a grandeur about the work that will add new lustre to the genius of Ball, while at the same time it will closely identify Forrest's name and fame with the best works of art."

After the statue was finished, the artist is reported to have said:

"If my countrymen will not accept this as a true representation, in marble, of our great national tragedian, it is not in my power to gratify their wishes."

We think the artist has done himself justice in his modelling and finish. The attitude is strong and well balanced. The drapery is gracefully managed in its falls and folds; and the other details of the dress show accurate chiselling. The head also is vigorously shaped and cut. The height of the figure is six feet six inches, which is some eight inches taller than Mr. Forrest. The extreme height of the figure and pedestal is eleven feet, and the weight is over three tons.

The statue represents Coriolanus in act v. scene iii. The tent of Coriolanus. Enter in mourning habits, Virgilla. Volumnia, leading young Maricus Valeria, and attendants.

"My wife comes foremost; then the honor'd mould
Wherein this trunk was framed, and in her hand
The grandchild to her blood. But, out, affection!
All bond and privilege of nature break!
Let it be virtuous to be obstinate.
What is that curt'sy worth, or those dove eyes,
Which can make gods forsworn? I melt, and am not
Of stronger earth than others. My mother bows;

As if Olympus to a mole-hill should
In supplication nod; and my young boy
Hath an aspect of intercession, which
Great Nature cries: Decry not; let the voices
Plough Rome and harrow Italy; I'll never
Be such a gosling to obey instinct; but stand
As if a man were author of himself,
And knew no other kin."

In imagination we see the veterans of the stage, now the recipients of the munificent bounty of the founder of the "Forrest Home," standing in one of the vast rooms of the palatial mansion, gazing upon his "marble portrait statue;" and as they gather round it, relating many a tale of the past, wherein each and every one bore a part. Passing from this room into the library, there we see them poring over the books of the drama, and in almost every one the name of Edwin Forrest bears witness to that gentleman's love for the drama, and a proper appreciation of its literature. Passing from the library into the picture gallery, we find them gazing in silent wonder; there they see a vast collection of works of art—paintings, sculptured figures, souvenirs of admiring friends—embracing every walk and vocation of life. Passing from this, we imagine them rehearsing in the neat classic theatre. But why imagine all this? It is to be a reality, and not a vision—not an actor's dream of home, to be dispelled by the morning's dawn, but a realized Utopia—a place where the aged actor can lie down "in green pastures," and wander "beside the still waters"—one sweet spot, where the tired mind may rest and call it HOME.

CHAPTER XXVII.

EDWIN FORREST'S POLITICS.—DEMOCRATIC.—FOURTH OF JULY SPEECH.—A PAGE FROM JOHN W. FORNEY'S BOOK.—FORREST A HUMORIST.—HE IS ONLY AN ACTOR.—HENRY CLAY.—ANECDOTE.

MR. FORREST was the most consistent politician that we ever met. He was a Democrat of that good old school from which came forth the champions of right in the great battle of sustaining our government against a foreign foe; he was also the warm friend of that great man whose sword flashed over the battle field in 1815, and drove the minions of monarchy from our shores; that man, the model warrior and statesman was GENERAL ANDREW JACKSON. In politics he was Mr. Forrest's tutor.

Mr. Forrest had been, during the course of his public career, on several occasions, invited to stand as a candidate for Congress, but all such proposals he had declined, his expressed wish being that he should be known in no public capacity that was not strictly professional. In 1838, in compliance with a request made by the Democratic Republican Committee of New York, he delivered a Fourth of July oration, remarkable for the purity and force of its diction, and the originality and patriotism of its sentiments. One paragraph from this oration defines the speaker's political views so well, and expresses so much of his character, that we reprint it. "To Jefferson belongs exclusively and forever the high renown of having framed the glorious charter of American liberty. To his memory the benedictions of this and all succeeding times are due for reducing the theory of freedom to its simplest elements, and in a few lucid and unanswerable propositions establishing a groundwork on which men may securely raise a lasting superstructure of national greatness and prosperity. But our fathers, in the august assemblage of '76, were prompt to acknowledge and adopt the solemn and momentous principles he asserted. With scarce an alteration—with none that affected the spirit and character of the instrument, and with but few that changed in the slightest degree its verbal construction—they published that exposition of human rights to the world as their Declaration of American Independence, pledging to each other their lives, their fortunes, and their sacred honor in support of the tenets it proclaimed. This was the grandest, the most important experiment ever undertaken in the history of man. But they that entered upon it were not afraid of new experiments, if founded on the immutable principles of right, and approved by the sober conviction of reason. There were not wanting then—indeed, there are not wanting now—pale counsellors to fear, who would have withheld them from the course they were pursuing, because it tended in a direction hitherto untried. But they were not to be deterred by the shadowy doubts and timid suggestions of craven spirits, content to be lashed forever round the same circle of miserable expedients, perpetually trying anew the exploded shifts which had always proved lamentably inadequate before. To such men the very name of experiment is a sound of horror. It is a spell which conjures up gorgons, hydras, and chimeras dire. They seem to know that all that is valuable in life—that the acquisitions of learning, the discoveries of science, and the refinement of art—are the result of experiment. It was experiment that bestowed on Cadmus those keys of knowledge with which we unlock the treasure houses of immortal mind. It was experiment that taught Bacon the futility of the Grecian philosophy, and led him to that heaven-scaling method of investigation and analysis on which science has safely climbed to the proud eminence where she now sits dispensing her blessings on mankind. It was experiment that lifted Newton above the clouds and darkness of this visible diurnal sphere, enabling him to explore the sublime mechanism of the stars, and weigh the planets in their eternal rounds. It was experiment that nerved the hand of Franklin to snatch the thunder from the armory of heaven. It was experiment that gave this hemisphere to the world. *It was experiment that gave this continent freedom.*

* * * * * * * *

"Where does the sun, in all his compass, shed his beams on a country freer, better, happier than this? Where does he behold more diffuse prosperity—more active industry—more social harmony—more abiding faith, hope and charity? Where are the foundations of private right more stable, or the limits of public order more inviolately observed? Where does labor go to the toil with a step more alert, or a more erect brow, effulgent with the heart-reflected light of conscious independence?

"Where does Agriculture drive his team a-field

with a more cheery spirit in the certain assurance that the harvest is his own? Where does commerce launch more boldly her bark upon the deep, aware that she has to strive but with the tyranny of man?

"But above all, let us be careful by no political interference with the pursuits of industry and improvement, to violate that grand maxim of equality, on which, as on a corner stone, the fabric of democratic freedom rests. *That we should frown indignantly on the first motion of an attempt to sunder one portion of the Union from another, was the parting admonition of Washington;* but with deeper solicitude, and more sedulous and constant care, should we guard against a blow being aimed, no matter how light, or by what specious pretext defended, against that great elementary principle of liberty, which, once shaken, the whole structure will topple to the ground."

Mr. Forrest's address bears all those strong evidences of mental culture which so distinguished his speeches in after years. There is a Shakesperian style about them which at once would tell a stranger this man is a student of the immortal bard's vast conceptions. His works were the text of the orator—*this man must be an actor.* A writer, speaking of one of Mr. Forrest's speeches, made on the occasion of a complimentary dinner tendered him, said: "*Although protesting he was no actor here (at the festive board), yet he never acted so well in his life as during this reply to the compliments profusely showered upon him.*"

The writer of this knew not the difference between Nature and Art—what was natural here, he attributed to the latter.

"This man must be an actor," was applied to Mr. Forrest simply because he spoke well and was an orator, and yet why is not an actor eligible to the highest offices in the gift of a free people? Is the profession of such a character as this to debar a man of culture, intelligence, honor and probity, as capable as a petty lawyer, or a corrupt precinct politician? So far from any absurd stigma being attached to the profession, when Æschyles wrote his Sophocles and Euripides wrote for the stage, no one could become a member of a company who had been dishonored by any offence committed against the laws. Enjoying all the privileges of a free citizen, an actor might aspire to the most honorable employment of the State. Some actors possessed great influence in the public assemblies. A celebrated performer, named Aristodemus, was sent on an embassy to Philip, King of Macedon; and Æschyles, Sophocles and Aristophanes, like Shakespeare, held it no degradation to act a part in the pieces they had composed. It is well known to the learned at what expense the Athenians supported their theatres, and how often from among their poets and actors they chose governors of their provinces, generals of their armies, and guardians of their liberties.

We have said that Mr. Forrest was the most consistent politician that we ever met with; perhaps we should have said the most consistent in politics. The last time Mr. Forrest voted, was at the October election, 1872, *and for the first time in his life scratched his ticket!* This was for the purpose of casting his vote for Gen. H. H. Bingham for Clerk of the Court of Quarter Sessions. "I vote for him," said he, "because I like the man from the opinion you have expressed of him, and as your friend, for every friend of yours I consider mine." This we considered one of the highest compliments Mr. Forrest ever paid us.

Gen. Bingham and Mr. Forrest were to have met, but the excitement of the election, and the former just entering upon the duties of his new office, delayed the interview; in the meantime death entered the mansion of the great tragedian, and shut out visitors forever.

There was another gentleman whose character Mr. Forrest much admired, and with whom he was not personally acquainted; this was M. Hall Stanton, Esq. "When I return from Boston," said he one day to us, "I want you to make an arrangement with Mr. Stanton to dine with me. He is a man whose acquaintance I very much desire." The very week the noble actor died was the one selected for this interview. *Had they met, the fortunes of the writer of these "Reminiscences" would have been materially changed.*

Well has it been said by an old writer: "Which of us setting out upon a visit, a diversion or an affair of business, apprehends a possibility of not arriving at the place of destination, yet at the same time does not apprehend himself at liberty to alter his course in any part of his progress? There is a certain destiny of everything."

Colonel John W. Forney relates the following incident in his "Anecdotes of Public Men." Perhaps I cannot better terminate this desultory anecdote than by giving you the following copy of an autograph letter now before me, written by Edwin Forrest, in 1856, when he sent a subscription of two hundred and fifty dollars to the Treasurer of the Democratic Committee of Pennsylvania, to help defraying the expenses of electing James Buchanan. It is very carefully composed, and indicates the business exactitude which marked him throughout life:

"BOSTON, November 29th, 1856.

"MY DEAR SIR:—You must excuse me for not replying sooner to your letter of the 21st. instant, but unusual press of business, and other matters, prevented me from doing so at an earlier period.

"I herein enclose you a check for two hundred and fifty dollars, which you will apply to the liquidation of the debt incurred by the Democratic Committee during the late political canvass.

"Truly yours, "EDWIN FORREST."

Shortly after the death of Mr. Forrest, Colonel John W. Forney published a few anecdotes and reminiscences of his friend. In one article he said:

"He has generally voted the Democratic ticket in his ward, and contributed largely to Mr. Buchanan's election in 1856. An autograph letter, containing a subscription of $250 to that campaign, is now in the possession of Ferdinand J. Dreer, enrolled among his treasures, and also accompanied by a comical verse, which is pinned upon the letter, evidently cut by him from some country newspaper. But no one can doubt where he has always stood who will read his will, especially that part of it in which he commands the reading of the unexpurgated edition of the Declaration of Independence on every Fourth of July. Twenty years ago Mr. Forrest summoned his neighbors, when he lived at Font Hill, N. Y., on the Hudson, and gave them a handsome collation, after which he read this very Declaration, himself, from a platform which he had erected. The company was most distinguished, and the event will still be recalled by the survivors. Still another additional proof of his patriotism may be stated. On the 24th of July, 1862, at the great war meeting, the largest meeting ever held in Independence Square, Mr. Forrest sent a check for one thousand dollars, which the editor of this paper had the honor of presenting."

We annex the "comical verse." Mr. Forrest had a

natural *penchant* for every thing humorous, and his clippings from newspapers, and extracts from periodicals of this character, would make a volume far more interesting than that of Joe Miller's. Mr. Forrest, himself a humorist, appreciated it in others:

> "When Fremont raised a flag so high
> On Rocky Mountain's peak,
> One little busy bee did fly
> And light upon his cheek;
> But when November's ides arrive
> To greet the Colonel's sight,
> Straight from the Democratic hive
> *Two* B's will on him light."

"He was but an actor!" How often this sentence has been uttered as a slur; as if an actor was incapable of being anything else. Actors were honored in Rome. The great Brutus thought his time not mis-employed in a journey from Rome to Naples, only to see an excellent troupe of comedians; and was so pleased with their performance, that he sent them to Rome, with letters of introduction to Cicero, to take them under his patronage;—this, too, was at a time when the city was under no small confusion from the murder of Cæsar. Yet amidst the tumults of those times, and the hurry of his own affairs, he thought having a good company of actors of too much consequence to the public to be neglected. And in such estimation was Roscius held by the public men of the day, that in public debates his name was mentioned in the most honorable manner.

If the great actors of the eighteenth and nineteenth centuries, whose names now adorn the dramatic pages of stage literature, had turned their attention to other pursuits, they might have reached the highest honors bestowed on men of genius and enterprise. Talma, Garrick, Kemble, Cooke, Cooper, Kean, Macready, Forrest, and others, would not have had the sarcastic phrase applied to them, "He is only an actor!" had they entered the list to contend with the political element, and battle for high reward, they would have gained it. This they did not do, hence they lived and died—only actors!

John W. Forney, in his "Anecdotes of Public Men," relates the following incident, which goes to show that our own great men understood the profession of an actor. In the year 1844, when Henry Clay visited Philadelphia, Mr. Forney, John Swift, and Edwin Forrest called upon him at the American House, on Chestnut Street; we will let Mr. Forney speak:

> "He looked feeble and worn—he was then over seventy years old—but he soon brightened. Anxious to rouse him, I quietly ventured to suggest that I heard the speech of Pierre Soulé, Senator in Congress from Louisiana—an extremist especially distasteful to Mr. Clay—and I thought it a very thorough and able presentation of the side adverse to the compromise measures. I saw the old man's eye flash as I spoke; and was not surprised when, with much vehemence, he proceeded to denounce Soulé. After denying that he was a Statesman, and insisting that there were others far more effective in the opposition, he wound up by saying: 'He is nothing but an actor, sir; a mere actor.' Then suddenly recollecting the presence of our favorite tragedian, he dropped his tone, and waved his hand, as he turned to Forrest—'I mean, my dear sir, a mere French actor.' We soon after took our leave; and, as we descended the stairs, Forrest turned to Swift and myself, and said, 'Mr. Clay has proved, by his skill with which he can change his manner, and the grace with which he can make an apology, that he is a better actor than Soulé.'"

How true it is said by the immortal bard:—

"All the world's a stage,
And all men and women merely players;
They have their exits and their entrances;
And one man in his time plays many parts."

CHAPTER XXVIII.

STATE OF THE DRAMA.—AMERICAN ACTORS.—A REVIEW OF THE CAUSE OF THE ASTOR PLACE RIOTS.—MACREADY'S FIRST AND SECOND MOVE.—THE APPROACHING STORM.—LAWYER'S ADVICE.

THE state of the drama in the year 1849 was much better than it had been for many years previous. This, in a great measure, was owing to the re-appearance of Mr. Forrest and Mr. Macready, and the character of the pieces in which they appeared. The public taste for what was then, and now, called sensational pieces, was gradually dying out; and the production of legitimate plays gave goodly evidence of a better state of things in the "Mimic World." The word legitimate we have often thought very appropriate to stage plays. It would be very difficult, however, for us to fix upon any one period in dramatic history, which would apply the word to the stage, simply because, what we term legitimate, is in direct opposition to a modern style of drama now in vogue; dramas so called, and which are a disgrace to our stage and its literature. As we are unable to fix upon any particular period in stage history, from which we can date what is called the legitimate, we must necessarily select out those eras in which good plays were performed; and probably no other than that of the Elizabethan age can be named. Indeed, you cannot go back beyond this period to find in a class of plays anything to carry out the word legitimate, which literally means, an appreciation of all that is beautiful in art, legal and lawful, in construction and in direct contradistinction to whatever is spurious, low or immoral. Shakespeare's plays come directly under the head of legitimate, not in the sense in which the word is used now; but from the fact that there were no plays at that period other than that class. In ancient Greece, it is true, they had what is called the "Classic Drama." The elements of the Grecian drama are to be sought in an age antecedent to all historic record. Mythical legends and episodic narrations of the virtues and achievements of those gods with which that age teemed, and filled every stream with Naiads, woods with Dryads, and the mountains with the Oreads and the Graces, were the first principles of representing life by action. Wild and poetical as these productions were, they certainly possessed better elements of dramatic *morale* than that of the Songs of Bacchus, amid the drunken revels of the wine growers, and from which sprang the first germs of tragedy.

It was long subsequent to the age of Shakespeare that the word legitimate was used to distinguish good plays from the bad; or rather we should say, from the low and vulgar class of dramatic productions. In our day the legitimate drama means the good old standard plays of the English school, as well as those of our own; and in this age of sensational trash, unrefined, low, vulgar, and immoral, the word legitimate is a distinguishing mark, that should be recognized and respected.

In speaking of the drama, with reference to its moral influences, we lay down the principle that the spirit of the legitimate drama is favorable to human improvement, and the stage under its auspices, could be made

> "The mirror of a nation's virtue,
> And the enlightened and polished school of a free people."

We have no disposition to conceal the fact that it has sometimes been abused for unworthy purposes; still less are we disposed to extenuate those abuses; though its history discloses the remarkable truth, that where it has conducted, and not followed the spirit of the age, it has uniformly been a school of virtue and refinement. It did not stamp the licentious character of Charles the Second's reign; it rather received and gave again the very body and pressure of the times. The drama should be regarded as a great instrument for the accomplishment of great ends. The nature of those ends will depend upon the character of those who employ the instrument. That it has at times been converted to an improper use, will not be denied. But is the candid mind prepared, from partial and temporary effects, to infer that the cause should be denounced and rejected forever? It is not upon reasoning like this that the convictions of mankind are usually based. Philosophy has been contaminated, and her fruits have been evil. Eloquence has been made to serve the cause of the demagogue, and has stood in ranks opposed to patriotism. Even the simplicity and purity of our holy religion have been made subservient to the ambition of unprincipled men. But where is he who will cast a shade upon the integrity of philosophy herself? Who will unhesitatingly pronounce eloquence a curse? And is the spirit of true religion less beautiful and less divine, because its principles have sometimes been perverted or misapprehended? The legitimate purpose of the drama is to improve, not to corrupt our virtuous sensibilities; but like every other human institution, it is imperfect. Its object has been sometimes misapprehended, and abuses have been the consequence. Yet "more in sorrow than in anger" do we deprecate that disingenuous spirit, which pronounces upon the uncorrupted drama those judgments which should be passed only upon its abuses. Let these be arraigned and condemned; justice, and that charity "which rejoiceth in the truth," command that rebuke extend no further.

"Thus many plays," says a learned divine, "instead of ennobling the soul with generous sentiments, sully the imagination by describing lust with all its incentives and allurements, and awakens those passions which lay dormant before." It is granted that good writers make the deeper impression, when they make court to the fancy, by bribing it with agreeable metaphors, paintings, and lively imagery. The same writer, in a sermon preached on "The Government of Thought," speaking of plays, says:—"Some of them are rational and manly entertainments, and may be read with improvement as well as delight. As to the rest, I would offer to the consideration of virtuous persons, whether it be consistent with their character, as such, to read in the closet, or hear on the stage, such lewd and immodest sentiments as it would not be consistent to hear in private conversation?"—"Seed's Sermons," IX

This character of plays has kept back many talented artists and writers, and thus materially injured the legitimate, by leaving the stage to mediocre actors and authors. The stage was never intended to be made the arena for the display of licentiousness, indecency and vulgarity; its object was to ennoble the mind by bringing forth the mental stores of gifted men, and place before an audience gems of bright thoughts, clothed with poetic beauty, instead of those vile abortions emanating from diseased imaginations. Plato, whose words of wisdom are as apples of gold, says, "that if men could behold virtue, she could make all of them in love with her charms," and adds, "a right play draws her picture in the most lively manner."

The minds of our youth have become corrupted; the Camille's of the French stage have filled our streets with wantons; the Jack Sheppard's of the English school furnished its victims for the House of Refuge and the Penitentiary.

To Thomas Althorpe Cooper, William B. Wood, William A. Conway, William Warren, Joseph Jefferson, J. W. Wallack, Junius Brutus Booth, Edwin Forrest, and his imitators, is the American stage indebted for all the good we have derived from exhibitions, and the effect they had upon the moral and intelligent. In no instance did they ever step from the sublime productions of gifted minds to the ridiculous sensational trash of the day.

We now approach one of the most important events that ever occurred in the history of our stage. It finds no parallel in that of any other. We head this sad portion of our Reminiscences·

AN IMPARTIAL REVIEW OF THE LAMENTABLE OCCURRENCES AT THE ASTOR PLACE OPERA HOUSE,

On the 10th of May, 1849.

In another part of these Reminiscences we gave the cause of the original quarrel between Mr. Forrest and Mr. Macready. We have shown conclusively that it originated in feelings of professional jealousy on the part of the latter, who insidiously strove to have the former driven from the British stage. It is also said that this natural jealousy was still further aggravated by Mr. Forrest's domestic relations. As an Englishwoman, his wife was still mindful of her having been born on the same soil with Mr. Macready, and it is a proverbial fact that no nation upon earth clings so obstinately to their native prejudices as the English. A writer says: "If we may believe rumor, Mrs. Forrest on many occasions allowed her prejudices to interfere with the most serious duty of a wife to sympathize with and uphold her husband."

It will be remembered that on Mr. Forrest's former visit to England, he was not only well received, but the press, with but one or two exceptions, was enthusiastic in his praise. All this to Macready was gall and wormwood; and in consultation with his friends —and more particularly John Forster—a plan was adopted to crush his successful rival—with what success we have already detailed. Mr. Forrest, on English ground, resented the insults offered him, and openly accused Macready of being the instigator of them. The hissing of Macready at Edinburg, although not endorsed by us at the time, was the climax to the *emeute* between these two popular tragedians. The quarrel between them had now assumed something of a national character, and when Macready's visit to this country was announced, there was a low murmuring sound heard throughout the land of an approaching storm; and had the great English tragedian kept his tongue still about their quarrel in England when he was called before the curtain, we question if the storm would have burst and caused so serious a calamity as that of the Astor Place Opera House Riot, on the 10th of May, 1849.

Mr. Macready, after an absence of three years, re-appeared at the Astor Place Opera House, then under the management of Chippendale & Sefton; Lessee, William Niblo. The play was announced—Mr. Macready's first appearance, on Monday, September 4th, 1848, as Macbeth, supported by Mr. Ryder, as Macduff, and Mrs. G. Jones as Lady Macbeth. This engagement closed on the 25th, when he appeared in the Merchant of Venice. This engagement, *unmolested*, was a brilliant one.

The Park Theatre was under the management of Mr. Simpson, being the last season of that highly esteemed gentleman and actor. It opened on the 4th of August, 1847. On the 31st of August, Mr. Forrest commenced an engagement as King Lear, but his triumphant career was interrupted by an attack of hoarseness, so severe, that it compelled him to withdraw for several nights.

He did not perform again until October 27th, when he opened in Metamora, and on the 28th as Spartacus, being his last appearance on the Park boards.

Mr. Macready, after playing an engagement at Baltimore, Philadelphia, Boston and other cities, and receiving a public dinner in New Orleans, arrived in New York on Friday, April 27th, 1849, and almost immediately made an engagement with the lessees of the Astor Place Opera House (Messrs. William Niblo and James H. Hackett), for four weeks, commencing on Monday, May 7th. This was announced some days previous, in the following card, in the city papers:

"Astor Place Opera House, Monday, May 7th, 1849. First night of Mr. Macready's farewell engagement will be presented Shakespeare's Tragedy of Macbeth. Macbeth, Mr. Macready."

In the meantime Mr. Forrest had been playing a splendid engagement at the Broadway Theatre, opening there on the 28th of August, 1848, as Othello. During this engagement, which lasted until the 22nd of September, he appeared in Virginius, Richelieu, and Damon. On the 23rd of April, 1849, he commenced a three weeks' engagement. The houses were crowded, and his reception, on every occasion, was an ovation to his genius, and a tribute to his merit as an actor and an American gentleman. This engagement, beginning with that of Macready's, naturally excited the public mind. Discussion and dispute ran high between the friends of the two rival tragedians. Not only the journals which usually devote a large portion of their columns to the drama, but even the commercial papers, took up the theme, and tended to fan the flame of discord to a burning point. There was one element far more dangerous to the English actor than that of the one controlled by the press; it was an element as mysterious in its origin, as it proved to be fearful when aroused. It was a human motive-power propelled into action by surrounding circumstances, composed in part of American prejudices and national associations connected with certain events which are patriotically recorded under four ominous figures, viz., "1776." Not to leave our readers in the dark, or continue the mystery, this element was the Boys of New York, known then and up to the present by a phrase more suitable to the element producing them —"The B'hoys." A writer, speaking of them, says: "To those abroad it may be necessary to state that the term does not by any means imply extreme youth. On the contrary, the class to which it is applied, consists, for the most part, of those who have already attained the years of manhood."

MR. MACREADY'S FIRST MOVE.

On the 4th of October, 1848, at the conclusion of the performance, being called before the curtain, he delivered the following speech:

"LADIES AND GENTLEMEN:—It is not my custom on such occasions as the present to address an audience, but I am moved to do so by an impulse which I cannot resist, and which is strengthened by the judgment just pronounced by a gentleman in the gallery (referring to somebody who had hissed) on the performance of the evening. I feel much gratified by the kind reception with which you have honored me, and I value it, as well on its own account as because on my arrival in your country, which, believe me, I always visit with pleasure. Some journals in New York asserted that I am *superannuated*, and am incapable of presenting the impersonation of Shakesperian character. Ladies and gentlemen, I appeal to your judgment."

MR. MACREADY'S SECOND MOVE.

On the night of the 25th of October, 1848, in answer to the call of the audience, he delivered a speech of some length, from which we make the following extract:

"But I have a *motive* for trespassing further on your patience. There is something apart from this, for which I would thank you. It cannot be disproved, however the failure of the plan may be quoted in denial of its existence, that a project was on foot to excite on this, my farewell visit to the American stage, a hostile feeling against me with the American public. Your most kind and flattering reception of me has baffled the intentions of my unprovoked antagonists," etc.

The imagination of Mr. Macready, excited by the recollection of the wrong he did Mr. Forrest in England, conjured up this hostile faction. The reader will remember that both of these speeches were delivered during his first engagement (during the performance of which he met no opposition or interference worthy of notice), and nearly one month before he appeared in Philadelphia. The last speech, so uncalled for, and of such singular character, induced the publication of the article in the Boston *Mail*, on the 30th of October, 1848, which Mr. Macready's counsel considered sufficient grounds for a libel. This article was headed: "More about McReady—His Abuse of Mr. Forrest in Europe—Endeavors to put him down in Paris, London and Edinburg—His intrigue with Bulwer to prevent Forrest Playing in Bulwer's Plays—His Abuse of Americans," etc., etc.

In Chapter XVIII. of these Reminiscences, we gave an account of Mr. Forrest's reception in England, and the part Mr. Macready took in provoking the quarrel. As our account differs very little from that of the *Mail*, we need not repeat it here. One passage, however, we give, as it shows, in connection with the whole article, how Macready provoked an *emeute*, which his friends so persistently denied: "Although Macready saw fit on his opening night in New York, on being called out by some friends, to slur a '*certain penny paper*' that had 'dared' to express an opinion regarding his talents and conduct, we shall not, by any means, give him the retort churlish; we only pity his ignorance of the institutions of this country, and hope, for his own credit's sake, that he will not, when he gets home, write a black book about American manners, etc., *à la* Trollope, and others," etc.

Immediately after the publication of the article in the Boston *Mail*, Macready committed to his counsel, Messrs. Reed and Meredith, of Philadelphia, authority to commence such legal proceedings as they might deem advisable; and preparatory thereto, he obtained from England certain documentary evidence relative to the quarrel between him and Mr. Forrest in England. All this was a mere trick of the actor and his counsel; no suit was ever begun, nor did the required proofs arrive from England. True, one or two letters came—one from a man signing himself A. Fonblanque, another from a John Mitchell, and one intended to terrify Mr. Forrest and his friends from the High Sheriff of Edinburg. As the Persians say, it was all BOSH!

These letters were all directed to W. C. Macready, Esq., Philadelphia, and were never used in court, but were published as evidence of Mr. Macready's childlike innocence. If these letters told anything as we read them, they told how far Mr. Macready's English friends could falsify truth and pervert facts. Reed and Meredith knew this, for no more was heard of the suit at court. They no doubt thought with Virgil, who said on a somewhat similar occasion:

"*Non nostrum inter vos tantas componere lites.*"

20

CHAPTER XXIX.

MACREADY'S THIRD MOVE.—FORREST'S CARD.—MACREADY'S REPLY.—WILLIAM B. REED'S LETTER.—DIGNIFIED SILENCE.—THE B'HOYS.—MAY 7TH, 1849.—ASTOR PLACE.—FIRST SYMPTOMS OF A RIOT.—JOHN BULL DEFYING BROTHER JONATHAN.

ON the 20th of November, 1848, Mr. Macready appeared at the Arch Street Theatre, Philadelphia. It was then, and for the first time, that an unsuccessful attempt was made to drive him from the stage. Upon his being called before the curtain he addressed the audience as follows:

"He had understood, at New York and Boston, that he was to be met by an organized opposition, but he had abiding confidence in the justice of the American people." [Here the noise and confusion completely drowned his voice, and three cheers were attempted for Forrest, and three hearty ones were given for Macready.] He resumed by saying, "It was the custom in his country never to condemn a man unheard." [Cheers and calls, a voice crying out, "Did you allow Forrest to be heard in England?"] He said, "I never entertained hostile feelings towards any actor in this country, and have never evinced a feeling of opposition to him. The actor alluded to had done that towards him, what he was sure no English actor would do—he had openly hissed him." [Great noise and confusion, hisses and hurrahs.] "That up to the time of this act he had never entertained towards that actor a feeling of unkindness, nor had he ever shown any since." [Collision in boxes and great uproar throughout the house.] He said,

"That he fully appreciated the character and feelings of the audience, and, as to his engagement, if it was their will, he was willing to give it up at once; [no, no, cheers and hisses;] but that he should retain in his memory the liveliest recollection of the warm and generous sentiments of regard shown him, and should speak of the American people, whom he had known and studied for the past twenty years, with the same kind feelings that he ever had done."

This, the third speech delivered by Mr. Macready, before Mr. Forrest had uttered a syllable, called forth from the latter gentleman this scathing card. The editor of the *Pennsylvanian*, of Nov. 22nd, 1848, introduced it thus: "We received the following card last evening. It is a reply to the speech of Mr. Macready, at the Arch Street Theatre, on Monday evening:"

A CARD FROM EDWIN FORREST.

"Mr. Macready, in his speech, last night, to the audience assembled at the Arch Street Theatre, made allusion, I understand, to 'an American actor' who had the temerity, on one occasion, 'openly to hiss him.' This is true, and, by the way, the only truth which I have been enabled to gather from the whole scope of his address. But why say 'an American actor?' Why not openly charge me with the act? for I did it, and publicly avowed it in the *Times* newspaper of London, and at the same time asserted my right to do so.

"On the occasion alluded to, Mr. Macready introduced a fancy dance into his performance of Hamlet, which I designated as a *pas de mouchoir*, and which I hissed, for I thought it a desecration of the scene, and the audience thought so too, for in a few nights afterwards, when Mr. Macready repeated the part of Hamlet with the same tomfoolery, the intelligent audience of Edinburg greeted it with a universal hiss.

"Mr. Macready is stated to have said last night, that up to the time of this act on my part, he had 'never entertained towards me a feeling of unkindness.' I unhesitatingly pronounce this to be a wilful and unblushing falsehood. I most solemnly aver and do believe that Mr.

Macready, instigated by his narrow, envious mind, and his selfish fears, did *secretly*—not *openly*—suborn several writers for the English press to write me down. Among them was one Forster, a 'toady' of the *eminent tragedian*—one who is ever ready to do his dirty work; and this Forster, at the bidding of his patron, attacked me in print even before I appeared on the London boards, and continued his abuse of me at every opportunity afterwards.

"I assert also, and solemnly believe that Mr. Macready connived when his friends went to the theatre in London to hiss me, and did hiss me with the purpose of driving me from the stage—and all this happened many months before the affair at Edinburg, to which Mr. Macready refers, and in relation to which he jesuitically remarks that 'until that act he never entertained towards me a feeling of unkindness.' Pah! Mr. Macready has no feeling of kindness for any actor who is likely, by his talent, to stand in his way. His whole course as manager and actor proves this—there is nothing in him but self—self—self—and his own countrymen, the English actors, know this well. Mr. Macready has a very lively imagination, and often draws upon it for his facts. He said in a speech at New York, that there, also, there was an 'organized opposition' to him, which is likewise false. There was no opposition manifested towards him there—for I was in the city at the time, and was careful to watch every movement with regard to such a matter. Many of my friends called upon me when Mr. Macready was announced to perform, and proposed to drive him from the stage for his conduct towards me in London. My advice was, do nothing—let the superannuated driveller alone—to oppose him would be but to make him of some importance. My friends agreed with me it was, at least, the most dignified course to pursue, and it was immediately adopted. With regard to an 'organized opposition to him' in Boston, this is, I believe, equally false; but perhaps in charity to the poor old man, I should impute these 'chimeras dire' rather to the disturbed state of his guilty conscience, than to any desire upon his part wilfully to misrepresent. "EDWIN FORREST.

"PHILADELPHIA, Nov. 21st, 1848."

The only mistake we think Mr. Forrest made in this letter, was the expression calling Mr. Macready a "superannuated driveller." Mr. Macready was born in the year 1793, consequently at the time this article was written, 1848, he was but fifty-five years of age. A man cannot be called or considered superannuated at that age.

To this letter, Mr. Macready replied in a card "to the public," dated Jones' Hotel, Nov. 22nd, 1848:

"In a card, published in the *Public Ledger* and other morning papers of this day, Mr. Forrest having avowed himself the author of the statement, which Mr. Macready has solemnly pledged his honor to be without the least foundation, Mr. Macready cannot be wanting in self-respect so far as to bandy words upon the subject; but, as the circulation of such statements is manifestly calculated to prejudice Mr. Macready in the opinion of the American public, and affect both his professional interests and his estimation in society, Mr. Macready respectfully requests the public to suspend their judgment upon the questions, until the decision of a legal tribunal, before which he will immediately take measures to bring it, and before which he will prove his veracity, hitherto unquestioned, shall place the truth beyond doubt. * * * * *

"For the other aspersions upon Mr. Macready, published in the Boston *Mail*, and now, as it is understood, avowed by Mr. Forrest, Mr. Macready will, without delay, apply for legal redress."

Mr. Forrest's reply to this card, goes over the whole ground of the reception he received at the Princess' Theatre, in 1845; Mr. Macready's complicity with "Forster," the "toady," the influencing of Bulwer, etc. He quotes from the several London papers to show that Mr. Macready's "veracity" was at fault. Our readers will remember that we have, in a former number, gone over the grounds of the quarrel between these two gentlemen in 1845—a quarrel which Mr. Macready foolishly revived in 1848–9.

As regards the threatened law suit, Wm. B. Reed's letter to Mr. Macready, dated May 1st, 1849, settles the matter. The letter is just such a one as an acute and sensible lawyer would write to a client he did not intend to fleece; and Mr. Reed showed his good sense in advising his excitable client to keep away from the courts. We give an extract from Mr. Reed's letter:—

> "Our opinion was, that the publications were libellous, and that an action would lie. But we could not reconcile it to our sense of duty to you, as a stranger, and one who could not remain here to watch the inevitable delay of litigation, to advise you thus to assert your rights. In my own mind, I was entirely satisfied that none of the attacks made on you could in the end do you the least harm, and there was, therefore, on my part, no hesitation in advising you not to bring a suit. All that since has occurred satisfies me that I was right. Your discreet and dignified silence under provocation of no ordinary kind, has won and kept you many friends, etc. * * *
>
> "William B. Reed."

This "dignified silence" consisted in his client making injudicious speeches—talking loudly at private dinners against Mr. Forrest—compelling managers to refuse free admissions to persons connected with the press who wrote against him—influencing the press by flattering the critics, who in return, praised, puffed, and fawned on the *great actor*, at the expense of our own tragedian, and independent criticism.

Mr. Reed's letter is worthy a Philadelphia lawyer; he knew there were no grounds for a libel suit, and gets quietly out of the matter by flattering his client with such sugared expressions as "your discreet and dignified silence," and having "won and kept many friends." The actor swallowed the bait, and the suit was withdrawn. The hook, however, was in his gill and rankled there. His next move was to publish letters from England, commenting on the *emeute*, and complimenting his speeches as manly and dignified.

The English view taken of the whole matter was not endorsed by the American press. Even E. Bulwer Lytton's letter to his "dear friend" Macready, dated December 16th, 1848, did not explain away his refusal to allow Mr. Forrest to play Richelieu and Claude Melnotte. In fact, all his attempts to throw the whole blame of the attacks made upon him here on Mr. Forrest, most signally failed, and the commencement of his second engagement foreshadowed a storm that his friends like our own "Old Probabilities," should have apprehended by examining the nation's barometer. We have spoken of the "B'hoys" of New York. In addition to what we have said, let us give an extract from Mr. William Knight Northall's "Before and Behind the Curtain," published in New York, in 1851. Speaking of this class known as the "B'hoys," he says: "It embraced, however, a very wide variety, both of age and of character, from the complete rowdy, whose only vocation is to 'pick a muss' and 'run wid der machine' —he rarely works with it—to the intelligent young mechanic, who on an occasional 'lark' finds a relief from the monotony of his daily labor. But when these discordant materials are brought to harmonize, and act upon any occasion in a mass, they form a most effective force, whose power in a riot nothing short of military discipline can withstand. We have no evidence whatever that an understanding existed between the celebrated Captain Rynders and the 'B'hoys,' or that the Empire Club was cognizant of the coming storm."

The first night of Mr. Macready's second engagement, was on May 7th, 1849, at the Astor Place Opera House.

MESSRS. WILLIAM NIBLO AND JAMES H. HACKETT...DIRECTORS.
MACBETH.......................................MR. MACREADY.
LADY MACBETH.......................................MRS. POPE.

BROADWAY THEATRE.

PROPRIETOR...............................MR. E. A. MARSHALL.
MACBETH.......................................MR. FORREST.
LADY MACBETH...................................MRS. WALLACK.

The announcement card of Messrs. Niblo and Hackett, of Mr. Macready's appearance, caused considerable excitement, inasmuch as "The Boys" talked loudly, and the speeches of Mr. Macready were quoted as affording sufficient cause to create a "muss." Mr. Forrest's letter exposing the English "Ring's" endeavor to have him hissed, and the success attending it in London, also added to the excitement; and as the evening approached, it was manifest that a spirit of determined resistance to the "Kid-glove" gentry (who upheld the English actor at the expense of Mr. Forrest) on the part of the class we have already described, was prevalent. Another thing that excited the fears of the manager was the avidity with which Opera House tickets were purchased by those who had never before been seen in its luxurious interior. That "The Boys" were bound to be there, was evident. They probably dreamed as little as any one of the extent to which the disturbance would go. They looked upon it in two lights—first, as a piece of fun, and secondly, as the means of teaching foreigners a lesson, and not to trifle with the people when national pride had aroused the spirit of their sires to put down English attempts to govern the "mimic world." The love of country in this case overcame the good sense and second thoughts of those who took upon themselves the right of redressing grievances.

Another cause—an error of the managers—provoked the ire of the crowd. *They had sold more tickets than the whole "Opera House" could accommodate.* This completed the alarm of Mr. Niblo, who immediately sought the Chief of Police, and requested the presence of a strong detachment of his men for the evening. They were granted, but came, for the most part, too late to be of much service in the scenes which followed. As this evening laid the foundation for the dreadful scenes of the 10th of May, we give our readers some account of Mr. Macready's reception.

As the ominous hour of half-past seven, P. M., drew near, the regular "tramp" warning, peculiar to the Chatham and Bowery, commenced. Mr. Niblo was behind the scenes, in consultation with Mr. Hackett. As the first slight echo of the unusual stage reveille sounded in his ear, he stepped lightly to the wing, and pulling the edge of the drop curtain slightly towards him, took a brief but earnest survey of the scene before him. Officer Bowyer, of the chief's bureau, who had just at that moment arrived, was standing beside the veteran manager as he was surveying the scene of action, and turning to the officer, said:

"This looks rather dubious, Mr. Bowyer!"

"Yes; the 'Boys' are here, certainly! What induced you to sell so many tickets? People are making a tremendous rush at the doors yet, and the house is full, over-full, already."

At that instant the orchestra commenced an overture, and the "tramp, tramp," of the "Boys" throughout the house, for a moment, ceased.

"What do you think, Mr. Hackett? Is there going to be a disturbance?"

Hackett did not know, but passed the question to Bowyer, who took Mr. Niblo's place at the wing, and took a survey at the entire audience.

"There is mischief in the parquette and amphitheatre," he remarked; "but, probably, no actual violence will be attempted. 'The Boys' will make a noise, and endeavor to prevent the play from proceeding, but possibly will do nothing further. They seem to be patient and very good-natured, but Mr. Macready may expect a rough reception."

The band of the orchestra ceased, and almost instantly the ominous "tramp, rap, rap," was recommenced, but louder and more determined. Mrs. Pope, dressed as Lady Macbeth, at this moment, made her appearance, pale with real excitement and agitation. "My God! Mr. Hackett!" she exclaimed, "what is the matter? Are we to be murdered? Murdered here to-night?"

"Keep calm, my dear madame; there is no cause for alarm; everything will go on smoothly."

Just before the rising of the curtain, the "tramp, tramp—rap, rap!" had entirely ceased; the house was perfectly quiet; but, alas, it was a lull in the storm—a calm that bore a significance, which neither the managers nor the police understood.

The curtain rose upon the first scene, when the appearance of Mr. Clarke, who personated the character of Malcolm, elicited three loud and enthusiastic cheers from the parquette and gallery. From the moment that the cheering, hissing and whistling, and other expressions of feeling began, not a syllable was heard during the remainder of the scene, nor the succeeding one, till the entrance of Macbeth, passed in dumb show. When Macbeth and Banquo entered in the third scene, the uproar was deafening. A perfect torrent of groans and hisses assailed Mr. Macready, and a deluge of assafœtida was discharged upon him from the gallery, filling the whole house with its pungent and not particularly fragrant odor. A rotten egg, *à la* Montreal, was projected against him, but missing his face, bespattered the stage at his feet. The friends of Mr. Macready, who appeared rather to outnumber those opposed to him, now manifested their feelings by cries of "Shame!" "Shame!" Cheers and waving of handkerchiefs provoked a response in the form of renewed groans, hisses, and a half dozen rotten potatoes on the part of the others. "Three cheers for Edwin Forrest!" were called for by some one in the pit, and were given with great enthusiasm by those unfriendly to Mr. Macready. Then came the cry of "Three cheers for Macready!" which were responded to with equal enthusiasm by the opposite side of the house. The scene now beggared description. Hisses, groans, cheers, yells, screams, and all sorts of noises, in the midst of which, Mr. Macready still maintained his position in the centre of the stage. "Off! off!" shouted one party. "Go on! go on!" screamed the other. Mr. Macready approached the lights. He was greeted by roars of ironical laughter and reiterated hisses and groans. A banner was exhibited in front of the amphitheatre, bearing on one side: "No apologies; it is too late!" and on the other: "You have proved yourself a liar!" From this it was evident that the whole programme of the attack had been quietly prepared. The appearance of the banner was the signal for a perfect tornado of uproarious applause, laughter, cheers and groans, in the midst of which an old shoe and a cent piece were hurled at Mr. Macready, who picked up the copper coin, and, with a kingly air, put it into his bosom, bowing at the same time with mock humility to the quarter of the gallery from which the visitation had descended.

Several of Mr. Macready's friends now became much excited, and shouted to him to "go on," and "not give up the ship," which elicited tremendous groans, hisses, and cries of "three groans for the codfish aristocracy," cries of "down with the English hog," "take off the Devonshire bull!" "remember how Edwin Forrest was used in London!" Thus passed the whole of the first and second acts. The greater portion of the audience opposed to Mr. Macready seemed in excellent humor. They chanted snatches of the Witches' Choruses, and amused themselves by asking and answering all kinds of ridiculous questions. When the curtain rose on the third act, and Macbeth appeared, the uproar was greater than ever. Smash came a chair from the gallery, strewing the stage with its fragments, within a few feet of Mr. Macready. Another chair fell at his feet, with a crash which resounded through the house. The few ladies in the boxes started up from their seats, and grew quite pale. Another chair was hurled on the stage, and the curtain suddenly fell. The ladies hurried from the boxes. Thus ended the first attempt of Mr. Macready to play in opposition to the popular voice.

One act of Mr. Macready's during the noise and confusion had a tendency to provoke the audience, and was no doubt the origin of the subsequent sad and fatal disaster. Finding that the hisses were becoming more energetic, and the groans fast rising into yells, he suddenly stepped forward to the foot-lights, and with a glance of defiance at the amphitheatre, gradually dropped his gaze, until his eyes rested full upon the midway occupants of the parquette seats. Then, with his arms folded, and his brow contracted with a scowl of mingled derision and scorn, he slowly paced the breadth of the stage, eyeing, as far as possible, each individual who so pertinaciously opposed his proceeding with the play. This was in bad taste—it was a mistake. The "Boys" became aroused—it was not the way to conciliate them. Had he adopted a different course—one more suited to our National feelings, and the well known good nature of the American people,—we question if the scenes which followed would have occurred. Allegorically speaking, it was the Lion defying the Eagle—practically, however, it was

JOHN BULL DEFYING BROTHER JONATHAN.

It was an imprudent act, and the last one terminating the performance on the evening of May 7th, 1849.

CHAPTER XXX.

THE 19TH OF MAY, 1849.—JAMES WATSON WEBB.—APPEAL TO THE WORKING MEN.—THE MILITARY PREPARE TO FIRE.—THREATS OF THE MOB.—ALARM IN THE GREEN-ROOM.—THE WORD GIVEN.—FIRE!—THE FEARFUL CLOSE OF THE RIOT.—DEATH!

A PORTION of the press on Tuesday, the eighth of May, made the most unfounded charges against

Mr. Forrest, and endeavored to hold him responsible for the conduct of the oppressors of Macready on the night previous. The New York *Courier* and *Enquirer* was particularly personal, asserting that Mr. Forrest had said "that Mr. Macready should never be permitted to appear again on any stage in this city."

To this charge Mr. Forrest, through his counsel, Theodore Sedgwick, Esq., replied: "I am instructed to say, that every charge against Mr. Forrest, contained in the article in question, is absolutely and grossly false, and as the attack is coupled with reflections of a most improper and offensive character, I hope you will see the propriety of retracting and withdrawing the accusation in the most immediate, direct and ample manner," etc.

Before this letter was received by the editor, he had actually made an apology, retracting what he said. To this article he appended the following P. S.

"Since the foregoing was written, we have received the following letter (an extract we have given above) from Mr. Sedgwick, to which we cheerfully give place, and only regret that any charge against, or allusion to Mr. Forrest, in connection with this disgraceful riot, should have been made. It is quite certain that there is no evidence of Mr. Forrest being a party to the proceeding; and we are bound to assume that he was not; and it is also evident that such was our conviction previous to the receipt of Mr. Sedgwick's note, from the fact that the foregoing had been already prepared for publication by our associate, and we so apprised Mr. Sedgwick's messenger.

"JAMES WATSON WEBB."

We have stated that the original cause of riot and bloodshed were the grossly insulting speeches of Macready, particularly the one delivered in the Astor Place Opera House, on the 25th of October. But justice to Mr. Macready requires us to say, that after the demonstration on the night of the 7th, he would have retired without further contest with the public, but for the officious interference of a few persons who were prompted by various motives to sustain him. On the 9th of May, the following letter, signed by forty-eight gentlemen of different degrees of respectability, was addressed to Mr. Macready:

"To W. C. Macready, Esq.

"Dear Sir:—The undesigned having heard that the outrage at the Astor Place Opera House, on Monday evening, is likely to have the effect of preventing you from continuing your performances, and from concluding your intended farewell engagement on the American stage, take this public method of requesting you to reconsider your decision, and of assuring you that the good sense of and respect for order prevailing in this community, will *sustain* you in the subsequent performances."

The journals favorable to Mr. Macready were enthusiastic in their praise of the *distinguished* citizens who signed this letter, and equally fierce in their denunciations of those who had the temerity to hiss him off the stage. The *Courier*, the *Commercial*, the *Mirror*, the *Express*, and the *Day Book*, fairly dared any one to attend at the Opera House on the night of the 10th, to hiss Macready. Those who hissed him on the night of the 7th, were denominated "rowdies," "ruffians," "blackguards," "rabble," "lower classes," and "the worst kind of *Loco Focos*." The *Mirror* invited them to the theatre to have another "trial of strength," and the *Courier* assured Mr. Macready that he was not opposed "by any portion of the American people *of whose approbation and esteem he would be at all desirous*."

Thus it will be seen that the friends of Mr. Macready, and the personal and political enemies of Mr. Forrest, united in giving an invitation to those who felt aggrieved by the conduct of Macready, to meet them at the Opera House, on the evening of the 10th, and try which party was the strongest! The distinguished forty-eight thought their names alone sufficient to subdue any outbreak on the part of the "lower classes."

The sequel proved that they did not estimate sufficiently the strength of Macready's opponents, nor the depth of feeling which had been excited against him. On a trial of strength the distinguished forty-eight, and the aristocracy, generally, were no match for the "Boys."

On Tuesday evening, May 8th, for which Mr. Macready had been announced in Richelieu, the Opera House was closed. On Wednesday, Mr. Hackett himself played in The Merry Wives of Windsor. Mr. Macready having consented to play again after the reception of the letter, Thursday night was fixed for his re-appearance in Macbeth. Both parties prepared for the struggle. As we have said, it was to be a trial of strength—"Aristocracy and the English Clique *vs.* The Lower Classes." The lessees, with some of the signers of the letter, called upon Mayor Woodhull and concocted measures for defending the Opera House in case of a riot. They also secured large quantities of tickets, and distributed them freely for the purpose of securing a favorable reception. Their opponents in the meantime were not idle. Placards were posted about the walls, some pretending to favor Mr. Macready, and couched in language adapted to excite prejudice against him—some were more openly hostile, of which the following is a specimen:

WORKING MEN,
SHALL
AMERICANS OR ENGLISH RULE
In this city?

The crew of the *British Steamer* have threatened all Americans who shall dare to express their opinion this night at the *English Aristocratic Opera House!!*

We advocate no violence, but a free expression of opinion to all public men!

WORKING MEN! FREEMEN!!
STAND BY YOUR
LAWFUL RIGHTS.
AMERICAN COMMITTEE.

On Thursday morning, May 10th, the rival placards were placed side by side:

ASTOR PLACE OPERA HOUSE.
DIRECTORS.
Messrs. Wm. Niblo, & Jas. H. Hackett.
This evening will be performed
MACBETH.
Macbeth, Mr. Macready. Lady Macbeth, Mrs. Pope.

BROADWAY THEATRE.
Proprietor—E. A. Marshall.
This evening will be performed
THE GLADIATOR.
Spartacus, Mr. Forrest. Julia, Miss Wallack.

From a work entitled, "Before and Behind the Curtain," by William Knight Northall, New York, 1851, we give an extract describing this terrible night-scene, which, for brevity and force, surpasses all others that were given on the morning after the riot. It will close our account of the

ASTOR PLACE OPERA HOUSE.*

"It was peculiarly unfortunate that just at the time

* Shortly after the trial of the supposed rioters, the whole proceedings were published, but as the details are dry and technical, and given in law phraseology, we deem the statement given here fully sufficient to furnish our readers some idea of this most terrible riot.

the new Mayor, but a day or two installed, was scarcely versed enough in the duties of his position to act with all the decision that was required. Still, dispositions were made on Thursday to meet any emergency, by detailing a body of three hundred men to the Opera House, and ordering two regiments of citizen soldiery to be under arms, and at their quarters on that evening. The Opera House was carefully occupied, the men posted, and the windows barricaded; and thus they awaited for the conflict to commence.

"As soon as the doors were opened, a rush commenced, which, in a very short time, nearly filled the house. Most of the doors were soon closed again, and the complaint was made that none were admitted but those who bore tickets with the private mark of the Macready party.*

"An attempt was made by a party outside to batter down one of the doors, but was prevented by the police. The glass lamps were broken, and stones were thrown through a single window that had been left unbarred, falling inside among the audience. The play commenced, amid a storm of cheers and hisses. But, on the whole, the scene within the house was of a less exciting character than on the previous night. The audience had been carefully picked, and "the Boys" were in the minority. Still they maintained a determined noise. The play proceeded almost in dumb show until after the commencement of the second act. Then, just as the rioters were about to jump in a body

* It appeared in evidence, upon the trial of Edward Z. C. Judson (Ned Buntline), who, it was said, headed the mob outside, and called upon them to stone the building, that some of these tickets were obtained by his opponents and supplied to the friends of "Ned Forrest." This was termed, "Shooting the Egyptians."

from the parquette to the stage, the chief of police gave the preconcerted signal by raising his hat. In an instant the police sprang to their work. The house was quickly cleared of all but a few of the most violent, the doors were closed again, and the latter found themselves very cleverly caught, and most effectually prevented from helping their friends outside. Thus ended the play within."

The *Herald*, speaking of the scene, said: "At this time, the scene within the house was indeed most exciting. In front and rear, the fierce assaults of the mob, as they thundered at the doors, resounded all over the theatre, while the shouts and yells of the assailants were terrific. Inside, however, all was comparatively quiet."

As the mob increased in magnitude, and in the ferocity with which they assailed the building, the cry arose inside, and also outside, among the peaceable citizens—"Where are the police? Cannot anything be done to disperse the rioters? Where is the Mayor? Military?"

Let us renew our extracts from Mr. Northall's account:—

"The Seventh Regiment marched up Broadway, led by a body of horse. Their arrival upon the scene of action only made the mob more furious, and they were attacked with stones and missiles of all descriptions. The horse were soon forced to withdraw, but the infantry stood their ground like veterans. The civil authorities delayed the order to fire; and meanwhile the troops were exposed to the most incessant annoyance, without the power of defending themselves.

"At last it become evident that they must fire or

withdraw. It was even doubtful whether they could withdraw—whether, on the first symptoms of retreat, the mob would not overwhelm them and wrest the muskets from their hands. As a last effort, Recorder Talmadge boldly went forward and harangued the rioters. But it was in vain!—in vain! although with a voice, Stentorian and trumpet-toned, he informed the frenzied masses that in the eye of the law they were all rioters; that if blood were shed, if life were taken, they alone were responsible for the consequences; that the military were present to protect the theatre, to protect Mr. Macready, to preserve the peace of the city, and their *duty would be performed at all hazards!* that the muskets of the National Guards were loaded with *ball cartridges*, and that, in *one minute*, unless they ceased that disgraceful tumult, the painful, but necessary order would be given to FIRE! and that the troops *would obey that order!* He then appealed to them as good citizens—as members of the great family of Americans, worshipping at freedom's altar—he adjured them no longer thus to desecrate her sacred temple. He concluded with saying: 'Retire instantly to your homes—depart, each one of you! I warn you, upon your peril, remain in this vicinity not one moment longer! Depart, I adjure you, and let this street be cleared, or the soldiers here beside me—your own brothers—the armed citizens of New York—*will fire upon you*, as sure as there is a God above us! This building *will be protected*, whatever consequences ensue; the sacred majesty of the law *will be vindicated!* Disperse! Don't wait for the fearful order! Disperse! Every good citizen will linger here no longer. Go home! each one

—go home! For God's sake, fellow-citizens! brothers! —quit this spot, and let this tumult—this cruel and dastardly attack—cease!'

"The only replies to those humane and philanthropic efforts were renewed abuse, scoffs, hoots, yells of defiance, and fresh vollies of stones!

"In truth, such was the diabolical uproar, that even the strong voice of the Recorder could be heard but a few feet from the spot where he stood; and probably few, very few, of the mob ever understood a word of the remonstrance—the earnest request, or the menace!

"'Gen. Hall,' said the Recorder, as he slowly struggled through the crowd up to the spot where that officer was standing, at the right of the battalion under his immediate charge, 'you must order your men to fire! It is a terrible alternative, but there is no other!'

"'Is the Mayor here to issue the order?' queried the careful soldier.

"'Sheriff Westervelt's authority is sufficient. Mayor Woodhull, as I am just informed by Justice Mountfort, has left the theatre and taken up his headquarters at the New York Hotel.'

"'Had not the Mayor best be sent for?' asked one of the minor magistrates present.

"'The National Guards cannot stand here another minute!' responded simultaneously General Sanford and Col. Duryea, who had just joined the conference. 'Nearly one-third of the force is disabled already.'

"'You need not send for the Mayor; he will not come here again to-night,' interposed a policeman, his head bound with a handkerchief, beneath which the blood was trickling down his cheek, from a severe blow of a stone over the temple.

"'What say you, Sheriff Westervelt?' asked General Hall.

"'Has the Riot Act been read?' interrupted a well-dressed 'sympathizer,' dodging his head out of the door-way. 'I warn you never to fire upon the people until they hear the Riot Act!'

"'The Riot Act has been *heard* sufficiently all the evening,' replied the Recorder. 'Mr. Sheriff, I consider your duty plain and imperative!'

"'Gen. Sanford!' was Mr. Westervelt's response, 'you have my permission to act as you consider indispensable in this emergency!'

"'Do you give me the order to fire?'

"'I do, sir! It is the only resource left!'

"'Mr. Matsell, call in your policemen—we shall be forced to employ bullets in half a minute!' And stepping in front of the line, Gen. Sanford, with some difficulty, made himself understood so as to bring the troops to the position of 'ready,' at the same time warning the mob to fall back, as *the guards would most assuredly fire!* He was accompanied by Gen. Hall and Col. Duryea, who exerted themselves to the utmost in inducing the people to retire, and thus save themselves and force the painful alternative!

"But all this was of no avail. The rioters would not understand that the movement was sincere, or else, in their mad passion, they seemed determined to brave even death itself, rather than desist from their infamous assaults.

"'Fire and be d——d!' 'Fire if you dare!'

'To Hell with your guns!' 'Shoot away, you infernal sons of ——!'

"'Fire into this,' yelled a grimed and heavy-headed rioter, holding a large stone between his knees, while with both hands he tore open the bosom of his red shirt. 'Take the life out of a free born American for a bloody British actor! Do it, aye, you darsen't.'

"'Fire, will ye!' screamed another, hurling a missile at Gen. Sanford, which took effect upon his sword arm, rendering it powerless for the time—'take that, ye chalk-livered oakum-faced rat.' 'Ho! all together, now boys! Hit 'em again! Give the counter jumping sogers hell,' and other similar, but more outrageous language, was the only response to their humane efforts.

"At the moment when Sheriff Westervelt indicated to Gen. Sanford the determination of the authorities to resort to the extreme remedy, the police, with their stars concealed, were intermingled with the crowd, immediately in front of the theatre. They had just restored the captured muskets to the troops, and occasionally singling out a rioter more violent and disorderly than the rest, they would manage to jostle him from the mass, when, by a sudden and concealed movement, they were sometimes successful in effecting his arrest and removal to the interior. It was a matter of imminent necessity, that these policemen should be called within the lines immediately, but the task proved not at all an easy one, since at the time the chief received his caution from Gen. Sanford, a pretty energetic fight was progressing for the possession of a prisoner, between the officers and the rioters.

"As it was, the first volley was fired while many of the policemen were still in the midst of the mob, and even at the second discharge, several of them were exposed, they being still within the range of the military.

"The pause for the last but fatal command was brief —yet those few moments were almost hours of fearful suspense to those who *knew* that death brooded over that mass of criminality and violence! Certainly, the general aim was not a murderous one; yet none could tell the mischief about to be occasioned by a glancing ball or stray bullet. Friends and relatives, possibly, were amid the multitude before them! And besides, a dangerous and delicate experiment was about to be tried! If this demonstration did not serve to intimidate, what would be the result? Would the guards obey the order if commanded to pour a point-blank volley into the bosoms of their fellow-citizens?

"These were startling questions! Nay, they were terrible!

"A moment or two would decide all!

"'Fire!'

"The word came from Gen. Hall, clear and distinct. It was heard above the din and confusion, along the whole line.

"A single musket, on the extreme left, responded!

"'Fire!' exclaimed Gen. Sanford, with all the energy of voice his lungs would afford.

"Three more pieces on the right were discharged almost simultaneously.

"'Fire! Guards!! Fire!!!' shouted Col. Duryea —and the remainder of the volley flashed forth, the pieces speaking with that sharper and fuller toned report which distinguished the service charge from the mere powder and paper of field day!

"The instant glare lit up a sea of angry faces on

Astor Place—of human forms clustered in the windows and on the roofs of the adjacent buildings; the tattered and broken lamps in front for a moment were seen clear and distinct—the shattered windows of the theatre itself were for a twinkling visible, and then all again was darkness! while the blue sulphurous smoke rolled outward among the crowd, or curled in dim eddies around the Guards themselves!

"And thus ended the Astor Place riots. The mob soon broke and fled; for they knew now the authorities were terribly in earnest. The obnoxious player was vanquished and driven out; but it had cost thirty American lives to do it. The majesty of the law was vindicated!

"Peace to the memory of those who fell; let us not judge harshly of the dead."

CHAPTER XXXI.

THE CAUSES LEADING TO THE DIVORCE BETWEEN MR. FORREST AND HIS WIFE.—DOMESTIC DIFFICULTIES.—DIFFERENCE BETWEEN AMERICAN AND ENGLISH LIFE.—MRS. FORREST.—STATE OF THE DRAMA.—ENGLISH ACTORS, AND ACTRESSES.—A LEGAL OPINION.—CORRUPT LEGISLATURE.

WE had purposed to pass over in silence that painful episode in the life of Mr. Forrest, known in criminal records as "The Forrest Divorce Case," but as it placed that gentleman in a false light through a biassed court and jury, a few of the leading facts of the case we deem necessary in connection with these Reminiscences. It may also be mentioned that many members of the theatrical profession, particularly at that period, were not considered as models of good husbands, nor their wives "angels of the household."

We do not deny but that the stage has furnished many grave reasons for critical censure, by sustaining actors and actresses whose conduct was gradually lessening its moral tendency. This, however, is not the general character of those of the theatrical profession, but it has been sufficient to elicit censure from the opponents of the stage. They have gone so far as to say, the "theatre is a school of vice," "a place to learn wickedness," and "that corruption and debauchery are the truly natural and genuine effects of stage entertainments." This domestic difficulty of Mr. Forrest's, is only one of a hundred grievances traceable to the detestable influence of the French and English school of morals which have flooded the land for years. It is well known that the English and French, or at least many of them, have none of that refined sense of what constitutes the real pleasure of the domestic circle. The manners and customs of a country are the criterions by which we form our opinions of those who practice them both at home and abroad. The influence of education properly exercised, with a strict eye to the observances of the rules of etiquette, are readily discernible in those whose parents direct the education of their children. Mrs. Forrest's parents, or at least the father, was a professional man, and had all those notions of life derived from a stage point. It was English life as exemplified both on the stage and off, but totally unsuited to that of the American.

If Mr. Forrest had established in his household certain rules, and taught his wife the difference between English and American habits, much of the evil, arising out of their misunderstanding, might have been obviated. The effect, however, of this neglect soon became apparent, all of which for awhile, Mr. Forrest bore in silence, the time came, however, when he found it necessary to remonstrate.

It was said on the trial that when Mr. and Mrs. Sinclair came to this country, with their daughters, they made Mr. Forrest's house their home, where they made themselves perfectly happy, not only in the enjoyment of what the wealth of the son-in-law afforded, but drawing around them men and women with whom Mr. Forrest had little or no acquaintance. This in a manner estranged man and wife, for Mr. Forrest as it is well known, was never fond of home company, unless of his own immediate household.

During the whole course of Mr. Forrest's dramatic career, his object was to maintain the dignity, character and morality of the drama, and to make the theatre a source of noble and useful entertainments. As a professional man, few ever enjoyed a higher reputation, both on and off the stage, for upwards of fifty years, than did Mr. Forrest, and when this sad episode in his private life occurred, no one ever suffered more mentally and physically than he did, for as he said: *"this state of things has destroyed my peace of mind, and is wearing out my life."*

As Mrs. Forrest is still living, and usefully employed, occupying a position in society alike respectable and honorable, we shall refrain from making use of the witnesses who testified so strongly against her on the trial. We do this because, to speak candidly, we think some of them magnified the social parties of Mrs. Forrest materially, and not understanding the difference between actors and actresses from those of other professions, felt shocked at their free and liberal manners. That these witnesses were so influenced, we have no doubt, and indeed we might say with that eccentric author of "Tristam Shandy," that these witnesses were like the armies spoken of in that incomparable work—"Who Swore terribly in Flanders."

As a specimen of the evidence, and we may say the most important, showing the gradual working up of the case, and the beginning of Mr. Forrest's change of behavior to his wife, we give the following evidence as sworn to by their house-keeper:

"At all times previous to the month of January, 1849, the said Edwin Forrest had always treated his wife in a kind and affectionate manner. I considered him a very indulgent husband; whenever he was in the city, and not absent upon his professional engagements, he was very domestic in his habits; and during the whole time that I have known them, up to January, 1849, their intercourse was extremely confidential, affectionate and intimate.

"And I further say, that while I was in Mr. Forrest's house in Reade Street, the demeanor of both him and his wife was most kind and affectionate, and I had not the slightest reason to doubt that they were mutually very much attached to each other.

"When I returned to live as house-keeper with the said Edwin Forrest, in the month of January, 1847, the said Forrest and his wife went to the south, where they remained for about two months, and shortly after they returned, in the spring of the year 1847, I heard conversations among the servants about the late hours kept by Mrs. Forrest and the gentlemen admitted to the house at such late hours, and I soon perceived that the state of things between Mr. Forrest and his wife had entirely altered."

* * * * * * *

Other portions of the evidence as given on the trial are totally unfit for publication. But as the jury ignored this evidence in rendering its decision, so will we (except in one instance), but will confine ourselves simply to the statements made by each of the parties and that of a few friends. There is enough in these to show that, guilty or innocent of any actual crime, there is sufficient in these statements to satisfy the reader that Mr. Edwin Forrest and Mrs. Catharine Sinclair Forrest *could never again live together as man and wife!*

> "Of all the passions, jealousy
> Exacts the hardest services, and pays
> The bitterest wages."

The scenes as detailed on the trial were of such a nature as to horrify our American ideas of propriety, and yet are thought nothing of in France and England. The servants, not accustomed to this mode of entertaining guests, viewed the whole affair in a criminal light, and indeed to them it so appeared. That pure moral tone which should produce harmony in the household, and strengthen love, is made discord, by repudiating the marriage vow, and the refinement so essential to the female character.

A true woman is the embodiment of virtue; she stands like the sun—

> "And all which rolls round
> Drinks life, and light, and glory from her aspect."

Virtue may be assailed, but never hurt. It is vice that spreads its poison through the soul, and closes up all the avenues leading to the portals of purity. It is vice that demoralizes society, pales the fair face of virtue, and though

"Well perfumed, and elegantly dressed,
Like an unburied carcass tucked with flowers,
Is but a garnished nuisance, better far
For cleanly riddance than for attire."

Shortly after the conclusion of the trial, Mr. Forrest visited Philadelphia. We were at that time writing a series of dramatic articles for the *Pennsylvanian*, the editor and proprietor of which was our much esteemed and valued friend, John W. Forney, Esq. We give the following article entire, which we wrote at that time, 1852. Then, as now, we endeavor to shield the lady from the serious impression the trial had made on the minds of the community, by attributing the cause to levity and improper training in her youth:

THE DRAMA.

Mr. Edwin Forrest, with some remarks on the morality of the Drama.

BY COLLEY CIBBER.

"The visit of Mr. Edwin Forrest to his native city—his home, his residence, in despite of the New York clique, has been one of a pleasurable character, although the mantle of sorrow weighs heavily upon him. A review of the extraordinary trial through which he had passed, its extraordinary result, the triumph of a clique, the prejudice of a court, and the hostility of a jury, fully satisfies us that the whole scene was a base attempt to subserve the interests of that clique, at the expense of truth and justice. The enormous amount of alimony—an amount predicated on the interest of a man's estate, guessed at by ex-parte witnesses, has astonished and confounded every one.* The real cause of Mr. Forrest's complaint, the breaking up of his domestic peace, the ruin of his prospects in the connubial state, were thrown aside, and his errors, made so under the English law, which still exists in New York, to sustain a subject of that ilk, and

* Alimony, an allowance to which a married woman is entitled upon a legal separation from her husband, when she is not charged with adultery or an elopement

satisfy its adherents. We ask, what else is the construction that can be put upon this most extraordinary case and its results? Malice did its work; a jury made up of Mr. Forrest's enemies—a jury determined to *crush him*, accomplished the rest. Mr. Forrest had been made the easy tool of designing men; his noble, generous nature abused, household invaded, himself cheated. These are the friends of the unwary, the confiding.

"Has this trial and its result lessened him here? No. His English foes have got a portion of his wealth—it was their aim—they can now revel on it. * * *

"It will be understood that we take the view of those scenes described by the witnesses as occurring in Mr. Forrest's house, already expressed by us, from an English stand-point, both as regards their social and public habits. The English stage, never too pure, furnishes us a history that is calculated not only to effect the moral, but the literary character of an institution, intended to be the noblest in the world.

"Take a glance even now around among our different theatres; managers as well as actors figure largely as bigamists, and many of the women as their partners in the crime. We have now two or three Mrs. B——. We have the husband of one of them keeping a tavern in Georgia, and another sojourning in other lands. We could unfold the history of another whose crimes have grown gray in the annals of our drama; we could speak of one who has turned his wife and children out of doors, and takes in her place another man's wife! We could tell of one whose name is allied to vice in every shape and form—we could tell of females, one who lived with the *murderer of her husband*, and whose death transferred her to infamy and still deeper in vileness. We could speak of one who left her husband, and now passes as the wife of a man who has two other wives living. Another manager, bought the wife of a musician engaged in the orchestra of his own theatre, for a new suit of clothes and fifty dollars cash!

"Are not these dreadful things? Do we not live in an age of crime? Is there any wonder why the drama is debased, and the moral tone of a theatre destroyed? Crime and depravity, vice and immorality attract, while modest talent, allied to virtue, is disregarded. Such is the character of that class, from which spring those evils which are demoralizing society. Little crimes become as nothing, and larger ones fashionable; we adopt the manners of the foreigner, and learn to imitate his vices. Whatever may have been the character of those who visited the house of Mr. Forrest during his absence, such at least is the character of two-thirds of those who now sway the destinies of the drama and the stage!

"We have never joined in the hue and cry against Mrs. Forrest. That she erred in judgment, acted without reflection, there can be no doubt. A jury has pronounced her innocent, but let her glance back; let her review calmly and dispassionately a career of life commenced under the brightest and most cheering of prospects; let her recall those happy moments when, with youth and innocence, she clasped the noble form and heart of the husband of her choice to her arms—then contrast the rest. If the fault was mutual which first chilled the 'fever of love,' mutual should have been their resolve; the man might have deviated—the man could have forsook his home and found peace, such as it was, in other places, but the wife never.

"But alas! from out of this strange and mixed-up affair, what has not come? The victim, the sufferer to English habits and customs is our countryman, our townsman; the vices of that school, have nearly corrupted our own; and it is now the duty of the American people to ask the question—*How much longer will we tolerate English vice and immorality on the stage?*

"In the city of New York, there have been managers of theatres, whose histories are the best commentaries that can be offered or given on English dramatic habits, manners and customs. Connected with these men are the wives of some dozen poor debased actors, whose habits and contemptibility are such that the crimes of their better halves are as nothing. It is from such a state of things many of our national vices spring. But how is it when an American actor is accused of such a thing! How is it when he asks for redress from domestic evils! Does the law wink at his acts as it does at those of the English! Oh, no—he is persecuted and prosecuted—perjury, and the combined efforts of the clique that rules in Gotham, are all brought to bear; and thus, while vice and immorality are winked at, and sanctioned when they are confined to foreigners, an AMERICAN ACTOR IS MADE TO PAY THREE THOUSAND DOLLARS per annum to sustain the cause of these English customs in our midst!"

Such was the state of the stage at the period named and from out of which came the "Forrest Divorce Case." Is it therefore to be wondered at, that a deep-rooted prejudice against the stage should be the result of these abuses.

New York and Brooklyn, at the present writing, are sad illustrations of this state of things, the publication of which in the papers, has shocked the whole country, as high-toned men and women are scandalously mixed up. The demon of Free Love has flapped his wings in triumph over cities once celebrated for their moral and religious tendencies. In many cases a divorce is not asked for by parties guilty of unlawful acts, for it not unfrequently happens that man and wife are equally culpable, and an exposure would only tend to a conviction of both. In the "Forrest Divorce Case," both husband and wife accused each other of the grossest misconduct. A verdict, however, was given in favor of the wife, and the court ordered her husband to pay three thousand dollars alimony per annum; the lady was declared innocent by verdict of the jury. If the law admitted her claim to a wife's share of the husband's property then — a law peculiar, probably, to New York—what hinders her from obtaining the same, if not all of his property now? She is, *de facto*, the sole heir, as no relative of the deceased lives to claim it, or is any blood relation named in the will. The court sustained her then; why not sustain her now? If it was right before the death of Mr. Forrest, is it not right now? It may be asked here, why the divorce was not granted in our State when brought before the Legislature. We regret to say, and it is with feelings of deep sorrow we assert the fact, it was because Mr. Forrest was too honorable to yield to the demand of some of its members for "certain considerations" before the question was brought before them. A member of the Legislature told the writer of this, and others, that for five thousand dollars he could have had the bill passed! This man was friendly to Mr. Forrest, and was willing to serve him, and for that sum he could have the whole thing settled. Where is a man to look for justice when he has to pay his way to the very portals of legislative halls? Hence we infer that this same sort of influence would have materially changed the aspect of the case in New York. It was not used; hence the result.

As we have stated, it is not our purpose to go over the whole ground of this case; but in justice to the memory of Mr. Forrest, it is necessary to give here the cause which induced him to propose a separation from his wife. Sometime before the trial, in open court, the proposition was to this effect; to avoid scandal, he would allow her fifteen hundred dollars per annum, to all of which she agreed, and for awhile the terms were strictly adhered to. As the first grounds of suspicion a husband has of a wife's infidelity, are either true or false, the proof of the latter should be positive before a single movement on his part should be made. Circumstances not unfrequently have placed an innocent woman in a false position in the sight of her husband, whose hasty conclusions have entailed upon both, long mental agony and physical suffering. It was not so in

Mr. Forrest's case. Let us give his version of the first cause which led him to suspect his wife's infidelity.

CHAPTER XXXII.

THE FIRST-CAUSE OF SUSPICION.—STARTLING DISCLOSURES.—JAMIESON AT BAY.—THE PHRENOLOGIST.—THE DISCOVERY.—PRIVATE DRAWER.—THE LETTER.—SEPARATION.—MR. FORREST'S LETTER TO HIS WIFE.

IN the year 1848, Mr. Forrest went to perform a professional engagement in Cincinnati, and was accompanied by Mrs. Forrest and Mr. Jamieson. During this visit, on the 31st of May, 1848, Mr. Forrest left his hotel for an hour, for the purpose of having his portrait taken, but, disappointed by the artist, he returned suddenly. We will let him tell the rest: "When I entered my private parlor in the City Hotel, I preceded S. S. Smith, who was with me, some yards, and found Mrs. Forrest standing between the knees of Mr. Jamieson, who was sitting on the sofa, with his hands upon her person. I was amazed and confounded, and asked what it meant. Mrs. Forrest replied, with considerable perturbation, that Mr. Jamieson had been pointing out her phrenological developments. Being of an unsuspicious nature, and anxious to believe that it was nothing more than an act of imprudence on her part, I was for a time quieted by this explanation. After we left Cincinnati, I observed that Mrs. Forrest carefully preserved about her person a bundle of letters; and although it was unusual for her to do so, it made no very material impression upon me at the time. In the month of January, 1849, Mrs. Forrest went to a party at her sister's (Mrs. Voorhees), and I remained at home. In the course of the evening I opened a drawer with a key in my possession, and found the bundle of letters I had seen Mrs. Forrest preserve with so much care. They were, with but one exception, letters written by Mrs. Voorhees to Mrs. Forrest. Among them was the letter, in the handwriting of George W. Jamieson, written to her under the *soubriquet* of 'Consuelo.' Shortly afterwards, I charged her with having received this letter from Mr. Jamieson, when she acknowledged that Mr. Jamieson gave it to her while we were on board a steamboat, and about to leave Cincinnati for Pittsburg." [The time referred to by Mrs. Forrest, when she received this letter from Jamieson, was on the 14th of May, 1848.]

"I further state that the facts set forth in my petition for a divorce, and presented to the Senate and House of Representatives of Pennsylvania, are just and true.

"I have read the remonstrance of Mrs. Forrest, and solemnly declare that the statements therein made, especially the alleged ground of separation, are untrue.

"Since the separation, I have voluntarily allowed her the sum of fifteen hundred dollars per annum, for her support, which has been punctually paid her in advance. My present income is about forty-three hundred dollars per annum.

"Since I was about nineteen years of age, I have supported my mother's family, and still continue to do so. I do not state this to claim any merit, but to show that I have, in spite of all her grounds of complaint, made to Mrs. Forrest a most liberal allowance for her support."

Mr. S. S. Smith, in his deposition, said: "On the day referred to, in the month of May, at Cincinnati, I was present when Mr. and Mrs. Forrest, and Mr. Jamieson agreed to attend an interview with a phrenologist, at three o'clock in the afternoon. At two o'clock, of the same day, I went with Mr. Forrest to the studio of an artist, with whom it was understood he was to sit an hour for his portrait. The painter not being at home, Mr. Forrest and I immediately and unexpectedly returned to the City Hotel. In entering the hotel, Mr. Forrest preceded me about ten yards, and entered his private parlor a short time before me.

"Upon my entrance, I found Mr. Jamieson and Mr. and Mrs. Forrest there. Mr. Jamieson immediately afterwards, notwithstanding his previous engagement to attend the phrenological examination, precipitately and without notice left the room, and when I searched for him he was not to be found in the house or its vicinity. I have known Mr. Forrest well for many years, and after the interview above mentioned, I observed a high and unusual degree of excitement on the part of Mr. Forrest in relation to his wife—a feeling which, intimate as I was with him and his wife, I had never witnessed before. I firmly believe that something must have been observed by Mr. Forrest upon his entrance into the room, in the position or deportment of Mr. Jamieson and Mrs. Forrest, which produced this change in Mr. Forrest. Mr. Forrest walked more rapidly than myself, and he entered the room so far before me, that I had no opportunity of seeing or knowing what it was that produced the change in him. I had always known Mr. Forrest previously as a most affectionate and confiding husband, but from that time there was a manifest change in his demeanor towards his wife."

Mr. Forrest did not let his wife know that he had in his possession the celebrated letter of "Consuelo" notoriety, immediately after her return from the party alluded to, as the following evidence, given on the trial, will show. What his feelings were, can be better imagined than described. One of the witnesses said:—

"Mr. Forrest remained at home, alone; during the evening I heard him walking up and down, rapidly, in his library and bedroom; and I thought, from his disturbed manner, that he was uneasy, and had something on his mind. I went to bed about twelve o'clock, and before Mrs. Forrest had returned. Mrs. Forrest returned about two o'clock, A. M."

Another witness, the house-keeper, stated "that there was a violent altercation between Mr. and Mrs. Forrest, in the library, and that it lasted a long time. In the course of the same day, Catharine Forrest told me, substantially, what one of the servants had said; 'that she had had an angry dispute the night before with her husband; that she had never seen him so much excited before; that he said something terrible was going to happen; and she could not tell what he meant.'

"On the morning in question, Mrs. Forrest went to the bottom drawer of one of the bureaus, which was always kept locked, and began to examine some papers which it contained, when, of a sudden she started back and exclaimed, 'Good God, what a fool sister Katten is!' I then went out of the bedroom into the library. Almost immediately after, I returned and said to her, 'Why, what is the matter with you?' to which Mrs. Forrest replied, 'He has got that letter.' She then said something about Mr. Jamieson and 'Consuelo,' and continued, 'now I know what he meant by the conversation we had together, it is separation.' Mrs. Forrest then went immediately to another drawer, which she unlocked; it contained some letters; then she said, 'I am glad he did not open this drawer, he might have found some more letters.' And the same day, in my presence, Mrs. Forrest destroyed a quantity of letters and papers which she took from that drawer. A few days afterwards, Mrs. Forrest said to me, that Mr. Forrest had told her (Mrs. Forrest) the night before, that he had found the letter from Mr. Jamieson and had determined to separate from her."

Edwin Forrest and his wife separated on the first day of May, 1849, both leaving the house on Twenty-Second Street. We have adverted to the cause or causes leading to this unfortunate termination of what, at first, promised a long and happy wedded life. But there are some other facts necessary to allude to here, as having a powerful bearing on the part of the wronged husband to demand such a separation. Mrs. Forrest, in the absence of her husband, was in the habit of keeping open house, and several of her friends were in the habit of staying late at night. Among these, were Capt. Calcraft and young Richard Willis. These two, according to a witness, "remained in the house till two or three o'clock in the morning." The same witness stated "that in the fall of the year 1848,

Mr. Richard Willis was secreted in the house for three days."

Mr. James Lawson, in his evidence at the trial, wherein he stated that he endeavored to reconcile the parties, said: "I first became acquainted with Edwin Forrest in the fall of 1826, and ever since I have been on terms of the closest intimacy with him. I have known Mrs. Forrest, wife of said Edwin Forrest, since the first day of her arrival in this country, namely, in the fall of 1837.

"Until the month of January, 1849, I always thought and believed that the said Edwin Forrest and his wife lived on terms of kindness and affection. Mr. Forrest always treated his wife with great tenderness. In the said month of January, I first heard from Mrs. Forrest, that a separation between her and her husband was resolved on; about the last of April following, they parted.

"In my interview with Mrs. Forrest, endeavoring to obtain concessions which I thought important to bring about a reconciliation with Mr. Forrest, she said: 'You are working in the dark; you do not know what you are striving at; for it is an impossibility that Mr. Forrest and I can ever live together as man and wife.' * * On or about the second of November last, when at an interview, Mrs. Forrest had consented to send her sister (Mrs. Voorhees), from her house in Sixteenth Street—which I thought a necessary step before the question touching the reconciliation could be put to Mr. Forrest—I asked Mrs. Forrest: 'Now, since we have come to this point, pray tell me who was wrong in that unknown cause which separated you. I do not ask the cause; for that, you say, is never to be told. But, who was wrong?' Mrs. Forrest answered; 'I was.' To this I remarked: 'I am glad to hear you say so; for confession is the first step to repentance,'" etc.

To which we annex the sworn statement of the Rev. E. L. Magoon:—

Elias Lyman Magoon, of the city of New York, being duly sworn and examined, said: "I am a minister of the Baptist Church; I have been acquainted with Edwin Forrest and Catharine his wife, for about twelve years, and I have heretofore supposed them both eminently worthy of my highest personal esteem; I first became acquainted with the said Edwin Forrest and wife at Richmond, in the State of Virginia, where I then resided; afterwards I removed to Cincinnati, Ohio, and there resided until I removed again to this city.

"During this time, I have met Mr. Forrest and his wife at Richmond, Cincinnati, in London, Paris, and at his house in this city, and always on terms of personal intercourse and intimacy; until recently, and within about a year past, I have been accustomed to hear nothing from said Edwin Forrest and wife but expressions of mutual confidence, and to see nothing between them but indications of mutual love; some time in or about the month of December, 1849, the said Catharine Forrest told me that for several months previous to her late separation, she and her husband had known each other only as brother and sister."

Mr. Forrest gave no explanation to his friends, directly or indirectly, as to the cause of separation of himself and wife, and would hold no converse whatever on the subject. Subsequently, however, when Mrs.

Forrest began to give her reasons, or rather, as she said, cause of separation, Mr. Forrest said to a friend, in December, 1849, that the real cause of the separation of himself and wife was his conviction of her infidelity! On December 24th, 1849, Mr. Forrest determined to end the unpleasant position in which he was placed, and give the public the true cause of the separation—preparatory to which he sent to Mrs. Forrest the following letter, as found in the testimony of the "Forrest Divorce Case" before the Senate and House of Representatives of the Commonwealth of Pennsylvania.

LETTER OF EDWIN FORREST TO MRS. FORREST.

"I am compelled to address you by reports and rumors that reach me from every side, and which a due respect for my own character compels me not to disregard. You cannot forget that, before we parted, you obtained from me a solemn pledge that I would say nothing of the guilty cause—the guilt alone on your part—not on mine—which led to our separation. You cannot forget that, at the same time, you also pledged yourself to a like silence—a silence which I supposed you would be glad to have preserved. But I understand from various sources, and in ways that cannot deceive me, that you have repeatedly disregarded that promise, and are constantly assigning false reasons for our separation, and making statements in regard to it, intended and calculated to exonerate yourself, and to throw the whole blame on me, and necessarily to alienate from me the respect and attachment of the friends I have left to me. Is this a fitting return for the kindness I have ever shown you? Is this your gratitude to one who, though aware of your guilt, and most deeply wronged, has endeavored to shield you from the scorn and contempt of the world. The evidence of your guilt, you know, is in my possession. I took that evidence from among your papers, and I have your own acknowledgment by whom it was written, and that the infamous letter was addressed to you. You know, as well as I do, that the cause of my leaving you was the conviction of your infidelity. I have said enough to make the object of this letter apparent. I am content that the past shall remain in silence, but I do not intend, nor will I permit, that either you or any one connected with you shall ascribe our separation to my misconduct. I desire you, therefore, to let me know at once whether you have, by your own assertions, or by sanctioning those of others, endeavored to throw the blame of our miserable position on me. My future conduct will depend upon your reply. "Once yours,

"[Signed] "EDWIN FORREST.

"New York, December, 24th, 1849."

CHAPTER XXXIII.

MRS. FORREST'S LETTER.—REPLY.—THE CONSUELO LETTER.—SKETCH OF GEORGE JAMIESON.—HIS FEARFUL DEATH.—RETRIBUTION!

IN the last chapter we gave Mr. Forrest's letter addressed to his wife. We now give the lady's answer. We would observe here, that the lady's letters are generally written in a style of elegance, simplicity, and apparent innocence, that no one who reads them but regrets the cause that led to their publicity:

MRS. FORREST'S ANSWER.

"I hasten to answer the letter Mr. Stevens has just left with me, with the utmost alacrity, as it affords me at least the melancholy satisfaction of correcting misstatements, and of assuring you that the various rumors and reports which have reached you are false.

"You say that you have been told, that I am 'constantly assigning false reasons for our separation, and making statements in regard to it, intended and calculated to exonerate myself, and to throw the whole blame on you;' this I beg most distinctly to state is *utterly untrue.*

"I have, when asked the cause of our sad differences, invariably replied, that was a matter known only to ourselves, and which would *never* be explained; and I neither acknowledge the right of the world, nor of our most intimate friends to question our conduct in this affair.

"You say, 'I desire you therefore to let me know at once whether you have by your own assertions, or by sanctioning those of others, endeavored to throw the blame of our miserable position on me.' I most solemnly assert that I have never done so, directly or indirectly; nor has any one connected with me ever made such assertions with my knowledge; nor have I ever *permitted any one* to speak of you in my presence with censure or disrespect. I am glad you have enabled me to reply *directly* to yourself concerning this, as it must be evident to you that we are both in a position to be misrepresented to each other; but I cannot help adding, that the tone of your letter wounds me *deeply;* a few months ago you would not have written thus. But in this neither do I blame *you;* but those who have for their own motives poisoned your mind against me —this is surely an unnecessary addition to my sufferings; but while I suffer I feel the strong conviction that some day, perhaps one so distant that it may no longer be possible for us to meet on this earth, your own *naturally* noble and just mind will do *me* justice, and that you will believe in the affection which for twelve years has never swerved from you. I cannot nor would I endeavor to subscribe myself other than

"Yours, now and ever,

"[Signed] "CATHARINE N. FORREST.

"Dec. 24th, 1849."

Mr. Forrest never alluded to his wife or cause of separation, after the amicable settlement alluded to. Mr. Andrew Stevens, in his evidence, stated that "during the summer of the year 1849, I was in the habit of spending my Sundays with Mr. Forrest, but he made no explanation, directly or indirectly, as to the cause of the separation of himself and his wife, and would hold no conversation whatever on the subject with me. I remained in absolute ignorance, so far as the said Forrest was concerned, of the true cause of the difficulty between himself and his said wife."

In a second letter Mrs. Forrest sent, as given in Schedule B, she went more into detail. In one part she said:—"You know as well as I do that there can be nothing in my conduct to justify those gross and unexpected charges; and I cannot think why you should now seem to consider a foolish and anonymous letter as an evidence of guilt."

Mrs. Forrest closed up this letter in the following feeling manner:

"I cannot believe it, and implore you, Edwin, for God's sake, to trust to your own better judgment; and as I am certain that your heart will tell you I could not seek to injure you, so likewise, I am sure, your future will not be brighter if you succeed in crushing me more completely, in casting disgrace upon one who has known no higher pride than the right of calling herself your wife.

"[Signed] "CATHARINE N. FORREST.

"Dec. 29th, 1849."

This is Mr. Forrest's answer to Mrs. Forrest's letter, marked B:

"I answer your letter dated the 29th, and received by me on the 31st ultimo, solely to prevent my silence from being misunderstood.

"Mr. Godwin has told me that the tardy reply to the most material part of mine of the 24th, was sent by his advice. I should indeed think from its whole tone and character that it was written under instructions. I do not desire to use harsh epithets or severe language to you. It can do no good. But you compel me to say that all the important parts of yours are utterly untrue. It is utterly untrue that the accusations I now bring against you are 'new.' It is utterly untrue that since the discovery of that infamous letter, which you so callously call 'foolish,' I have ever in any way expressed my belief of your freedom from guilt. I could not have done so, and you know that I have not done it. But I cannot carry on a correspondence of this kind. I have no desire to injure or to crush you; the fatal wrong has been done to me, and I only wish to put a final termination to a state of things which has destroyed my peace of mind, and which is wearing out my life. "[Signed] "EDWIN FORREST.

"New York, Jan. 2nd, 1850."

As this letter closed all correspondence between the parties, and terminated their private arrangements, and resulted in a trial in open court to prove charges made against the lady too gross for publication, we dismiss the whole subject—the worst of scandals, and give the celebrated Consuelo letter, the first cause of Mr. Forrest's suspicions of his wife's infidelity. We leave it to any husband—any high-minded man—to say, if finding such a letter in the possession of his wife, whether it would not create serious cause for suspicion; this letter speaks for itself, and so we end this sad episode in our Reminiscences:

LETTER OF MR. JAMIESON TO MRS. FORREST.

"And now, sweetest Consuelo, our brief dream is over—and such a dream! Have we not known real bliss? Have we not realized what poets love to set up as an ideal state, giving full license to their imagination, scarcely believing in its reality? Have we not experienced the truth that ecstasy is *not* a fiction? I have, and as I *will not permit myself to doubt you*, am certain *you* have. And oh! what an additional delight to think—no, to *know*, that *I* have made some hours happy to you. Yes, and that remembrance of me may lighten the heavy time of many an hour to come. Yes, our little dream of *great account* is over, reality stares us in the face. Let us peruse its features. Look with me, and read as I do, and you will find our dream is 'not all a dream.' Can reality take from us when she separates and exiles us from each other? Can she divide our souls—our spirits? Can Slander's tongue or Rumor's trumpet summon us to a parley with ourselves, where to doubt each other we should hold a council? *No! no!* a doubt of thee can no more find harbor in my brain than the opened rose could cease to be the hum-bird's harbor. And as my heart and soul are in your possession, examine them and you will find no text from which to discourse a doubt of *me.* But you have told me (and oh! what music did your words create upon my grateful ear), that you *would not doubt me.* With these considerations, dearest, our separation, though painful, will not be unendurable; and if a sombre hour should intrude itself upon you, banish it by knowing there is one who is whispering to himself, *Consuelo.* There is another potent reason why you should be happy—that is, having been the means of another's happiness, for I am happy, and with you to remember, and the blissful anticipation of seeing you again, shall remain so. I wish I could tell you my happiness. I cannot. No words have been yet invented that could convey an idea of the depth of that passion, composed of pride, admiration, awe, gratitude, veneration and love, without being earthy, that I feel for you.

"Be happy, dearest; write to me and tell me you are happy. Think of the time when we shall meet again. Believe that I shall do my utmost to be worthy of your love: and now, God bless you, a thousand times my own, my heart's altar.

"I would say more, but must stow away my shreds and tinsel patches—ugh! how hideous they look after thinking of you.

"Adieu! adieu! and when thou art gone,
My joy shall be made up alone,
Of calling back with fancy's charm,
Those halcyon hours when in my arm,
Clasp'd Consuelo.

"Adieu! adieu! be thine each joy,
That earth can yield without alloy,
Shall be the earnest constant pray'r
Of him who in his heart shall wear,
But Consuelo.

"Adieu! adieu! when next we meet,
Will not all sadness then retreat,
And yield the conquer'd time to bliss,
And seal the triumph with a kiss,
Say, Consuelo?"

We have said this trial ended the sad episode in the life of Mr. Forrest; but, alas! not its consequences. The verdict was rendered by the jury on the 24th of January, 1852, adding thereto: "and that the alimony to be allowed to the said plaintiff shall be three thousand dollars per year." Perhaps, this side of Hades, no such verdict was ever rendered; the defendant was actually found guilty of the very charges brought against the plaintiff, she was found not guilty of adultery in the fifth question in the specification, and the defendant was so declared on the first and third to have been the guilty party!

In heathen mythology it is said there are judges in hell who hold court in the tribunal opposite the entrance of the infernal regions; on it were seated Minos, Rhadamanthus and Æacus. The imagination, without any extraordinary degree of extravagance, could readily transfer this Court of Judges to New York, and invest the presiding officers of an earthly tribunal with those of Tartarus.

Mr. Forrest appealed from this decision, and used every effort to defeat the order of the court; appealed to higher courts, and failed; a final verdict compelled him to pay the full amount, and to her allowance as alimony one thousand dollars more, making in all an annual income of four thousand dollars! This amount was faithfully paid up to the day of his death, and which the executors still continue to pay. What will be the result of Mrs. Forrest's future claim upon his property can only be decided by the courts.

GEORGE JAMIESON.

As this individual's name is mixed up in the Forrest Divorce Case, as one who took a leading part in destroying the peace and happiness of the man who had been his friend—loaned him money, and befriended him every way—something of his history may not be out of place here. We knew this man Jamieson; he was what we should call a *bon-vivant,* fond of good living and drinking at the expense of others. He was, however, a first-class boon companion. We were at a private dinner given in New Orleans to a favorite comedian. Jamieson was present. He was the life of the company—gave imitations of actors, sung comic songs, imitated the negro minstrels; in fact, delighted and amused all who were present. The next night he played Macbeth in a manner that surprised those who, on the evening previous, were amused at his comicalities.

George Jamieson was born in New York, in 1812, and made his *debut* in his native city, January 23rd, 1837, in a farce called The Chameleon, in which he personated five characters. It was on the occasion of the benefit of Charles Eaton, at that time a young tragedian. In 1839, he became a member of the National Theatre, at the corner of Church and Leonard Streets, New York. He first appeared in Philadelphia, October 9th, 1840, at the National Theatre. In 1861 he visited England. Returning to this country, he appeared with much success at the Winter Garden Theatre, New York, as Pete, in the Octoroon. Jamieson was well known in the dramatic profession—unreliable, careless, and regardless of the proprieties of dramatic, social, or moral life. He met with a sudden and awful death, October 3rd, 1868, near Yonkers, by being run over by a Hudson River Railroad train. *Was it retribution?*

> "Where be your jibes now? your gambols? your
> Songs? your flashes of merriment, that were
> Wont to set the table in a roar?"

CHAPTER XXXIV.

AFTER THE TRIAL.—HIS APPEARANCE AT THE BROADWAY THEATRE.—RECEPTION.—SPEECH.—FIRST APPEARANCE OF MRS. CATHARINE N. SINCLAIR (FORREST) AS AN ACTRESS.—AN OLD PLAY-BILL.—UNJUST CRITICISM.—MR. FORREST AS AN ARTIST.

MR. FORREST was not idle during the progress of the trial, he was fulfilling his engagements in various portions of the country, and found friends and sympathizers everywhere.

The Broadway Theatre, New York, under the management of Mr. Marshall, with Thomas Barry, formerly of the Park, for stage manager, re-opened on the 27th of August, 1851, with an excellent company.

On the 15th of September, 1851, Mr. Forrest made his first appearance in two years, at that theatre, as Damon, and his last on the 27th, as Spartacus. These two characters were always received by the audience with much applause, and were considered the most striking pictures of the histrionic art that were ever presented on the stage. We have already alluded to them in former parts of these Reminiscences. We now come to another very important era in the life of Mr. Forrest; it is his first appearance after the termination of his divorce suit, January 24th, 1852.

In despite of the verdict, and all the evidence produced on the trial against him, there were but few who placed implicit confidence in that to which some of the witnesses swore. Indeed, the same may be said of those who gave evidence against the lady. Public opinion was about equally divided, and each had the benefit of the doubt.

February 9th, 1852, he commenced as Damon. This engagement lasted sixty-nine consecutive nights, during which time the houses were crowded. On his entrance, the first night, bouquets were showered upon the stage. Small American flags were thrown, and, mingling with the flowers, made the whole scene appear as a garden. A large flag was also displayed in the parquette, with this motto:—"This is our verdict!"

Mr. Forrest was called before the curtain and made a brief speech, as pensive as it was effective; he made no allusion to the past, but he spoke of the drama, and its future prospects, cherished as it would be by such intelligence as evidently was now maturing the sensational literature of the day, fostered with care, its future destiny could easily be foretold.

In conclusion he said:—"I thought my path was covered with thorns, but I find you have strewed it with roses." This engagement was the longest, as well as the most memorable, ever recorded in the history of the stage. The house—one of the largest and most magnificent in America—was crowded nightly to the utmost of its capacity, and with audiences whose enthusiasm remained unabated.

On the fiftieth night of this engagement there was a jubilee. The theatre was illuminated in front; an appropriate transparency was exhibited; many persons in the neighborhood, sympathizing with the general feeling, illuminated their dwellings. Inside there was one continued triumph for the great actor, while the street was crowded by admiring thousands, who could not gain admittance.

Before Mr. Forrest again appeared at the "Broadway," another event took place, which possessed a degree of interest almost equal to that of the one given. It was the first appearance of Mrs. Catharine N. Sinclair on any stage, the 22nd of February, 1852, at Brougham's Lyceum, New York, as Lady Teazle, in The School for Scandal, with Chippendale, Lynne, C. Mason, Walcott, Brougham, Skerrett, and Mrs. Maeder in the cast. Mrs. Sinclair's *debut* was a triumphant one, and her performance of Lady Teazle attracted full audiences for eight successive nights. She subsequently appeared as Pauline, Margaret Elmore, Lady Mabel and Beatrice, but without a corresponding success. Had she sustained these several characters as well as she did that of Lady Teazle, there is not the least doubt that she would have been a leading actress, if not a star, on the American stage. The propriety of her appearance on the stage, at this critical juncture, was very generally questioned. Mr. George Vandenhoff, who had been her instructor, appeared on the 23rd, as Claude Melnotte. Her engagement was not what might be termed a profitable one. The season ended abruptly on the 17th of March.

The Broadway Theatre reopened on the 30th of August, 1852, with the play of The Hunchback. On the 20th of September, Mr. Edwin Forrest appeared as Richelieu; on the 21st, as Damon; closing on the 30th of October. After playing at Philadelphia and elsewhere, Mr. Forrest returned to New York, and commenced another engagement at the Broadway Theatre, February 24th, 1853, opening with Othello. During this splendid engagement the manager produced Macbeth, May 2nd, 1853, with new scenery and dresses, at a cost of $8.000, taking rank with Charles Kean's getting up of King John and Richard III. This was played twenty nights in succession. We give the cast as played on that occasion as worthy a place in the records of our stage history.

MACBETH..MR. FORREST.
MACDUFF..F. CONWAY.
DUNCAN..MR. DUFF.
MALCOLM..A. DAVENPORT.
BANQUO..C. POPE.
HECATE..MR. GROSVENOR.
WITCHES........................DAVIDGE, WHITING AND BARRY.
LADY MACBETH..MRS. PONISI.

In connection with this cast, we will give that of its first performance in this country, March 3rd, 1767:

MACBETH..MR. HALLAM.
DUNCAN..MR. GRENVILLE.
MACDUFF..MR. DOUGLAS.
MALCOLM..MR. HENRY.
BANQUO..MR. MORRIS.
HECATE..MR. WOOLS.
LADY MACBETH..MISS CHEER.
LADY MACDUFF..MRS. DOUGLASS.

The names in this cast are among the pioneers of

the drama in this country; they are all familiar to those who take an interest in our early stage history.

The scene of Mr. Forrest's great success was the Broadway Theatre. Whenever his name was announced, it was the precursor to crowded houses. On the 17th of April, 1854, he commenced another long engagement, during which his Virginius won golden opinions from all sorts of people.

Shortly after Mr. Forrest's first appearance after the "divorce," certain would-be critics made some wonderful discoveries in his style of acting, intimating also that his readings of certain passages in the plays of Shakespeare were so emphasized as to convey allusions to his wife, or, at least, to show his opinion of women generally. These absurd constructions became marked features by those who are too apt to follow the opinions of others, rather than adopt those of their own. Not only this, they also made the discovery that Mr. Forrest was not the great actor that fame had heralded. He was accused of being merely a physical actor—"a vast animal bewildered by a little grain of genius," "a muscular tragedian of body without brains." Such language, uttered at a time when the fame of the great actor was ringing in the ear of nations, it assumed the tone of personal enmity, rather than that of criticism. With us, however, criticism had not attained the certainty and stability of science. With such low expletives, as given above, was Mr. Forrest greeted on his reappearance, and by whom? A few hirelings of the press, whose ideas of criticism were based on their own imperfect knowledge of this scientific art. They ridiculed the dramatic powers of the man whose genius had flashed over two hemispheres—the man whose voice and action brought back to a London audience the echo of those who had made "Old Drury" a classic temple—the man whose Lear paled the lustre on the laurelled brow of a Garrick. The man whose Othello startled an English audience, and as one of their most eminent critics said: "The effect was electric, and shot through the vast assemblage with a thrill of terror."

In the art gallery of the stage, Mr. Forrest's splendid pictures of Damon, Virginius, Coriolanus, Richard, Othello, Hamlet, Macbeth, William Tell, Carwin, Lear, Jack Cade, Spartacus, Richelieu, and others, will always be referred to as the highest specimens of histrionic talent.

With the stage, its character and its literature, the name and fame of Edwin Forrest are closely connected. It is not altogether a national feeling we have upon the subject, it is one that is sustained by the most accomplished critics in this country and in Europe, which induced us at an early period to speak of Mr. Forrest's acting as being superior to that of many who, with far less genius, elicited fulsome praise from the uninformed. True criticism is the proper estimate made of the works of art and of letters; it brings with it a warmth of feeling which, genial-like, makes true merit blossom in the sunshine it throws around it. It is the rain to give life and vitality to the early seed, the light to consummate its growth. True criticism can effect this; the false, never. Hence, criticism, as it is generally received, must, from the very nature of men's souls, be commensurate with the exercise of the judgment. A true critic is one who examines closely his own feelings before he grasps the pen, and by a delicate and nice examination, endeavors to discover if his judgment would endorse the motions caused by the action of the scene and the incidents of the story. This is considered the strongest test by which the truth of criticism can be tried. It was a critical knowledge of nature and of man which enabled Homer and Shakespeare to instruct and to astonish. Few critics in modern times have been enabled to do anything of the kind; hence, we have no standard of criticism among us.

Mr. Forrest's acting has seldom been tested by the rule of analysis; men of little minds could never comprehend the genius of the actor, nor the truthfulness of his art. They had no idea of its being an art calculated to refine taste, exalt the mind, and depict with a true artist's skill the emotions of the heart when following the author through the various phases of the passions evoked by the "cunning of the scene." Perhaps no one ever imparted so much knowledge of the drama to the million than did Mr. Forrest, and no one ever studied harder to attain the power to do so. That he did attain it, his fame while living, and the tribute paid to his memory are the proofs.

> "No pyramids set off his memory,
> But the eternal substance of his greatness
> To which I leave him."

We have alluded to certain criticisms on Mr. Forrest's acting as being of an extremely low order of that art. Caricature an artist, and you insult art; hold up the learned man as a target for folly to fire at, and you mislead the ignorant in regard to the source of education. True art is a very delicate subject for the uninformed to write about, it is beyond their reach. Can they follow it through fields of air—or criticise one

> "*Who writes his name on clouds,*
> *And treads the chambers of the sky?*"

or follow genius

> "*In his eagle flight,*
> *Rich dew drops sparkling from his plumes of light?*"

We think not.

The stage and the drama, identified with all that appertains to the arts and sciences, poetry, painting and music, command the respect of all who value and can appreciate, not only the "best words of the best authors," but all those pleasing auxiliaries we have named.

CHAPTER XXXV.

COMPLIMENTARY BENEFIT TO JAMES W. WALLACK.—MR. FORREST AS CLAUDE MELNOTTE.—THE ORIGINAL IN THE CHARACTER.—CAST.—RETIRES TO PRIVATE LIFE.—HOME ON BROAD STREET.—THE POOR SOLDIER.—FORREST'S LIBERALITY.—RENEWS HIS PROFESSION.—GREAT SUCCESS IN SHAKESPERIAN CHARACTERS.

MR. FORREST'S reputation was now at its height; he was acknowledged the greatest actor living. Every engagement was a perfect ovation; he not only mastered all the difficulties of texts, annotations and criticisms upon Shakespeare, but overcame the prejudices of those who had for years repudiated native talent. This was his final triumph. From his first reappearance on the stage after the divorce, up to the year 1854, his career was a brilliant one; he was emphatically the star of the "Mimic World." It would be but a repetition of what we have already said were we to follow him from place to place, and quote the note of praise accompanying his every movement. One event occurred during his engagement in New York, to which we refer with pleasure.

On the 29th of May, 1855, a complimentary benefit was given to James W. Wallack, Sr. This event came off at the Academy of Music, on which occasion Mr. Forrest deviated from a course he had strictly followed for years, and tendered his valuable services to one of the most finished and accomplished actors of the day. This was partly in return for the kindness and attention that gentleman showed him while in England, and that, too, at a time when friends were most needed. For this, and also for the necessities of the veteran actor, he broke through a rule which on several occasions he was highly censured for adhering to so strictly. Among the names of those who also volunteered on that occasion, were Mr. E. L. Davenport, Mr. F. Conway, Mr. Walcott, Mr. Henry Hall, Mr. Borani, Miss Louisa Pyne, Miss Fanny Vining, Mrs. F. Conway, Mrs. Buckland, Miss Kate Reignolds; and others volunteered, whose services could not be made available. The play was Damon and Pythias—Forrest as Damon, and Davenport as Pythias.

On the 27th of September, 1855, Mr. Forrest enacted Claude Melnotte, a character we thought one of the finest of his youthful impersonations. Mr. Forrest was the first Claude Melnotte in this country. It was produced at the Park Theatre, on the 14th of May, 1838. The popularity of the author, and the success of the play in England, and being its first representation in this country, attracted a crowded house. The cast was perfect in every respect:

CLAUDE MELNOTTE	MR. FORREST.
COL. DUMAS	MR. PLACIDE.
BEAUSEANT	MR. RICHINGS.
GLAVIS	MR. WHEATLEY.
DESCHAPELLE	MR. CLARKE.
MME. DESCHAPELLE	MRS. WHEATLEY.
PAULINE	MRS. RICHARDSON.
WIDOW MELNOTTE	MISS CHARLOTTE CUSHMAN.

Placide, Richings, Wheatley, and Mrs. Richardson had parts peculiarly adapted to the several styles in which they had excelled, while Miss Cushman's talents raised an insignificent character to an interesting and prominent position. We have witnessed the representation of this play in almost every city in the Union, in many of them with most excellent casts, but never saw any one to approach the Claude of Mr. Forrest, or a lady to equal Miss Cushman, as the Widow. Mr. Francis Courtly Wemyss, in his "Twenty-Six Years of the Life of an Actor and Manager," says: "On the 18th of May, 1838, Bulwer's play of 'The Lady of Lyons,' was acted *for the first in the United States, at Pittsburg, Pa.*, for my benefit. Mrs. Shaw, as Pauline. Then it was a failure, for on a subsequent representation, the proceeds of the house were only $126."

In the year 1855, Mr. Forrest purchased the handsome brown stone mansion, at the south-west corner of Broad and Master Streets, Philadelphia, which has since been his home, and for a while he retired from the stage. This property originally belonged to Frederick Gaul, Esq., the eminent brewer, and was not quite finished when Mr. Forrest purchased it. It has an extensive garden, in which tall, stately trees and weeping willows vied with the flower beds for supremacy. Mr. Forrest paid more attention to the trees than he did to the flowers. He cultivated the grape, and erected a hot house for their especial growth. Speaking to him one day about the garden, we asked why he did not pay more attention to the beautifying of it by arranging the flower-beds in accordance to the modern poetical arrangements, for there is poetry in them; why not illustrate it?

"Because," he replied, "I prefer the trees; I love to hear the wind whistling through their branches, and when alone in my library, it sounds like a voice from another world."

Subsequently Mr. Forrest purchased two adjoining lots, which he used as a vegetable garden. After the war, he gave a one-armed soldier the sole use of this lot. We have seen him working in it, planting and cultivating the growth of cabbages, potatoes, tomatoes, beans, peas; in fact everything that is required for the table for either rich or poor. All the profit arising from the production of this lot went to the sole use of the maimed soldier and his family. We said to him one day:

"What is the value of this lot—the one used by the old soldier?"

"Well, I don't exactly know."

"Suppose," we observed, "we say $25,000."

"Well, what then?"

"Simply this; the man is occupying a piece of ground for a vegetable garden, the interest of which, if sold, would bring you in fifteen hundred dollars per annum."

"True, but as I never intend to sell it while living, what matters it; he may as well have the use of it, as the other portion of my ground is sufficiently large for my purpose."

Few rich men ever did as much for an old soldier as Mr. Forrest did for this one.

His front on Broad Street was one hundred and ninety-eight feet, depth two hundred feet, the house and picture gallery occupying one hundred feet of the front, and there was an iron railing extending the length of the balance, in front of the garden, thus giving to passers-by a full view of the interior. We one day asked him why he put up the stone wall inside of the railing, thus giving to the exterior a prison-like appearance. His answer was—but not until he laughed heartily as a sort of prelude—"One day," said he, "I was in the garden, having on an old hat and light linen coat, which extended almost down to my feet, working away, with my back toward the street: I heard a sound, a sort of murmur; I paid no attention to it, however, when suddenly a shrill, boyish voice shouted out, 'There he is;' and then another, more manly, exclaimed, 'It is Richelieu.' I turned suddenly round, and to my utter astonishment saw the whole length of the iron railing lined with a gaping crowd, some shouting Macbeth, Rolla, Richard, and the devil knows what; and as I rushed into the house the sounds followed me. That, sir, is the reason why I put up that wall."

During Mr. Forrest's retirement, numerous inquiries were made when it was likely he would again appear. In answer to them, we published the following:

"TO CORRESPONDENTS. EDWIN FORREST."

"The question is so frequently asked in relation to the probability of this gentleman's appearing again on the stage, that we feel it a duty to answer such questions to the best of our knowledge, as we know it is not an idle curiosity which prompts them.

"These inquiries, written in many instances by persons evidently anxious to witness his powerful impersonation of character, are highly flattering to this inimitable artist. They also develop to us the fact that thousands are so sickened, and, in some instances, disgusted at the present state of the drama, and the paucity of genuine talent in our midst, that a change for the benefit of the whole body politic is most anxiously desired.

"To end the anxiety manifested, we can state, with confidence, that Mr. Forrest will appear on the stage again, and this event, so long looked for will most probably take place in the fall or winter season of the present year, *June*, 1860."

In the year 1860, he accepted a very tempting offer made by James M. Nixon, to perform one hundred nights (three nights each week) in the principal cities of the Union, Mr. Forrest receiving a clear-half of the nightly receipts. He opened on the 17th of September, 1860, at Niblo's Garden, as Hamlet. In 1861, Mr. Nixon engaged the Academy of Music, in Philadelphia, with Mr. Forrest as the star, and, as on the occasion of his New York engagement, seats were sold at auction. This was one of the most brilliant engagements ever performed by Mr. Forrest in his native city, during which he won golden opinions from all sorts of people, and, with but two exceptions, elicited the warmest encomiums from the press. This engagement closed on Monday, January 13th, 1862, with Othello. In consequence of the great success attending Mr. Forrest's impersonation of Shakesperian characters, the manager a few nights before the close, issued the following card:

"From the decided preference given by the public to Mr. Forrest's Shakesperian impersonations, the manager has determined, for the few remaining nights, that none but Shakespeare's plays will be produced."

This was a compliment paid alike to the author and the actor. The success attending this engagement with Mr. Nixon, was unparalleled in the history of the American stage.

Having concluded his engagement with Mr. Nixon, Mr. Forrest commenced a short one with Mr. William Wheatley, at the Chestnut Street Theatre, commencing January 26th, 1863, with Virginius, on which occasion Mr. Wheatley being called out, made the following speech:—

"If fortune does help the bold as the Roman proverb says, and the old English one, 'Resolution and success are cater cousins,' has any thing in it, then indeed do I feel certain that my honest ambition cannot and shall not be belied by my failure. Indeed, it seems to me that the blind goddess of the wheel and money bags, was in one of her most loving moods, since she enables me to commence my season in conjunction with the most powerful attraction as an artist, that could be found in this country—nay! by the world. You are of course aware that I am now alluding to Mr. Edwin Forrest!"

In consequence of the universal desire to obtain

seats on the occasion, tickets were sold by auction at high premiums from the auctioneer's rostrum.

During this engagement, Mr. Forrest produced Dr. Bird's celebrated play of The Broker of Bogota; speaking of which, he said—"Mr. William Wheatley's impersonation of Antonio de Cabero was one of the most finished pieces of acting I ever witnessed. The applause of the audience was equally divided; he receiving, I really believe, the greater share."

After fulfilling this engagement, Mr. Forrest again appeared at the Academy of Music, Mr. J. T. Ford, manager. The success attending this engagement was not so good, owing to the paucity of talent in the company.

Mr. Forrest continued playing throughout the country from this period, up to 1866, when he made his great tour to California, opening at San Francisco, at the Opera House, as Richelieu. Prior to his departure to the Pacific coast, he played an engagement at Chicago, Illinois, for five nights, to immense houses; the whole proceeds yielding $11,600—one night's performance alone being over $2,800!

Passing over the intervening years, we come to his last great engagement, commencing in Philadelphia, at the Walnut Street Theatre, October 2nd, 1871.

CHAPTER XXXVI.

MENTAL AND PHYSICAL LABOR.—FORREST'S ENERGY.—GREAT WESTERN AND SOUTHERN TOUR CONTEMPLATED.—PREPARES HIMSELF FOR THE TASK.—STARTS FROM PHILADELPHIA.—COLUMBUS.—CINCINNATI.—OHIO.

THOSE who have been used to a career of comparative idleness, can never know how men of busy lives seek for employment; and those whose days have been spent in constant labor from their youth up, cannot bear sudden and entire cessation without great suffering. Time is a dismal void to them. Young says, "Time destroyed, is suicide, where more than blood is spilt." The muscles and brain crack with rust, and man falls into the "sere and yellow leaf" before his time. How thoroughly Mr. Forrest appreciated this, can be seen by a glance at his professional career. From October 2nd, 1871—being then in the sixty-fifth year of his age—up to the 18th of March, 1872, he acted in fifty-one different towns and cities, playing five nights a week, performing one hundred and twenty-one nights; and in that time travelled not far from seven thousand miles; and in this campaign, accompanied by his able and efficient agent, Joseph McArdle, Esq., they suffered all the fearful calamities of railroad and steamboat disasters, putting up most of the time in hotels barren of ordinary comforts and convenience. The amount of vitality demanded in the representation of the characters acted by Mr. Forrest during the last campaign of his professional life was enormous.

Now let us contrast the present custom with an earlier epoch in the history of the drama. Formerly, the theatres were opened but three nights a week; then the actors had time for study and duly to rehearse their parts. Now they are called upon for eight performances a week, including matinees; and, in some instances in the South, they are asked to perform on Sunday evenings. When John P. Kemble took his farewell of the stage, he acted but fifty-four nights during the whole season, which lasted from October 25th, 1816, to June 23rd, 1817, during which time he was living quietly in his comfortable home in London. Mr. Kemble was then in his sixtieth year.

David Garrick never at any time played more than one hundred and thirty-eight nights, during any theatrical season; and for the last five years of his professional life, he acted but fifty-four nights in all, and was the manager of the theatre. He, like Kemble, left the stage in his sixtieth year. Compare with this, the mental and physical labor done by Mr. Forrest, who had just passed his sixty-sixth birth-day, and no one can dispute his intellectual or physical superiority. He one day remarked to an intimate friend, while speaking of the demands made upon him in the performance of some of Shakespeare's plays:—

"Why, I part with more vitality in one performance of Lear, than would keep an Alderman *alive* for a *lustrum!*" Upon another occasion he said: "I have wept more over the wrongs of Lear and Othello, within the last ten years, than I have ever wept before in my life." His friend remarked—"There was a sadness and a pathos in the tones of Forrest's voice as he gave utterance to these words, more touching and of deeper import than any of his acting I had ever seen." There certainly is a charm and music in the low marvellously sympathetic tones of Forrest's voice, that bring to our mind the criticisms of Hazlitt on Edmund Kean's farewell in Othello—(which by the way, was one of the most beautiful things we ever heard or witnessed on the stage)—when he compared the voice of that peerless actor to the "Sighing of the South wind through a Cypress Grove!"

It was stated of Thomas A. Cooper, that he visited every State in the Union, played in sixty theatres, acting four thousand five hundred nights, and travelled twenty thousand miles. James H. Caldwell, the great Southern manager, unfurled the banner of Thespis in thirteen States as proprietor, built four theatres, and travelled sixty thousand miles, as actor and manager, in thirteen years. From the 15th of May, 1820, to the 14th of July, 1821, he performed in the following route, travelling with a dramatic corps every mile—Washington City, Alexandria, D. C.; Fredericksburg, Richmond, Petersburg, and Norfolk, Virginia; Charleston, S. C.; New Orleans, La.; Natchez, Miss.; Nashville, Tenn. His annual journey, as given above, when completed, amounted to six thousand miles.

Mr. Forrest, anticipating this great undertaking, had, in a measure, prepared himself. He visited the most celebrated springs, rested on mountain tops, passed over lakes and valleys, sought places having legendary and historic interest—thus strengthening the body as well as the mind. The pure fresh air from the mountains, the salubrious gale that swept across the lake, a plunge into the vapor baths of Virginia, all contributed to aid and sustain him for the task.

The love of the profession, the desire to extend the legitimate drama, and to gratify the wishes of thousands living in the distant cities South and West, was the object of this great dramatic tour. His name, so closely identified with our drama, and written in golden letters on the histrionic page made it familiar to all. New stars had appeared in the "mimic world;" new names been added to the list of great actors, which, for a while, elicited criticism, but, lacking the mental glow, the mind's light, they have long since passed away in meteoric flashes. Forrest's star was in the ascendant, and the drama wore it like a jewel on her brow. Travelling through sections of our country, where the drama, some years ago, had scarcely a local habitation and a name, suffering the many privations incident to such a journey, Mr. Forrest gave another portion of a long and useful life to the cause of the legitimate drama, and to the interest of the American stage, furnishing to the many who had read only about plays and actors, the evidence of what true art can do in the nineteenth century; made stage illusions a seeming reality —showed them Lear panoplied in all his majestic grandeur—a living portrait of Shakespeare's creation; presented to their astonished view the wily Cardinal, who ruled France, in the place of a weak king; drew with the power of his genius, Virginius, Damon, Coriolanus, and also the Jealous Moor, and other of Shakespeare's great characters, making them startling pictures for admiring thousands.

We will glance slightly over this tour, from its start until its close. Alas! how nearly did that word connect itself with that of his own life? No coming events cast their shadows before him in that bright hour of his dramatic triumph; no dark pall resting on some sculptured marble was conjured up to his mental vision; and yet these shadows were before him—moving on, darkening, and closing gradually into eternal night!

Mr. Forrest commenced this mapped out engagement at the Walnut Street Theatre, on the second of October, 1871. To say it was a success, would be simply to repeat what we have already said of his other engagements. This engagement closed on the 16th of October. He then proceeded to Columbus, Ohio; opened there on the 23rd of the same month, and thence to Cincinnati, the Athens of the West. When Mr. Forrest first appeared in Cincinnati, nearly fifty years before, the city, as well as the drama, were in their infancy. To him these remembrances must have been pleasing. He could look back to the time when the boatman's song was heard on the waters of the Ohio, and these notes were re-echoed from the forests lining its shore:

"Hard upon the beach oar,
She moves too slow,
All the way to Shawneetown,
Long while ago."

These scenes and these notes echoing from the bluffs of the beautiful Ohio, had a charm for his youthful mind which time on its onward course could not dispel. Indeed, he often spoke of them as among the most pleasing reminiscences of his past life. It is not, perhaps, generally known, that Mr. Forrest indulged, when alone in his library, writing, or as he said "attempting to write poetry," and almost as soon as finished, found its way into the waste basket. One poem, however, may be found among his papers, descriptive of the scenes alluded to above, which we are satisfied never met the fate of the others. It commences with an invocation to nature; and we could almost venture to give the opening lines, but fearful of trusting too much to memory, we refrain, lest the loss of a word might mar the harmony and rhythm of the lines, and thus lessen the claims the great actor had to be ranked among our poets.

Mr. Forrest commenced his engagement in Cincinnati, at Wood's Theatre, October 30th, 1871, as King Lear. The editor of the *Commercial*, speaking of his Lear, says:

"And yet we think the glorious quality of his acting has never been surpassed in this city. Forrest still has his magnificent voice with its stirring compass; he has health and gnarly strength; he has his old faculty of intense and unflagging concentration; he has all his wonted power to thrill an audience and sway its sympathy; and speaking for the enchained spectators of last evening, we can say that his delineation of King Lear is a creation to remember and to venerate. The picture once seen must hang forever among the old masters. A man will sooner rust out than wear out, runs the old proverb; and to a man of Mr. Forrest's massive mould inaction is hateful. Avarice, 'the last vice of a noble mind,' has no place in his motives. He is blessed with large wealth, spends it freely for life's comforts and refinement, and gives nobly. Ambition cannot bestow further rewards; he has long ago secured the highest. He stands in the front rank of tragedians. It was but a few days ago that he concluded a flattering season in Philadelphia, the city of his residence, and he has busy engagements extending henceforward until summer again brings a vacation to all his brother professionals, old and young. He continues to act, not for the incitement of money, nor the incense for applause, but because he was born an actor, and loves art for its inner and loftier rewards. Perhaps he thinks it is time enough to retire when audiences slip away from his controlling authority. That moment has not arrived, and we cannot detect its near approach. The career of Edwin Forrest on the stage has hardly a parallel for tension of effort and prolonged vitali ty, and still it marches on triumphant. The Lear of his mellow age is grander than the Gladiator of his early prime."

From Cincinnati he proceeded to New Orleans, and opened there on the 13th of November, 1871. From New Orleans, Mr. Forrest proceeded to Galveston, Texas, commencing there on December 4th, 1871; from thence to Houston, opening on the 11th; and from thence he started for Nashville, Tennessee, where he commenced a splendid engagement on the 18th of December, 1871. The *Union and American*, speaking of the last night of his engagement, December 23rd, said:

"FORREST'S CLOSING NIGHT."

"Last night closed the engagement of the justly renowned Edwin Forrest, one of America's famous actors, and, in many respects, one of the greatest men known in his profession throughout the world. It is more than probable that he will never appear again before a Nashville audience; but he has left an impression upon our theatre-going public that will be remembered for time to come. In years past, Nashville audiences have been favored with visits from numerous brilliant lights in the dramatic firmament some of whom might be compared to the momentary blaze of a rocket; or, rather, the flash of a meteor, which is only seen when falling, or the Northern lights, which appear to flash and flicker in ragged confusion. Not so with Forrest. His brilliancy resembles the diamond of genius; and like the constant flood of light which emanates from some wildly waving torch, casts broad illumination into the dark places of nature. As in the sea shell, long separated from its native sea, there yet lingers, or seems to linger, when you apply it to the ear, the distant and far-off murmur of the main, so, in the recollection of a man of genius, like Mr. Forrest, there lingers an echo of that which is vast and infinite. There is a language in his face, a meaning in every gesture, and new and striking conceptions in every sentence that he utters.

"In the different characters represented by Mr. Forrest during the week, he has made himself simply a looking-glass to nature, and has earned a title to the applause of all who appreciate true greatness. In his personation of Lear, last evening, there was observable the same mellowness that characterized other parts in his role; and it was, if anything, more effective, producing the same wrapt attention on the part of the audience, who seemed to realize the fact that the voice of genius, though often rugged, sometimes wrathful, despairing, is always a cry from its own heart. Low, sometimes as the sob of the dying deer, and again as loud as the crash and darkness of a thousand storms, bursting their inaccessible abodes of crags and thunder-clouds. In that vast audience at Masonic Hall last night could scarcely be found a single individual who was not willing to accord to the distinguished actor the highest meed of praise for the truthful and faithful rendition of Shakespeare's sublime conception, and there were many, no doubt, who regretted the close of this season of dramatic grandeur."

CHAPTER XXXVII.

KANSAS CITY.—FORRESTANIA.—ST. LOUIS.—HIS GREAT SUCCESS.—CRITICISMS. — A MINISTER CONVERTED BY HIS ELOQUENCE. — ACCEPTS AN INVITATION TO BOSTON.—SICKNESS.—JAMES OAKES' LETTER.—RETURN HOME.

MR. FORREST'S next engagements were at Omaha, Kansas City, St. Joseph's, etc.; commencing at the former place, December 25th, 1871. The excitement at Omaha, to witness his acting, brought people from distant parts of the country, and the theatre was crowded. But a few years ago, this whole section of country was a wilderness. What is it now? Not only a growing country as regards agriculture and commerce, but in the mind's culture. In every place his King Lear was received with the greatest enthusiasm; not so much from its being the production of Shakespeare, but from the powerful acting of Mr. Forrest. He gave a truthful, lifelike picture of the old King, which flashed before the eyes of his audience as a meteor from the skies, and presented one of the most extraordinary efforts of genius and dramatic talent that was ever made by any actor since the days of Betterton; and we have tradition only as an evidence of his superiority over all others in this character. During Mr. Forrest's engagement at Kansas City, excursions were ran into the city upon all the railroads centreing at that place, at greatly reduced prices. The New River, Fort Scott and Gulf Railroad, brought excursionists from Baxter's Springs, a distance of one hundred and fifty miles, for three dollars each, the round trip, including omnibus fare to and from the depot—a supper, a hotel, and admission to the Opera House. Does history furnish a parallel to this?

The following anecdotes were related of Mr. Forrest during his western tour. We will head the article.

"FORRESTANIA."

Without doubt, it is a very pleasant thing to be famous; but to have your acquaintance sought by everybody becomes tiresome after a while, and the "known to fame" sighs in vain for quietude and freedom from the persecution. Probably Edwin Forrest never visited a town or city where he was not assailed by bores, and because he refused the intrusion, was declared discourteous. Some of the more persistent had a faculty of presenting themselves, upon the first occasion, of catching a glimpse of the tragedian.

"Mr. Forrest, I believe."

"No, sir!" invariably interrupted Forrest. "That is Mr. Forrest," indicating Mr. McArdle, his business manager.

When Mr. Forrest visited Bloomington, Illinois, Dr. Shroeder, the eccentric Teutonic proprietor of the opera house, ventilated his opinions in regard to the relative merits of Mr. Forrest and McKean Buchanan.

"McKean Boochanan," said the doctor, "is the greatest actor that ever came to Bloomington, and I always says to him, 'Mr. Boochanan, whenever you want to come to my opera house, you can have it without costing you a cent.'"

"Don't you think," asked Mr. Holland, "that Mr. Forrest's Lear is a most wonderful effort?"

"Yaw, yaw," answered Shroeder, "Mr. Forrest is a pooty good actor, and I liked him foost rate; but when you come right down to hollerin', Forrest ain't nowhere."

The following was spoken of in connection with the above:

"If there is one thing above all others for which Mr. Forrest had a great distaste, it was a sea voyage.

While making the passage to California, a fearful storm arose, and among the few who braved its fury on deck, were the tragedian and a clergyman. The winds shrieked, the waves lashed furiously, and the vessel tossed and trembled, while Mr. Forrest vented an occasional oath. This greatly shocked the pastor, who, clinging to a rope's end to maintain his position, turned with the solemn rebuke:

"Don't you know, sir, our Saviour went to sea in a vessel, and a great storm arose?"

The vessel gave a great lurch, and the sea thundered over the deck. When the vessel righted and regained her course, the great actor turned with the response:

"Yes, so he did; but when he got tired of it he got out and went a-foot. We can't."

Mr. Forrest's next engagement was at St. Louis, where he opened on the 8th of January, 1872, at

DE BAR'S OPERA HOUSE.

Mr. Forrest's reception in St. Louis was most flattering. His engagement closed on Friday evening, January 12th. The editor of the *Republican*, speaking of it, said:

"Long before the curtain rose last evening, there was not a single vacant seat in the theatre above or below, and every inch of available standing room in the aisles and lobbies was occupied. We have rarely seen a more splendid audience on any occasion than gathered to honor Mr. Forrest's farewell appearance, and see him in what is, in many respects, his noblest character. The public seemed to understand that this might be the last time they would have an opportunity of saluting a famous actor, and that, live as long as they might, there was small chance of ever witnessing a greater Lear.

"And, taking all in all, it was a grand performance—worthy alike of the subject, and of the reputation of him who delivered it. The man who can play Lear as it deserves to be played, must not only possess high genius, fine taste, and uncommon physical energy, but he must have passed into the shadow of age, and endured sharp trial and bitter sorrow. Mr. Forrest has all these requisites, and they blend together in an impressive picture whose sombre yet powerful colors are stamped upon the soul of him who looks thereon. The tremendous grief of the crownless king, his awful wrath, his madness, his tears, his death—all these are drawn with a wonderful vividness and reality, which go straight to the heart. We remember nothing more touching on the stage than the struggles of the poor old man when he feels reason tottering upon her throne, and then yielding to the irresistible pressure of a mighty woe, sinks into the semi-oblivion of harmless lunacy. And in the climax of the closing scene, where he bends over the corpse of his daughter, looks into her still eyes, presses her pulseless heart, watches for the dumb lips to open once more, and then whispers in broken, tremulous voice: '*Cordelia! Cordelia! stay a little!*'—what an infinite depth of pathos is there in it all! It is the sublimity of sorrow, the acme of an anguish whose appropriate consummation is death."

On the 15th of January, 1872, Mr. Forrest opened at Quincy, and on the 22nd, at Pittsburg. It is almost needless for us to say that his advent at any town and city was the assurance of crowded houses. The press was equally warm in his praise. The editor of the *Post*, at the close of an article on his Lear, said:

"Does the ordinary man of business keep his highest place for fifty years? Does the author do this? or the clergyman? or the doctor? And yet the merchant, or the author, the clergyman, or the lawyer, do they, or either of them, perform their heaviest labor each day from 8 til' 12 P. M.? Do they travel on *off days* and *nights*, to meet new engagements? Yet all this the actor has to do, and the more eminent is his ability the more exacting and unceasing are his labors. And such has been Mr. Forrest's life of labor, through which he still retains his mental and physical vigor."

On the 5th of February, 1872, he opened at Cleveland, Ohio, in the character of Richelieu, to one of the most fashionable houses of the season. The *Daily Herald* spoke in the highest terms of his impersonation of the *Wily Cardinal.* On the 12th of February, 1872, he opened at Detroit, and from thence he proceeded to Buffalo, where he played one of the most successful engagements made during his tour. The criticisms on Mr. Forrest's acting, which appeared in the several papers of the city, bear evidence of superior minds and intellectual culture on the part of the writers—far superior to those of many other cities. This is readily accounted for, from the fact that Buffalo has always been distinguished for her public schools, and has the honor of being among the first cities in the State of New York in introducing and perfecting this system of popular education. Her libraries, her educational and benevolent institutions, her university, medical colleges, the Young Men's Association, with a library of over 7,000 volumes, connected with a lecture room; with a newspaper press unequalled for the talent displayed in the editorial columns, Buffalo may well claim the title of a literary city—a modern Athens for learning and intelligence.

On the 26th of February, 1872, he opened in Rochester; on March 4th, in Syracuse, closing at Utica, Troy and Albany, where he commenced on the 18th—thus closing one of the most extensive and arduous engagements ever attempted by any actor.

A correspondent of the Syracuse *Daily Standard*, speaking of Mr. Forrest's advent in that city, said:

"Those who have heard Mr. Forrest, need no suggestion to hear him again. A gentleman who has heard him often during a long residence in New York, remarked to me recently that he would like to hear him every evening the year round. Those who have not heard him, and have an ear for the music of speech, should not neglect the opportunity. His elocution is a master-piece of perfection. His majestic presence and wonderful voice are unimpaired by the lapse of time. His style combines the most perfect finish with a natural simplicity that pleases alike the rudest as well as the most cultivated taste. It is nature itself, speaking to nature, and carrying away the soul a willing captive. All attempts at description are vain. Words are idle. As well attempt to photograph the rainbow, as to describe the rich, sweet, and every-varying melody of his deep and powerful voice, expressing every shade of emotion, from the gentlest sympathy to the most terrible storm of passion, which finds in his earthquake utterance ample power and to spare. An amusing incident illustrates the magic effect of his acting. I heard him about four years ago, in New York, in the character of Virginius. A gentleman from New Jersey sitting at my elbow told me that he was a clergyman, and that he had never been in a theatre before in his life, but he could not resist his desire to hear Mr. Forrest; and added that he hoped that none of his congregation would recognize him. Before the close of the play he said 'he did not care who recognized him. He wished his whole congregation was present, as he thought that the moral lesson taught by Mr. Forrest was far superior to anything he could do in the pulpit.'"

It is an old saying that "actors represent fiction as truth; and preachers represent truth as fiction;" such being the usual careless manner in which they preach. Fortunate, indeed, would it be for the cause of religion, if its advocates possessed the eloquence of Mr. Forrest; and the legal profession might have taken lessons of him with advantage.

At the solicitation of numerous friends in Boston, Mr. Forrest was induced to forego his intention of returning home, and play an engagement in that city. During this engagement, Mr. Forrest was attacked with an illness, so severe that for awhile his life was in danger. In answer to a letter we wrote at that time to James Oakes, Esq., of Boston, one of Mr. Forrest's old and most intimate friends (and now one of the executors of his estate), we received the following:

"BOSTON, April 18th, 1872.

"Mr. Forrest arrived in Boston on Saturday, March 23rd, in pretty good condition, save the wear and tear incident to his herculean professional efforts during the previous six months. He opened in Lear, on Monday evening, March 25th, to an immense audience, and he played the old King, five nights the first week, to audiences composed of the brightest intelligence of Boston. He could have filled the theatre for two weeks longer with Lear, had the strain on him permitted its continuance. On the following Monday and Tuesday evening he acted Richelieu superbly, notwithstanding he was laboring under the effects of a sudden and severe cold that caused him to be very hoarse. On Wednesday, he was to have acted Virginius, but during the day the hoarseness increased, and towards evening, congestion of the throat was so severe, that it was deemed advisable to call a physician, as Mr. Forrest seemed unwilling to abandon acting on that night, as he said he could not bear the thought of disappointing a public who had ever been so kind and generous to him. When, after the physician had examined him thoroughly, he gave it as his medical judgment that if Mr. Forrest attempted to perform that night, if he did not die on the stage, he probably would not survive until morning, then, and not till then, did Mr. Forrest yield and give himself up to his physician. Within twenty-four hours he was attacked by pneumonia, and for several days a fatal termination was feared. With the aid of his excellent constitution, his iron will, and unfaltering courage, through God's mercy, he is now nearly well, and will be able to go home in the course of a week. The sympathy for him during his illness has been general, not only in our city but throughout our whole Commonwealth. No man ever received a truer or more general sympathy than has been manifested towards Mr. Forrest. He never in all his life acted better than he did on each of the seven nights; and had this engagement been the close of his professional career, those seven representations would have stood in history as a monument to his splendid genius, more enduring than any of marble or of brass that could have been raised."

From this severe attack Mr. Forrest slowly recovered; and when he emerged from the sick room, his health was shattered, and he was incapacitated, by a paralysis of his limbs, from again—at least for a time—appearing upon the stage. He reached his home, and in the quiet of his extensive library, surrounded by his favorite authors, or seated calmly in his picture-gallery, gazing upon gems of art of his own selection—or working in his garden—his mind tuned to harmony, he found health and strength reviving under these cheering home influences.

We conclude this part of our Reminiscences with the following beautiful tribute to the dramatic genius of Mr. Forrest, written by one highly valued and esteemed in the literary world—a struggling bard for that fame which cruel death deprived him from reaching. Yet he died with a wreath of poetic beauty on his brow—placed there by those who knew his worth and mourned his loss. The article was written when the author was under the impression that Mr. Forrest was about retiring from the stage:

"Every lover of the drama will hope that the day may be far distant when his professional displays will terminate; and the plaudits of his admiring countrymen ring upon his ears for the last time. Whenever that event occurs, and he ceases to be a hero of the actual present, his memory will become enshrined in the hearts of myriads, as being connected with the most inspiring and exalted moments of their lives; and they will look back at this great star of scenic splendor, and recall with delight those varied and intense emotions, which, with magic power, he had often produced within them, when portraying so impressively, the joys and sorrows, the hopes and fears, the grandeurs and the vicissitudes of humanity.

> "'Thus, by the mighty actor wrought
> Illusion's perfect triumphs come;
> Verse ceases to be airy thought,
> And sculpture to be dumb!"

CHAPTER XXXVIII.

RETROSPECTION. — YOUTHFUL REMINISCENCES. — FAIRMOUNT.—OLDEN TIME. — PLACE OF REHEARSAL.— A CLOSE STUDENT.— PRIVATE LIFE. — COAT OF ARMS.—THE IDIOT BOY.—POEM.

THE dark shadow that fell upon his early pathway of life, had a certain influence over his otherwise genial nature. It was then he turned his attention stronger than ever to the stage, and endeavored, by constant action, to drive away the gloom that was gradually settling on his mind. And yet, how often do the stern realities of every-day life o'ertop the fictions of romance and the stage! Where the latter presents one Mrs. Haller, the great world produces thousands; and when we see portrayed the seducer and the plausible libertine of the drama, do we not recognize their counterparts multiplied *ad infinitum* in real life? During Mr. Forrest's visit to the Springs, and other places, on his pleasure tour, one or two writers spoke of his taciturn manner and gloomy aspect; and, as one asserted, as "if laboring under mental depression." Much of this was simply imaginary. Mr. Forrest did not court the acquaintance of strangers, nor intrude himself in their company, like many of the profession do. He might have been called distant, cold and formal, at a first glance; but a warmer heart and friendlier disposition, prone to familiarity, did not exist; but that familiarity was not the growth of an instant; it was progressive, and few men possessed a greater amount of true wit and humor than did Edwin Forrest. Those who knew him, and visited him in his "hours of ease," free from the "fitful thoughts" of the past, can readily contradict the statements of transient travellers and letter writers. It was the nature of Mr. Forrest to be social, and to be a boy again—when we were talking over the bright days of our youth—how we wandered on the banks of the Schuylkill, climbed the huge rocks that towered above our heads, which seemed as monuments reared to honor Nature; but are now supplanted by ornamental trees, beauteous walks, and a basin of water from which flows to all parts of the city the pure water of the river Schuylkill. What is Fairmount now? In the days of our youth it was a wild, romantic scene of rocks and mammoth trees. The hand of man has transformed the wilderness to a parterre of flowers.

It was beneath the huge oaks, whose spreading branches shaded us from the sun, that Edwin Forrest first tried his voice in "public speaking." As it were but yesterday, we can see him, in all his boyish pride, reciting the speech from Douglas: "My name is Norval," etc., his voice echoing far and wide, and through the arena Nature's self had made. Nor was he alone in this. There was Jack Moore, practising to play Alexander the Great; but whose voice was harsh and unmusical, while the former's was all harmony. Moore enacted Alexander the Great, at Tivoli Garden, in 1818, and Edwin Forrest, Young Norval, at the Walnut Street Theatre, 1820.

Fairmount was a favorite resort of the young men of the day. It was our custom to meet on a Sunday at Palmer's printing office in Locust Street, above Eighth, and make arrangements for a ramble in the country—Fairmount was the country then. Well do we remember meeting in the composing room of this printing office, with Benj. Mifflin, Washington Dawson, Edwin Forrest, Anthony Seyfert, J. H. Campbell, Joseph C. Neal, and others, with whom all our earlier associations are pleasingly connected. We may as well state here, that being four years older than Mr. Forrest, we looked upon him at that time as a "boy," and that our *age* entitled us to consider him our *protegé*, which he soon discovered, and resented as being presumptuous. Since then, when laughing over our boyish days, and contrasting the great actor with ourselves, we indeed thought it the height of presumption. We cannot leave this subject without referring once more to Fairmount. Those who look back to their boyhood days, and remember some well-remembered play-ground, can readily appreciate our feelings while contrasting the present view of this beautiful place with what it was then. We give an extract from a letter written by William Penn to James Logan, in 1701, showing his fancy for the site of the present water works, and his intention to settle there if he returned, saying: "My eye, though not my heart, is upon Fairmount, unless the unworthiness of some spirits drive me up to Pennsburg or Susquehanna for good and all." Watson, in his Annals of Philadelphia, speaking of Fairmount, says: "All this change of Fairmount, by the hand of art, is a fair exchange for the loss of its original rugged, woody and romantic cliffs; then all solitary and silent, now all busy with active life, and useful, by its poetic utility, sustaining the health, and blessing the city inhabitants."

Our readers can readily pardon this digression when they take into consideration that it is a remembrance of our youth which calls up a scene so dear to us, and as the play-ground of one with whom our earliest predilections of the stage are associated; as also with others, who, like him, have passed away, and left us in age to wander alone amid scenes, which, although much altered, still bear the traces of their former "rugged" grandeur.

As we have said, it was the nature of Mr. Forrest to be social; but the profession to which he belonged had drawn a curtain between him and the real world. The actor lives and breathes in an atmosphere of his own—a sort of lesser world, different, far different from that of the great; he peoples it with the spirits of the dead, talks to them through books, and on the stage assumes their person and character. Thus the mind becomes so imbued, as it were, with the philosophy of the world of letters, that it contracts, rather than expands, when it comes in contact with that of the world of art. It was supposed by many that the seeming sternness and gravity of Mr. Forrest was of recent origin. Not so; for when a boy he associated but little with others, unless with those who, like him, had a penchant for the stage. His chief companion was a play-book, a character in it, his study. Wrapt up in the pleasure derived from such companionship, he found but little to amuse him beyond its pages. We called him the "philosopher in petticoats." We have said that Mr. Forrest possessed a rich fund of wit and humor. So he did, but it was more of a refined than of a coarse nature. He would illustrate in a truly artistic manner the peculiar characteristics of a "Jakey," without his low expletives. He was equally felicitous in imitating a Frenchman; and would keep the table in a roar by giving imitations of the modern mode of teaching elocution. His rendering of the "Sailor Boy's Dream," in imitation of that peculiar school of recitation, was a perfect gem.

> "A merrier man,
> Within the limit of becoming mirth,
> I never spent an hour's talk withal."

Col. John W. Forney, in his "Anecdotes of Public Men," speaking of Mr. Forrest, says: "He needed no solicitation to display his varied stores of humor and of information. Sketches of foreign travel; photographs of Southern manners, alike of the master and the slave; his celebrated French criticism upon Shakespeare; his imitation of the old clergyman of Charleston, South Carolina, who, deaf himself, believed everybody else to be so; his thrilling account of his meeting with Edmund Kean, at Albany, when Forrest was a boy; his incidents of Gen. Jackson; his meeting with Lafayette, at Richmond, in 1825. Few that heard him can ever forget that night. But nothing that he did will be remembered longer than the manner in which he recited 'The Idiot Boy,' a production up to that time unknown to everybody in the room except Forrest and myself, and to me, only because I heard him repeat it seven years before, when I lived on Eighth Street, in the house lately known as the Waverly."

Another writer said:

MR. FORREST WAS A GREAT STUDENT.

"Having received but little instruction in his boyhood, from the time fortune dawned upon him, he sought by every means that wealth and determination could give him to make himself an accomplished man. His library in Philadelphia, of which everybody has heard, was his home, his resting-place; and here he gathered such a store of literary knowledge as but few men acquire, even in a longer life than sixty-seven years. Mr. John W. Forney has been heard to say, on returning from a visit to Mr. Forrest, that Forrest was a fresh surprise to him each hour he spent in his company. His knowledge was not confined to dramatic literature alone. He was a good classical scholar, a remarkably acute and learned lawyer, and his knowledge of science and arts alone would have made him a foremost man in any country."

The writer of these Reminiscences, during this interregnum in the professional life of his friend, and while he was preparing for his readings, spent much of his leisure time with him, and occasionally partook of a "quiet supper" at his house. Mr. Forrest had, in a measure, shut himself out from society; and it may well be said, he lived a lonely life. How many of his old friends would have been delighted to render his loneliness more cheerful?

MR. FORREST'S COAT OF ARMS.

One day we found him busily engaged drawing something on a card; it was a design, tastefully, if not artistically arranged. "Look at that," said he, holding it up to our view; "What do you think of it?"

"Why, it is your coat of arms!"

"How do you like the design?"

"Very well; and the trees and the leaves, entwining, quite appropriate. Is it your own design?"

"Certainly; it requires but a little stretch of the imagination to get up such a thing as this;" throwing it scornfully, it seemed to us, on the table. "These things," he continued, "savor too much of foreign aristocracy, which, I am sorry to say, too many of our people follow. With us, true nobility lies in the heart, the soul, and mind of man, not in ancestry." Here he recited a passage from some author, which we forget, forcibly illustrating the folly of boasting of rank and descent. Forrest was to our "manor born," and eschewed everything of a foreign character, calculated to corrupt and demoralize our "manners" and customs. He was an American, heart and soul. The card represented a tree, resting on a closed helmet, around and about which were wreaths of oak leaves. Portions of the lower part of the helmet rested on a shield; and instead of the usual Argent bars, azure, and gules, there were three trees placed in circular form, standing on a green ground, which color characterized the other portions of the crest. Immediately beneath the shield, was the following motto: "*Vivunt dum Virent;*" and underneath this was a tablet, sustained as it were by the wings of a bird, on which was engraved the name "FORREST." Altogether, it was a beautiful design. The original is now in our possession.

We allude to these peculiarities here for the purpose of doing away with an impression that Mr. Forrest was a melancholy man; he may have had his hours of sadness and of gloom; he may have looked despondently back over the past, and traced upon its surface those shadows that still dim memory's mirror, despite of all our attempts to erase them; with all this, the true nature of the man was there.

> *"His bold brow*
> *Bore the scars of mind, the thoughts*
> *Of years,*
> *But not their decrepitude."*

Even the silence and quiet of his library, surrounded by the still monitors of the world of letters alone, the pale light streaming down upon the open pages of a book, could not put out the flame of youth which lingered in his heart. Still the influence of the stage and the dramatic school, more or less, had its effect upon him, making him at times less cheerful, and uncompanionable; but when the spirit of the once "wild dreaming boy" was aroused, you found him a different being, and as Col. John W. Forney said, "he was one of us," and not the misanthrope, letter writers would make him.

Again, if you touched an intellectual chord, you awakened within him those hidden fires of genius which shone so brightly in mimic scenes. Among men of mind, Mr. Forrest could maintain, nay lead the conversation upon any subject; for he had not only studied books, those epitomes of the world, but he had read the great book of creation in its original text. Conversant with the classics, familiar with the writers of every age, his deductions were made not from the ideas of the superficial, but from those of minds capable of forming, reasoning, and classifying. His arguments were listened to with attention; for he was bold, energetic, original, and at times unanswerable. Such, in fact, was Mr. Forrest in the private circle. There are those who imagined Mr. Forrest a Hamlet in private life; a sort of melancholy prince of the household, and put the meaning of words into his mouth to suit their own critical notion. They would have him say:

> ———"Oh, that this too, too solid
> Flesh would melt,
> Thaw, and resolve into a dew."

When, in fact, he would have it do no such thing. They would synonymal passages of Shakespeare expressly for him—passages that only affected him as the actor, not as the man. We have heard people say how suited is such and such a passage to Mr. Forrest —how apt, and illustrative, and how forcibly and pointedly did he deliver them. One we quote:

> "And yet, to me, what is the quintescence of dust? Man delights not me—nor woman neither; though by your smiling you seem to say so."

It is here Hamlet spoke truth; but that the actor should be accused of placing particular stress upon the lines to suit himself, is ridiculous. We said Hamlet spoke the truth, as regarded himself, and it is to be regretted that Shakespeare, in connection with this beautiful passage, should have made Rosencranz tell a most deliberate falsehood, for he immediately answers:

> "My Lord, there was no such stuff in my thoughts,"

and turns off the questioning with another lie, by making an allusion to the players. Passages of Othello have also been quoted, as being pet subjects for the display of Mr. Forrest's peculiar temperament. Edwin Forrest, in personal appearance, was a man who did not ask, but demanded attention; he was tall, dignified, grave, and at times absolutely majestic; courteous in speech, affable in manner; in thought, feeling, and action, a gentleman. His eye was full of fire and expression. His voice possessed remarkable compass, both for power and melody; from the awful curse of Lear, and the passion of jealousy depicted by the Moor, down to the delivery of the simple story of the "Idiot Boy;" there never was such a voice, so tuned to pathos, so aroused to torrents of passion, invoked by the emotions of the character he had to portray, heard upon the stage. There are many passages in Shakespeare whose sublimity and grandeur are only surpassed by those of the Bible, which no actor, either living or dead, that we ever heard, could approach Edwin Forrest in the delivering of them.

THE IDIOT BOY.

Those who have heard this touching effusion recited by Mr. Forrest will never forget either the pathos with which he rendered it, or his simple affecting introduction to it. In speaking one day of this poem, and its author, Mr. Forrest stated that he was under the impression it was written by a brother of the poet Southey.

"It had pleased God to form poor Ned
A thing of idiot mind,
Yet to the poor unreasoning boy
God had not been unkind.

Old Sarah loved her helpless child,
Whom helplessness made dear,
And life was everything to him
Who knew no hope nor fear.

She knew his wants, she understood
  Each half artic'late call;
For he was everything to her,
  And she to him was all.

And so for many a year they lived,
  Nor knew a wish beside;
But age at length on Sarah came,
  And she fell sick and died.

He tried in vain to 'waken her:
  He called her o'er and o'er,
They told him she was dead: the words
  To him no import bore.

They closed her eyes and shrouded her,
  Whilst he stood wond'ring by;
And when they bore her to the grave,
  He followed silently.

They laid her in the narrow house,
  And sung the funeral stave;
And when the mournful train dispersed,
  He loitered by the grave.

The rabble boys that used to jeer
  Whene'er they saw poor Ned,
Now stood and watched him at the grave,
  And not a word was said.

They came and went and came again,
  And night at last drew on;
Yet still he lingered at the place
  Till every one was gone.

And when he found himself alone,
  He quick removed the clay,
And raised the coffin in his arms
  And bore it swift away.

Straight went he to his mother's cot,
  And laid it on the floor;
And with the eagerness of joy
  He barred the cottage door.

At once he placed his mother's corpse
  Upright within her chair;
And then he heaped the hearth and blew
  The kindling fire with care.

She now was in her wonted chair,
It was her wonted place,
And bright the fire blazed and flashed,
Reflected from her face.

Then bending down he'd feel her hands,
Anon her face behold;
Why, mother, do you look so pale—
And why are you so cold?

And when the neighbors on next morn
Had forced the cottage door,
Old Sarah's corpse was in the chair,
And Ned's was on the floor.

It had pleased God from this poor boy
His only friend to call:
Yet God was not unkind to him,
For death restored him all!"

CHAPTER XXXIX.

OUR DRAMATIC AUTHORS. — THE STAGE. — RICHARD PENN SMITH'S CAIUS MARIUS.—WHEN FIRST PRODUCED.—HOW IT WAS RECEIVED.—AN AUTHOR'S TRIALS.—HIS GOOD NATURE.—EXTRACT FROM THE PLAY.—ANECDOTES.

IN the last chapter we left Mr. Forrest enjoying the comforts of home; but he was not idle; his spirit could not brook complete inanity, and, in consultation with his friends, he decided to give Shakesperian readings. At first we objected to this step. "Wait," we said, "a little longer. You are now improving in health so rapidly, that you will in a very short time be enabled to enact Lear, Richelieu, and the Broker of Bogota, three of your best characters, as well as ever. Your lameness will not be perceivable, as age and infirmity are essential in giving due effect to their impersonation."

"I have thought of that," he said; "and if this medicine should effect a cure"—alluding to some vile nostrum he was taking—"I will follow your advice; in the meantime, these readings will not interfere with my future arrangements."

Alas! that future to him was oblivion. The future! alas! who can look into that dark unfathomless gulf and stay his footsteps on its brink?

"Out, out, brief candle!
Life's but a walking shadow; a poor player,
That struts and frets his hour upon the stage,
And then is heard no more; it is a tale
Told by an idiot, full of sound and fury,
Signifying nothing."

Before we bring Mr. Forrest before the public as a reader, let us introduce the names of those American authors and their productions which the genius of the great actor brought so eminently before the American people.

OUR DRAMATIC AUTHORS.—THE STAGE.

"For thee, the bard shall draw from every clime,
The swelling triumph and the curtained crime;
Death's moss-grown gates unbar, the sleepers wake,
To charm the good, and bid the guilty quake."

The name of Mr. Forrest is closely identified with what is aptly termed the American Drama. Several fine productions have been written principally through his instrumentality, which else, perhaps, would never have found their way into existence. Instead of hoarding the profits of his industry (which were earned solely by hazardous toil, and which, truly, none had a better right to retain), he devoted a part of it to the rise of dramatic literature; and while he thus held forth a sufficient stimulus to rouse the inactive to action, had himself exerted his own talent in support of these productions. If in one or two instances the pieces failed to meet the public approbation, it was not owing to any fault of the actor; still he gave to them the finishing touch of art, thus rendering their dramatic imperfections less apparent. Those that were successful will still retain their place on the stage; but we question, even with all their merit, whether others will be enabled to sustain the character so ably as did that great master of the histrionic art. It will be long before the impression Mr. Forrest made in such characters as Metamora, Spartacus, Jack Cade, Broker of Bogota, Oraloosa, and Caius Marius, will be erased from the public mind. Mr. Forrest has done more individually, than all the theatres in the country combined, to draw forth and reward the talents of native dramatists. Identified thus with our literature, and possessing wealth sufficient to do much good, Mr. Forrest, of course, received the just praise, of just men, for the manner in which he used his position to advance the interest of our dramatic literature. Well was it said by the late Judge Conrad, that "The drama here is yet in its infancy. Let it be fostered, and who can foresee its destiny? Let it be fostered not with false tenderness, or indiscreet indulgence, but with a care, vigorous but parental, frostly but kindly."

RICHARD PENN SMITH'S CAIUS MARIUS.

This play was produced at the Arch Street Theatre, January 12th, 1831. It was not fairly treated by the actors, many of whom were imperfect in the words of the author. Mr. Forrest, always perfect in his part, fought bravely, and almost alone, to save the piece. Even after a careful rehearsal, its success was questionable, and Mr. Forrest had to drop it from his repertoire. The tragedy possesses sterling merit as a literary production, the language is uniformly vigorous, and the sentiments poetical and just. With all these, the very attributes of a good play, it lacked the most important—action and effect; the curtain falls gracefully on each act to some beautiful sentiment, but no tableaux to create applause; a sound that falls upon the author and actor as refreshing as the dew of Heaven.

Richard Penn Smith was a native of Philadelphia, and a member of the bar. From his father, William Moore Smith, a gentleman of the old school, of highly polished education and manners, and a poet of considerable reputation in his day, he inherited a taste for letters, and was early distinguished for the extent and variety of his acquirements. His first appearance as an author was in the columns of the *Union,* where he published a series of letters, moral and literary, under the title of the "Plagiary." About the close of the year 1822, he purchased the newspaper establishment, then well-known throughout the country, as the *Aurora,* from Mr. Duane, and assumed the arduous and responsible duties of an editor. At this dray-horse work he continued about five years, when, finding it both wearisome and unprofitable, he abandoned it, and resumed his profession. A good classical scholar, and a tolerable linguist, with a decided bent for the pursuits of literature, his mind was well stored with the classics, both ancient and modern; and amid the vexations and drudgery of a daily newspaper, he wooed the muses with considerable success. Perhaps to the discipline which editorship necessarily imposes, and the promptness which it requires, may in part be attributed the great facility he possessed in composition. While engaged in the duties of a profession, generally considered uncongenial to the successful prosecution of literary adventure, he produced a number and variety of pieces, both in prose and verse, which showed considerable versatility of talent. His favorite study was the drama, and with this department of literature he was thoroughly familiar. With the dramatists of all nations he had an extensive acquaintance, and in the dramatic history of England and France he was profoundly versed. Perhaps there are few who studied the old English masters in this art with more devoted attention, and with a keener enjoyment of their beauties. But it is not alone in the keen enjoyment and appreciation of others that he deserves attention. He has given ample evidence that he possessed no ordinary power for original effort in this most difficult department of literature.

We do not know how many plays he has produced, but the following, all from his pen, have been performed at different periods: Quite Correct; Eighth of January; The Disowned, or the Prodigals; The Deformed, or Woman's Trial; A Wife at a Venture; The Sentinels; William Penn; The Triumph of Plattsburg; Caius Marius; The Water Witch; Is She a Brigand; My Uncle's Wedding; The Daughter; The Actress of Padua; and The Bravo.

As an evidence of his facility in composition, it

may be mentioned that several of his pieces were written and performed at a week's notice. The entire last act of William Penn was written on the afternoon of the day previous to its performance, yet this hasty production ran ten successive nights, drawing full houses, and has since been several times revived. His Deformed, and Disowned, two dramas, which may be compared favorably with any similar productions of this country, were both performed with great success in London.

If green-room anecdotes can be depended on, Mr. Smith was blessed with a much thicker skin than usually falls to the lot of the *genus irratabile vatum.* It is said that on one occasion he happened to enter the theatre, during the first run of one of his pieces, just as the curtain was falling, and met with an old school-fellow who had that day arrived in Philadelphia, after an absence of several years. The first salutation was scarcely over, when the curtain fell, and the author's friend innocently remarked, "Well, this is really the most insufferable trash that I have witnessed for some time." "True," replied Smith, "but as they give me a benefit to-morrow night as the author, I hope to have the pleasure of seeing you here again." At another time, a friend met him in the lobby as the green curtain fell, like a funeral pall, on one of his progeny, and unconscious of its paternity, asked the author, with a sneer, what the piece was all about. "Really," was the grave answer, "it is now some years since I wrote that piece, and though I paid the utmost attention to the performance, I confess I am as much in the dark as you are."

In 1831, Mr. Smith published a work in two volumes, called the "Forsaken," the scene of which was laid in Philadelphia and the adjoining country, during our revolutionary struggle. At that time, American novels—with the exception of Cooper's, were not received with the same favor as now; but a large edition of the "Forsaken" was even then disposed of, and it obtained from all quarters strong commendation. In our judgment, it is a work highly creditable to the author. The story is interesting, and in its progress, fiction is blended with historical truth with considerable skill and force.

Mr. Smith also published two volumes, entitled "The Actress of Padua, and other Tales," which have been eminently successful. As a writer of short tales, he was natural and unaffected in manner, correct in description, concise in expression, and happy in the selection of incidents. He possessed, moreover, a quiet humor, and an occasional sarcasm, which made his productions both pleasant and pungent.

Mr. Smith wrote much for the periodical literature of the day, both political and literary, and his poetical pieces, if collected, would make a large volume; but these appear to have been scattered abroad, without any purpose of reclamation. His name is attached to a limited number, which are distinguished by a healthy tone of thought, neatness of expression, and harmony of versification; but as, generally, they were produced for some particular occasion, they have —most of them, at least—passed into oblivion with the occasion that called them into existence.

The following extract from Caius Marius, may be considered a fair specimen of his style:

ACT V.—SCENE V.

The Capitol. A Festive Board decorated. MARIUS *and* SOLDIERS *seated with goblets before them.* MARTHA, *the Sybil, near* MARIUS. CINNA *and* SULPITIUS *standing at the wing.*

Marius.—"Fill up your goblets, till the rosy wine
Sparkles like Sylla's blood. Drink to the shades
Of the Ambrones and the Cimbril; drink
To those whom Marius vanquished. See, they come;
The yelling spirits of the savage Teutons,
And mad Jugurtha, foaming 'neath his chains,
Arise to join the pledge. Drink deep, I say,
To th' enemies of Rome, for they are now
The friends of Marius.

Sulpitius.—How his eyes glare!

Marius.—Who was it saved ungrateful Italy,
When swarms of savages like locusts came,
To batten on her fertile fields and vineyards?
Whose name struck terror through the countless horde,
And checked the progress of the sweeping deluge,
And turn'd its fearful course? 'Twas Marius!
Who was it led proud Afric's haughty king,
In triumph, at his chariot wheels, through Rome,
Until the monarch, who for years defied her,
Became imbecile, and deprived of reason?
'Twas Marius!"

Mr. Forrest paid much better for original plays than the managers, who being able to purchase the best plays of English dramatists for a few dollars, felt little disposition to risk hundreds on native productions, which, unaided by the talent of an acknowledged star, seldom outlive the first night of representation.

ANECDOTES.

There are numerous anecdotes related of Richard Penn Smith, all of which display the most ready wit, and sarcastic humor. Indeed, he was so celebrated for repartee and off-hand sayings, that he was actually dreaded in company, and very few had the courage to measure lances with him when wit was the prize. A few we give here:

When Mr. Smith was a young man, he was introduced by his father to a well-known Philadelphian, by the name of Wharton, who, from the fact of having a very large nose with a wart on it, was called, "Big nosed Wharton," to distinguish him from another gentleman by the same name. When out of hearing, the father said to the son, "They call that gentleman big nosed Wharton." The son quickly replied, "They have made a mistake, they should call him *Wart-on big nose.*"

Upon going one day into a hotel in which some of his friends were holding an argument about the city of Dumfries, Scotland, they made an appeal to him to decide the question. "I know nothing of *the* Dumfries of Scotland, but I know *a Dumb-freas* of Germantown." Mr. Freas of the Germantown *Telegraph*, was sitting within hearing at the time.

He was one evening sitting at the table of a dinner given to the Judges of the Supreme Court by the Bar of Philadelphia. Mr. Smith had his health drank, and when he arose to reply, a well-known lawyer by the name of Robert M. Lee, pulled him by the coat and urged him to toast him. As Mr. Smith closed his remarks, he said:

"Gentlemen, *you* have toasted the Binneys', Rawles', and Sergeants' of the bar, allow me to offer the *lees* —'Here is to the health of Robert M. Lee.'" Mr. Lee did not see the joke, and replied to the amusement of all present.

Mr. Smith always raised his own pork. On one occasion he had them killed on the eighth of January. The next day he met a friend who remarked: "Smith, yesterday was a fine day for killing pigs." "Yes," replied Smith, "but it was a bad day for Packingham."

Mr. Smith died on August 12th, 1854.

CHAPTER XL.

DR. ROBERT MONTGOMERY BIRD.—HIS BIRTH AND EDUCATION.—STUDIES MEDICINE.—BECOMES A POET.—CELEBRATED AS A NOVELIST.—FAMOUS AS A DRAMATIST.—THE GLADIATOR A GREAT SUCCESS.—FORREST AS SPARTACUS.—ORALOOSA.—BROKER OF BOGOTA.

IN Chapter VII. allusions were made to Dr. Bird, in connection with the subject of these Reminiscences. We will now give some further account of the beautiful productions of this highly accomplished gentleman and scholar.

Dr. Robert Montgomery Bird was born in Newcastle, Del., in the year 1805, and died in the city of Philadelphia, January 23rd, 1854. It is too often the case, and we deeply regret it, that the memory of our literary men, as well as their works, are permitted to pass away from us, without an effort to keep them before the world, and remain as finger-posts, to point the ambitious to that "majesty of worth," from whence immortality springs. Fame, literary fame, with us is evanescent, a mere streak of sunshine over the dark scenes of dull plodding life. Few live in favor of the world; few die who are remembered afterwards, unless some peculiar and striking feature, in their literary career, is calculated to repay the trouble of re-producing their works. Having no standard of literature of our own, no national feeling upon the subject, it is not to be expected that the works of an author will live in after ages, when the estimate of an age with us—*is a season.*

Dr. Bird was a pupil of Mount Airy College, Germantown; after leaving which, he studied medicine, and received his degree of M. D., from the University of Pennsylvania; but, we believe, never experimented with human life, to test his ability to cure. This, we conceive to have been one of the most humane traits in his character.

His first appearance, as an author, was in 1828, when he published in the *Philadelphia Monthly Magazine*, three spirited tales, entitled, "The Ice Island," "The Spirit of the Reeds," and the "Phantom Players," besides several short pieces of poetry, the best of which was "Saul's Last Day." At this time, Dr. Bird had already written several tragedies, in imitation of the old English Drama, but none of his labors at that period had ever been submitted to the public. We recollect perusing the manuscript of two, which gave promise of the distinction that awaited him as a dramatist. They were entitled "The Cowl'd Lover," and "Caridorf." If these productions were now to be revived, we have no doubt they would advance the author's reputation as a poet. At this period he had also written two or three regular comedies, but it struck us that his comic powers did not bear him through as triumphantly as his talents for delineating the terrible and sublime had done. Edwin Forrest, who has done more individually, than all the theatres in the country combined, to draw forth and reward the talents of native dramatists, was the means of introducing Dr. Bird at his very onset, as a writer, triumphantly to the whole American people. This was on the first production of the tragedy of the Gladiator, written with a view to the powers and talents of Mr. Forrest; and it has seldom occurred that author and actor were so much indebted to each other, as on this occasion. The piece was eminently successful throughout the Union; and, although written exclusively with a view to the stage, it abounds with poetic passages, and possesses no ordinary share of literary merit. The scene in the arena, at the close of the second act, when the gladiators break loose from their tyrants, and raise the standard of freedom, is not surpassed on the score of originality and effect, by any scene in any modern drama. This tragedy was speedily followed by another, entitled, Oraloosa, founded on the cruelty of the Spaniards in Peru, but it never acquired the popularity of its predecessor, though received upon the stage with every mark of public favor. Oraloosa, was succeeded by the Broker of Bogota, which we consider the most finished of Dr. Bird's dramas. It did not create the decided impression that was produced by the Gladiator, for there was nothing of the drums and trumpets, and battling for freedom, which this play affords, to put the spirit in motion; but the Broker of Bogota, viewed as a specimen of dramatic art, surpasses either of the other pieces. All these tragedies were written expressly for Mr. Forrest, and were performed by him with eminent success. Prior to the production of either, Dr. Bird had written a tragedy, entitled, Pelopidas, fitted to the powers of our tragedian, and every way calculated to enhance the author's reputation.

This play has never been produced, and probably, although it is said to be far superior to Oraloosa, never will, having been condemned by the author himself.

In 1833, Dr. Bird became a candidate for public favor, in another department of literature, and he met with the same decided success as a novelist, that had attended his labors as a dramatist. His first novel was entitled "Calavar, a Romance of Mexico." This was followed by "The Infidel," "Nick of the Woods," and "The Hawks of Hawk Hollow," the scene of which was laid in Pennsylvania. These productions at once placed him in the front rank of American novelists, in the estimation of the intelligent, both at home and abroad. All his novels have been republished in London, and have been reviewed in terms of high commendation. His language is eloquent, imaginative, and powerful. His characters are well contrasted, boldly conceived, and happily and consistently sustained throughout; while his plots are constructed with dramatic skill, and his subjects and scenes present a freshness and originality in striking contrast with the *racifimentoes* of some of the novelists of the day.

He was the author of several pieces of poetry, all of which were remarkable for great delicacy, simplicity and sweetness. He was a good classical scholar, possessed a knowledge of several languages, and his reading was extensive and various, and more familiar with the history of South America, and Spanish North America, than any other man in the country.

It has been said by some critics, envious of Dr. Bird's fair fame, that his style, though energetic, is coarse. There are passages in "Calavar," and "Nick of the Woods," which, in point of eloquence, pathos, and all the elementary rules of composition, will compete with any work of a similar kind in the English language. In fact, we would quote "Nick of the Woods" throughout, and contrast it with any one of Bulwer's novels, nor have any fears of the result. "Nick of the Woods" is a compliment to the literature of our country.

Dr. Bird was much esteemed for his urbanity and unostentatious demeanor. There was about him none of that poetical nonsense which clings to so many who lay claim to a literary character. He had less egotism than any man we ever met with; like the farmer, he cultivated the soil of literature for its fruit, not its blossoms; he garnered up the seed, while others made bouquets out of their productions, and paraded them as they would a diamond breastpin, or a new coat; things seldom, however, available with them for such a purpose. In stature, Dr. Bird was about five feet ten inches high; robust, with a mild, amiable countenance, hair slightly tinged with silver gray.

Something like Dominie Sampson, Dr. Bird was a complete book-worm, and, at times, so absorbed in literary pursuits, that he paid little or no attention to worldly matters. As an instance of this, we might cite facts to show how prone he was to the wiles, or rather sly jokes of some of his intimate friends, who took delight in what they called "drawing him out." The doctor was, in fact, so single-minded in all that related to the rascality of the age, that it would seem that he, like Rip Van Winkle, had been asleep for the last twenty years, and just woke up in time to become acquainted with men and things as they existed around him. Correct himself, and truly honorable, he naturally believed all the world to be so. On one occasion, and we believe the only time the doctor ever witnessed the representation of his play of the Broker of Bogota, a gentleman who was seated near him, observed—"The author of this piece, whoever he is, must be a d—d scoundrel himself, or he never could have sketched such a villain as that," alluding to a character in the play. The doctor started, gazed on the speaker, and satisfied that the man spoke without a knowledge who he was, made some remark in reply, and left the theatre in disgust. This incident the doctor himself related.

These little grievances are the trials of poor authors, and neither the actors, managers, or audiences, have any sympathy for them. The fact is, an author can be likened to a dyspeptic—his disease creates laughter and sarcasm, instead of kindness and sympathy.

In all the social relations of life, Dr. Bird maintained a steady uniform character, and it is a remarkable fact, that although his productions placed him in a high position before the people, and his dramatic ones attracted crowded houses every time they were played, he was less known to the mass of the people than any other literary man in Philadelphia.

At one time, Dr. Bird became part owner and editor of the *North American*, a highly popular paper of Philadelphia; and many of the able editorials, which tended to give it tone and character, were the productions of his classic pen. But he has gone to that "undiscovered country from whose bourn no traveller returns."

"His was the merit—seldom shows
Itself bedeck'd with tinsel and fine clothes;
But, hermit like, 'tis oftener used to fly,
And hide its beauties in obscurity."

THE GLADIATOR.

The first performance of this play was at the Arch Street Theatre, Philadelphia, on Monday evening, October 24th, 1831. It was thus announced:

ARCH STREET THEATRE.

MONDAY, OCTOBER 24TH, 1831.

First night of the new prize tragedy, by Dr. Bird, called

THE GLADIATOR.

Mr. E. Forrest will appear in the character of Spartacus.

The managers have the pleasure of announcing the first representation in this city of the new prize tragedy of The Gladiator, written by Dr. Bird, which was received in New York with unprecedented success. Neither pains nor expense have been spared to produce the tragedy with all possible splendor. The whole of the dresses, decorations and mountings are new, and designed by Mr. Andrew J. Allen, the American costumer.

The new scenery by Mr. Leslie. The arena scene being historically and magnificently set and arranged from the best authorities.

This Evening

THE GLADIATOR.

The Prologue will be spoken by MR. THAYER.
The Epilogue by MISS E. RIDDLE.

MARCIUS LUCINIUS CRASSUS......MR. DUFFY.
LENTULUS......MR. QUINN.
JOVIUS......MR. JONES.
BRACCHIUS......MR. HORTON.
FLORUS, SON TO LENTULUS......MR. J. E. MURDOCH.

GLADIATORS.

SPARTACUS......MR. E. FORREST.
PHASARIUS......MR. J. R. SCOTT.
SENONA......MRS. STONE.
JULIA......MISS E. RIDDLE.

Gladiators, 20; Roman Guards, 16; Lictors, 6; Patricians, 6; Ladies, 8; Female Slaves, 6; Children, 2.

ORALOOSA.

The play of Oraloosa was produced at the Arch

Street Theatre, on the 10th of October, 1831. On the same evening, Charles Kemble made his first appearance at the Chestnut Street Theatre, as Hamlet. With attractions so equally balanced, the town was fairly divided. Everybody was anxious to see Mr. Kemble, whose name alone was sufficient to attract a crowded house, associated as it was with one of the brightest eras in the history of the English stage. On the other hand, Dr. Bird's great success in the Gladiator excited a no less degree of curiosity to witness his second attempt as a dramatic poet. Both theatres drew crowded houses for a succession of nights, during the respective engagements of Mr. Kemble and Mr. Forrest. The following is a copy of the original bill of the first performance:

ARCH STREET THEATRE.

MONDAY EVENING, OCTOBER 10TH, 1831,

Will be presented the new Tragedy, written by Dr. Bird, called

ORALOOSA.

Founded on the cruelty of the Spaniards in Peru.

With entire new South American scenery of the most gorgeous character; splendid new costumes of Spanish and Indian style, from the most correct drawings by travelled artists and publications on the subject.

A Tragedy, in five acts, entitled

ORALOOSA;

OR, THE LAST OF THE INCAS.

FRANCISCO PIZARRO....DANIEL REED.
FRANCISCO DE ALCANTARA....JAMES E. MURDOCH.
CARVOHAL....CHARLES S. PORTER.
DIEGO DE ALMAGRO....JOHN R. SCOTT.
DON CHRISTOVAL....F. C. WEYMSS.
SOTELA....WILLIAM JONES.
JUAN....MR. SPRAGUE.
VACA DE CASTRO....MR. QUINN.
MARCO CAPAC....MR. HORTON.
ORALOOSA....EDWIN FORREST.
OCÆLLIA....MISS ELIZA RIDDLE.
FEMALE ATTENDANT....MRS. BUCKLEY.
A FRIAR....JOHN RICE.

The prologue was written by Richard Penn Smith, and spoken by Mr. Duffy; the epilogue, written by a friend of the author's, was spoken by Miss Riddle. The piece, however, did not increase the reputation of the author of the Gladiator; something better was anticipated, and the play of Oraloosa fell beneath the previous productions of Dr. Bird's muse. Neither plot, incident, or dialogue, would bear comparison with the Gladiator. The audience was evidently disappointed, and Mr. Forrest subsequently struck it from his roll of acting plays, remarking: "It was unworthy of the author, and would never produce anything but mortification to the actor."

We think Mr. Forrest was too hasty in arriving at this conclusion, as Oraloosa certainly deserved no such censure. Its incidents are strikingly dramatic, and the young hero a character that is calculated to win the approbation of an audience. Had Mr. Forrest taken as much interest in Oraloosa as he did in the Gladiator, it would not have met this fate. On its first reception in New York, on the 7th of December, 1832, it was a most decided success. In the hands of that talented young actor, Edwin Adams, Oraloosa would find an able representative.

THE BROKER OF BOGOTA.

This followed soon after Oraloosa, which we consider the most finished of Dr. Bird's dramas. Viewed as a specimen of dramatic art, it surpasses all of his other pieces. All these plays were written expressly for Mr. Forrest. This great tragedy ranks in point of poetical and dramatic interest with the Lear of Shakespeare. Mr. Forrest produced the Broker of

Bogota during one of his splendid engagements in New York, at the "Bowery." In consequence of the Park Theatre being engaged for the Kembles', Woods', and Power, he accepted the "Bowery," where he had not played for four years. He opened there on the 27th of November, 1833. This engagement closed on the 23rd of December. On the 5th of January, 1834, he commenced a new engagement, during which he played Jaffier, to Cooper's Pierre, and Mrs. McClure's Belvidere; also Pythias, to Cooper's Damon. Dr. Bird's fine tragedy, the Broker of Bogota, was brought out with great success on the 12th of January, 1834, with the following cast:

BAPTISTA FEBRO........................MR. E. FORREST.
ANTONIO DE CABRERO........................MR. H. WALLACK.
MARQUIS DE PALMERA........................MR. H. GALE.
FERNANDO........................MR. G. JONES.
RAMON........................MR. INGERSOLL.
FRANCISCO........................MR. CONNOR.
MENDOZA........................MR. FARREN.
PABLO........................MR. MCCLURE.
JULIANA........................MRS. MCCLURE.
LEONER........................MRS. FLYNN.

With such a cast as this, a far inferior play would have succeeded, but the Broker of Bogota required just such a company to render it as perfect as true art is susceptible of imparting to the works of genius. Mr. Forrest frequently told us that he was compelled to forego the pleasure of producing this play, in consequence of the paucity of talent in theatres in which he was called to play during his engagements. There is not a name in the above cast but is familiar to our readers. Six of the males even at that period, and long subsequent, were well-known stars, and the two ladies were alike celebrated for their talent, and one especially for her beauty. To her how applicable are these lines:

"'Twas such a face
As Guido would have lov'd to dwell upon;
But, oh; the touches of his pencil, never
Could paint her perfect beauty. In his home
(Which once she did desert) I saw her last;
* * Her brow was fair, but very pale, and look'd
Like stainless marble; a touch methought would soil
Its whiteness * *."

CHAPTER XLI.

ROBERT T. CONRAD.—SKETCH OF HIS LIFE.—HE STUDIES LAW.—A POLITICIAN, POET, AND DRAMATIST.—BECOMES AN EDITOR.—WAS RECORDER OF THE NORTHERN LIBERTIES.—IS APPOINTED JUDGE OF THE COURT OF QUARTER SESSIONS.—IS ELECTED MAYOR OF THE CITY OF PHILADELPHIA.—RESUMES THE PRACTICE OF THE LAW.—JACK CADE.—ITS GREAT SUCCESS.—A COMPLIMENT TO OUR LITERATURE.—EXTRACTS FROM THE PLAY.—G. H. MILES, AUTHOR OF MOHAMMED.

IN another part of these Reminiscences we have alluded to this gentleman and the play which immortalized his name. It may not be considered a repetition if we add something more to the memory of one who was so highly esteemed by all who knew him, more particularly as he added one more play to the dramatic library of our country, that has been, and ever will be, a credit to our literature. The following article was written by us a few days after his death; and we deem it necessary to republish it, as it connects the gifted author of Jack Cade with the subject of these Reminiscences. We have, in speaking of this play, stated that its original title was Aylmere.

"HON. ROBERT T. CONRAD."

"'One night
Rack'd by these memories, methought a voice
Summon'd me from my couch.'—*Jack Cade.*

"The sudden death of the Hon. Robert T. Conrad, which occurred on Sunday evening, the 27th of June, 1858, created a melancholy sensation throughout the community, among whom, for a long period of years, he held high and prominent positions. Indeed, we were scarcely prepared for such an announcement, for within a few days we saw him in the evident possession of good health; and we imagined the time was not far distant when the world of letters would again be charmed with some emanation from his gifted pen, conceived by a mind brilliant in thought, and glowing with genius; but alas!

"'His spirit, with a bound,
Burst its enchaining clay;
His tent, at sunrise, on the ground
A darken'd ruin lay.'

"Robert T. Conrad was born in the city of Philadelphia, June 10th, 1810. His father, John Conrad, was known by the writer of this, in his active business day, as a book publisher, and in after years as one of the Aldermen of the Northern Liberties. At a proper age, young Conrad was placed in the law office of Thomas Kittera, Esq., one of the most accomplished lawyers of his day. He was a gentleman of refined manners, pleasing address, and possessed a voice that set words to music. With such a man young Conrad studied law, and received those lessons which stamped the gentleman in after years; and although the mildew of the dark shade of life may blight the impress of the man, still the mind and its cultivation remain, even amid the ruin and wreck it caused.

"Young, ardent, full of poetry, imaginative and fiery, young Conrad looked upon the drudgery of a law office, as a sort of mechanical exercise, in which the mind had little to do. With this idea, he not unfrequently perpetrated a verse of poetry, instead of copying a page from Blackstone. His first attempt at anything more elaborate than a poem, was his Conrad of Naples, which was produced at the Arch Street Theatre. It was played on the evening of the 17th of January, 1832, with Mr. James E. Murdoch as the hero. John R. Scott also enacted the part afterwards. Conrad of Naples was a youthful effort, but gave promise of something in the dramatic way that would reflect credit on its author and the city of his birth. That he achieved, and his great play of Jack Cade places him first among our native dramatists.

"He was also a frequent contributor to the various periodicals of the day, and started a daily paper called the *Commercial Intelligencer*, which was remarkable for the spirit and pungency of its political articles. The *Intelligencer* was afterwards united with the *Philadelphia Gazette*, and Mr. Conrad continued for some time as co-editor of the joint concern, with Condy Raguet, Esq. A few years afterwards, he produced a second tragedy at the Walnut Street Theatre, entitled, Aylmere. This piece was altered and adapted to the peculiar powers of Mr. Forrest, and under the name of Jack Cade, was produced, with the most astounding

27

success, at the Arch Street Theatre, June 16th, 1841. Robert T. Conrad's fame (if not his popularity) was predicated on this play—it brought him immediately before the public in a new and brilliant light—it placed him on the list of those who had made a world within a world, at the head of which stood its creator—WILLIAM SHAKESPEARE. It gave him position, character and popularity; and had he properly used all these, the name of Conrad would have been, in its connection with our literature, the Addison of our country. But we will not speak of causes, the effects of which lessen the labor of the historian."

When Jack Cade was produced, its style was criticised, and its language commented upon. All this was, no doubt, evoked by that spirit of rivalry which existed here, at that time, between the friends of American and British literature.

In 1845, the author of this article published a small volume, entitled "The Dramatic Authors of America." Speaking of Robert T. Conrad, in connection with Jack Cade, we observed:

"He has written much occasional poetry, and several of his pieces bear internal evidence of the possession of no ordinary poetical talent. The lines on a Blind Boy soliciting charity by playing on a flute, are worthy of the pen of Wordsworth. Mr. Conrad is better known as a political writer than for his labors in the flowery paths of literature. He writes with a pen of steel, dipped in aquafortis—a dangerous talent, and one which, when freely exercised, seldom garners any other than a harvest of tares. We look upon this gentleman as possessing talent of no ordinary calibre. He thinks deeply, sees clearly, and is not disposed to imbibe received opinions, because endorsed by weighty names, without first casting them into the alembic of his own mind. His prose is distinguished for its perspicuity, fullness of its sentence, happy illustration and forcible expression; and if he were to turn his attention to history, political or otherwise, we have no doubt that he would produce such a work as would at once secure him an enviable place among the literary characters of the country. We understand that he has commenced a romance founded on important incidents of the Revolution, and look forward with impatience for its completion, knowing that whether it prove popular or otherwise, it will be no ordinary production.

"Jack Cade is undoubtedly destined to rank among the very highest dramatic productions of our language. The plot, though elaborate, is simple and undeveloped; the incidents are striking and effective; the characters are drawn with the utmost vigor, and contrasted with admirable skill; the sentiments are noble and manly, and the diction is marked with the truest perceptions of poetical excellence. There are passages in this piece which would not suffer by comparison with the choicest extracts from the ablest of the older dramatists.

"It is to be regretted that the state of our dramatic literature is so low as to keep such productions from the stage as the mind of Conrad could furnish. The true spirit of dramatic poetry breathes through this beautiful play, and it is with regret we say, being in heart and soul an American, that the careless, cold, apathetic feeling manifested for genuine poetry among us, is one of the chief causes of the decadency of the drama, and the absence of men of learning and of genius from the dramatic walks. We have in another portion of this work stated that to Mr. Edwin Forrest was this piece indebted for its existence upon the stage. And we venture to say, that the vilest trash of the English school will be more applauded by the audience when enacted by a regular stock company, than would Judge Conrad's Aylmere in the absence of Mr. Forrest! All writers have an individual as well as a national pride. Hence, to write a play for an actor, depending on the uncertainty of life, and his popularity, for your fame, is certainly not a very enviable situation, or a pleasing position for a sensitive man. Such is our dramatic character—such the state of its literature!"

Alas! it is so still! Our readers are all, or nearly all, familiar with the history of Robert T. Conrad. He was one of us in the great party question whether native or foreign influence was to control us as a nation and a people. How far and to what extent this question was carried, and its results, our readers are equally familiar with.

After his retirement from the *Commercial Intelligencer*, he resumed the profession of the law. He at one time was Recorder of the Northern Liberties, and shortly afterwards was made one of the Judges of the old Court of Quarter Sessions, in connection with Judges Barton and Doran.

At one period after his exodus from the bench, he became a constant contributor to the columns of the *North American*, and other papers. The beauty of his style, the elegance of his diction, and the spirit of true poetry which meandered through his writings, gave character and dignity to the papers that published them.

In June 1854, he became the candidate of the American party for Mayor, and was elected by a large majority.

In 1856, Governor Pollock appointed him Judge of the Quarter Sessions. When his term was out, he resumed the practice of the law, and the equally pleasing task, at least to him, of wooing the muses as evidenced in the publication of some very pretty poetic effusions. But death stepped in, put out the light, and all was dark! Name and fame do not go out however, with the light of life. They are "extinguished, not decayed."

Judge Conrad has passed from amongst us; and his name, which was associated with the drama and poetry, and all that is pleasing in art and nature, is now to be spoken of in connection with

"The knell, the shroud, the mattock and the grave;
The deep, damp vault, the darkness, and the worm."

Yet, beyond all this, there is a brighter home to which his spirit long ere this, has winged its flight; and we are left to recall many, many scenes and pleasant hours that were passed in his company while living.

What is termed Mr. Forrest's version of Aylmere, or Jack Cade, was first performed in New York, at the Park Theatre, on the 24th of May, 1841, with the following cast:

AYLMERE (JACK CADE)	MR. FORREST.
CLIFFORD	MR. MURDOCH.
LORD SAY	MR. WHEATLEY.
BUCKINGHAM	MR. A. ANDREW.
FRIAR LACY	MR. NICKINSON.
WAT WORTHY	MR. CHIPPENDALE.
MOWBRAY	MR. C. W. CLARKE.
COURTNEY	MR. W A. CHAPMAN.
JACK STRAW	MR. BELLAMY.
DICK PEMBROKE	MR. FISHER.
ARCHBISHOP	MR. BEDFORD.
MARIAMNE	MRS. GEO. JONES.
WIDOW CADE	MRS. WHEATLEY.
KATE	MISS MCBRIDE.

The tragedy of Jack Cade contains many passages of rare beauty. We annex the following as being peculiarly beautiful, and at the same time highly dramatic:

EXTRACTS FROM JACK CADE.

AYLMERE IN THE COLISEUM.

"One night,
Rack'd by these memories, methought a voice
Summon'd me from my couch. I rose—went forth.
The sky seem'd a dark gulf where fiery spirits
Sported; for o'er the concave the quick lightning
Quiver'd, but spoke not. In the breathless gloom,
I sought the Coliseum, for I felt
The spirits of a manlier age were forth:
And there, against the mossy wall I lean'd,
And thought upon my country. Why was I

Idle and she in chains? The storm now answer'd!
It broke as Heaven's high masonry were crumbling.
The heated walls nodded and frown'd i' the glare,
And the wide vault, in one unpausing peal,
Throbb'd with the angry pulse of Deity.
Lacy.—Shrunk you not 'mid these terrors?
Aylmere.—No, not I.
I felt I could amid this hurly laugh,
And laughing, do such deeds as fireside fools
Turn pale to think on.
The heavens did speak like brothers to my soul;
And not a peal that leapt along the vault,
But had an echo in my heart. Nor spoke
The clouds alone: for, o'er the tempest din,
I heard the genius of my country shriek
Amid the ruins, calling on her son,
On me! I answered her in shouts; and knelt
Even there, in darkness, 'mid the falling ruins,
Beneath the echoing thunder-trump—and swore—
(The while my father's pale form, welted with
The death-prints of the scourge, stood by and smiled),
I swore to make the bondman free! * * *

SAY AND ALMERE.

Say.—Sirrah, I am a peer!
Aylmere.—And so
Am I. Thy peer, and any man's! Ten times
Thy peer, an' thou'rt not honest.
Say.—Insolent.
My fathers were made noble by a king.
Aylmere.—And mine by a God! Their people are
God's own
Nobility; and wear their stars not on
Their breasts—but in them! But go to; I trifle.
Say.—Dost not fear justice?
Aylmere.—The justice of your court?
Nursed in blood! A petty falcon which
You fly at weakness! I do know your justice.
Crouching and meek to proud and purpled Wrong,
But tiger tooth'd and ravenous o'er pale Right!"

There are other passages in this play of a very high order of poetry, which would not suffer in comparison with the choicest extracts from the ablest of the oldest dramatists.

As rendered by Mr. Forrest, in tones that have never been equalled by any actor on the stage, their beauties became sublime. We read of Demosthenes, and also of his defects, and how he had to substitute pebbles for the loss of teeth! If Demosthenes was a great orator with pebbles for teeth, what was Mr. Forrest with fine teeth? The public speaker, whether he be simply an orator, a preacher, or an actor, must be natural and easy in his delivery, otherwise the effect he intended to make is lost. Shakespeare, who never lost sight of an occasion to give advice and instruct, thus speaks of one who lacked the power to appear natural, though ashamed:

> "Pleads he in earnest? Look upon his face:
> His eyes drop no tears; his prayers are jest;
> His words come from his mouth, ours from our breast:
> He prays but faintly, and would be denied:
> We pray with 'heart and soul,'
> 'Heart and soul!'"

Yes, this is the great actor's cue.

G. H. MILES—MOHAMMED.

Mr. Forrest made several efforts to procure another play suitable to his peculiar style; but as our dramatic writers did not feel disposed to run the risk of failure, the attempt was not made to meet the views of the actor, until he publicly offered a prize of three thousand dollars for a play written by an American, which would be well adapted to representation; and promising one thousand dollars for that play among the number (provided none realized his first intention) which should possess the highest literary merit. In answer to this invitation, Mr. Forrest received upwards of seventy plays. Each one of these he carefully read. None of them answered his original design. He, however, awarded to Mr. G. H. Miles, one thousand dollars for his play of Mohammed, deeming it to be the best literary production in the collection.

The reader will not be surprised at the above statement if he is at all conversant with the nature of the subject. The production of a *successful* play, not only requires ample leisure and freedom from all care in reference to subsistence, during the progress of composition; but also a more rare and difficult combination of intellectual qualities than belong to most other species of composition. First there must be genius—the poet's heaven-born fire; the grace and beauty of dramatic versification; a familiarity with classical, historical, and mythological learning; the well trained powers of the practiced thinker and writer; and a deep insight into the hidden springs of human action, feeling, and passion; while other attainments, less lofty or imposing, are equally indispensable—a knowledge of stage effect; a constructive ability whereby to avoid impossible or absurd situations, which would violate the known relations of time and space; the resources of inventive genius which furnished constant novelties and striking surprises on the stage, and an ability to intersperse the grave and gay, the solemn, the ludicrous, the pathetic, and the sublime, in judicious variety. To possess all these qualifications, falls only to the lot of the highest, and therefore the rarest, dramatic genius.

If these and many other qualities are essential to the successful dramatist, need we wonder that so few succeed? Need we be surprised that Mr. Forrest sought, in vain, among the seventy original plays before him, for one in which he felt he could do himself or his design justice?

The selection of this play from seventy others, and not calculated for stage representation at that, is a sad commentary on the dramatic literature of our country. Still, Mr. Forrest deserved much credit for awarding this sum for the best literary play out of the seventy offered. The following specimen of the author's style will afford our readers some idea of his poetic abilities. Its dramatic construction will be better understood, when we say it totally failed when it was brought out by Mr. Neaffie at the Lyceum—Brougham's Theatre, New York. Mr. Forrest loaned the play to Mr. Neaffie, who produced it on the 27th September, 1852. Mohammed, Mr. Neaffie; Omar, Mr. Lynne; Cadyah, Mrs. Maeder. It was performed but three times.

EXTRACT FROM MOHAMMED.

Abubeker (*to Saad and Osaid*).—"Obey the prophet.
Moh.—Teach them how to do it.
Exeunt Abubeker, Saad, Osaid.
Remorse or poison, which?—by Heaven, I know not
All, I half repent,—it is remorse!
Can poison rend *bowels of the past,*
And drag out blood, and blasphemy, and lust,
And mix them with the brain? Can poison shape
Imposture with its long and demon train,—
The slaughtered Bedouin and the ravished virgin—
A future pledged to sacrifice and fraud—
Insulted Heaven and deluded earth?
Poison?—O God! 'twere honey to remorse!—
Avenging Allah! double all my pains;
Heap pang on pang, till crushed affliction groans!
Make *every nerve an adder*—but shut out
The spectral, impious landscape of the past!"

CHAPTER XLII.

MR. FORREST AS A READER.—HAMLET.—HIS CONCEPTION OF THE CHARACTER. — WONDERFUL POWERS OF DELINEATION.—HIS LAST APPEARANCE BEFORE THE PUBLIC AS AN ACTOR AND A READER.

AMONG the ancients it was a fundamental principle, and frequently inculcated—"*Quod omnibus disciplinis et artibus debet esse instructus orator;*" that the orator ought to be an accomplished scholar, and conversant in every part of learning. October 15th, 1872, Mr. Forrest gave his first reading at the Academy of Music, in the city of Philadelphia. Contrary to general expectation, the house was only moderately filled; but those that were present composed the intellect of the city, and applauded the reader, as they were wont to applaud the actor. The editor of the *Sunday Dispatch*, speaking of Mr. Forrest's advent as a reader, on the evenings of October 15th and 18th, said:

"The audiences on both occasions were small; and yet there is a vast number of persons to whom religious scruples forbid attendance at the theatre, who were not strangers to Mr. Forrest's fame, and were presumably desirous to see him. That they did not fill the Academy is perhaps as much due to bad management as to any decline in Mr. Forrest's popularity; and, indeed, the field seemed to be so wide and fertile that, only a year or two ago, Mr. T. B. Pugh had offered to pay Mr. Forrest twelve hundred dollars a night for a series of readings under his management. Similar non-success attended Mr. Forrest's readings in other cities and towns. He appeared in Wilmington, Delaware, unsuccessfully, and afterwards in Steinway Hall, New York, where he read Hamlet, on November 19th, to about four hundred people, and Othello, on the 22nd, to an audience of not more than two hundred and fifty. His final appearance was on November 30th, in Boston."

Hamlet on the stage, and Hamlet at the desk, become distinct characters, unless the reader can embody within himself the whole *dramatis personæ* of this great tragedy. To illustrate the peculiar characteristics of this play, the reader should not only possess the faculty of imitation, so as to give individuality to the characters, but also the power of illustrating by action those questionable passages in the play which have exercised the mind of commentators and actors ever since its first introduction on the stage (1596). These requisites are so essential to the correct rendition of the various characters in the tragedy, that no one, unless he is a Shakesperian reader, should undertake it. Few actors, however, possess the power of making Hamlet a stage feature; failing in this, how would it be with them in the reading of it? The man who comes before an audience to read Hamlet, should thoroughly understand, and be enabled to present the character, *as it is*, and not as he imagines *it should be*. He must be able to distinguish the difference between the assumed madness of Hamlet, and that which, to a certain extent, existed before, as evinced in that great soliloquy, wherein he meditates suicide, the dawn of insanity, commencing:

"Oh! that this too, too solid flesh would melt."

This distinction is a nice one, and unless the reader has fully analyzed the character, he will not, nor can he convey to an audience the cause of his actions, or give a cue to his motives. To account for Hamlet's harshness to Ophelia, it is necessary that the mental condition of the prince should be considered as a cause for his unjust as well as unmanly conduct. The mind of Hamlet is weak—weak, because it is diseased; hence, not being healthy, his acts are but the effect of a defect, or as he says of himself—"Sense is apoplexed." He even goes further, and says: that he has not only "the outward pageants and the signs of grief, but I have that within which passeth show." If the reader overlooks these peculiarities and gives us words and actions merely, under the impression that Hamlet simply assumes madness—he will fail. Goethe says of Hamlet:

"A beautiful, high, noble, pure, moral being, without the mental strength which makes the hero, travels under a burden which crushes him to the earth, one which he can neither bear nor cast aside. Every duty is sacred to him, but this is too heavy. The impossible was demanded of him—not that which was in itself impossible, but that which was impossible to him. How he writhes and turns, filled with anguish: strides backwards and forwards, ever being reminded, ever reminding himself, and at last losing sight of his purpose, without ever having been made happy."

Hamlet, as read by Mr. Forrest, was one of the most beautiful and striking illustrations of the character that was ever given. He stood before the audience the embodiment of the whole play, giving to each character its distinctive feature, tone of voice, changing from the deep philosophy of words, as uttered by Hamlet, to the more light and less harmonic of that of the others, giving to each a different tone, thus calling up the creations of Shakespeare's fancy in a series of pictures, as striking as they were artistic. Thus, by the mere effort of genius, blended with art, the *dramatis personæ* of this noble tragedy, the illusions of the stage were transferred to the desk. The scene where Hamlet encounters the Ghost was not only read by Mr. Forrest, but acted; his every look, action, and tone of voice invested it with thrilling interest. Beautiful as the language of Hamlet is, it was doubly enhanced by the voice of the reader and his impassioned eloquence. Another scene we particularly refer to, is the interview Hamlet has with his mother, in what is called the "Closet Scene." This is one of the most extraordinary dramatic scenes that is to be found in any play that was ever written. Let us more particularly speak of it, as it has always been considered the test of an actor's power. What can be more striking, and at the same time so startling, to a mother, when thus addressed by a son!

> "Look here, upon this picture and on this;
> The counterpart presentment of two brothers.
> See what a grace was seated on this brow!
> Hyperion's curl's, the front of Jove himself;
> An eye like Mars, to threaten and command;
> A station like the herald Mercury,
> New lighted on a heaven-kissing hill.
> * * * This was your husband! Look now what follows—
> Here is your husband, like a mildewed ear,
> Blasting his wholesome brother. Have you eyes?" etc., etc.

The Queen, overcome with his terrible denunciation, exclaims:

"No more!"

Hamlet proceeds:

"A murderer and a villain; a slave, etc. * * *
A cut-purse of the empire and the rule,
That from the shelf the precious diadem stole,
And put it in his pocket.
A king of shreds and patches."—[*Enter Ghost.*]

It is here the wonderful power of the actor displays itself. The sudden transition from the stern and pathetic, the angry and impassioned, to that of horror at the appearance of the Ghost, can only be realized when the reading of the words are accompanied by the voice and action of the actor, for we contend that no one but the most accomplished of the profession can do justice to Shakespeare. Hamlet sees the Ghost, his mother does not. Struck with the altered looks of her son, and his strange actions, she exclaims:

"Alas! he's mad!"

Then when she says:

"Whereon do you look?"

And he answers:

"On him! on him!—Look you, how pale he glares!" etc.

The Queen asks:

"To whom do you speak this?
Hamlet.—Do you see nothing there?
Queen.—Nothing at all. Yet all that is I see.
Hamlet.—Nor did you nothing hear?
Queen.—No, nothing but ourselves.
Hamlet.—Why—look you there! Look, how it steals away!
My father in his habit as he liv'd!
Look, where he goes, even now, out at the portal!"

As Mr. Forrest read this portion, with eyes fixed, finger pointed, the audience instinctively followed the motion of the latter, and looked towards the "portal," to see if the power of the actor had realized this wonderful picture as drawn by the author by conjuring up the ghost. For a moment the illusion seemed reality; the next it passed away with the flash of light so wonderfully thrown upon it by this great master of the dramatic art. Such was Mr. Forrest's reading of the play of Hamlet.

Mr. Forrest's reading in New York was extolled by intelligent critics, but not appreciated by the many. In an article, written by Mr. T. H. Morrell, of New York, published November 20th, 1872, speaking of Mr. Forrest's advent as a reader, he said:

"Within the past two months Mr. Forrest has given readings from Shakespeare in Philadelphia, Brooklyn, Wilmington (Del.), and other cities, and last evening for the first time in New York. Everywhere, with one exception only, he has been greeted with genuine heartiness of feeling and tokens of pleasure. The exception referred to was, it is to be regretted, that of our neighbor, Brooklyn. On the occasion of the veteran's appearance at the Academy of Music there, an audience, select and appreciative, assembled to honor one whose memory, associated with the drama, had been enshrined in their hearts as being connected with the most inspiring and exalted emotions.

"But it was a *Spartan few* that met there; not such an assemblage as the city of Brooklyn should have gathered together to render homage to the genius of that noble artist, who, still in the full possession of his intellectual power, his superb voice—strong, resonant, musical, as of yore—with his emotional nature deepened by the teachings and sorrows of time—had re-appeared before them to give an interpretation to the grandest poetry ever penned by mortal man. And those who *were* present, will not soon forget the tones of that voice, when, at the conclusion of the reading, Mr. Forrest, 'with thanks for the marked attention that had been bestowed, bade our sister city respectfully farewell.'

"Forrest's reception last night partook very much of the character of an ovation. That welcome, so cordial and so unmistakable in its sincerity, has proved, to the credit of our city, which, on the night of the 23rd of June,

1826, hailed with delight and enthusiasm this our actor, as 'he placed his foot on the first round of young ambition's ladder,' that in his *declining* years, with all those wondrous powers yet unimpaired, that have swayed and charmed the myriads who have gathered near his throne, to the credit of New York, let it be said, that by *her* citizens, Edwin Forrest, the 'Garrick of America,' is not to-day—forgotten!"

Another critic, not very friendly, it was supposed, to the actor, wrote the following:

"It is our deliberate opinion that Mr. Forrest not only cannot play Hamlet, but that he does not understand what Hamlet means. His utter incompatibility with the part was shown in many ways as this reading proceeded—not the least significant token being what we may describe as a ponderous commonplace of personality, relieved now and then by a kind of suppressed ferociousness. It is our choice, however, not to linger on this point. The strife as to Mr. Forrest's Hamlet is an old one, and it is very idle now. We do not wish to disturb any person's belief, and would express our own—since the necessity arises—in the kindest manner. It was a great pleasure to hear Mr. Forrest's magnificent voice. Its soft tones are delicious, and its strength remains unimpaired. That poetry which hovers about the sound of words he could always feel; and this he conveyed last night. There were no recondite or unusual 'readings.' Mr. Forrest says 'in the dead *vast*,' instead of 'in the dead *waste*,' and also makes Hamlet apostrophize, 'thou *dead* corse,' instead of the more common, but not more authentic, 'thou *dread* corse.' Other peculiarities there were none—unless we denote the irrelevant mood, in the first soliloquy, indicated by the colloquial accentuation of 'my father's brother,' and the altogether foreign stroke of satire on the word 'philosophy,' in the well-known speech to Horatio about the things in Heaven and earth. These, though, were peculiarities of meaning, not of text, and the discussion of them would lead us from the direct path, which is to say, simply, that Mr. Forrest gave a reading of 'Hamlet,' in which his physical advantage of voice was finely manifested, and in which he furnished several exceedingly fine bits of elocution—without, as we think, shedding any new light either upon Shakespeare's great play, or upon the generally accepted critical understanding of his idea of it. A reading by this gentleman of 'Alison's History of Europe,' or 'Baxter's Call,' would be equally impressive with his reading of Hamlet."

The last appearance of Edwin Forrest before the public, as a reader, and never again to appear as an actor, was in Boston, on the evening of Saturday, November 30th, 1872.

CHAPTER XLIII.

THE LIBRARY.—DESCRIPTION OF THE PICTURE GALLERY. — RELICS. — CURIOSITIES. — SHAKESPEARE'S CORNER.—SAD EVENTS ANTICIPATED.—PERSONAL RECOLLECTIONS.—THE LOST FOLIO.—LOVE OF POETRY.—LINES ON THE DEATH OF A FRIEND.

WE have alluded to Mr. Forrest's library and picture gallery in a former chapter, and as it was the scene of many happy hours we spent with him, and his picture gallery the subject for mutual comments, opinions and criticisms, we will devote a little more space to speak of both. The first was probably more complete in every department of literature than any other private library in the country. We say was, for the most important portion of it—the dramatic, no longer exists.

No one of refinement and taste with the means to gratify both, could possibly neglect the works of art in connection with that of literature. The intimate and indissoluble connection which subsists between the Fine Arts in general, and practically between Poetry and Painting, which for that reason, are demonstrated Sister Arts, together with the immediate reference, which this latter branch of the Fine Arts has to the stage, will, it is presumed, fully justify us in connecting Mr. Forrest with every thing, which so essentially contributes to embrace the attractions of scenic representations.

Some two years ago, accompanied by several ladies, we visited the distinguished actor, for the purpose of showing the ladies his splendid collection of books, paintings, and other works of art. As the following account of the visit embraces nearly all the objects of interest, both in the library and the gallery, we give it as it originally appeared in one of the Philadelphia papers:

A WALK THROUGH THE ART GALLERY AND LIBRARY IN THE MANSION OF EDWIN FORREST, ESQ.

BY MISS L. L. REES.

"There is no study more interesting than that which traces the progress of the arts and sciences from the earliest stage of rude and yet efficient workmanship, down to the beautiful and too often delicate handicraft of the present day.

"Being a devoted admirer of relics, not (I may as well state by way of parenthesis) easily gulled by the million specimens that came over in the Mayflower, nor Washington's many body-servants, I spent a very pleasant afternoon, with several agreeable friends, in walking through the spacious library and well-arranged picture gallery of Mr. Edwin Forrest's palatial residence, while the great tragedian performed admirably the part of cicerone.

"We stood for a few moments before a case in which rested a Scottish claymore, and fancy carried us back to the blood-stained field of Culloden; there was also the sword which Talma, the greatest of French actors wielded on the mimic stage, and there was also the original knife which, on the world's stage, bears the name of its inventor, Colonel Bowie; a clumsy two-barrelled pistol lay there, a silent memento of the Revolutionary war, alongside of a cane once in the possession of Washington; while another handsome cane, a present to Mr. Forrest, and the hoof of the celebrated trotter, Edwin Forrest, will, in the lapse of years, become relics for the future antiquary.

"A complete suit of ancient armor brought before our mind's eye the halls of a baronial castle, while pieces of armor, exact copies of those in the tower of London, hanging on the walls, added to the illusion, and we were no longer modern damsels, but *ladyes* of the age of chivalry, expectant of the tournament.

"A quaint and strangely-carved Prie Dieu, from an old monastery, might have told us of many an agonizing prayer rising from its desk to a prayer-answering God, and the 'Conversion of St. Paul,' represented by the carving on its dark panels, grotesque as it seems to us, might have whispered 'Hope' to the suppliant.

"We held in our hands a black-lettered Bible, printed in the year 1578; and in this connection I might as well mention Mr. Forrest's most precious book, which is kept in a glass case, and of which he said, 'If this house was burning he would want this book saved, if all else perished;' the first folio edition of Shakespeare's works, dated 1623.

"A pearl-backed missal, an inch and a half long and an inch wide, claimed our attention. The type was perfectly clear and distinct, and I should think the book would prove quite a convenience to church-goers.

"A carved high-backed settle of sturdy oak, which has done duty since 1620, interested us, and we wished some magician's wand would roll back the curtains of the past and let us trace the history of that piece of furniture. Just imagine the love scenes, the conspiracies, the partings, which it had witnessed; and yet it stood solemn, grim, and ancient, *sub silentio*.

"We saw the original portrait of Nell Gwynne, the famous beauty of her time; but I can safely say that Philadelphia belles can boast of equally fine faces. Perhaps it was the manner which fascinated, which was the one charm of the dark Cleopatra.

"Also, the copy of a gorgeous altar-piece, painted by Raphael, at the order of a duke, who presented it to the church in commemoration of the preservation of his life during a battle. Of course, the duke himself figured in the memorial picture. Copies from Murillo, exhibiting his varied style—the solemn and the comic—were seen in that collection from all art galleries of the world.

"The last picture from Gilbert Stuart's failing fingers, a portrait of Mr. Forrest, was an interesting remembrance of the painter, exhibiting his rare talent even in old age, but as a likeness it was a failure.

"Among other relics of the past are two statues, representing Tragedy and Comedy, which once sentinelled the entrance to the 'Old Drury,' in Chestnut above Sixth, now no more, and are now the presiding deities of a neat little theatre fitted up by Mr. Forrest in his mansion.

"A devotee to the memory of William Shakespeare, the tragedian possesses every book or picture which contains any item of interest in reference to the Bard of Avon, and in his library we saw the plays of the immortal dramatist, complete in sixteen volumes, published in 1865, printed in clear type, on massive paper, which cost five hundred dollars. Only one hundred and fifty copies were struck off, and then the types were destroyed, making this book a rare one for posterity.

"The statue of Mr. Forrest, carved from fine white marble, weighing over three tons, and in height six feet and a half from the pedestal, represents him as Coriolanus.

"The graceful folds of the drapery, the perfect delineation of the muscles, the symmetry of the figure, and the striking resemblance of feature, make it a correct specimen of the perfection to which the sculptor's art has arrived.

"We could trace the progress of photography also, while we gazed at Mr. Forrest as King Lear, Macbeth, Othello, Richelieu, Hamlet, Richard the Third, and Metamora—each picture the counterpart of the being the genius of authors had evoked. But the triumph of the art which makes the sun its workman was a life-size photograph of Edwin Forrest.

"So perfect, with hat in hand, as if making a morning call, you almost expected to see the other hand move toward yours in friendly greeting.

"Portraits of others whose names were household

words in the mimic world greeted us at every step, until we felt as if we were ghosts haunting this home of the living.

"But now we approach the gem of the collection. A little, laughing rivulet, flowing through the forest shades, with a gleam of sunlight edging its way through the green leaves, dashing against the tree's brown trunk, throwing its golden sheen on the rippling water; but in its glittering way it falls upon the light brown hair of a little girl, making it a beauteous auburn; it kisses the bare neck and gilds the white garment which she holds daintly up, while the tender little feet touch delicately the cold, shaded water. Another little girl, sitting 'neath the shadow of the tree, has just commenced at shoe and stocking, and when disrobed, she, too, can venture for a wade in the brook.

"The pen is but a poor substitute for the artist's pencil, so when I say that the present owner has been offered eight thousand dollars in gold for this painting, the production of Meyer, a German artist, I am giving my readers a better appreciation of its value than my meagre description attempts to do.

"'Morning, Noon and Evening,' from the pencil of Mr. Bellowes, gives the gradations of human life in three beautiful landscapes.

"First, we have the river; a boat moored to the shore, the village church, with its modest spire, in the distance, toward which are moving the christening party. All nature is glowing with the balmy breath of Spring on this lovely morning, when the little babe will receive the benediction of the baptismal rite.

"Next, we see the same river, and from thence to the shore is stepping the bride in her pure dress and orange flowers, to be married in the same church which witnessed her baptism. The glowing sun betokens the noon tide hour, the ploughed fields on the hill-side, the busy Summer time, and life's youth, full of happiness, is before us.

"Now we stand before the river again, but it ripples no longer in the sunlight; the unbroken surface of ice reflects only the silver crescent in the winter's sky. No boat is moored to the snow-clad shore, but from the icebound river, over the white covered earth, comes the funeral procession, wending its way to the desolate-looking church, that the solemn service for the dead may be recited over the babe of the Spring morning, the bride of Summer noon, and the corpse of the Winter evening; while, bowed with age and grief, walks as chief mourner the widowed husband.

"Come with us now to ancient Rome. The immense amphitheatre is crowded to witness a gladiatorial show. But where is he who is to make the sports for lords and ladies? Asleep in his dungeon, his naked dagger by his side. His brawny chest displays his muscular power—his ghastly face and pallid lips betoken the dread of the coming hour—and yet he sleeps! In the next cell you can see but the claws of the ferocious lion, who soon is to be the victor or victim.

"Across the limbs of the sleeper falls the streak of light from the opening door where stands the Lanistoe to bid him to his doom. Oh, close the door! Shut from us all sights and sounds of a barbarous past, and let not even a streak of its faint light mingle with the golden beams of the present, nor throw its sickly glare across a brighter future."

Strange that so soon after his death the most interesting and highly-treasured portion of his library so identified with his own stage history, and set apart to be incorporated with his memory, should be destroyed by a fire that took place in his library, and pass away with him. Go out as it were with his life, leaving scarcely a dramatic work left, or at least of any account, toward which the old veterans of the stage could gaze upon and say: "These were the pride of our noble patron—these the silent, though faithful friends who were with him in his lonely home." A few scattered leaves, essays, etc., on the drama remains, it is true; but where are the works of the great masters? Alas! they are no longer a part of the vast library of Edwin Forrest.

After the fire we visited the scene of destruction; there among the *debris*, with its crisped and charred leaves, not a page of which was complete, lay the folio of Shakespeare's plays—1623! This valuable book was kept in a glass case with the greatest care, to keep away moth, dust and damp. Mr. Forrest's charge to his servants and others was, that in case of fire or robbery, they should think of nothing else, until they had saved the folio of Shakespeare, and a single picture in the gallery, by Meyer, to which we have already alluded.

There were also among the *debris*, the burnt, crisped volumes of Halliwell's great edition of the plays of Shakespeare (sixteen volumes folio). These splendid volumes were illustrated by numerous plates, *fac-similes*, and wood-cuts accurately taken from the original sources. Only one hundred and fifty copies of this work were printed. One volume only of this work escaped, and that was in a distant part of the library.

The following editions of Shakespeare's plays were among the collection destroyed: Pope's, 1725; Warburton's, 1747; George Stevens', 1766; Robinson's, 1797; Miller's, 1807; Malone's, 1790, and various editions by Samuel Johnson, George Stevens, Isaac Reed, Boydell's great edition of 1802; Collier, 1853, etc. The catalogue of the dramatic works destroyed by this fire would fill a volume. As we had free access to his library at all times, this department, which was designated

THE SHAKESPEARE CORNER,

possessed great attractions; the recollections of the many happy hours we spent there can never be forgotten.

During Mr. Forrest's engagement in the South and West, in 1871, we had charge of his house, and very reluctantly received the keys of his library and picture gallery. Knowing the great value he placed upon both, we thought the responsibility too great, although we felt complimented for the confidence he placed in us. He was away several months. That folio edition of Shakespeare and the one picture, both of which he so highly valued, were ever in our mind. If there was an alarm of fire in the dead hour of the night, we would rush to the window and glance in the direction of Mr. Forrest's house, listen to the roll of the engines, and felt a sense of relief when the sound died away in the distance. These two objects were our "John Jones," and when he returned and found his library all bright and cheerful, we both felt happy. The one, to find himself once more at home, and the other, that he could return the keys and say: "All is safe. The folio in its place—the picture still hanging in the picture gallery." How applicable to man are these beautiful lines—for what are human calculations but day dreams, which the light of the morrow dispels? What are bright thoughts but the gleam of a moment, to pass away the next?

"To-morrow, and to-morrow, and to-morrow,
Creeps in this petty pace from day to day,
To the last syllable of recorded time;
And all our yesterdays have lighted fools—
The way to dusty death. Out, out, brief candle!
Life's but a walking shadow; a poor player—
That struts and frets his hour upon the stage,
And then is heard no more; it is a tale
Told by an idiot, full of sound and fury,
Signifying nothing."

Who but Shakespeare could have written such lines? and who but a Forrest read them?

He is no longer with us—no longer to be seen, that stalwart figure—the piercing eye and lofty brow. No longer to be seen, the proud representative of the heroes of the past ages—no longer to be seated in his vast library, a lonely man, looking around with honest pride, and bowing his head in silent admiration to the thousands of master spirits contained in the bound volumes before him. These were his trusty friends, for they neither fawned nor flattered. Where are those true friends now? Go ask the *debris* that lie scattered around his spacious library—go ask the flames as they cracked and blazed for three long hours, rioting and revelling in huge volumes of smoke as they rolled through the halls and chambers of his dwelling—go ask these, and their answer will be—ASHES!

As Mr. Forrest's library was the scene of many pleasant hours in our life, we cannot leave it hastily. Our readers are aware, ere this, that our Reminiscences of Mr. Forrest are of a desultory character, hence we give them as they rise up in memory before us.

So few knew Mr. Forrest outside of the theatre, where, amid the glare of light, sound of music, and all the paraphernalia which make up the "mimic world," he was so panoplied in "armor bright," or dressed in regal robes, that his private character was judged from a stage point of view. It is, therefore, not unlikely that a portion of play-goers would form an opinion of the actor from the character he impersonates. They take the ideal for the reality. We remember when the elder Kean was playing an engagement in Philadelphia, in the year 1826, a young girl cried out, during the performance of Richard III., "Take away that wicked man." And yet the actor is but a representative of what are supposed to be the real personages of history, and if he carries along with such impersonations his own individuality, he ceases to be an artist. The young lady could not realize the fact that a small man with a smooth face, terrible eyes, and a hunchback, could be other than a "wicked man." But the actor, such a one as Forrest in *repose*, is "himself again," and no more like the imperious characters of the drama than was David to Goliah.

We never entered his library but we found him either with a book in hand or engaged at the writing table. The former, however, was his chief employment in his hours of ease. No one could have imagined for a moment that the quiet, calm student before him was the terrible Lear and Othello of the stage. To hear him talk—to listen to his glorious voice as he read some passages from a favorite poet—listen to his anecdotes and his masterly imitation of all the great actors of his time—hear him in the pathetic scenes of the drama and of fugitive poetry, particularly that of "The Idiot Boy"—no one would ever imagine that the stern Roman of the stage, could draw tears by his wonderful display of feeling and pathos in the reading of a simple poem.

Mr. Forrest was a great admirer of good poetry, and had quite a collection of poems cut from the newspapers of the day. To have heard him read Whittier's beautiful lines of "School Days," no one would have imagined for a moment, that this same voice startled a theatre full of people in delivering the awful curse of Rome, in the great play of Richelieu.

The man who could read "The Idiot Boy," so as to draw tears from the eyes of his hearers, and recite

"School Days," to conjure up the days of our youth—to make old age forget its decrepitude, must needs be a poet. We often thought that Mr. Forrest indulged in the pleasing walks of Parnassus, but we never discovered his footprints there. Perhaps the following lines are the only ones that were ever published as coming from his pen. They were written in New Orleans, in 1829, and published in the *Louisiana Advertiser:*

LINES

On the lamented death of HENRY KEPPELE BUNTING,

Whose virtues gained him the esteem of all who knew him.

"How slow they marched—each youthful face was pale,
And downcast eyes disclosed the mournful tale,
Grief was depicted on each manly brow,
And gloomy tears abundantly did flow
From each sad heart, for he whose breath had fled,
Was loved by all—in honor's path was bred;
I knew him well, his heart was pure and kind,
A noble spirit and a lofty mind!
Virtue cast round his head her smiling wreath,
Which did not leave him on his bed of death.
His image lives—and from my grief-worn heart,
While life remains, will never, never part!
Weep, soldiers, weep! with tears of sadness lave
Your friend and brother's drear, untimely grave."

EDWIN.

CHAPTER XLIV.

FORREST IN HIS PICTURE GALLERY.—LOVE OF ART.—THE LIBRARY.—REPEATING THE LORD'S PRAYER.—THE MINISTER AND THE ACTOR CONTRASTED.—WINE AND GRAPES.—THE OLD BIBLE.—REFERENCE TO THE FOLIO OF 1623.—THE RESULT.—THE HISTORY OF THIS EDITION OF SHAKESPEARE'S PLAYS.—UNJUST CRITICISM.—THE LAST SCENE IN THE LIBRARY.

THE landscape mentioned in our last, painted by Meyer, is considered the gem in the Forrest Collection. The principal figure is a girl, as already described, which, for natural beauty and artistic skill in its portraiture, has few equals in ancient or modern schools. The artist seemed to have invested it with a sort of etherial beauty, which had taken such a hold of Mr. Forrest, that he made it, not only a study, but apparently a thing to worship. With him this picture became, as it were, a part and portion of himself—the lovely girl recalled some passage in his life to which he had alluded on several occasions, but never explained. For hours would he sit in the gallery, gazing upon it. What his thoughts were when there alone, all around him still as the silence of death, no one ever knew. Picture him in your mind's eye gazing upon that child—life-like by the painter's art—dreaming, perhaps, of some bright object long since passed away from him—

and earth; picture him the lone man seated in his gallery, with numerous portraits around him, some so natural that you could almost hear them whisper! there he sits gazing, thinking, dreaming of the past—its sunshine and joys; and then awakens to find them again in that picture. We could never gather, by word or action, any clue to this strange morbid feeling. He has been known to get up in the dead hour of the night, go into the gallery, turn on the gas, and sit gazing on that picture for hours. The mystery connected with it, died with him.

No one, after seeing him as we did, would ever accuse Mr. Forrest of being ascetic or rough. Few gave him credit for possessing those "soft parts of conversation that chamberers have;" they associate him with the sternness of tragedy, the might of Damon, the inflexibility of Brutus, the dignity of Coriolanus, or the *Diabola* of Richard III."

These, indeed, seem to throw around an actor a sort of tragic gloom. See him, however, when the stage illusion has passed away, and you find him as fit for comedy and farce as the most facetious would require. Such was Mr. Forrest. We knew him, Horatio—a fellow of Infinite jest, of most excellent fancy. "Mr. Forrest," says one, "was rough in his manner." To whom? At rehearsal he was strict, for he could not recognize in a well-regulated theatre the necessity of trifling with any part of an actor's duty so essential to the interests of the stage and drama. He would have all men artists, or at least the lovers of an art which they were to follow as a profession. Although mere art cannot give the rules that make art, study and application can. Men would come to rehearsal of a morning, to use the term mildly, *drunk*. Others, again, without having the least knowledge of what they had to do or say. Forrest's impulsive nature could not stand this; he would speak plain and to the purpose, perhaps not quite so complimentary to the delinquents. As the founder, we may say, of our national drama, he had the right to check abuses, correct errors, and establish rules for the dramatic school of which, although he knew not then, he was in time to become its master!

Seated in his library one Sunday afternoon, when the windows were open, and the numerous birds in his garden were sending forth their happy notes as hymns to their Creator, and the voice of a preacher in an open lot on Broad street adding discordance to all that is sweet and harmonious in nature, he would express his regret that nature and the dramatic art were not more studied by the ministry. "Now," said he, "for instance"—and he stood up, not with an air of mockery, but with the confidence that his great art would so impress holy words as to bring them home to every heart —"I'll recite the Lord's Prayer." We never heard, and probably will never hear again, this great and solemn prayer read or recited, we may say, as it was on this occasion. His full-toned voice, the depth of feeling displayed, although given as an illustration, seemed to invest the great actor with almost prophetic power. The voice of the preacher in the open lot sounded harsh; his yells and screams to win sinners were those of an alarmist; there was no harmony in their sounds, no true sense of religion to give them effect. The *actor*, not the *preacher*, seemed to us, then, the only exponent of divine things.

Some of our preachers have a way of their own,

artificial, pompous and unnatural. There is a want of truth and nature in their reading and delivery, an absence of feeling in the expression of sorrow and suffering. Every passion or emotion of the mind has from nature its proper and peculiar countenance, sound or action; and the whole body of the man, his looks, and every tone of his voice, like the strings of an instrument, receive their expression from the various impulses the subject evokes. We have heard passages of Job read by an actor, which, if given from the pulpit, would have thrown over that splendid dramatic poem a new light—a light brought forth by the power of action on the sealed book, and opening its leaves to sybilline the world! The ancients excelled in action; many of their actors, by the mere exercise of their body and arms, and expression of countenance, could describe a whole story, and excite an audience by these qualities alone. An actor will melt an audience to tears by his reading the "Prodigal Son," while a preacher will not excite a single emotion. When Garrick was asked by a celebrated bishop how it was that an actor could produce such an effect on an audience, so as to cause them to weep, while preachers were unable to create a similar manifestation, he answered: "*Ministers speak truths as if they were fictions, while actors speak fictions as if they were truths.*" This seems to have been a fault in pulpit oratory for ages. An old writer thus quaintly describes an orator; "*An oratour is he that can or may speke in every question sufficiently elegantly and to persuayde properly, accordynge to the dygnytie of the thyng that is spoken of, the opportunity of tyme, and pleasure of them that be hcrers.*"

Mr. Forrest, with all his ponderous grace, elegance and tragic power, was remarkable for the beauty of his reading pathetic pieces and Biblical gems. A writer, speaking upon this subject, says: "Your action must appear natural as the general offspring of the things you express, and the passion that moves you to speak in that manner; in short, the actor, pleader or preacher, must possess that discrimination in the management of his actions, that there may be nothing in all the various motions and dispositions of his body which may be offensive to the eyes of his auditors, nothing grating or unharmonious to the ear in his pronunciation; in that case his person will be less agreeable, and his speech less efficacious, by wanting that grace, truth and power it would otherwise attain."

We are still in the library, "There," said he, "are some of the finest grapes in the country; they are from Springbrook; those on the other side are from my hot-house in the yard; try both." Beside the grapes were oranges, lemons, cakes, apples, pears, old brandy, and rich wines of the choicest brands; cigars, the perfume of which gave zest to the feast. Such was the scene Mr. Forrest's library presented to welcome friends. We indulged in all save the liquor and cigars. "I will never ask you to drink a drop in my house," he said, "for the man who for over fifty years resisted the temptation of the bottle, shall never say; 'It was here I yielded.'"

"You need not," was our reply: "although not what is called a 'temperance man,' no inducement under heaven can shake my resolution *never to taste liquor again.*"

As Mr. Forrest, during our numerous visits, scarcely touched a glass of liquor, we are pleased to add here that no one can ever accuse him of having been an intemperate man.

"There," said he, "do you see that old Bible?" an old relic of some by-gone age. "That, I picked up in Africa; it belonged to a priest attached to some mission. He wanted money, I wanted the book. I value it not so much for its antiquity, but finding it, as I did, so far from the land of civilization."

In conversation upon topics of the day, Mr. Forrest never interlarded his language with quotations from plays, as many actors do. He was easy, natural and unaffected, never using high-sounding words or unnecessary oratorical display. Hyperbole, so frequently resorted to by actors, and loud talkers, formed no part of his conversation. You hear many exclaim, "By all the Gods," and something about "high Olympus," "the thunderbolts," "dogs of war," "shake not your gory locks at me." This is all acting off the stage, and in many instances much better than it is done on. To hear a man talk thus might give the few some exalted notion of his genius from a narrow point of view, but the many would incontinently set him down as an *ass*.

Between gentlemen and scholars, unless the subject of conversation tends that way, all these hyperboles and expletives are discarded, and when conversing with the educated actor you learn one fact; that he, like the merchant when away from commercial business, invariably "sinks the shop."

It is Shirley Brooks, we believe, who says: "When engaged at my trade, I require all my tools; when remitted to leisure, I rejoice to lay them aside." This is true logic in its application to the avocations and business of life.

We had occasion some few years ago to allude to Mr. Forrest's private habits, and speaking upon the subject, after a visit, similar to one given before, we wrote the following:

"During our conversation allusions were frequently made to his foreign travels. To us his account was interesting, because he occasionally spoke of places and of men more or less connected with the drama's history. He had trodden on classic ground, and visited places where the first dawn of the Grecian drama came upon the mimic world. It was only, however, when something occurred in our conversation, that he alluded to his travels, but when some particular scene or incident connected with them was called up, then would his eyes brighten, and his full-toned voice, rich in melody, dilate upon the subject, not egotistically, but to illustrate some peculiar national trait of character, or manner of the people. When we say that Mr. Forrest's tour extended to portions of Africa, and also among the Moors, even beyond the line of European civilization, it may be imagined that he was enabled to tell us something of a people which the genius of Shakespeare presents to us in the character of Othello.

"We never met with a traveller, if we except the late John Howard Payne, who spoke less of his travels than did Mr. Forrest. It might be that he considered it as savoring too much of egotism to speak of his personal adventures in foreign lands. Be this as it may, we were reminded strongly of our first interview with the author of Brutus, whose history in connection with his foreign travel was never uttered while living, nor written since his death. Mr. Forrest just said enough to arouse our attention to this fact, that it was not all labor lost; and we have no doubt that when a life of him is written, his notes of travel will furnish the historian with many interesting sketches, apart from the local interest naturally attached to it. Mr. Forrest's vast library room has several centre tables and desks; these are laden with all the paraphernalia of a man of letters and of business. Books, pamphlets, and newspapers are scattered around, but arranged in perfect order; everything tells you at once he is no idler. Every table has its history. Here is one that looks as if it was arranged for business matters; here another, evidently used for literary purposes, for we see books open for quotation or reference, and slips of paper, evidently notes and memorandum. A glance, however, showed us that the matter was more of a practical than a dramatic selection of items. Near to a window, in the rear of the library opening out into his extensive gardens, stood a table laden with much solid matter, and we at once set it down as his *autobiographical table.* Here, we said to ourselves, will be written the life of *Edwin Forrest, the tragedian, by the author himself.*

"Although nearly the whole of this vast room is filled with books and some rare relics, all bearing evidence of mental culture, industry, and study, still there were certain mysterious-shaped things that denoted some attention to physical culture, such as Indian clubs, used for the purposes of exercising the muscles of the arms, dumb-bells, etc. In fact, Mr. Forrest told us of the various exercises in which he indulged, apart from these visible evidences, that would in our opinion, kill two-thirds of those who attempted them, but in his case they act as charms to give him health and strength.

"As ours is a mere pen-and-ink sketch of Mr. Forrest and his surroundings, attractive and pleasing as they are, it must necessarily be very imperfect. We had purposed to give our readers a more extended notice of Mr. Forrest's inner life, there is so much to see, to admire, and so much to covet, if we may confess our sin, that we found it impossible to confine our pen to him altogether. Books, engravings, photographs, pictures, paintings, sculpture and relics meet the eye at every turn; and when we left the house it was with mingled feelings of pride and admiration, for the visit only tended to strengthen our opinion of the stage, and that with such men as Mr. Forrest as its head, it would soon become, to use the language of John Stiles, 'the mirror of a nation's virtue, and the enlightened and polished school of a free people.'"

We were speaking one day, when seated in his library, about some of our early scenes in the happy days of boyhood. The subject gradually turned to the stage. We called his attention again to the oft disputed passage in Hamlet, to which we have alluded in another chapter, "I'll call thee Hamlet," etc.

"Why do you continue to read as you do, when satisfied in your own mind that it is not correct?"

"Well," said he, "I have an idea, sometimes, it is the most proper; still, as I have been so accustomed to read it so, I doubt if I were convinced of my error, I would read it so still."

"Custom," we remarked, "should never sustain error. We differ, however, and so let the matter rest. But," casting our eyes toward where lay the folio of 1623, of which he set so high a value, not in money, but in its age and close affinity with those who had it printed—"have you ever referred to that edition? if not, let us look for the passage now." It appeared he never had, strange as it may sound.

We both went to where the "sacred volume," in a dramatic sense, was, and its leaves were carefully turned over until we came to Hamlet, and to my great satisfaction, and Mr. Forrest's surprise, we found the passage marked thus:

> "I'll call thee Hamlet!
> King! Father! Royal Dane!—Oh, answer me!"

This edition of Shakespeare—the first folio—was published in 1623, by Heminge and Condell, two prominent members of the company, who were still connected with the theatre at the time it was going through the press; hence it is to be inferred that the punctuation was in accordance with the manner with which it was spoken on the stage.

Forrest gazed on the page, and quietly observed: "You are right;" and yet, when he gave his readings in Philadelphia and in New York, he read it as he had on every occasion of his playing Hamlet.

The fate of this volume is well known to our readers. The destruction of the dramatic library by fire so shortly after his death, is of a more serious nature than at first was imagined. The very books which were so essential to the "Edwin Forrest Home" were destroyed—works that cannot be replaced, or if some of them could, they would not be like those lost, for on the margin of the leaves of many, particularly Malone's edition of Shakespeare, Mr. Forrest had made numerous notes—notes that marked the intellectuality of the man, and the great Shakesperian scholar that he was. When we last saw the crisp-burnt copy of this folio smouldering in its ashes, a few leaves only remaining to tell its sad story, we thought of its owner lying there in the deep vault, his last resting-place, while all that he most valued was now, what he soon would be —ashes. How he valued that book—venerating alike its age and its author! How often had he said to us: "If this house took fire, and I could save that book, and one picture, in the gallery, all the rest might go." Nearly all the rest *did* go, at least of those books so essential to the "Edwin Forrest Home," but with them went the folio of 1623. The picture he so highly valued was saved, as the fire did not reach his picture gallery. The burning of Mr. Forrest's library has elicited much comment, and as yet no satisfactory account of it has been given to the public. One other reason that induces us to allude to it now, is that many persons are under the impression that the folio of Shakespeare's plays (1623), and other valuable dramatic works, *were not destroyed*. Crisped and rendered forever useless, is all that remains of the folio of 1623.

As a relic of the burning, it can be shown to strangers; *a sad memorial, it is true.*

As this, the first folio edition of Shakespeare's plays, is now so rare, and commands such fabulous prices, some account of it may not be out of place in these Reminiscences.

THE FIRST FOLIO EDITION OF SHAKESPEARE'S PLAYS, PUBLISHED IN 1623.

John Heminge, and Henrie Condell, brother actors with Shakespeare, and Directors of the King's Company of Comedians, published the first edition.

The following is an actual copy of the title page of Shakespeare's plays complete, known as the folio of 1623. It is faced, on a fly leaf, by the verses of Ben Jonson, on the head of Shakespeare, engraved by Droeshout, which occupies the centre:

"Mr. William Shakespeare's Comedies, Histories, & Tragedies. Published according to the True original copies. London. Printed by Isaac Jaggard, and Ed. Blount, 1623."

At the bottom of the fly leaf of the volume is the following Colophon:

"Printed at the charges of Wm. Jaggard, Ed. Blount, J. Smithweeke, and W. Aspley, 1623."

The following are the verses of Ben Jonson:

TO THE READER.

"This figure that thou here sees't put
It was for gentle Shakespeare cut;
Wherein the Grauer had a strife
With nature, to out-doo the life:
O, could he but haue drawne his wit
As well in brasse, as he hath hit
His face; the print would then surpasse
All that was ever writ in brasse,
But since he cannot, Reader, looke
Not on his picture, but his booke."

We give Ben Jonson's testimonial exactly as it stands in the folio of 1623, for it afterwards went through various literal changes. There are other commendatory verses, prefixed to the folio of 1623, from different authors, viz., L. Digges, J. M. (perhaps the initials of John Marston) and Hugh Holland.

This edition is dedicated "To the most Noble and Incomparable Paire of Brethren, William Earle of Pembroke &c., Lord Chamberlaine to the King's most Excellent Majesty. And Philip Earle of Montgomery, &c., Gentlemen of his Majestie's Bed Chamber. Both Knights of the most Noble Order of the Garter, and our singular good Lords."

This dedication is signed by John Heminge and Henrie Condell. Accompanying this is an address:

TO THE GREAT VARIETY OF READERS.

As both the dedication and address are lengthy, and not of sufficient interest, we will give a short extract from the latter, as containing the only portion more particularly connected with the immortal bard:

"It had bene a thing, we confesse, worthy to haue bene "wished, that the Author himselfe had liu'd to haue set "forth, and ouerseen his owne writings; But since it hath "bin ordain'd otherwise, and he by death departed from "that right, we pray you doe not envie his Friends the of-"fice of their care, and paine, to have collected, and pub-"lish'd them; and so to have purtis'd them, as where (be-"fore) you were abus'd with divers stolne, and surrepti-"tious copies, maimed, and deformed by the frauds, and "stealthes of injurious imposters, that expos'd them; even "those are now offer'd to your view cur'd and perfect of "their limbs; and all the rest, absolute in their numbers, "as he conceiued the; Who, as he was a happie imitator "of Nature, was a most gentle expresser of it. His mind "and heart went together: And what he thought, he vt-

"tered with that easinesse, that wee haue scarse receued "from him a blot in his papers. But it is not our prouince, "who onely gather his works and give them you, to praise "him. It is yours that reade him." * * * *

This is signed by JOHN HEMINGE and HENRIE CONDELL.

As we close the chapter which we head "The Library," the last interview we had with our lamented friend in it, may not prove uninteresting to our readers. On the Tuesday previous to his death, we had a long and pleasant conversation. His reference to our early days; the old South Street Theatre; the Tivoli, and his first appearance at the Walnut Street Theatre, was spoken of with a sort of foreshadowing of his coming end. It did not affect us then, but since his death the shadow assumes reality. Mr. Forrest had concluded his readings in New York. In a pecuniary point of view they were not successful, nor did the "critics" of that city give him credit for the correctness of the rendition of the text. On this afternoon these criticisms were the subject of our conversation; and we would observe here that Mr. Forrest manifested not the least temper on the occasion, on the contrary, he laughed heartily at a critic accusing him of reading Hamlet in this manner:

"Thus was I sleeping by a brother's hand."

instead of—

"Thus was I, sleeping, by a brother's hand
Of life, of crown, of Queen at once despatched."

"Is there a man," he said, "in this community, could imagine for a moment that I, who have made

Shakespeare a life's study, would render his text in this ridiculous manner!"

Then we came to another. The writer says, "Mr. Forrest read, 'dead vast,' instead of 'dead waste.'" The folio edition, and some of the quartoes have it "wast," and "waist." In the first folio, the only authority, it is "vast." Mr. Forrest uses it, as it is evident Shakespeare intended, to denote "the vacancy and the void of night," the "deserted emptiness," and "the still of midnight." "*Vast*" being taken in its primitive sense for desolate, void, and not in the sense of "waste," as expressed in this sentence, "*They* made the waste—the waste wilderness." Vast is Nature's vacuity of space, and as Milton uses it, "the vast of Heaven," and as Shakespeare uses it in "The Tempest," as "that vast of night."

Then our attention was called to another supposed correction of Mr. Forrest's reading:—"*Thou dead corse*," the critic said, should be read "*dread corse*." The latter is a modern interpretation of the text, based on the idea of the first being tautological. The definition of the word corse, fully sustains Shakespeare's use of the word, while at the same time it confutes the theory of being tautological. "A dead human body, a corse," etc. Dead corse is Shakespeare. The old authors also used the word "dead," in connection with "corses," as will be seen from the following:—

> "That ye say'd ii deed corses were drawe downe the steyers without pytie, and layed in ye court that all men myght beholde that myserable spectacle."

This passage will be found in Fabyan. K. John. an. 8.—

Again, a critic said, Mr. Forrest read a passage thus:—"You know sometimes he walks *four hours* together, here in the lobby," instead of, "he walks for hours," etc.

The Shakesperian scholar knows full well that "*four hours*" is the proper reading. In many of the old English plays, as well as those of Shakespeare, the words "four hours," "three hours," "two hours," are invariably used, and seldom do you find "for hours" in connection with the specification of time and place.

Connected with this interview are one or two other incidents which we will name. He had been reading the Provoked Wife, by Sir John Vanbrugh (1697). He had marked a passage, as he said, "for our especial notice," showing the immoral state of the drama at that time. He read the passage marked, and gave one of his peculiar laughs, which, apart from the subject, made one laugh with him. It was the laugh of a man at peace with all the world.

He handed me on the same day an envelope with this inscription:—"Bill of the play, George Fred. Cooke, Boston." The play-bill is dated February 5th, 1812, "Merchant of Venice."

Beside the Provoked Wife lay a MSS. play we loaned him to read a few days previous, written by John Howard Payne, entitled The Italian Bride. It lies there now, for he had no time to finish it—death was in haste, and he had to leave.

The last words he uttered, as we parted at the door of his library, were—"God bless you!" God *had* blessed me in the friendship of such a man as Edwin Forrest.

We have frequently thought, since the death of

Mr. Forrest, that these criticisms, so unjust, so uncalled for and evidently personal, had some effect upon him. Although he strove to hide it, there were times we knew when they were conned over in a bitter spirit. These "unfledged critics—hirelings of the press," who only know Skakespeare from a stage point of view, dared to criticise the readings of a man who had made the original texts a life study. They had performed their dirty work, pocketed their hire, and were content.

The tongue of calumny and the pen envenomed with the poison of "envy, malice and all uncharitableness," can never touch him more.

"After life's fitful fever, he sleeps well."

In connection with this portion of our Reminiscences, the following article from the pen of T. H. Morrell, Esq., of New York, will be read with pleasure, as an able vindication of the distinguished tragedian from the attack of a *pseudo* critic.

MR. FORREST'S LATE READINGS IN NEW YORK.—"FREE LANCE" SHIVERED, IF NOT BROKEN.

King.—Have you heard the argument? Is there no offence in 't?
Hamlet.—* * No offence i' the world.
Hamlet, Act III. Scene 2.

"In replying briefly to an article contributed to a daily contemporary, a few days since, its correspondent bearing the pseudonym of 'Free Lance,' and in which the writer 'takes up arms against a sea of troubles,' and wildly brandishes his weapon in the hope of annihilating all, whether 'native, to the manor born,' or of foreign extraction, who have recently attempted in our city to honor by interpretation the creations of the mighty Bard—and yet so skilfully *modifying* his hypercriticism in the endeavor to see how near he may come to the mark without *hitting* it—I propose only to recur to the remarks respecting the veteran of the American stage, Mr. Forrest, they forming the opening portion of his lengthy and certainly not uninteresting paper.

"An admirer of the great tragedian, though having no personal acquaintance with the gentleman, it is not my intention to take up the gauntlet in defence of Mr. Forrest as an artist, nor do I propose to enter into any controversy in the matter, believing that, at this late day, no such step is necessary, and least of all, desired.

"But in justice to the intelligence and culture of a large portion of our citizens who have in years back flocked to witness this actor's delineations (among which the character referred to has always been a prominent feature), whatever difference of opinion may exist in regard to Mr. Forrest's rendition of the *role* of the 'Melancholy Dane' (the right to criticise which is freely acknowledged), it is but proper that the sweeping assertion made by a certain critic, that '*Mr. Forrest does not understand what Hamlet means,*' should be promptly refuted as utterly devoid of consistency, fairness and candor.

"'Free Lance' (unlike, however, the critic), while diverging somewhat from the actual statistical and historical facts, has certainly evinced a considerable display of ability, proceeding no doubt from earnest and candid conviction.

"And first, while he has undoubtedly been allured by the fascinations of such plays of 'singular construction and cotemporaneous events' as have been produced by our youngest manager, it is very evident that in making the assertion that 'England's *neglected* Shakespeare is preferable to America's *murdered* one,' he has never witnessed, or perhaps heard of, certain Shakesperian characters, as represented by the following *American* artists, viz.: The Falstaff of Hackett, Forrest's Lear, Booth's Iago, Davenport's Hamlet, Adams' Mercutio, Gilbert's Dogberry, and Miss Cushman's Lady Macbeth, creations which to-day stand side by side with the same impersonations, in times long past, by Henderson, Garrick, Cooke, Kemble, Cooper, Moody, and Mrs. Siddons. And, again, in stating that 'Mr. Forrest was born at a time when lungs meant more than art,' he displays an almost inexcusable ignorance of the history of the English stage, which from the year 1800 to 1820 was illumined by the most brilliant meteors that ever graced the histrionic firmament, all of which were pre-eminent for their *intellectual* rather than their *physical* powers. The stately Kemble (John Phillip) and his peerless sister, Mrs. Siddons, the gifted, though unfortunate, George Frederick Cooke, the classical Vandenhoff, the gentlemanly Charles Kemble, the handsome Wallack, Junius Brutus Booth, Young, Miss O'Neill (buried only a few days since), and others, not to forget that wonderful genius, Edmund Kean, who, bursting forth before the foot-lights of bankrupt Drury Lane, on the night of February 26th, 1814, like some golden aurora upon the frozen regions of barren northern wilds, startled by his originality, his fiery impetuosity, his devilish subtlety, and his sublime pathos, the very foundations of dramatic England.

"'Free Lance' demurs also at the tragedian's rendition of the *text* of Hamlet, especially noting the well-known lines:

"'Or that the Everlasting had not fixed
His canon 'gainst self-slaughter.'

"And if *not* regarding with sacred awe the commandment of the Omnipresent and All-Seeing One—*His* canon above all others, and who *alone* has warned us of that

"'Dread of something *after* death—
The undiscover'd country, from whose bourn
No traveller returns,'

of *what* avail would be all human and moral prohibition?

"Surely Mr. Forrest might well pronounce, with reverential emphasis, '*His* canon' only, the *fiat* of Him who can make and unmake judges, and who has written in imperishable characters on tablets unchangeable, immortal as his own Divinity, '*Thou shalt do no murder.*'

"If the said correspondent of 'cotemporaneous and singular construction' will refer to the original folio of the great Bard (or to the admirable fac-simile reprint made by Booth, of London, not long since), he will find that Polonius thus addresses the King:

"'You know sometimes
He walks FOURE houres together, heere
In the Lobby.'

"This is as Shakespeare *wrote* it, not as 'Free Lance' would read it.

"The other readings objected to are but of little importance, being possibly, defects of hearing, for while 'all his reports go with the naked truth,' I say it in a spirit of Christian charity, they may not have accompanied the unvarnished *facts*.

"Again, I cannot coincide with the bearer of a

'Free Lance' (though, I fear, a *frail* one) in his regret that 'Mr. Forrest should not retire to a life of elegant leisure,' believing that the new field the veteran has chosen will only add renewed lustre to his wondrous intellectual powers, still undimmed and unimpaired. Without a rival near his throne, our actor may yet pursue 'the even tenor of his way,' assured that there will never be but one Edwin Forrest."

CHAPTER XLV.

CLOSE OF A BRILLIANT CAREER. — THE UNCERTAINTY OF LIFE. — FAREWELL. — OUR LAST INTERVIEW, TUESDAY EVENING, DECEMBER 10TH, 1872.—TERRIBLE ANNOUNCEMENT.—DEATH.

THE close of Mr. Forrest's dramatic career was as brilliant as was the light that shone upon his youthful beginning fifty years gone by. The bright dream of the boy was realized in age. He had attained the height to which his youthful ambitious aspirations aimed; he had mastered all the difficulties that beset his pathway, and climbed young ambition's ladder until he reached its utmost round. From thence he looked down upon the great moving panorama of the drama, as section after section passed away from him, and wondered if ever again he should take part in its revolving course. No! never again—never here. The curtain fell on the last act of his dramatic life, and the great tragedian passed from the busy scenes of an actor's career, to the quiet inactive one of private life

Was it his intention to retire from the stage? Had the curtain indeed fallen forever between him and the public? Was the sound of applause that greeted him on every occasion of his entrance on the stage, in some favorite character, to be heard no more? Was the image of Lear to disappear with this great representative—the only portraiturest of that creation of Shakespeare's genius? Was Richelieu's startling picture to be copied by some vile pretender? No! the great master was only resting from his labors. Three-score and six years had not dimmed the fire of his eye, nor the lustre of his mind. Physically, he was strong; and with a frame of vast muscular power, many, very many years were set down *by him* in life's calendar yet. His only enemy was the gout; this, he thought to conquer; "and when I do," said he, "I shall go upon the stage again a better actor than ever." How applicable to this period of his life is the following speech, made by him some twenty years before, on his contemplated retirement from the stage, to turn his attention to farming. It was delivered during what he called his farewell engagement in New Orleans:

"LADIES AND GENTLEMEN:—The little bell which told the falling of the curtain also announced my final departure from among you. For the last quarter of a century you have cheered my efforts. From the time that I landed, a nameless stranger among you, until the present period—I have been crowned by you with most brilliant success. I wish to change my pursuit—I would not 'lag superfluous on the stage.' I have chosen a pursuit congenial to my feelings—that pursuit which the immortal Washington pronounced one of the most noble, most useful ever followed by man—the tilling of the soil. And now, ladies and gentlemen, I have to say that little word, which is often said in this sad, bright world—'Farewell!'"

Farewell! yes, it was a word that made him feel sad then, for he was so overcome by emotion that he was forced to retire from the stage. His eyes were moist with tears of parting friendship.

But how different now! At the very moment when he was planning schemes for the future; surrounded with all that wealth and taste could bestow; with all the implements of his great art scattered around him—Shakespeare in every form of type and binding, from the earliest folio to the last edition published here and in Europe. There, amid the treasured works of past ages, books, pictures in oil, and engravings, sculptured figures, added to objects of *vertu*, stood the representative of the heroes of Shakespeare, a rich, popular, and, as we thought, a happy man. Happiness does not always accompany wealth; still, with the memories of the past crowding his mind, the strong will of the man subdued every emotion that was calculated to impress its workings on his countenance. He had ever an open hand and a smile for his friends to welcome them.

It was thus we parted from him on Tuesday evening, December 10th, 1872: when he said, as he grasped our hand—"God bless you!" Was it our last meeting—our last parting in life? Was the dark wing of death fluttering o'er his head? Was the bell to strike, and the curtain to fall between him and life's future, to rise no more? The dawning of two more suns told the fearful tale.

On Thursday morning, the 12th of December, 1872, about nine o'clock, we were called upon by a faithful servant of Mr. Forrest's, who gave the alarming intelligence that he was lying senseless, and apparently dead. She gave the information in wild accents, almost unintelligible. In ten minutes we stood at his bedside. We had sent word by a messenger to Col. John W. Forney and Daniel Dougherty ere we left our house, requesting them to come immediately.

The appearance of the body—the calm features, flesh still warm—had none of those indications which the death-stricken have. We looked around for the means of restoring him to consciousness, fully impressed with the conviction that it was a stupor from which he might readily be aroused. We bathed his head and neck with Cologne water. Finding this did no good, we raised his head gently, in the hope that the motion would cause a reaction in the dormant state—lethargic we thought. Still there were no signs of life. All this time his two female servants and his coachman stood anxiously watching the result. At last the awful truth flashed upon us, and we exclaimed: "My God! he is dead!" The moment these words escaped us, there was a cry of agony from the women that was heart-rending. No time, however, was to be lost. In less than fifteen minutes we had a doctor beside the bed. Anxiously we watched his every motion; the placing of the ear over the region of the heart—the close examination of the eyes—the raising up of the arms—and then, their falling heavily on the bed—we knew, then, that it was the sleep of death, from which there was no awakening on earth.

The great tragedian had passed away in the light of the morning sun, whose rays came down through the lofty windows upon his noble brow, and shed over him, and the whole scene, a radiance that seemed almost preternatural. The great actor was dead; the lightning-flash was no more rapid in its course than was that of the breath when it left its earthly tenement.

> "He died, not as men who sink,
> Before our eyes, to pulseless clay;
> But changed to spirit, like a wink
> Of summer lightning, pass'd away."

About an hour afterward, Col. John W. Forney, and Daniel Dougherty, Esq., stood beside us, gazing upon the features of one we had so often watched when he was depicting some great character of the drama. We will now let Col. Forney speak of this melancholy scene:

"His breakfast was ready at the usual hour (8.30) on Thursday morning, and the bell was rung; there was no reply. His heavy tread descending the broad stairs was unheard, and the bell was rung a second time without response. When the faithful Kate entered the library, and proceeded towards Mr. Forrest's bedroom, adjoining it, she heard a strong breathing, and on entering found him stretched across his bed, apparently in a swoon, and a livid streak on his right temple. He could not answer her call, and when she called in his friend and neighbor, Mr. James Rees ('Colley Cibber'), who summoned a neighboring physician, Dr. Corbet, the great actor was dead. Word was immediately sent to James Oakes, of Boston, an associate of Mr. Forrest, to Daniel Dougherty, his lawyer, and to Colonel Forney, of the *Press*, and last evening the two latter, with Mr. Rees, Mr. Parkinson, Mr. Elvins, and a few others, saw the great man laid out in his bedchamber, his face as quiet as if in sleep, and his broad forehead recalling the magnificent brow of Shakespeare. Indeed, all about the dead man was Shakesperian. His dressing-case was literally covered with pocket volumes of the plays of the immortal bard, and in the library, at the west end, the broad pages of Halliwell's magnificent edition were open at Hamlet, with notes in Mr. Rees' handwriting, showing that he and Mr. Forrest were on Tuesday comparing some of the criticisms on Forrest's late reading of that play in the New York *Tribune* and *Herald*. His intellect was clear till struck by the fatal blow."

As every thing connected with the deceased possesses more or less interest, the following extracts from a letter written to the New York *Herald* by its regular correspondent, will be found equally interesting:

"PHILADELPHIA, Dec. 13.—Seated at the desk where the dead tragedian has so often sat, and grasping in my hand the pen so often directed by that hand now nerveless I look around Forrest's 'home,' his library, and endeavor to fathom that austere existence, the secret of that life, the causes of the things that were through the medium of the things that are, his books, his pictures, and the many reminiscences of that stormy life. The library was emphatically Forrest's home, other apartments of the large, rambling mansion on the south-west corner of Broad and Master streets being nothing to him save as parts of a great whole. I doubt if he visited his picture gallery more than once a week, and then only because the central figure there is a marble statute of himself by Ball. His library was all in all to him, and it was here alone that he came out of the shell of his melancholy, and lived and thought his nature out. A long room running from east to west across the south wing of the mansion, having on either side ten rows of book shelves, inclosed by glass doors, contained his literary treasures.

"Near the east window, on the table at which he often sat and poured over his books, lay an open book, the fifteenth volume of Halliwell's 'Criticisms and Commentaries on Shakespeare.' The book is opened at the one hundred and sixth page, and a scene from Hamlet had last engaged his attention. Mr. Forrest, on Wednesday last, had received a *Herald* containing a criticism on his reading of Hamlet, and in company with Mr. Rees ('Colley Cibber') he had been comparing the before mentioned authority with the criticism alluded to. Clarke's and White's 'Notes on Shakespeare' also lay on the table, opened at the index page. Both books remain as they were left, fitting evidences of the fact that Mr. Forrest 'died in harness.'

Scattered around, in reckless profusion, on the tables, chairs, and main shelf of the bookcases, lay letters, notices, papers, books, articles of *vertu*, wearing apparel, and one or two tin boxes, containing valuable papers.

"His writing-table, where I am seated as I write, was used as a receptacle for anything and everything. A copy of Shakespeare, printed in 1632; one or two unopened letters, a 'Walker's Dictionary,' a check-book, receipted bills, a letter—the last one he ever wrote—addressed to a gentleman in Yonkers; telegrams, a private seal, and a motley collection of newspapers lie before me now. In a glass case on the outside shelf of one of the bookcases is a copy of Shakespeare, one of the very first ever printed, bearing date 1623. A like copy was recently sold in London for £800, or $4000. But Shakespeare abounds here in many forms. Forrest worshipped the great bard, as his life and reading amply testify.

"Passing from the library by a door in the eastern extremity, the visitor steps into the bath-room, and thence into the sleeping apartment where Mr. Forrest died. Mr. Forrest's personal tastes seem to have been of a simple nature. A plain mahogany bedstead, a dressing case of antique design, a bureau and two or three chairs complete the furniture. A portrait of his mother hangs near the head of the bed—a kindly, sympathetic face. In this room he died alone. The circumstances of his death are full of sadness and replete with useful lessons. At nine o'clock yesterday morning the breakfast bell rang, and Mr. Forrest answered the summons in his usual manner by a sort of affirmative ahem! 'Katie,' his tried and trusted domestic of many years' standing, went down stairs and awaited his coming. As he did not appear, Katie became a little impatient, and went up stairs to ring the bell a second time. As she approached the door she heard him breathing heavily, and groaning. Much alarmed, she called out, 'O, Mr. Forrest! Mr. Forrest, are you sick? What is the matter?' But no answer came to her summons; and, thinking both the library and bedroom doors were fastened, she stood spell-bound with fear and anxiety. As she related the story of his death, she said, 'I was almost crazy—the poor man dying, and I not able to get near him.' Almost unconsciously she tried the library door, and it opened. She rushed through the library to the bedroom, and found Mr. Forrest stretched on his back, and apparently suffering intense pain. 'Oh! speak to me, Mr. Forrest! What is the matter?' she called; but still no answer. Almost frantic by this time, she ran down stairs and surprised her sister, the cook. 'Mr. Forrest is almost gone!' she said. 'Send for Mr. Rees! Telegraph Mr. Oakes! Send for a doctor! Send for Mr. Dougherty!' she cried out in turn; but her sister dropped whatever was in her hands, and ran up stairs to the dying man. She raised his feet from the side of the bed, and put them on a chair. She sponged his head with cold water, and opened his collar, and tried to get a word from him. He could not speak, but gave her a look of such unutterable meaning, in which despair, desire to speak, and mental suffering were combined. He lived but a few moments after the cook came up. Even as he looked in the face of his servant, the film of death settled on the 'windows of his soul,' and with one last despairing sigh, he settled back on the bed and was gone.

"The immediate cause of his death is not positively determined. Dr. Gross, a surgeon of note in this city, in his certificate of death, says: 'Cause, apparently apoplexy of the brain.' From what I can learn from the servants, I incline to the belief that Mr. Forrest burst a blood-vessel. It was a very favorite habit of his to dress himself in the morning with the exception of his coat, and stretching himself on his back in bed, in front of a movable mirror, exercise with a pair of eight-pound dumb-bells. When found yesterday the dumb-bells were lying at his side. The cook says 'a red streak' appeared at the side of his neck just before he died. It would appear from this that he had been taking his accustomed exercise, and possibly with more violence than usual, and had burst a blood-vessel when attempting to rise from a reclining position.

"Thus he died, without a word, without one parting glance from the eyes of love. Surrounded by all that wealth and taste could give, deprived of that in his last moments that all the wealth and all the power of the world could not have given him—a friend to return the last pressure of that stiffening hand."

When Mr. James Oakes, of Boston, arrived at the instance of our telegram, it was, as stated above, to find the friend so much loved and admired, lying, like some sculptured figure of pure Italian marble, classic even in death, before him. His emotion, his tears, were those of a man true to one with whom, for years, he had been so intimately associated. From James Oakes these were tributes of the heart—gems of true friendship.

EDWIN FORREST'S LAST LETTER.

The last letter written by Mr. Forrest was penned by him on the day before his death. It was directed to James Oakes, Esq., Boston, but was returned to Philadelphia, Mr. Oakes, the moment he heard of the demise of his old friend, coming on at once. Mr. Oakes had sent Mr. Forrest the caricature of a clergyman who had so many calls for locks of hair, that he was almost shorn bald by his admirers. "Kate" and "Lizzie," who are mentioned, were his two faithful Irish servants.

"PHILADELPHIA, December 11th, 1872.

"DEAR FRIEND OAKES:—I have received your three letters with the enclosures. That poor devil of a parson was *barber*ously treated by his congregation. He ought to have known to do what he thought was right—was his only course—one can't serve God and Mammon too. The sheet of foolscap, with water-mark of 1801, is a rare thing; thanks for it. I got to New York on Sunday, just before six A. M., and went to the Metropolitan Hotel; ordered a room and a fire, and went to bed, and there lay thinking what a pleasant time I was indebted to you for in Boston. Why, the next week passed away like an ecstatic dream, without any let or hindrance. Yesterday was the coolest day of the season here, and I found the scarf, wrought by the fair hands of Miss Georgie, a true comforter; and again gratefully thanked her for it. The bouquet brought me by Mrs. Lane is now on my dressing-table, with scarcely a leaflet blighted, and its perfume breathes upon the air night and day, telling me of her kindness. The girls, Lizzie and

Kate, were delighted to receive your kind remembrance of them, and thank you very much. The article from the *Traveller* is good, and vows nothing but truth, and it does *blow*—so does Gabriel's horn—and at the right time, too. It needs something to wake the dead.

"I hope you have been vaccinated, as you promised me, for that terrible pest—the small-pox—is a hideous and fearful thing. Don't neglect yourself in this duty, which you owe to all who love you.

"Remember me to your sister, to Mrs. Lane, and to Miss Georgie, and also to Mr. Lane, with whom I was much pleased.

"God bless you ever, my dear and much valued friend.

"EDWIN FORREST.

"JAMES OAKES, Esq., Boston."

CHAPTER XLVI.

THE EULOGIES OF THE PRESS THROUGHOUT THE COUNTRY.—THE SUNDAY DISPATCH.—THE FUNERAL.—THE BODY.—THE COFFIN.—SURROUNDING OBJECTS.—THE IVORY CRUCIFIX.—EXCITEMENT AMONG THE CROWD.—THE DOORS THROWN OPEN.—INCIDENTS AT THE FUNERAL.—TESTIMONIALS.—LOTUS CLUB, OF NEW YORK.—THE VAULT.—THE LAST CEREMONY.—BEAUTIFUL POEMS.

THE moment the death of Mr. Forrest was announced, the press everywhere teemed with articles speaking of his merits as an actor, and the popularity he had gained as being one of the ablest representatives of Shakesperian characters of the age in which he lived and died. Biographical reminiscences, eulogistic notices, and appropriate verses to his memory, occupied the columns of the papers for days and weeks after he was laid in the still and silent grave. Fame and glory to him were things of the past.

"If," said the editor of the *Sunday Dispatch*, of Philadelphia, "to be famous were to be happy, then Edwin Forrest was to be envied. It cannot be said of his death, as it was of Garrick's, that 'it eclipsed the gayety of nations;' but it startled not only this city, in which he was born, but the whole nation. The death of such a man has the effect of a great disaster—the dethronement of a king, the defeat of an army, the burning of a city; the surprise and shock of the sudden death of Mr. Forrest has been felt in every part of this country, for he had impressed his age not only by his intellectual force, but by a strongly-marked character and actions which were independent of his career upon the stage. It is certain that the death of no other actor of our time could have commanded equal attention from the world. For fifty years he bore his part in a personal drama which had millions of spectators. It was a play in which splendor and gloom, triumph and defeat, pain and pleasure, were strangely contrasted, and which became mournful as it drew near its close. Now the great tragedian, who acted death so often in jest, has played that tragedy in earnest, and the curtain has fallen upon the drama."

We quote this passage, with more than ordinary pleasure, from the fact that a very unpleasant litigation between the actor and the publishers of the *Dispatch* grew out of an article which appeared in that paper, intended, it seems, as a burlesque, giving imaginary interviews between the actor and the critic. Mr. Forrest felt himself aggrieved, hence the suit. The following manly card, from the proprietors of the

Dispatch, settled the unpleasant affair, and Mr. Forrest admitted to us that a more satisfactory acknowledgment of what he considered at the time an insult, could not have been made:

"To the Public.—It will perhaps be remembered by most of our readers that Mr. Edwin Forrest brought a libel suit against the proprietors of this paper, for articles which appeared in our issues of the tenth, seventeenth, and twenty-fourth of November, 1867. The solicitations and representations of mutual friends have induced Mr. Forrest generously to consent to the withdrawal of the case.

"Under these circumstances it becomes our duty, as it is our pleasure, to express our regret at the publication of the articles in question. The articles complained of were, we frankly admit, beyond the limits of dramatic criticism, and the present proprietors, who saw them first when printed, were at the time, and still are, sincerely sorry they appeared.

"Though not personally acquainted with Mr. Forrest, we do know—what the world knows—that he has always been prompt and faithful in his professional engagements; and his bitterest enemies—if he have any—must admit that he is not only eminent in his profession, but especially free from the vice of intemperance."

The funeral took place on Monday morning, December 16th, 1872. As if the spirit of Shakespeare exercised an influence here below—great ruler of the "mimic world"—this passage from King Henry VI. would almost seem to connect it with the solemnities of the day. "Hung be the heavens with black!" was literally so on the morning of the funeral.

The body lay in a large reception room, directly beyond the main entrance from Broad Street. The casket was covered with black cloth, and was silver-mounted—six silver handles being distributed on its sides. The lid bore this simple, modest inscription:

"EDWIN FORREST.
"Born March 9, 1806. Died December 12, 1872."

The body was laid out in a full dress suit of black; and the hands, whose gestures had so often led on applause, were folded restfully upon its breast. Most natural and life-like was the countenance—hardly subdued with the pallor of death, exhibiting no trace of pain, and presenting all its well-known energetic firmness.

Trimmed and constructed of the choicest and most fragrant flowers, crosses, wreaths, and other floral emblems lay upon the casket and upon the body it enclosed. Their odor, funereal yet sweet, penetrated all the atmosphere of the room.

There was one other object in this room which, while it attracted the attention of those present, elicited whispered comments, such as "Was he a Catholic?" "Where will they bury him?" etc. This object was an ivory-carved figure of our Saviour on the cross, about one foot in length. This beautiful piece of art was sculptured by a monk in Italy, from whom Mr. Forrest purchased it. He paid for it three hundred dollars. This ivory crucifix occupying so prominent a place in the chamber of death, gave rise to the report that he was a Roman Catholic. On one side of the room was a large mirror, on the other a piano, an old-fashioned sideboard stood back. There were no pictures in this room, nor ornaments, besides those named.

The body and the room in which it lay, was under the immediate charge of the following gentlemen: Messrs. James Oakes, Daniel Dougherty, John W. Forney, James Rees, John McArdle and Gabriel

Harrison. The formal invitation to the funeral was in these words:

"DEAR SIR:—You are requested to attend the funeral of the late Edwin Forrest, which will take place on Monday next, December 16th, at one o'clock P. M., from his late residence, No. 1346 North Broad Street."

To carry out the well-known wishes of Mr. Forrest, the purpose was to admit no one into the death chamber but his immediate friends. It had been the intention to exclude the general public from the house of death and a review of the remains, but this determination had to be abandoned. Several causes conspired to this. First, there was the strong pressure of a conviction that they who had been the admirers and applauders of the great tragedian during his life, had almost a right, certainly were entitled to the privilege of looking upon him, lying in that death he had so often simulated; and then there was the difficulty, the impossibility of obtaining police officers to keep cleared of the populace the front of the house, since all of them were engaged in the taking of the census of the school children on that day.

By ten o'clock, a large number of the sad and curious had gathered on the Broad Street sidewalk, and hemmed in the entrance to the house. The doors were kept vigilantly barred to all save those having the right of entrance—the friends and acquaintances of the deceased, the gentlemen having the obsequies in charge, and those specially invited to participate in the last funeral rites. These were admitted, but with difficulty. The difficulties increased as the throng augmented, and at length grew to be insufferable. Then the original programme of privacy had to be cast aside, the populace admitted in order to free the pressure upon the doors, and the body of the distinguished dead exposed to public gaze. A line of people extending from the main entrance to the room in which Mr. Forrest's body lay, was formed, and kept unbroken by those coming in and those going out, until the funeral services began. Surely fifteen hundred, probably two thousand persons passed in to look upon his remains.

These — the hundreds of visitors — were made up of all classes. They were the general public. Not a few among them were members of the dramatic profession, and to these were added those who had business relations with Mr. Forrest, the neighbors of Broad Street and other streets of the vicinity; those to whom he had shown kindness in his lifetime, and then the rude, vulgar crowd of the curious. Ladies predominated in the multitude.

INCIDENTS AT THE FUNERAL.

Among those who came into the room to take a last look upon all that remained of the great actor, was an old lady, who approached the coffin and stood gazing upon the features of the deceased for several moments — gazing intently. She was weeping, too; but as others wept, this attracted no particular attention. It was not until after tearing herself away from the side of the body, she thought of something which she could retain as a memento of the deceased: approaching us, she said: "Could you let me have a lock of his hair, sir?"

"No, madam, that is impossible, as the body is now prepared for its last resting-place."

"O! sir, if you only knew what a good friend he was to me and mine, you would try to let me have it—something to keep as a remembrance," and again she shed tears. Who she was we knew not, but that she had good reason to remember him, was evident from her desire to have some memorial of one for whom she grieved so much.

Another lady came to us on that sad morning, and stated that Mr. Forrest owned a lot in a cemetery in the lower part of the city, and when her husband died—who was an old friend of Mr. Forrest's—he generously offered her his lot for a place of burial. "I have," she said, "a son buried there also. Do you think," she asked, "the executors will cause the bodies to be removed?"

"No, madam," we replied; "the lot in which no member of Mr. Forrest's family is buried, is yours, although it is in his name. This, we can assure you, madam—rest satisfied. We will, however, mention this to the gentlemen who will have charge of Mr. Forrest's affairs, and can vouch for their respecting the dead who lie there, as they will respect the memory of him who so generously tendered its use for your family."

Another old lady—and strange as it may seem, all those who seemed the most distressed were aged—walked up to the coffin, gazed for a moment on the marble features, life-like, in death; then gently reclining her head, imprinted a kiss on his forehead, and silently walked away. Then there came an old actor—he stood gazing on the corpse; tears came into his eyes, a sigh escaped him, and wiping the former away, he passed hastily through the crowd—the very picture of one who had lost a near and dear friend.

Of all those who came and went on that sad occasion, these were the only ones, among the many, who seemed fully impressed with the loss they had sustained, and who might well have said with Hamlet:

> "We have that within that passeth show:
> These but the trappings and the suits of wo."

"MEETING OF ACTORS.—On Saturday, December 14th, on the stage of the Walnut Street Theatre, a meeting of the dramatic fraternity was held to take suitable action on the death of the great tragedian. The attendance was large. Mr. Thomas A. Hall temporarily presided, and after a sketch of the merits of the deceased as a man and as an artist, Mr. Lewis Baker was selected as permanent chairman, and Mr. B. W. Turner as secretary.

"It was resolved, on motion of Mr. Lewis Morrison, seconded by Mr. E. L. Davenport, that all the members of the profession attend the funeral, and that the gentlemen wear a band of crape on the left arm, and the ladies such a token of mourning as they might select. On motion, a committee was appointed to draft an appropriate testimonial, and publish it as the sense of the meeting, in regard to the great loss the stage has sustained in the death of Mr. Forrest. The committee consisted of Messrs. T. A. Hall, William H. Bailey, C. H. Morton, E. L. Davenport, and Lewis Morrison.

"Mr. Morton moved that notices be posted in the green-rooms of all the theatres, informing the members of the companies that the funeral would take place at one o'clock on Monday, the 16th, and invite them to attend.

"Mr. Davenport said that while he rendered every tribute to the memory of the great man, he thought, that all ostentation by the members of the profession ought to be avoided, and he moved to amend the resolution by providing that the notices should merely announce the time of the funeral, and that the members should attend individually, and not as a body. The motion, as amended, was adopted. The meeting then adjourned."

ACTION OF THE NEW YORK ACTORS.

At a meeting of actors held in New York on Sunday, 15th of December, at the Metropolitan Hotel, the following resolutions were adopted:

"*Whereas.* The Almighty has, in His good time, seen fit to remove from our midst, ripe in years and with an honored name, Edwin Forrest, the Nestor of the American stage:

"*Resolved,* That in the death of the man who may be said to have almost been the representative of the drama in his native country, and whose indomitable will, large intellect, and devotion to his profession, have rendered him an honor to the walk of life which he adopted, that not alone the stage, but the entire intelligent portion of the community, have sustained a loss that will be deeply and profoundly felt.

"*Resolved,* That we recognize in the career of Edwin Forrest, a bright incentive to those who have entered upon the actor's life—a life which has already given many examples of goodness and rectitude, and, in the case of the deceased, has tended to elevate the stage and call attention to its objects by the votaries of the drama in his native land.

"*Resolved,* That while we deplore his taking off as a loss to his profession, still we bow our heads in submission to a mightier will, and find consolation in the fact that Edwin Forrest was taken from a life of suffering to one where trouble cannot reach him further. The life-string may be snapped, but the memory of the actor, the scholar, and the man, cannot perish, but will live to a bright and glorious future."

The Lotus Club, of New York, having signified its intention of sending on a delegation of its members, headed by Mayor Hall, as a mark of respect for the deceased tragedian—preparations were made for the reception of the delegation, and a place assigned it in the funeral cortege.

The delegation left New York at seven and a-half o'clock in the morning, and were met at the West Philadelphia depot on their arrival by Mr. Harrison and Mr. McMinn, and taken to Mr. Forrest's residence, at Broad and Master streets, in carriages.

The following gentlemen were designated as pall-bearers:

Mr. James Oakes, of Boston; Mr. James Lawson, of New York; Daniel Dougherty, Esq.; Colonel John W. Forney; Dr. Jesse R. Burden; Dr. Samuel D. Gross; George W. Childs, Esq., and Colonel James Page, of Philadelphia.

Ex-Mayor John Swift, one of the earliest friends of Mr. Forrest, would also have served as a pall-bearer had his age and infirmities permitted. A carriage was sent to his house for him in the morning, but he was too feeble to venture out.

At the appointed hour the usual funeral service of the Church of England was performed over the body, conducted by Rev. Mr. Newlin, of the Church of the Incarnation, and Rev. Mr. Boyer, of St. Paul's.

The body was then borne to the hearse in waiting, and the funeral cortege, consisting of about fifty carriages, moved off in the following order: Pall-bearers, domestics of the house, near friends of the deceased, the Lotus Club, members of the dramatic profession, and others invited.

As the solemn procession moved along, throngs of people lined the streets, gazing sorrowfully upon the hearse containing the body of one who for upwards of forty years enchanted them with his great histrionic powers. The cold drizzling rain did not deter them from following the funeral cortege to the place of burial. On its arrival at the church, the crowd was so large that there was great difficulty in entering the graveyard. On every countenance there was an expression of sadness, and when the last words were said, "dust to dust, and ashes to ashes," the pent up feelings of the crowd gave way in an audible sigh.

Beneath a weeping sky, and in the midst of a chilling atmosphere, the remains of America's greatest tragedian were consigned to their last resting-place. In a vault in the old graveyard attached to St. Paul's church, along with the mouldering bones and the decaying coffins of those who had gone before him, rests the earthy form of one whose name, though lowly and humble at first, became great in "mouths of wisest censure."

"What monument
Is wanted, where affection has enshrined
The memory of the dead? Grief must have spent
Itself, before one thought to such poor theme is lent."

"The curtain falls. The drama of life
Is ended. One who trod the mimic stage
As if the crown, the sceptre and the robe
Were his by birthright—worn from youth to age—
'Aye, every inch a king,' with voiceless lips,
Lies in the shadow of death's cold eclipse."

The following beautiful poem, from Lippincott's Magazine, adds another incident to those we have given of the kindness of heart of that distinguished gentleman:

A TRUE INCIDENT.

BY LUCY H. HOOPER.

All night long the baby voice
Wailed pitiful and low;
All night long the mother paced
Wearily to and fro,
Striving to woo to these dim eyes
Health-giving slumbers deep;
Striving to stay the flutt'ring life
With heavenly balm of sleep.

Three nights have passed—the fourth has come,
 Oh, weary, weary feet!
That still must wander to and fro—
 Relief and rest were sweet.
But still the pain-wrung, ceaseless moan
 Breaks from the baby breast,
And still the mother strives to soothe
 The suff'ring child to rest.

Lo, at the door a giant form
 Stands sullen, grand, and vast;
Over that broad brow every storm
 Life's clouds can send has past.
Those features of heroic mould
 Can awaken awe or fear;
Those eyes have known *Othello's* scowl,
 The maniac glare of *Lear*.

The deep, full voice, whose tones can sweep
 In thunder to the ear,
Has learned such softness that the babe
 Can only smile to hear.
The strong arms fold the little form
 Upon the massive breast.
"Go, mother, *I* will watch your child,"
 He whispers, "go and rest."

All night long the giant form
 Treads gently to and fro;
All night long the deep voice speaks
 In murmured soothings low,
Until the rose-light of the morn
 Flushes the far-off skies,
In slumber sweet on *Forrest's* breast
 At last the baby lies.

* * *

Low lies the actor now at rest
 Beneath the summer light;
Sweet be *his* sleep as that he gave
 The suffering child that night!

CHAPTER XLVII.

THE WILL OF EDWIN FORREST.

I, EDWIN FORREST, of the city of Philadelphia, State of Pennsylvania, do make and publish this my last will and testament. I give, bequeath, and devise unto my friends, James Oakes, Esq., of Boston, James Lawson, Esq., of New York, and Daniel Dougherty, Esq., of Philadelphia, all my property and estate, real and personal, of whatsoever description and wheresoever situated, upon the trusts and confidences hereinafter expressed; and I also appoint them my executors to administer my personal estate and bring it into the hands of said trustees; that is to say, upon trust.

First. That they, the said trustees, the survivors or survivor of them, shall be authorized to sell all my real estate, at public or private sale, at such times as in their judgment shall appear to be for the best advantage of my estate, excepting from this power my country-place in the Twenty-third ward of the city of Philadelphia, called "Springbrook," and to convey to purchasers thereof a good title in fee simple, discharged of all trusts and obligation, to see to the application of the purchase moneys; and such purchase moneys, and the proceeds of all the personal estate, shall be invested in such securities and loans as are made lawful investments by the laws of Pennsylvania, and shall be in the joint names of the trustees under my will. The investments which I shall have made my executors or trustees may retain or change, as they may think for the best advantage of my estate.

Secondly. Upon trust to pay to my two sisters Caroline and Eleanora, jointly, while both remain single, and to the survivor of them, until her marriage or death, which shall first happen, an annuity of six thousand dollars, in equal quarterly payments in advance, from the date of my decease; and should one marry, then to pay the said annuity of six thousand dollars unto the other until marriage or death, whichever event shall first happen; said annuity, however, not to be a charge upon any real estate which shall be sold, but only upon the proceeds, and upon trust to permit my said sisters and the survivor of them to use and occupy my country place, called Springbrook, with the necessary furniture and utensils and stock, until marriage or death as aforesaid, free of all charge for rent, and to take the income and profits thereof; and the said trustees shall pay the taxes thereon and keep the same in repair.

Thirdly. To take and hold all said property and estate in trust for an institution which they will call "The Edwin Forrest Home," to embrace the purposes of which I hereinafter give the outline, which institution shall be established at my country place called Springbrook, certainly within twenty-one years after the decease of the survivor of my said sisters, and sooner, if found judiciously practicable. The following is an *Outline of my Plan* for said Home, which may be filled out in more detail by the charter and by-laws:

Article 1. The said institution shall be for the support and maintenance of actors and actresses, decayed by age or disabled by infirmity, who, if natives of the United States, shall have served at least five years in the theatrical profession, and if of foreign birth, shall have served in that profession at least ten years, whereof three years, next previous to the application, shall have been in the United States, and who shall in all things comply with the laws and regulations of the Home, otherwise to be subject to be discharged by the managers, whose decision shall be final.

Article 2. The number of inmates in the Home shall never exceed the annual net rent and revenue of the institution; and after the number of inmates therein shall exceed twelve, others to be admitted shall be such only as shall receive the approval of the majority of the inmates as well as of the managers.

Article 3. The said corporation shall be managed by a board of managers, seven in number, who shall in the first instance be chosen by the said trustees, and shall include themselves so long as any of them shall be living; and also the Mayor of the city of Philadelphia for the time being; and as vacancies shall occur, the existing managers shall from time to time fill them, so that, if practicable, only one vacancy shall ever exist at a time.

Article 4. The managers shall elect one of their number to be the president of the institution; appoint a treasurer and secretary, steward and matron, and, if needed, a clerk; the said treasurer, secretary, steward, matron, and clerk, subject to be at any time discharged by the managers. Except the treasurer, the said officers may be chosen from the inmates of the Home, and the treasurer shall not be a manager, nor either of his sureties. The managers shall also appoint a physician for the Home.

ARTICLE 5. Should there be any failure of the managers to fill any vacancy which may occur in their board for three months, or should they in any respect fail to fulfil their trust, according to the intent of my will and the charter of the institution, it is my will that, upon the petition of any two or more of said managers, or of the Mayor of the city, the Orphans' Court of Philadelphia county, shall make such appointments to fill any vacancy or vacancies, and all orders and decrees necessary to correct any failure or breach of trust, which shall appear to said court to be required, as in case of any other testamentary trust, so that the purposes of this charity may never fail or be abused.

ARTICLE 6. The purposes of the said "Edwin Forrest Home" are intended to be partly educational and self-sustaining, as well as eleemosynary, and never to encourage idleness or thriftlessness in any one who are capable of any useful exertion. My library shall be placed therein, in precise manner as it now exists in my house in Broad Street, Philadelphia. There shall be a neat and pleasant theatre for private exhibitions and histrionic culture. There shall be a picture gallery for the preservation and exhibition of my collection of engravings, pictures, statuary, and other works of art, to which additions may be made from time to time, if the revenues of the institution shall suffice. These objects are not only intended to improve the taste, but to promote the health and happiness of the inmates and such visitors as may be admitted.

ARTICLE 7. Also, as a means of preserving health, and consequently, the happiness of the inmates, as well as to aid in sustaining the Home, there shall be lectures and readings therein, upon oratory and the histrionic art, to which pupils shall be admitted upon such terms and under such regulations as the managers may prescribe. The garden and grounds are to be made productive of profit, as well as of health and pleasure; and, so far as capable, the inmates, not otherwise profitably occupied, shall assist in farming, horticulture, and the cultivation of flowers in the garden and conservatory.

ARTICLE 8. "The Edwin Forrest Home" may, also, if the revenues shall suffice, embrace in its plan, lectures on science, literature, and the arts; but preferably, oratory and the histrionic art, in manner to prepare the American citizen for the more creditable and effective discharge of his public duties, and to raise the education and intellectual and moral tone and character of actors, that thereby they may elevate the drama, and cause it to subserve its true and great mission to mankind as their profoundest teacher of virtue and morality.

ARTICLE 9. The "Edwin Forrest Home" shall also be made to promote the love of liberty, our country, and her institutions; to hold in honor the name of the great dramatic bard, as well as to cultivate a taste and afford opportunity for the enjoyment of social rural pleasures. Therefore, there shall be read therein to the inmates and public, by an inmate or pupil thereof, the immortal Declaration of Independence, as written by Thomas Jefferson, without expur gation, on every fourth day of July, to be followed by an oration, under the folds of our national flag. There shall be prepared and read therein, before the like assemblage, on the birthday of Shakespeare, the 23d of April in every year, an eulogy upon his character and writings, and one of his plays, or scenes from his plays, shall on that day be represented in the theatre. And on the first Monday of every June and October, the "Edwin Forrest Home" and grounds shall be opened for the admission of ladies and gentlemen of the theatrical profession and their friends, in the manner of social *picnics*, when all shall provide their own entertainments.

The foregoing general outline of my plan of the institution I desire to establish has been sketched during my preparations for a long voyage by sea and land; and, should God spare my life, it is my purpose to be more full and definite; but should I leave no later will or codicil, my friends who sympathize in my purposes will execute them in the best and fullest manner possible; understanding that they have been long meditated by me, and are very dear to my heart. They will also remember that my professional brothers and sisters are often unfortunate, and that little has been done for them, either to elevate them in their profession, or to provide for their necessities under sickness or other misfortunes. God has favored my efforts and given me great success, and I would make my fortune the means to elevate the education of others and promote their success, and to alleviate their suffering, and smooth the pillows of the unfortunate in sickness, or other disability, or the decay of declining years.

These are the grounds upon which I would appeal to the Legislature of my native State, to the chief magistrate of my native city, to the Courts and my fellow-citizens to assist my purposes, which I believe to be demanded by the just claims of humanity, and by that civilization and refinement which spring from intellectual and moral culture.

I, therefore, lay it as a duty on my trustees to frame a bill which the Legislature may enact, as and for the charter of said institution, which shall ratify the articles in said outline of plan; shall authorize the Mayor of the city to act as one of its managers, and the said court to exercise the visitatorial jurisdiction invoked, and prevent streets from being run through so much of the Springbrook ground as shall include the buildings and sixty acres of ground. Such a charter being obtained, the corporation shall be authorized, at a future period to sell the grounds outside said space, the proceeds to be applied to increase the endowment and usefulness of the Home. And so far as I shall not have built to carry out my views, I authorize the said managers, with consent of my sisters, or survivor of them, having a right to reside at Springbrook, to proceed to erect and build the buildings required by my outline of plan, and toward their erection apply the income, accumulated or current, of my estate. And should my sisters consent, or the survivor of them consent, in case of readiness to open the Home, to remove therefrom, a comfortable house shall be provided for them elsewhere, furnished, and rent and taxes paid, as required in respect to Springbrook, at the cost and charge of my estate, or of the said corporation, if then in possession thereof.

Whensoever the requisite charter shall be obtained, and the corporation be organized and ready to proceed to carry out its design, then it shall be the duty of the said trustees to assign and convey all of my said property and estate unto said "Edwin Forrest Home," their successors and assigns forever, and for the latter to execute and deliver, under the corporate seal, a full and absolute discharge and acquittance forever, with or without auditing of accounts by an auditor of the court, as they may think proper, unto the said executors and trustees.

In testimony whereof, I have hereunto set my hand and seal this fifth day of April, eighteen hundred and sixty-six.

[L. S.] EDWIN FORREST.

Signed, sealed, delivered, and published as and for his last will and testament, by Edwin Forrest, in our presence, who, at his request and in his presence and in presence of each other, have hereunto set our hands as witnesses thereto.

ELI K. PRICE,
H. C. TOWNSEND,
J. SERGEANT PRICE.

Whereas, I, Edwin Forrest, of the city of Philadelphia, State of Pennsylvania, having made and duly executed my last will and testament, in writing, bearing date the fifth day of April, 1866, now I do hereby declare this present writing to be as a codicil to my said will, and direct the same to be annexed thereto, and taken as a part thereof:

And I do hereby give and bequeath unto my friend James Lawson, Esq., of the city of New York, the sum of five thousand dollars; and also to my friend Daniel

Dougherty, Esq., the sum of five thousand dollars; and also to my beloved friend Miss Elizabeth, sometimes called Lillie Welsh, eldest daughter of John R. Welsh, broker, of Philadelphia, the sum of five thousand dollars ; and also to my friend S. S. Smith, Esq., of Cincinnati, Ohio, the sum of two thousand dollars ; and also to the benevolent society called the "Actors' Order of Friendship," the *first* one of that name established in Philadelphia, I will and bequeath the like sum of two thousand dollars.

In witness whereof, I, the said Edwin Forrest, have to this codicil set my hand and seal, this fifth day of April, 1866.

[L. S.] EDWIN FORREST.

Published and declared as a codicil to his will in our presence, by Edwin Forrest, who, in his presence and at his request, have signed as witnesses, in the presence of each other.

ELI K. PRICE,
H. C. TOWNSEND,
J. SERGEANT PRICE.

Whereas, I have this day, October 18, 1871, provided my friend, James Oakes, with an annuity of twenty-five hundred dollars during his life, I have erased from this codicil, and do revoke the five thousand dollars legacy to him, and now do bequeath the said sum of five thousand dollars intended for James Oakes to my beloved friend, Miss Elizabeth, sometimes called Lillie Welsh, eldest daughter of John R. Welsh, broker, of Philadelphia. This five thousand dollars is to be given in addition to the sum of five thousand dollars already bequeathed to the said Miss Welsh, making in all to her the gift of ten thousand dollars ($10,000).

In witness whereof I set my hand and seal.

[L. S.] EDWIN FORREST.

Witnesses present at signing:

GEO. C. THOMAS,
J. PAUL DIVER.

STATE OF PENNSYLVANIA,
CITY OF PHILADELPHIA, *ss:*

Be it remembered that on this nineteenth day of October, in the year one thousand eight hundred and seventy-one (A. D. 1871), before me, J. Paul Diver, a notary public, resident in the city of Philadelphia, duly commissioned and qualified by the Executive authority, and under the laws of the State of Pennsylvania, personally appeared before me Edwin Forrest, to me known to be the individual named in and who executed the foregoing codicil to his will, and acknowledged that he signed and sealed the same in the presence of witnesses.

In witness whereof, I have hereunto set my hand and affixed the official seal as such notary public, the day and year aforesaid.

J. PAUL DIVER, Notary Public.

[Notarial Seal.]

CHAPTER XLVIII.

AN ACT TO INCORPORATE THE "EDWIN FORREST HOME."

SECTION 1. *Be it enacted by the Senate and House of Representatives of the Commonwealth of Pennsylvania, in General Assembly met, and it is hereby enacted by the authority of the same,* That JAMES OAKES of Boston, JAMES LAWSON of New York, DANIEL DOUGHERTY, JOHN W. FORNEY, JAMES H. CASTLE, JOHN H. MICHENER, and the Mayor of Philadelphia, and their successors, are hereby made a body politic, by the name of "The Edwin Forrest Home," with perpetual succession, and have and use a common seal, and be capable to sue and be sued, in law and equity, and to take, hold, and convey real and personal estate of an annual income not exceeding thirty thousand dollars: As vacancies shall occur the existing managers shall from time to time fill them, so that, if practicable, only one vacancy shall ever exist at one time, and the board may consist of seven managers; the Mayor will be a manager only during his term of office.

SECTION 2. The said "Edwin Forrest Home" shall be established at the country seat of the late Edwin Forrest, called Springbrook, and shall be for the support and maintenance of actors and actresses, decayed by age, or disabled by infirmity, who, if natives of the United States, shall have served at least five years in the theatrical profession, and if of foreign birth, shall have served in that profession at least ten years, whereof three years next previous to the application shall have been in the United States, and who shall in all things comply with the laws and regulations of the Home, otherwise to be subject to be discharged by the managers, whose decision shall be final.

SECTION 3. The number of inmates in the Home shall never exceed the annual net rent and revenue of the institution, and after the number of inmates therein shall exceed twelve, others to be admitted shall be such only as shall receive the approval of the majority of the inmates as well as of the managers.

SECTION 4. The managers shall elect one of their number to be the president of the institution, appoint a treasurer and secretary, steward and matron, and, if needed, a clerk—the said treasurer, secretary, steward, matron and clerk subject to be at any time discharged by the managers. Except the treasurer, the said officers may be chosen from the inmates of the Home, and the treasurer shall not be a manager, nor either of his sureties. The managers shall also appoint a physician for the home.

SECTION 5. Should there be any failure of the managers to fill any vacancy which may occur in their board for three months, or should they in any respect fail to fulfil their trust, according to the intent of the will of said Edwin Forrest and the charter of the institution, upon the petition of any two or more of said managers, or of the Mayor of the City, the Orphans' Court of Philadelphia county shall make such appointments to fill any vacancy or vacancies, and all orders and decrees necessary to correct any failure or breach of trust which shall appear to said court to be required, as in case of any other testamentary trust, so that the purposes of this charity may never fail or be abused.

Section 6. The said institution shall be so conducted as to carry into effect the following provisions of the will of the late Edwin Forrest, and the Orphans' Court for the county of Philadelphia shall have and exercise all the powers therein expressed.

"The purposes of the said 'Edwin Forrest Home' are intended to be partly educational and self-sustaining, as well as eleemosynary, and never to encourage idleness or thriftlessness in any who are capable of any useful exertion. My library shall be placed therein, in precise manner as it now exists in my house in Broad street, Philadelphia. There shall be a neat and pleasant theatre for private exhibitions and histrionic culture. There shall be a picture gallery for the preservation and exhibition of my collection of engravings, pictures, statuary, and other works of art, to which additions may be made from time to time, if the revenues of the institution shall suffice. These objects are not only intended to improve the taste, but to promote the health and happiness of the inmates and such visitors as may be admitted.

"Also, as a means of preserving health, and consequently, the happiness of the inmates, as well as to aid in sustaining the Home, there shall be lectures and readings therein, upon oratory and the histrionic art, to which pupils shall be admitted upon such terms and under such regulations as the managers may prescribe. The garden and grounds are to be made productive of profit, as well as of health and pleasure; and, so far as capable, the inmates, not otherwise profitably occupied, shall assist in farming, horticulture, and the cultivation of flowers in the garden and conservatory.

"'The Edwin Forrest Home' may, also, if the revenues shall suffice, embrace in its plan, lectures on science, literature, and the arts; but preferably, oratory and the histrionic art, in manner to prepare the American citizen for the more creditable and effective discharge of his public duties, and to raise the education and intellectual and moral tone and character of actors, that thereby they may elevate the drama, and cause it to subserve its true and great mission to mankind as their profoundest teacher of virtue and morality.

"'The Edwin Forrest Home' shall also be made to promote the love of liberty, our country, and her institutions; to hold in honor the name of the great dramatic bard, as well as to cultivate a taste and afford opportunity for the enjoyment of social rural pleasures. Therefore, there shall be read therein to the inmates and public, by an inmate or pupil thereof, the immortal Declaration of Independence, as written by Thomas Jefferson, without expurgation, on every fourth day of July, to be followed by an oration, under the folds of our national flag. There shall be prepared and read therein, before the like assemblage, on the birthday of Shakespeare, the 23d of April in every year, an eulogy upon his character and writings, and one of his plays, or scenes from his plays, shall on that day be represented in the theatre. And on the first Monday of every June and October, the 'Edwin Forrest Home' and grounds shall be opened for the admission of ladies and gentlemen of the theatrical profession and their friends, in the manner of social picnics, when all shall provide their own entertainments.

"The foregoing general outline of my plan of the institution I desire to establish has been sketched during my preparations for a long voyage by sea and land; and, should God spare my life, it is my purpose to be more full and definite; but should I leave no later will or codicil, my friends who sympathize in my purposes will execute them in the best and fullest manner possible; understanding that they have been long meditated by me, and are very dear to my heart. They will also remember that my professional brothers and sisters are often unfortunate, and that little has been done for them, either to elevate them in their profession, or to provide for their necessities under sickness or other misfortunes. God has favored my efforts and given me great success, and I would make my fortune the means to elevate the education of others and promote their success, and to alleviate their suffering, and smooth the pillows of the unfortunate in sickness, or other disability, or the decay of declining years."

SECTION 7. That it shall be lawful, and it is hereby required that the Councils of the City of Philadelphia shall cause to be laid out, in connection with the city survey of the public plan, an area of sixty acres, to be surrounded by a street of sixty feet in width, and to include the buildings now on said place; and the same being done, no streets or street shall ever thereafter be laid upon or run through said sixty acres without the consent of said board of managers: *Provided,* That said grounds shall be laid out with drives and walks, to be maintained in good order, upon which the public shall be admitted to enter for health and enjoyment, under rules and regulations to be established by said Board of Managers, for designated times, not less than thirty hours in each week. And the said corporation shall thereafter be authorized to sell the residue of the grounds of said Springbrook estate, in fee simple; the proceeds to be applied to increase the endowment and usefulness of said Home. The enclosure around said open ground shall always be such as to permit persons five feet in height to look into them from the foot-pavement outside; and there shall be at least four carriage-ways for entrance and departure, one on each side, and as many footways.

SECTION 8. The said Board of Managers shall have power to ordain by-laws, and establish rules and regulations, both for their own meetings and government and for the said institution, and the public admitted to visit the grounds; and the said grounds, plants, library, and objects of art, shall have all the protection that cemeteries have from contiguous nuisances and mutilations, as if the laws relating to them were here enacted for the protection of this institution.

SECTION 9. That said estate, so far as it shall go

to said charity, shall be exempt and is hereby exempted from the collateral inheritance tax.

W. ELLIOTT,
Speaker of the House of Representatives.
GEO. H. ANDERSON,
Speaker of the Senate.

Approved the seventh day of April, Anno Domini one thousand eight hundred and seventy-three.

J. F. HARTRANFT.
Governor of Pennsylvania.

OFFICE OF THE
SECRETARY OF THE COMMONWEALTH,
HARRISBURG, *December* 12, *A. D.* 1873.

Pennsylvania, ss:

I do hereby certify that the foregoing and annexed is a full, true and correct copy of the original act of the General Assembly entitled "An act to incorporate the Edwin Forrest Home," as the same remains on file in this office.

In testimony whereof, I have hereunto set my hand, and caused the seal of the secretary's office to be affixed, the day and year above written.

[SEAL.] JOHN B. LINN,
Deputy Secretary of the Commonwealth.

CHAPTER XLIX.

COMMENTS ON THE WILL OF EDWIN FORREST.—SOMETHING IN REGARD TO THE LOCALITY OF THE "EDWIN FORREST HOME."—WILL IT SUIT THE VETERANS OF THE STAGE?—TOO FAR OUT OF TOWN.—SPRINGBROOK IN THE MARKET FOR SALE!—THE WIFE'S CLAIM. — OBJECTIONABLE CLAUSE. — THE PROPER PLACE FOR THE HOME.

IN 1869, Mr. Forrest read to us the outline of a will, or at least that portion of it relative to the "Edwin Forrest Home." It differed in many respects from the one dated 1866. In it there was no allusion to the "farm" or "labor." We had frequent conversations upon the subject, and gave our opinion openly upon several points of it. We are satisfied that in the outline he read to us, Springbrook was not the *locale* he had then in view. We said to him when he alluded to it that "if the house was ready for inmates to-morrow, he could not get three persons to avail themselves of its advantages." In the first place it was too far out of town, and the veterans of the stage would not like to lose sight of a theatre with which all their early associations were connected.

A few years ago we had several old actors, who had retired from the stage, and who were nightly seen at our theatres enjoying some good old play. To them the theatre was an *oasis* on life's dreary sands. Many of our readers will recall the names of these gentlemen: William B. Wood, Charles S. Porter, Charles Durang and Edward N. Thayer; not one of these old actors were so situated as to become inmates of a Home of this kind. How many years will elapse before Springbrook, as part of our city, will have a theatre? A Home for sailors is generally near some river, thus giving the old tars an opportunity of seeing a vessel, commenting on the "dangers of the deep" and spinning long yarns to enliven the time.

So should the actors' Home be near to the scenes of their past labors; take them from it, and you take away the one little star that should shine upon the darkening cloud of age. One of the old actors named above, speaking of the age of actors and the causes of short life among the idle and dissipated, said: "This much, I may safely say, that while I know not how it may be in other professions, my observations prove that *artistes* generally, and actors particularly, live too long for their comfort, or enjoyment of existence."

Instead of idly believing in antiquated errors, as to the ages and fortunes of those of whom we have little knowledge, it is far more rational to conclude that age, in any situation, is seldom found productive of happiness; and the aged actor, like his fellow-sufferers in other labors, is often found to realize the beautiful lines in the Merchant of Venice, where Antonio sensibly prefers an early death to protracted years of want:

"Herein Fortune shows herself more kind
Than is her custom; for it is still her use
To let the wretched man outlive his wealth,
To view with hollow eye, and wrinkled brow,
An age of poverty. From which lingering penance
Of such misery doth she cut me off."

We have embodied in the above remarks much of what we said to Mr. Forrest on the occasion to which we have alluded. Now let us see the result, without arrogating to ourselves any degree of credit for his change of views.

In 1866, Mr. Forrest considered this place a Paradise; what was his opinion of it at a subsequent period?

In the year 1870, he submitted to us a statement of Railroad Stock which was offered in part payment for the Springbrook property, and so anxious was he to get rid of it, that he said to us he was willing to make a sacrifice of twenty thousand dollars on it, which amount he had expended on the property over the original purchase money, in erecting hot houses, furnaces, etc., for the cultivation of grapes. Among the papers of Mr. Forrest will be found an opinion of the value of the Railroad Stock offered in payment, which not being satisfactory, the sale was not consummated.

The codicil, dated October 18th, 1871, was made at the very time Springbrook was in the market for sale. His engagement at the Walnut Street Theatre closed on the 16th of October, 1871. The codicil was added two days afterwards to a will made five years before. Mr. Forrest left the city immediately after the signing of this document, at the same time giving instructions to Mr. Thomas Shallcross, his agent for this property, and ourselves, to look out for a purchaser for Springbrook. Why was a codicil placed to a will which Mr. Forrest had entirely repudiated, for its whole tenor was for the erection of a Home for Actors on land which was to be sold under his instructions, given two days after signing the codicil?

Shortly after Mr. Forrest's departure from the city, Mr. Shallcross found a purchaser for Springbrook, and he at once wrote to Mr. Forrest, saying, I have sold Springbrook for $95,000; $50,000 cash, and the balance in good city mortgages. To his surprise Mr. Forrest did not receive this information in the spirit with which the whole matter was conducted, nor did he answer the letter immediately, and when he did it was to have the sale postponed until he returned home. It was evident therefore to Mr. Shallcross, that Mr. Forrest must have had some reason for relinquishing a sale made under the most advantageous circumstances. The purchaser ultimately threw up the bargain. Mr. Forrest's course in this matter can be readily accounted for, which in the excitement and desire to get rid of Springbrook, he overlooked—*he could not give a clear title while the divorced wife had a claim upon his property!* Every piece of ground sold by Mr. Forrest was subject to her claim, which an *enlightened court* awarded, as alimony!

The question arises here, we think: does the alimony continue after the death of the husband? We are not sufficiently learned in the law to give an opinion upon this point; in the lady's case, a clause in Burrill justifies in a measure the decision given by the court in New York, which says: "Alimony is an allowance to which a married woman is entitled upon a legal separation from her husband, when she is *not charged with adultery or an elopement.*"

If the parties go to law to decide this question of the wife's claim to alimony after the husband's death, we are fearful that the landed estate of Edwin Forrest, —houses, library, pictures, bonds, mortgages, and all that was his, will be swallowed up in that vortex known as LAW. We should suggest a compromise with the lady, who, we are well informed, is willing to meet the Executors rather than go to law. This will settle the matter at once, and the will of the tragedian can then be acted upon immediately.

It is evident, therefore, from what we have said, that until a short time before Mr. Forrest's death, he had no idea of locating the Home at Springbrook. His mansion at Broad and Master streets possessed all conveniences—a vast library, a gallery of pictures, many of them peculiarly adapted to the object of the Home, portraits of leading actors, Cooke, Kean, Cooper, Wallack, Kemble, Caldwell, with those of Mrs. Siddons, Rachel, and other eminent actresses; a photograph gallery, illustrating Mr. Forrest in all the characters in which he appeared during the fifty years of his eventful career on the stage; there is also a neat little theatre under the picture gallery, with appropriate scenery, painted by that excellent scenic artist, Mr. John Wiser; these with extensive grounds attached, made it a Home ready at any moment for poor actors.

Had the sale to which we have alluded been consummated in 1871, what would have been the fate of the will of former date? It is true, another, which we most sincerely believe was the one, the outline of which he read to us in 1869, would have taken its place, and the Home would have been in the city and not twelve miles from it. He put off the day, the hour, the minute, until it was too late—too late!

It is well known that Mr. Forrest's will, as it now stands, was a sad mistake, the comments made upon it after its publication were of such a character as to lessen his memory with many who, previously, had a high opinion of him not only as an actor but as a man.

His fame as an actor was lost sight of, and a universal sentiment was expressed by no means complimentary to him. Our readers are aware that we have endeavored throughout these "Reminiscences" to place Mr. Forrest before them in such a light as to disabuse the minds of his censurers, who, judging him from an imperfect will, condemn a whole course of life for this one fault, which summed up in a few words—was, that he "put off until to-morrow what he should have done to-day." The neglecting of which duty has cast a shadow over his tomb that the sunshine of years can never dispel.

Edwin Forrest is in his grave. A man more sinned against than sining.

In article 7th of the will there is a clause which we feel assured old actors will never endorse, it is this:—"*The garden and grounds are to be made productive of profit as well as of health and pleasure, and so far as capable, the inmates, not otherwise profitably occupied, shall assist in farming, etc., etc.*"

According to another portion of the will, all that is expected of the inmates as regards indoor occupation is, either to lecture on oratory, or give readings, etc. This might be a source of revenue if the "Home" was in the city, but could scarcely be expected to yield much at Springbrook. Again, outdoor labor, working on a farm, could scarcely be expected from men who never did any thing in that line, but whose lives had been devoted to the cause of the drama. A man of seventy or eighty years of age needs quiet and retirement, and if he were able to work on a farm he certainly would be capable of performing on the stage, unless his habits were such as to debar him of the one and totally unfit him for the other. An actor is not considered in the light of a laborer, unless, as Shakespeare says, it is to "labor in his vocation." An old worn-out actor would seek such a Home as a cessation from labor, and if he can bring his intellectual abilities to be of service to the institution, it would be within the range of his artistic and dramatic education only, beyond that, it would be to insult the intelligence and age of the recipient of such bounty.

Lectures on science and the arts, at Springbrook, are things of the future. Isolated as the place is, miles away from the city, these pleasing themes to men of literary taste sound well on paper, but viewed from a practical point of view cannot be carried out for years to come. The drama's cause can never be advantageously elevated, if the means to do so are placed so far away from those, who, otherwise, would be delighted to participate in such a laudable undertaking. Were it in the city, as we feel assured that Mr. Forrest fully intended it to be, the "Edwin Forrest Home" would in a very short time be one of the Institutions of the Country.

THE END.

www.ingramcontent.com/pod-product-compliance
Lightning Source LLC
LaVergne TN
LVHW021317110826
845150LV00003B/597

* 9 7 8 1 4 2 5 5 5 7 3 7 9 *